Forest Resources

in

U.S. HISTORY

JAMES ARMSTRONG

West Virginia University

Kendall Hunt

publishing company

All cover photos courtesy of the author

Kendall Hunt
publishing company
www.kendallhunt.com
Send all inquiries to:
4050 Westmark Drive
Dubuque, IA 52004-1840

ISBN 978-0-7575-7250-0

Printed in the United States of America
10 9 8 7 6 5 4 3 2

Contents

Foreword

In the early morning light of August 14, 1765, the sight of an effigy hanging from a large elm tree on the lawn of Deacon Jacob Elliott startled the citizens of Boston. The effigy bore the initials "A.O." Andrew Oliver was one of the prominent citizens of Boston, which, with 15,000 inhabitants, was the largest city in the Massachusetts Bay Colony. Born into a wealthy family, he had spent most of his fifty-nine years adding to his considerable wealth through industriousness and shrewd business dealings, as well as obtaining various high paying positions within the royal government of the Colony. Like elitists throughout human history, Oliver tended to scorn those he considered his social inferiors. His imperiousness made him an unpopular man with the farmers, artisans and tradesmen of Boston. When he accepted the lucrative post as collector of the King's newly implemented Stamp Tax, the dislike shown by the common people turned to hatred. [Ferling 2003]

The market day crowds gathered around the tree through the morning. The atmosphere was festive with several hundred small children marching around the tree while their parents discussed the symbolism of the effigy and the issues of taxation and self-determination it represented. Citizens thought by some (like Oliver) to be disreputable troublemakers but calling themselves "patriots" delivered impassioned speeches filled with ideals of "personal security, personal liberty, and private property." [Fischer 1989]

As evening fell, the crowd's mood turned angry. A mob of Bostonians marched to the mansion of the Royal Governor shouting "liberty and property," then to the State House where the Governor's Council was meeting. The mob saved its full fury for Andrew Oliver. They tore down a building he had erected as his Stamp Office before marching to his house, breaking the windows, looting and vandalizing the Oliver family's possessions and burning the effigy hanging on Deacon Elliott's elm tree on a bonfire made up of lumber that was once his office. The Boston mob properly intimidated Oliver, who promptly resigned his post. Other mobs would gather in Boston over the next decade, elevating tensions between Massachusetts colonists and the mother country. In 1775, the friction would ignite a revolution. [Ferling 2003, Fischer 1989]

Deacon Elliott's elm tree would acquire a name, "The Liberty Tree." Its image would appear on medallions struck by Paul Revere that were worn by Boston's Sons of Liberty. Other New England communities soon followed Boston's example by naming the community's largest, oldest and most prominent tree a liberty tree. In the Revolution, a number of New England regiments carried flags adorned with the image of a liberty tree. A Liberty Tree appeared on the obverse of one of the first coins minted in America. Its designer, Joseph Jenks wrote, "What better thing than a tree to portray the wealth of our country!" [Fischer 1989, Youngquist and Fleischer 1977]

This book is about trees and forests. And it's about Americans. Mostly it is about how Americans have shaped forests and used the resources that forests provide to create the most prosperous nation the world has seen. This book is also about human attitudes, human ingenuity and the human experience. And it is about change; changes in the forest and changes amongst the people of the United States. Lastly, it is about freedom. For without the inherent belief in individual liberty represented by Deacon Elliott's elm tree, the United States would be a depressingly different place and we would be a depressingly different people.

I wrote this book as a text for my West Virginia University course Wood Science 100, "Forest Resources in U.S. History." Wood Science 100 is a freshman-level, general education course open to students in all majors at WVU. As such the intention of the book is to present a broad-brush overview of the history of Americans and our forest resources. And as the course title implies, I am a wood scientist. The book reflects my professional interests and my professional points of view as a wood scientist. The book does not attempt to fully explore all topics from all perspectives. Nor is its intention to go into great detail on any one topic or any particular aspect of that long history. There are better books written by more talented and knowledgeable authors that cover the details. I point out a few of my favorites as recommended readings. I refer to others in the bibliography. And I'm sure I missed some that I should not have missed.

Acknowledgements

There are some people who deserve my thanks for making this book possible. Bradford Cochran and Benjamin Dudik reviewed the draft and provided many ideas how to improve it for the benefit of its intended student audience. My wife, Rose, proofread several sections of the book that deal with controversial topics. I am grateful to Charles Mann, William Denevan and their publishers for giving permission to reprint articles that appear as Chapters 4 and 5. Bill Luppold, Jim Bowyer, and Thomas Bonnicksen were wonderful sources of information and, more importantly, sources of inspiration for this book. Colleagues in the Division of Forestry and Natural Resources at WVU imparted pearls of wisdom and fascinating pieces of information that inspired further research for inclusion in this book. These include Tony Tomkowski, Jim Rentch, Bruce Anderson, Bob Whitmore, Chad Pierskalla, Dave DeVallance, Elemer Lang, Jody Gray, Ray Hicks, Dave McGill, Shawn Grushecky, Jim Anderson, Ben Dawson-Andoh, Joe McNeel, Jingxing Wang, and a friend and colleague, the late Bill Grafton. I apologize to any I have inadvertently forgotten to mention. I am also grateful for the assistance provided by Christine Adair and Stephanie Moffett at Kendall-Hunt.

Dedication

This book is dedicated to my children, Rebecca, Amanda and Scott, and my grand-daughter, Emmarose. I ask the students who read this book to never forget that the world their generation creates is the world that Emmarose and her generation will inherit.

Chapter 1

Forests of the United States

The forests of the United States cover approximately 751 million acres (303.5 million hectares) or approximately one third of the total land area of the United States (Smith et al. 2009). The U.S. ranks fourth in the world in forest land, accounting for 8 percent of the world's forests (FAO 2009). Forest land statistics are not as straight-forward as one might think. "There are more than 250 definitions of the term 'forest'" (Illinois State Museum 2006). All definitions require tree cover and most include a percentage of canopy cover (overlapping crowns) that may range from 5 percent to 100 percent. Definitions may also require that trees cover a minimum area for land to fit the definition of a forest. For example, the U.S. Forest Service requires one acre of forest cover to consider land forested (Smith et al. 2009). There are differences between ecological, political, and legal definitions of a forest (Illinois State Museum 2006). These differences in how people define forests are a source of confusion and disagreement as humans consider how best to protect and use forest resources.

Approximately 52 percent of the forested land is located in the eastern United States and 48 percent is in the west, including Alaska and Hawaii (Smith et al. 2009).

America's forests are an ecologically diverse mixture of plant and animal species and constitute a number of forest types. The term **forest type** describes the forests that prevail in a given region, and the name for each forest type comes from the domi-nant tree species within that region's forests. For example, the forests that covered much of the eastern United States at the time of European contact were of the oak-chestnut type.

OWNERSHIP OF AMERICAN FORESTS

The federal government owns one third or 248 million of the 751 million forested acres of the United States. The National Forest system contains approximately 147 million acres or 19.6 percent of the nation's forest land. National Parks, Bureau of Land Management (BLM) land, Indian reservations, the military and other federal installations make up the remaining 101 million acres of federal forest land. An addi-tional 80 million acres are in state or local ownership, making a total of 43.6 percent of all forested land that is in public ownership (Smith et al. 2009).

Approximately 86 percent of the federal forest acres are in the west. Forty-four percent of the federal forest is in the Pacific Coast region (including Alaska), and 42 percent is in the Rocky Mountain states.

Approximately 74 percent of the privately-owned forest acreage of the U.S. is in the east and 44 percent of it is in the south. Private ownership encompasses all non-governmental owners including individuals, corporations, and non-governmental organizations. This pattern of private and public land ownership is a direct result of the pattern of westward expansion of settlement through American history (Smith et al. 2009).

PHOTOSYNTHESIS

The definition of a **tree** is a perennial plant, having a height of at least twenty feet at maturity in a given locality and usually, but not always, possessing a single, self-supporting stem (Panshin and deZeeuw 1980).

Trees depend upon the process of photosynthesis. The leaves take in carbon dioxide, and the roots take in water. Light enables the tree to combine the basic elements of carbon, hydrogen and oxygen to form simple sugars in the leaves. The tree transports those sugars down the stem through the inner bark or *phloem* where they combine into complex carbohydrates known as polymers that constitute the cell structure of the tree.

The trees that make up a forest are engaged in an intense competition for resources: water, carbon dioxide and light. Thus, the solar energy taken in to support photosynthesis is used to form the basic biochemical building blocks that enable the tree to grow taller. Then it may successfully compete with its neighbors for light so that it may spread its roots to acquire water and spread its canopy to support the leaf structure that absorbs carbon dioxide and light. The **xylem** or *wood* is the tissue that serves as the fluid conduction system for carrying water from the roots to the leaves and that provides the strength to hold the canopy erect above the competition.

There are some tree species that require a lot of light and tend to be the first trees to colonize a recently disturbed clearing or site. Other trees can grow in the shade of the taller trees. Eventually they will replace the taller trees as they grow old and die. Over time, they will dominate the stand.

Figure 1.1 Yellow-Poplar. *An example of a hardwood species.*

HARDWOODS AND SOFTWOODS

In the most general terms, hardwoods, softwoods or a mixture of the two may dominate a forest.

Hardwoods are *Angiosperms* (Latin for "encased seed"), broad-leafed trees that bear seeds in fruit, nuts and legumes. The oaks, elms, maples, ash and poplar are examples of hardwoods.

Softwoods are *Gymnosperms* (Latin for "naked seed"). These are the trees that have needles and cones. We also know them as conifers and include the pines, spruces, hemlocks, cedars, Douglas-fir and redwood.

Softwood timber makes up 57 percent of the nation's forest growing stock while hardwoods make up the remainder. Of this total, 68 percent of the nation's softwood growing stock is in the west, and 88 percent of the hardwood growing stock is in the east. Looking at it another way, two-thirds of the eastern forest consists of hardwood growing stock while 90 percent of the western forest consists of softwood growing stock. Approximately three-quarters of the softwood forests of the west are in federal ownership (Smith et al. 2009).

Figure 1.2 Eastern Hemlock. *An example of a softwood species.*

PRINCIPLES OF FOREST ECOLOGY

The forests of America have gone through a never-ending process of change. To understand that change, it is necessary to outline a few fundamental principles and definitions from forest ecology (Bonnicksen 2000a).

The random and often chaotic occurrence of disturbance dominates forest ecology. **Disturbance** is any process that clears away existing vegetation. Some examples include storms, fire and floods, mortality caused by insects or disease or the clearing of land by humans.

Trees fall into two general categories according to their strategies for occupying the land following a disturbance. **Pioneer** species are the earliest plants to occupy a recently disturbed site. These plants are generally shade-intolerant and employ the strategy of occupying recently disturbed sites where there is abundant sunlight. Some pioneers can grow in partial shade and some require full sunlight. **Settler** species are shade-tolerant. They are able to live in the shade in the forest understory and require moist litter for a seedbed. They "infiltrate stands or groups of pioneer trees and wait in the shady understory for the overstory trees to die" (Bonnicksen 2000a). Once older pioneers die, the settlers grow rapidly to dominate the stand.

A forest consists of patches. Bonnicksen (2000a) defines a **patch** as "a relatively uniform group of plants" of approximately the same age. Patches are created when a disturbance such as a storm, lightning strike, insect infestation, fire or human activity clears away an existing part of the forest. The size of a patch of forest depends upon the extent of the disturbance that created it. For example a single, large tree may die and fall, clearing a small opening for the establishment of a small patch or a catastrophic wildfire may clear thousands of acres. Patches may come in all shapes and sizes, and they change over time.

When a disturbance clears a patch within a forest, a process known as **forest succession** begins to take place. The first stage of succession occurs when grasses, forbs and shrubs begin to grow in a recently cleared patch. Pioneer trees that require bright

Figure 1.3 *Regenerating of red spruce following a disturbance (insect infestation).*

sunlight join them. The next stage of succession occurs as the pioneer trees reach pole size—a patch of "middle-aged pioneer forest." They are densely packed, growing straight and forming a close canopy that blocks light from the forest floor. The grasses, shrubs and forbs die. As the weaker trees in the patch die during the third stage of succession, this creates an "open old pioneer forest." As aging pioneers die and fall, they create openings in the canopy. (Some pioneers can live a thousand years; others survive a much shorter time.) Enough light gets through the canopy for settler trees to grow. As more pioneers die, small patches of young settlers take their place. This fourth stage of succession is an "old transitional" patch of forest. Eventually, all of the pioneer species die and are replaced by settlers. This is the final stage of succession—a "late-successional" or "self-replacing" forest (Bonnicksen 2000). (We sometimes call a late-successional forest an "old growth" forest. However, there are many definitions of the term "old growth" that may lead to confusion and become an obstacle to the resolution of conflicts over the use of forests.)

Forest succession is not always a predictable process. Random or human-caused disturbance can, and does, interrupt the process. New species may invade ecosystems and compete with existing species.

FORESTS OF THE U.S. IN THE 21ST CENTURY

The U.S. Forest Service estimates that 1.03 billion acres of forest existed in the U.S. in 1630. Remaining forest cover is approximately two-thirds of the 1630 estimate. The basis of the 1630 figures is the 1909 work of R. S. Kellogg, "as an estimate of the original forest area based on the current estimate of forest and historic land clearing information. These data are provided here for general reference purposes only to convey the relative extent of the forest estate, in what is now the United States, at the time of European settlement." Since 1909, the extent of America's forests has remained relatively constant (Alvarez 2007, Kellogg 1909, Smith et al. 2009).

The forests of the United States are a source of wood for residential construction, furniture, paper, energy, household and office items, musical instruments and countless other products used in everyday life. Wood is arguably one of the greenest materials that we can use for these purposes. However, timber harvest is a controversial issue with Americans who seemingly want wood products but don't want to cut the trees necessary to produce them.

Active conservation efforts are improving the quality of an estimated 20 percent of U.S. forests as compared to 11 percent worldwide. Twenty-five percent of productive forest lands are included in one of the major certification schemes that ensure their sustainable management. In addition, the volume of timber growing stock has increased almost 50 percent since World War II. Wildlife conservation efforts have led to increasing populations of numerous species over the last century. Recreational use of public and private forests is increasing (Alvarez 2007).

The condition of some American forests is poor, particularly the publicly-owned western coniferous forests. These forests are "overcrowded and unhealthy." Wildlife habitats have been fragmented and reduced in size, watersheds are threatened, and forests are vulnerable to "huge insect and disease epidemics" as well as to catastrophic wildfires. Insect infestation and fires that burned 50 million acres of forest between 1990 and 2002 have heavily damaged the forests of Arizona, the northern Rockies and California. California's magnificent giant sequoias are threatened and the pine forests of California's San Bernardino National Forest are all but gone. There are threats to a number of other historic forest types. The six worst years for forest fires since 1960 occurred between 2000 and 2008 (Alvarez 2007, Bonnicksen 2002, 2003a, 2003b, 2006, NIFC 2009).

Homework

Name: _____   Date: _____

1. List two or three problems that you might associate with the management of privately owned forest lands.

2. List two or three problems that you might associate with the management of federally owned forest lands.

Hint: There are no specific "right" or "wrong" answers to these questions. They are exercises in critical thinking.

America's Forests at the Time of European Contact

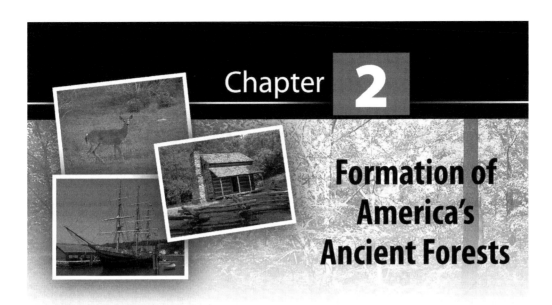

Chapter 2

Formation of America's Ancient Forests

The forests of the United States began to take form as the last ice age, the Pleistocene Epoch, was ending approximately 17,000 years ago. During the Pleistocene, two great ice sheets covered almost 6 million square miles and were as much as two miles thick. Glaciers extended over most of Canada into what is now the northern tier of the United States. To the east, the Laurentide Ice Sheet extended east from the base of the Rocky Mountains south into the Appalachians; it covered southern New England and the Lake States. To the west, the Cordilleran Ice Sheet extended across the west from the northern Rockies to the coast. Sea level was some 328 to 492 feet lower than today, and the Atlantic continental shelf was exposed as much as 62 miles farther than today's shoreline. The Pacific continental shelf was exposed as much as 31 miles beyond the current shoreline (Bonnicksen 2000a).

Coastal and central Alaska were free from the ice sheets, and a land bridge across what is now the Bering Strait, "Beringia," was exposed above sea level, connecting the Asian and American continents. In describing how changing climate affected North America, Pielou (1991) states, "One of the most interesting aspects of this never ending change from the ecological point of view is that, over the time interval we are considering (and probably for the whole of Earth's history), physical conditions on this continent (and everywhere else) have never repeated themselves."

The last glacial maximum occurred approximately 18,000 years ago (Pielou 1991, Bonnicksen 2000a). Since then the Earth has warmed, although this has not been a steady process. The Earth has undergone periodic cooling and warming periods within the past 18,000 years. One such warming period occurred approximately 7,000 to 4,000 years ago with mean temperatures estimated to exceed today's mean temperature by 1° to 2°C. Cooling followed this, and then came the "Medieval Warm Period," which lasted

Recommended Reading

Bennicksen, Thomas M. 2000. *America's Ancient Forests: from the Ice Age to the Age of Discovery.*

Thomas Bonnicksen is a forest ecologist and an advocate of "restoration forestry." That is the attempt to restore as much as possible America's forests to conditions that existed at the time of first European contact. *America's Ancient Forests* is the result of his exhaustive study of what the ancient forests were like. It was the primary reference for this chapter and should be a "must read" for forestry students and others interested in the health and management of forest resources.

from approximately A.D. 900 to 1200, when temperatures again might have exceeded modern levels.[1] A "Little Ice Age" lasted from approximately A.D. 1450 to between 1850 and 1880. Little Ice Age temperatures were approximately 1°C cooler on average than today (Bonnicksen 2000a, Fagan 2000, 2004).

Earth's climate is a complex phenomenon. In recent years it has become a topic of bitter debate in scientific and political circles. It is beyond the scope of this book to explore the topic of climate change; however, interested students may refer to the Climate Debate Daily (*climatedebatedaily.com*) website for a comprehensive bibliography of current essays and research discussing both sides of the issue. In addition, Pielou (1991) provides a relatively easy-to-understand explanation of the complicated concepts of glacial ages, glaciations and their causes.

THE PLEISTOCENE FOREST

The forest ecologist Thomas Bonnicksen (2000a) states, "The landscape beyond the glaciers would not be familiar to modern eyes. It was an alien world of modern and extinct animals living among well-known plants mixed in unusual ways." During the Pleistocene, seasonal differences were moderate because summers were cooler than today. Fossils, fossil pollen and carbon dating provide clues to the character of the vegetation that existed across the American landscape during the last ice age (Pielou 1991).

Tundra and cold steppes covered Beringia, Alaska, and the region immediately south of the glaciers. The characteristics of tundra are grass-like sedges (plants with triangular-shaped leaves), grasses, herbs, lichens, mosses and scattered small sages. Tundra dominated the southeastern edge of the glaciers and extended down the Appalachians as far south as Georgia. Cold steppes consist of sagebrush and grass, but very little sedge. Bare areas with dry soils were interspersed along the glacial front. There were patches of trees scattered through the tundra and cold steppes (Bonnicksen 2000a).

Forests dominated the American landscape south of the tundra and cold steppes. Ice age forests were mostly **boreal**, or northern forest types consisting predominately of softwood species that could tolerate cold winters and short, cool summers. White spruce dominated the Ice Age forest, occupying drier sites through most of what is now the Great Plains, east of the Mississippi and into the Southwest. Black spruce, while less common, occupied the wetter sites. Scattered through the white spruce forest were Colorado blue spruce, junipers, aspen, birch and limber pine. Sagebrush and fireweed existed in clearings within the forest. An unknown species of pine occupied the Texas panhandle and eastern New Mexico. These species are pioneers, and the forest was likely open and park-like, much like the forest of south-central Alaska is today. Wildfire was (and is) common in white spruce forests, sometimes consuming as much as a million acres. Lightning caused many of the fires, but after the arrival of man it is probable that humans caused at least half (Bonnicksen 2000a).

Western forests contained many of the same species as today, but in different mixes and locations. Subalpine species—Engelmann spruce, subalpine fir and lodgepole pine—existed on the lower slopes of the Rockies. The tree line[2] was approximately

---

[1] The existence and extent of the Medieval Warm Period is a debate within the scientific community. Some scientists argue that it did not exist, others that it was limited to the Northern Hemisphere and others that it was global. Scientists also disagree on whether or not temperatures during the Medieval Warm Period were greater than temperatures in the latter twentieth and early twenty-first.

[2] The "tree line" is the elevation marking the limit above which trees are capable of growing.

2,000 feet lower than it is today. In the Pacific Northwest, the coastline was further west and Puget Sound was an ice-filled basin. Coast species such as Douglas-fir and red alder were pushed into small areas south of the Puget Trough. Douglas-fir was scarce in northern California and probably existed on the coastal shelf off southern California. At times, 17,000-year-old Douglas-fir logs eroded out of gullies on the California Channel Islands. As is the case today, the giant redwoods occupied the coastal plain, which was farther west than it is today. Juniper-sage woodland and mixed conifer forests cov-

Figure 2.1 White Spruce Forest, Alaska.

ered much of the present-day desert of the southwest. The deserts of the Southwest were cooler and moister, allowing forests of pygmy conifers and oaks to exist. Engelmann spruce grew on the Mogollon Rim in northern Arizona where ponderosa pine now grows. A mixed conifer forest occupied Chaco Canyon in northwestern New Mexico. The ponderosa pine that now dominates the Colorado Plateau had retreated to the Santa Catalina and San Andres Mountains of southern Arizona and New Mexico and south into Mexico. Fir, spruce, limber pine and sagebrush covered the region. Small prairies existed in northern Texas in the Llano Estacado "within bands of forest like lakes of grass" (Bonnicksen 2000a).

Jack pine forests spread south of the white spruce forests in regions now occupied by the southern pines. Eastern hemlock and white pine forest existed along the present Continental Shelf, which is now, of course, beneath the Atlantic. Today's southern species—magnolia and southern pines—existed only along the Gulf Coast from northern Florida and south Georgia to the Rio Grande.

Hardwoods interspersed with coniferous species across the continent; however, the mixed hardwood forest we are familiar with existed in narrow bands in the uplands along the Mississippi Valley. Oak, hickory, beech and walnut occupied warmer sites in the south.

A diversity of wildlife unknown in today's American forests existed in the white spruce forest of the Ice Age. A multitude of wildlife existed in the Pleistocene, including the megafauna: woolly mammoths, mastodons, giant sloths, dire wolf, saber-toothed cats, short-faced bears, giant beaver and stag moose. The end of the Ice Age resulted in the extinction of many of these species. Small arctic mammals—arctic ground squirrel, arctic shrew, lemmings and ermines—were a part of the mix. These species, as well as musk ox, reindeer and caribou, existed much further south than their current ranges. Scientists have found caribou fossils from this era as far south as northern Alabama and Georgia. Beringia allowed species to migrate from Asia to America and vice versa. Migrant species from Asia included the long-horned bison (that evolved into the giant bison and later the modern bison), the ancestor of the bighorn sheep, the woolly mammoth and a two-legged creature known as *Homo sapiens.* The ancestors of the modern horse and camel migrated from America to Asia. "Pleistocene communities had a greater diversity of species, higher numbers of animals, more large animals, and larger animals than any that existed from then until now" (Bonnicksen 2000a).

TRANSITION FROM THE PLEISTOCENE TO THE MODERN FOREST

Retreat of the glaciers and disintegration of Ice Age forests began approximately 17,000 years ago. This was not a steady process but a sporadic one with frequent reversals. For example, the sea level rose until roughly 5,000 years ago when the coastlines of America reached their approximate present position. The period from approximately 9,000 to 5,000 years ago marked the time of the Great Drought, further disrupting forests through harsh climate and by creating conditions for catastrophic wildfire.

As the glaciers receded, tundra and cold steppe replaced glacier. White spruce advanced northwards into tundra. To the south, the climate became too warm for spruce, and it began to die out, replaced by warmer climate species. In places other pioneer species—dwarf birch, willow, poplar, juniper, silverberry and soapberry—preceded spruce. The white spruce forest reached what is now central Minnesota approximately 14,500 years ago. By 10,000 years ago, it had reached the foot of the glacier at the Canadian border. The white spruce forest moved in a band that stretched from northern Illinois east into Massachusetts at about the same time. In Maine, poor soil slowed the advance of spruce. Glaciers to the north and invading settler species from the south severely restricted the range of the spruce forest. Approximately 4,000 years ago, the ice sheets finally melted and the spruce forest again expanded across Canada and Alaska.

Prairie began to expand northward from the Llano Estacado approximately 12,000 years ago. Warming climate and drought across the southern plains caused the spruce to die. In the next 2,000 years, grasslands extended into the Dakotas. Prairies advanced further north to Minnesota and Iowa 8,000 years ago. Small colonies of white spruce survived at higher elevations and exist today in the mountains of northwest Montana. Small pockets of white spruce existed in canyons and on steep north-facing slopes in the ponderosa pine forest of the Black Hills.

Lodgepole pine was the pioneer species in the lowlands of the west, replacing tundra. It did not reach the current northern limit of its range in the central Yukon until less than a century ago. Red alder, Engelmann spruce and Sitka spruce also invaded the tundra along the Pacific Coast approximately 16,800 years ago. The settler species, western and mountain hemlock, invaded the pioneer forest, forming "patchy, open parklands of forest and tundra." The jet stream changed 14,500 years ago, creating a moister, warmer climate and forcing mountain hemlock into the Olympic Mountains. By 6,000 years ago, the northern coastal forest looked much as it does today except for the absence of western redcedar, a settler species that requires very moist soils. Redcedar appeared approximately 5,000 years ago but did not proliferate until 2,000 years ago when it made up 50 percent of the forest in some places.

Eastern larch (tamarack) migrated north to Canada, the Great Lakes region and New England where it exists today with black spruce on boggy sites, much like it existed during the Ice Age. Jack pine and red pine—fire species—spread north more rapidly than hardwoods, indicating that wildfires must have cleared white spruce forest in advance of the pines. Jack pine migrated north through New England where it is uncommon today and intermingled with hardwoods in the Great Lakes region. White pine moved from its refuge on the continental shelf into the Shenandoah Valley by 12,700 years ago, arriving in the north after red and jack pine. It spread west and north, reaching the White Mountains 9,000 years ago, through the Great Lakes and southern Canada, and reaching Minnesota 7,200 years ago. Eastern hemlock also spread north, occupying wet sites and arriving in southern Michigan about 7,000 years ago. The hemlock population crashed approximately 4,800 years ago—possibly due to a fungal disease—with trees rarely reaching thirty years of age. The species did not recover until 2,000 years later. Aspen, birch, and balsam fir also migrated north into Canada and the northern tier of the United States. The Rockies blocked balsam fir, a settler species, from moving west.

The eastern hardwoods—American elm, oak, maple and black ash—spread from the Southeast and up the Mississippi River Valley following the southern edge of the white spruce forest and arriving in the Great Lakes region approximately 11,000 years ago. Black ash—a swamp species—and northern red oak—an upland species—arrived in the north earlier than other hardwoods. Some scientists speculate that these pioneer species may have survived in scattered spots within the white spruce forest of the Ice Age. Oak, a pioneer species, and elm and maple—settler species—arrived in New England 10,000 years ago. Hickory arrived 5,000 years later. Blue jays must have helped the spread of oaks. Jays can carry three to five acorns while flying and carry them up to two and a half miles. Wildlife biologists estimate that jays store 67 percent of the acorns in open forest and 12 percent in nearby grasslands—burying them in places that favor the establishment of pioneer species. Beech—a settler species—spread slowly since it had farther to travel and its nuts are heavier. Blue jays and passenger pigeons probably helped its spread. Chestnut was one of the slowest species to advance, moving from its refuge in the lower Mississippi Valley at an estimated rate of 300 feet per year. Chestnut did not become abundant in southern New England until approximately 2,000 years ago. Its population increased abruptly, probably as a result of Indian burning practices. By the time of European settlement, it had spread from southern Missouri to southern Maine and was the dominant species in the oak-chestnut forest (Bonnicksen 2000a).

Southern pines began to replace hardwoods in the south approximately 6,000 to 9,000 years ago, with the modern forest established approximately 5,000 years ago.

AMERICA'S ANCIENT FORESTS

The formation of America's ancient forests,[3] like the retreat of the glaciers, was not a steady process. It was sporadic, with different species of plants and animals migrating in different directions and reaching their present range at different times. Like the glaciers, trees advanced and receded with fluctuations and climate. And as Pielou (1991) said, "conditions have never repeated themselves."

As we consider America's forests of the twenty-first century, we must understand that conditions always change. Thus, forest ecosystems are always changing. As we learned in the previous chapter, change is seldom predictable but dominated by disturbance. We may consider the Pleistocene disturbance on a grand scale. Today, our forests continue to change. And as we are about to learn, humans had and continue to have a hand in how that happens.

---

[3] Bonnicksen (2000) uses the term "ancient forest" to describe America's forests as they existed at the time of first European contact. Others define the term differently, but this book follows Bonnicksen's meaning of the term.

Homework

Name: _____   **Date:** _____

Do an Internet search and write down three definitions of "ancient forest" that you find that differ from that adopted by Bonnicksen and this book.

1.

2.

3.

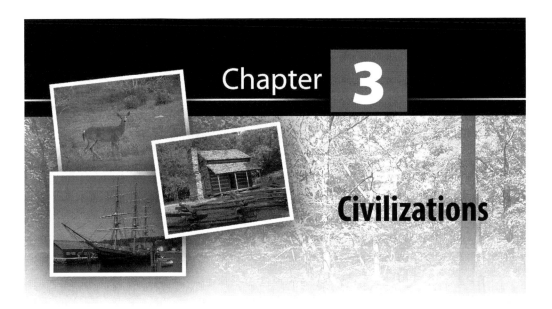

Chapter 3

Civilizations

PENETRATING THE MISTS OF TIME

On the Colorado Plateau in the Four Corners region where the states of Utah, Arizona, Colorado and New Mexico converge, a great civilization existed in the distant past. We call them the Anasazi (a Dineh word meaning "ancestors of our enemies").[1] They constructed large, multi-roomed, multi-storied, terraced stone structures. Some were in the shape of the letter "D." They built others into difficult-to-access ledges on the sides of cliffs and mesas. Their villages included circular, underground chambers known as kivas.

> ### Recommended Reading
>
> Mann, Charles C. 2005. *1491: New Revelations of the Americas before Columbus.*
>
> Mann's book, *1491,* is one of those rare gems that reveals new information in every chapter and challenges many preconceived ideas about Indians and the state of nature in the Americas before Columbus. Mann is not afraid to discuss controversial ideas and is honest in portraying why they are controversial. It is a fascinating book.

They made pottery ornamented with bold geometric designs. They built roads and irrigation systems. They constructed sophisticated solar calendars and carried on trade with distant peoples from as far away as Mexico.

There are thousands of similar archeological sites of various sizes scattered throughout the region. The locations of the most impressive sites are in Chaco Canyon, New Mexico, Canyon de Chelly, Arizona and Mesa Verde, Colorado. The locations of these sites are inhospitable. Chaco and Canyon de Chelly are in arid country that seems incapable of providing the necessities—especially water—for supporting the number of people required to build and inhabit the structures and to support the civilization they built. The spectacular ruins on Mesa Verde are constructed in cliff ledges on the sides of the mesa.

The Anasazi quarried stones used at all three sites from nearby cliffs, and they had to cut and transport timbers used to support the roofs at Chaco and Canyon de Chelly

---

[1] The more commonly known name for Dineh is "Navajo," a Pueblo word that translates roughly as "people of the great planted fields" (Sides 2006).

Figure 3.1 Cliff Palace. *Mesa Verde National Park, Colorado.*

from distances as far as fifty miles away (Frazier 1987). They appear to have done some of the masonry work with an eye to decorative features as well as to the structural integrity of the building.

Twenty-first century visitors are inspired to question who built these villages and how a pre-Columbian civilization could construct them without the wheel or domesticated draft animals. Why did they choose these locations? Why did they leave? Where did they go? Could war or climate change have been factors in the construction and abandonment of the sites? Perhaps the answers to these questions may be easier to discover if we can answer critical questions of time. When were they built? When were they abandoned?

The answer to who they were comes from contemporary Native Americans. Today's Pueblo Indians—including the Acoma, Zuni, Taos, Sandia, San Ysidro, Zuni and Hopi—understand that they are the descendants of the Anasazi. The "enemies" the Dineh were referring to are the Pueblo.

One of those fascinating accidents of science provided the answer to the question of "when." And the method used to answer this question involved the timber beams that supported the roofs of the pueblos.

Richard Wetherill, a rancher from Mancos, Colorado, led the first archeological expedition to Chaco Canyon in 1895. Earlier Wetherill had discovered the ruins at Mesa Verde, Colorado. Later expeditions revealed that Chaco was a sophisticated culture. According to Frazier (1987), scientists have inventoried 2,528 individual archeological sites in Chaco Canyon and found evidence of an extensive trade with Mexico. The Chacoans had a rich spiritual life as indicated by the many kivas. They built a sophisticated irrigation system with canals, dams and floodgates. A network of 26 to 40-foot wide, straight roads led from Chaco to outlier sites. Stairways carved into the surrounding cliff sides connect Chaco Canyon to the roadways to outlier sites. A solar calendar and other indications of an advanced understanding of astronomy exist in Chaco and on Fajada Butte. Two corner windows in Pueblo Bonito show the winter solstice when the light forms a rectangle on the north wall beginning at the room's corner.

Figure 3.2 Pueblo Bonito. *Chaco Culture National Historical Park, New Mexico.*

For a number of years, archeologists and anthropologists speculated about who built the ruins in Chaco. Why did they leave? When were they occupied? Among those most interested was Neil Judd, an archeologist with the Smithsonian Institution who began an extensive dig at Chaco in 1920 under the sponsorship of the National Geographic Society.

DENDROCHRONOLOGY

The question of time was answered in a most unlikely manner that is typical of how science often works. Andrew Ellicott Douglass (1867–1962) was an astronomer at the University of Arizona's Steward Observatory. Douglass was studying solar phenomena and developed a hypothesis that the eleven-year cycle of sunspot activity would affect plant growth, specifically in the width of tree rings.

The basis of the concept behind his theory comes from the fundamentals of plant physiology. Green plants grow through the process of photosynthesis in which the leaves absorb carbon dioxide and the roots take up water. The photosynthetic process combines the three component elements—carbon, hydrogen and oxygen—to form simple sugars such as glucose. Simple sugars are the basic building blocks of the polymers (large molecules formed by the combination of small, repeating structural units) that comprise wood: cellulose, lignin and hemicelluloses. The energy source for photosynthesis is the sun. Wood is solar. It was this reasoning that led Douglass to experiment with tree growth to determine if he could reconstruct a biological history of solar activity.

The woody tissue of the stems, roots and branches serves two primary functions in the living tree. The wood conducts fluids from the roots to the leaves. It also provides mechanical support to raise the crown above its neighbors, enabling the individual tree to successfully compete for light. Therefore, the stem and branches must thicken as the tree grows up in order to provide the strength required to hold the crown erect. The thickening of the stem occurs in the *cambium*. The cambium is a layer of reproductive cells located between the woody tissue and the bark where cells divide to form new wood and bark cells. Cell division occurs only in the cambium and not within the existing woody tissue.

In the temperate zones, tree growth is seasonal. Each winter, the tree becomes dormant. Wood consists of individual cells each shaped like a long, slender tube. Nearly all of the cells are oriented along the axis of the tree stem and serve as a series of pipes for fluid transport up the stem. In the spring, the cells formed by the cambium are large and have thin cell walls as well as large cell cavities. Later in the growing season, the cells tend to be smaller in diameter with thicker walls and smaller diameter cavities. This forms visible annual growth rings within the wood of temperate species. The inner, lighter-colored, less dense portion of the growth ring is known as *earlywood*. The outer, darker, denser portion of the ring is the *latewood*.

Douglass developed the optical instruments and microscopic techniques to catalog tree ring widths and precisely measure variations in growth from year to year. He discovered that the trees in his sample exhibited a remarkable consistency in the annual patterns across the region. His samples reflected a pattern of good and poor growing seasons. However, his hypothesis that scientists could determine solar activity by studying growth patterns in trees failed.

Douglass found no relationship between tree growth and solar activity. Other variables such as rainfall, openings in the canopy and disturbance have a greater influence on growth. He failed to prove his theory. In particular, Douglass noted rainfall as the dominant variable affecting the growth of trees in the arid Southwest. Despite his failure to prove his initial hypothesis, Douglass was quick to recognize the importance of the remarkably consistent growth patterns he had observed in his experiments.

Douglass observed that he could reconstruct a chronological record of the patterns of growth rings by matching patterns of an older sample of unknown age to similar patterns in a sample of known age. This was not a simple method. Ring width patterns of different ages can be confusingly similar. "It is necessary to be extremely careful not to be fooled. Douglass was a careful man, and the technique proved successful. Its application to archeology was inevitable" (Frazier 1987). Douglass named his new technique "*dendrochronology*," the study of time through trees.

Figure 3.3 Floor Beams in an Anasazi Pueblo. *Bandelier National Monument, New Mexico.*

In 1922, Neil Judd sought Douglass' help. Could he use Douglass' technique of matching tree rings to determine the age of the structures in Chaco Canyon? Ponderosa pine beams supported the roof systems of the pueblos. The logs must have been carried by hand to Chaco Canyon from the high country as much as fifty miles distant. Because of the dry conditions in the desert of northwestern New Mexico, the beams were well preserved. Douglass was able to find sufficient samples to reconstruct a timeline for the ruins in Chaco Canyon.

He discovered that construction of the magnificent Pueblo Bonito in Chaco Canyon began in 919 and remained occupied in 1127. Pueblo del Arroyo, a smaller Chaco ruin, was under construction from 1053 to 1103. The Anasazi were building Balcony House at Mesa Verde from 1190 to 1206 and built the Cliff Palace in 1073. They had constructed and occupied other Anasazi ruins in Canyon de Chelly, Arizona and elsewhere during the same era.

"By translating the story told by tree rings, we have pushed back the horizons of history in the United States for nearly eight centuries before Columbus reached the shores of the New World, and we have established in our Southwest a chronology for that period more accurate than if human hands had written down the major events as they occurred" (Douglass 1929).

INDIANS? OR NATIVE AMERICANS?

Before going any further, we must deal with the issue of what to call the indigenous people of America. Charles Mann (2005) calls it a "terminological quicksand." Are they Indians—an unfortunate misnomer stemming from the geographic ignorance of Columbus? Or should we call them Native Americans? Both are problematic.

Mann (2005) claims, "every native person I have met (I think without exception) has used 'Indian' rather than 'Native American.'" He quotes American Indian Movement activist Russell Means: "Anyone born in the western hemisphere is a Native American. . . . I abhor the term Native American." For this reason, I will respect Means' wishes and Mann's judgment, preferring the term "Indian" when generically discussing the indigenous people of the Americas.

However, I will follow Mann's example and refer to specific cultures or nations wherever appropriate. Most Indians refer to their specific tribal affiliation—Dineh or Haudenosaunee, for example—just as a European might describe herself as Polish or Swedish rather than European. I will also follow Mann's convention of referring to tribal groups by the names they use to describe themselves. For example, Mann uses "Dineh" rather than "Navajo" and "Haudenosaunee" rather than "Iroquois."

Although we do not know what the ancestors of modern Indians called themselves, we now refer to the first immigrants to America as "Paleoindians."

THE TRADITIONAL VIEW OF AMERICAN HISTORY

American history began in 1492 when Christopher Columbus landed on the shores of Hispaniola. Or so goes the traditional interpretation. The nature of human life in the Americas before Columbus was either ignored or clouded in mistaken perceptions. But recent, including numerous very recent, discoveries are revealing a rich diversity of human cultures more ancient and far more sophisticated than originally believed (Mann 2005, Taylor 2001).

The traditional view of North America in 1491 is that small bands of Stone Age people sparsely populated the continent. With a few exceptions, these bands were nomadic hunters or depended upon subsistence agriculture. Although there were differences in their customs and languages, they were a relatively homogeneous people unlike the diverse cultures of Europe. The predominant perception was that indigenous cultures were unchanged over the centuries.

The traditional perception extends to the pre-Columbian environment—what the geographer William Denevan (1992) has described as the "Pristine Myth." Under this interpretation, Indians were "noble savages" whose impact on the environment was minimal. The America "discovered" by Columbus was a vast wilderness (Krech 1999). Scholars have refuted the pristine myth although the myth persists in the minds of much of the public. We now understand that Indians were skilled managers of the plant and animal communities that surrounded them.

The perception of minimal Indian impact on the landscape originated with the recorded observations of early European explorers and settlers. Cronon (1983) describes the limited observations of North America by European explorers of the sixteenth century—Verrazzano, Gosnold, Pring and Champlain—as being confined to "within a few miles of the coast or along a few major rivers." Most were engaged in the search for "merchantable commodities"—gold, silver, furs, timber and fertile land for agriculture—that further limited their recorded observations of the American landscape. In this regard, they valued those resources that were scarce in Europe and that were useful to European lifestyles. There was a bit of salesmanship involved as well as colonial proprietors sought to encourage settlement and financial support by describing the New World as a vast wilderness, paradise or a "Garden of Eden" (Krech 1999).

But their recorded observations of Indian activity, particularly burning practices, seem to contradict the pristine description. They made their descriptions of the American wilderness with Europe as the point of reference rather than as a description of Indian activity. Much of the forests of Europe had been removed centuries before the birth of the earliest explorers of the New World. The landscape of their homelands in the sixteenth and seventeenth centuries was agrarian and urban. From that perspective, it is easy to understand the European perception of the Americas as a wilderness.

Europeans brought with them diseases that decimated Native American populations. However, spread of disease was rapid and decimated Indian populations well in advance of European arrival in a particular location. There is strong evidence that forests had ample time to reclaim grasslands or agricultural fields after abandonment by the survivors of the frequent epidemics and before the first observation of the landscape by European eyes. This factor also contributed to the perception of America being a vast untamed wilderness before European settlement (Denevan 1992, Mann 2005).

European and American authors of the late eighteenth and early nineteenth centuries romanticized the perception of America as pristine prior to European settlement. Michel de Montaigne, Jean-Jacques Rousseau, William Wordsworth, Samuel Taylor Coleridge, Henry David Thoreau, Ralph Waldo Emerson, James Fenimore Cooper and others romanticized Indians as "noble savages" living in perfect harmony in the American wilderness.[2] While some were portraying Indians as noble, others were portraying them as murderous, ignorant barbarians (Krech 1999). Both stereotypes are inaccurate and demean Indians as being naive and childlike or inhuman and without morals.

Indian cultures were diverse and dynamic (Taylor 2001). Perhaps Indian cultures at the time of Columbus were more diverse than their European counterparts. While Indians of the East lived in semi-permanent villages and subsisted on fishing, game, and agriculture, tribes of the Plains were nomadic hunters who followed the bison herds and made seasonal camps during winter. The Pueblo tribes lived in permanent villages dependent upon agriculture. The people of Acoma have lived in a pueblo atop a mesa east of Gallup, New Mexico, for a thousand years.

Some tribes lived relatively comfortable and affluent lives, comparable to or better than the lives of their contemporaries in Europe. Others lived on the brink of starvation. Indians spoke different languages, made alliances with some tribes and made war on others. The Haudenosaunee (Iroquois) and Hurons of the eastern Great Lakes region were in a constant state of warfare until the Iroquois virtually wiped out the Huron (Taylor 2001). The Haudenosaunee were a confederacy of five (later six) related tribal groups who had formed an alliance ending fratricidal warfare to live in political harmony with each other.

Cultures emerged, disappeared, merged and evolved over the thousands of years of Indian occupancy of North America prior to European contact. Mound builder cultures emerged, evolved and disappeared in the Mississippi and Ohio Valleys and in the Gulf States. Archeological excavations at Mesa Verde have uncovered the remains of primitive dwellings or "pit houses" that predate the construction of the great Anasazi cliff dwellings like Cliff Palace and Balcony House. The Anasazi abandoned Canyon de Chelly, Mesa Verde and Chaco Canyon for reasons that are unclear but most likely related to changing climate. Later archeological sites track their migration to today's Hopi villages in Arizona, into New Mexico's Rio Grande valley, to Taos in northern New Mexico or south to Acoma and Zuni Pueblos.

---

[2] Krech (1999) points out that the original meaning of the term "savage" was derived from the Latin "*Silvaticus*" and meant living in a "state of nature." The term's present derogatory connotation has evolved since it was first used to portray Indians.

Much of what we know about pre-Columbian civilization has emerged very recently. As new knowledge has emerged, the mysteries of these civilizations have deepened. The examples of the many theories of how and when humans first arrived in the Americas emphasize this point.

ORIGINS

Scientists believe that humans originated in Africa approximately 250,000 to 400,000 years ago. With the exception of Antarctica, North and South America were the last continents occupied by humans (Taylor 2001). Over the years, researchers proposed a number of theories about how and when Indians arrived in the New World (Jacobs 2002, Mann 2005), beginning with the quaint theory that the ancestors of modern Indians were descendants of Chinese, Phoenicians, Basques, Africans, "Hindoos," Greeks, Assyrians, Welsh, survivors of the lost city of Atlantis and the Biblical Lost Tribes of Israel. By the nineteenth century, the scientific disciplines of archeology and anthropology discarded these theories. However, the scientists of that era were inexplicably slow to discard the notion that Indians were not recent arrivals in the New World. Amateur archeologists had discovered artifacts that suggested much earlier origins, perhaps back to the Pleistocene. But others scoffed at their findings as the ignorant ramblings of "relic hunters." The most vocal critics of the new theories were scholars—William Henry Holmes and, later, Aleš Hrdlička of the Smithsonian Institution. (Mann 2005)

This is not an unusual phenomenon in the sciences and social sciences. Older generations of scientists frequently treat new ideas skeptically (not necessarily a bad thing) as they have built their careers and professional reputations on the theories newer ideas are about to replace. One of the more startling discoveries happened in 1908 near Folsom, in the northeast corner of New Mexico. George McJunkin, a ranch foreman, former slave and amateur geologist, discovered the bones of long-extinct animals in a washed-out creek bed. Later excavations near Folsom turned up elegantly crafted spearheads with a fluted base. If the spear points—the famous Folsom Point— and the fossils were contemporary, humans must have occupied North America as far back as the Pleistocene. Another discovery followed Folsom in 1929 in a dried out creek bed near Clovis, New Mexico, along the Texas border. Nineteen-year-old Ridgely Whiteman had discovered more "extinct elephant bones." Whiteman contacted the Smithsonian, but after cursory examination, that august institution considered the find "of no interest." Whiteman's find attracted the attention of Edgar B. Howard, a graduate student at the University of Pennsylvania. Howard began an archeological dig near Clovis that turned up evidence of human occupation that coincided with the fossils. Among the artifacts were beautifully crafted stone spear points.

A long, tapered point characterizes the Clovis Point. Clovis points were flaked from fine-grained stone such as flint, and researchers have discovered quarry sites with the best stone along the Canadian River of Texas, in the Knife River Valley of North Dakota and in southeastern Idaho. A good point has carefully chipped and rounded edges that could be as sharp as a scalpel. The center of the point is fluted to fit a spear shaft, fastened with sinew and coated with pitch. The longest point found is six inches long. Researchers consider the Clovis a work of art, yet it is a deadly projectile designed for killing mammoth and other big game. The general belief is that it originated in Alaska, where it is known as the Mesa point, but a simple Internet search illustrates that there are numerous theories revolving around the origin of the Clovis Point and the people who developed it (Campbell 2003). Scientists have since found evidence of what became known as the Clovis Culture at more than eighty sites in North America (Mann 2005).

The theory of "Clovis First" came into prominence in the 1960s. Proponents believed that the first humans in the Americas were Stone Age hunters, following the woolly mammoth and other game across Beringia into the interior of North America when the glaciers of the Pleistocene were receding.

In the 1950s, Willard F. Libby of the University of Chicago developed the technique of carbon dating.[3] The Earth's atmosphere always contains a certain amount of mildly radioactive carbon, C^{14}. Over time, C^{14} decays and becomes the non-radioactive C^{12}. Its half-life—the time it takes for half of the C^{14} to decay—is 5,370 years. Plants absorb a certain amount of C^{14} during photosynthesis. Animals take in C^{14} by eating plants. Carnivores take in C^{14} when they eat herbivores. But when a living organism dies, it absorbs no more C^{14}. Only the process of decay of C^{14} continues. Thus, scientists may estimate the approximate date when the tissue died from the proportion of C^{14} remaining (Mann 2005).

In 1958, the first carbon dating laboratory associated with archeological research was established at the University of Arizona. One of its scientists was the geologist, C. Vance Haynes. Haynes studied a number of Clovis sites, establishing relatively consistent dates of approximately 13,500 to 12,900 years ago. For the first time, dates of human occupancy of North America had been established (Mann 2005). Bonnicksen (2000a) lists estimated times of habitation in various locations: Wisconsin —13,400 to 12,300 years ago; western Washington and Oregon—12,000 years ago; Florida—12,000 years ago; Maine—11,000 years ago; southeastern New York—11,000 years ago; California—12,000 years ago; and New Mexico—11,600 years ago.

Haynes wasn't finished. He recognized a stunning coincidence in dates from his education in geology (Mann 2005). Approximately 14,000 years ago, the Cordilleran and Laurentide Ice Sheets receded, creating a corridor east of the Rockies into the interior of the continent. The Beringia land bridge disappeared into the sea, then reopened and closed twice before permanently disappearing 10,500 years ago, trapping both animals and people in Alaska. The new arrivals followed the game south. It took approximately a century for Paleoindians to emerge from the passageway through the ice (Bonnicksen 2000a). Haynes published his findings in an article in *Science* in 1964, winning popular acceptance for the theory that the Clovis Culture explained the origins of human beings in the Americas.

It did not take long for the "Clovis First" theory to fall apart under the weight of new evidence (Krech 1999, Mann 2005). In 1986, an article in *Current Anthropology* featured a proposed modification of Clovis First, suggesting that the ancestors of modern Indians descended from three migrations beginning with the Clovis migration across Beringia (Greenburg et al. 1986). Joseph F. Greenberg, a linguist at Stanford University, argued that North American languages originated from three linguistic sources and that the "three linguistic stocks represent separate migrations." Two Arizona State scientists, Christy G. Turner II, a physical anthropologist, and Stephen L. Zegura, a geneticist, added dental and DNA evidence respectively to support the three-migration theory (Mann 2005). This theory states that approximately 10,000 to 8,000 years ago, the Athabascan language stock migrated across the Bering Strait in small, hide-covered, wooden-framed boats (Taylor 2001). A number of tribal groups of the Pacific Coast from Alaska to California, as well as the modern Apache and

---

[3] Libby received a Nobel Prize for his work in 1960.

Dineh (Navajo) of the southwestern United States are the descendants of this group of immigrants. The next migration occurred approximately 5,000 years ago when the Inuits and Aleuts (often miscalled "Eskimos") arrived by boat (Taylor 2001)[4]. Scientists do not universally accept the three migration theory. The evidence was anything but conclusive, and soon new evidence would emerge that would push the horizons of human occupancy of the Americas farther into the past.

In the 1960s, anthropologists began to explore an alternative "Coastal Migration Theory" that the first Americans had migrated down the Pacific Coast (Fladmark 1979). Evidence supporting Fladmark's theory is scarce. The rising of ocean levels as the glaciers melted would have erased any evidence of coastal camps. The Coastal Migration Theory has been gaining acceptance in the scholarly community although there is much disagreement over the timing and number of migrations (Dixon 2002, Jacobs 2002, Mann 2005). A further area of disagreement is whether the migration was by land or by boat as humans followed the coastline south (Jacobs 2002).

Advances in the field of human genetics have generated new information and, ironically, added to the controversy concerning the origins of humans in the Americas. Human DNA exists in two forms, in the chromosomes that give us the inherited characteristics passed on from our parents, and in the mitochondrial DNA. Mitochondria are tiny worm-like structures that exist in the protoplasm of human cells. They resemble bacteria, which may explain their biological origin. The mitochondria possess distinctive DNA "with fewer than fifty genes" (Mann 2005). Human sperm cells contain relatively few mitochondria, most or all of which the egg destroys after fertilization. Egg cells, however, contain many more mitochondria that survive in the human embryo. Thus, mitochondrial DNA follows a strict matriarchal line of inheritance. A child's mitochondrial DNA is identical to his mother's, which in turn is identical to her mother's back through a continuous female line of ancestry.[5]

Geneticists began exploring the mitochondrial DNA of various ethnic groups during the 1970s. If people share similar genetic characteristics, they belong to a "haplogroup" and thus share common ancestry. Researchers have identified approximately forty mitochondrial DNA haplogroups, and five exist among the indigenous population of the Americas (Eshleman et al. 2003, Malhi et al. 2002). The genetic characteristics of prehistoric and contemporary Indians suggest that their ancestors may have arrived in a single wave of migration, although some geneticists argue that the evidence supports two or more migrations (Mahli et al. 2002). The Indian haplogroups are common in eastern Siberia, suggesting that migration originated from that region of the world (Eshleman et al. 2003, Mahli et al. 2002, Mann 2005).

DNA researchers hold differing conclusions on when immigration took place. The estimates range from 11,000 to 43,000 years ago (Mahli et al. 2002, Mann 2005). DNA research by Wallace and James Neel published in 1994 indicated that Paleoindians migrated from Siberia 22,000 to 29,500 years ago, long before the ice-free corridor opened up at the end of the Pleistocene. Brazilian researchers pushed the timeline

---

[4] A fourth and often ignored migration deserves mention. Polynesians arrived in the Hawaiian Islands from the Marquesas Islands, Tahiti-nui and Hiva approximately 1,500 years ago or earlier. The great Polynesian migrations across the Pacific were contemporary to the Viking migrations in the North Atlantic, both occurring during the Medieval Warm Period.

[5] We may trace patriarchal lineage through the DNA of Y-chromosome haplogroups. However, only male subjects carry the Y-chromosome, limiting the sample size available to geneticists by approximately 50 percent. In addition, mitochondrial DNA "mutates at an order of magnitude faster than does nuclear DNA" and is easier to work with in the laboratory (Eshleman et al. 2003). Therefore, mitochondrial DNA is the more powerful research tool.

back to 33,000 to 43,000 years ago in a study published in 1997 (Mahli et al. 2002, Mann 2005).

Monte Verde is an archeological site along a river bank in Chile. Research began there in 1977, and by 1989 scientists had uncovered evidence of human occupation dating back at least 12,800 years. Inconclusive evidence suggests that human occupancy at Monte Verde could have occurred as early as 32,000 years ago (Mann 2005). If, as postulated in the Clovis First scenario, humans had used Beringia and the ice-free corridor to reach the Americas, it would not have been possible for them to reach Chile 12,800 years ago. Other research added to the doubts about Clovis First. Geologists began to question the timing of the ice-free corridor between the Laurentide and Cordilleran Glaciers in the 1990s, believing that it opened up more recently than previously believed. In addition, the corridor may not have been hospitable to human occupation.

The Monte Verde study generated controversy among scholars (Eshleman et al. 2003, Fagan 1990). In 1997, a team of researchers, including Vance Haynes, journeyed to Chile to verify the research at the Monte Verde dig. No consensus emerged. Haynes and other supporters of Clovis First were adamant that the Monte Verde research was flawed. Others agreed that Monte Verde was indeed a breakthrough. The controversy continues, but Mann (2005) reports that support for Clovis First is diminishing, especially among younger generations of scientists.

Although the timing and number of migrations is unsettled, it appears that most scholars now believe that the ancestors of Indians migrated from Siberia and that the most likely point of entry was along the Pacific Coast (Eshleman et al. 2003, Mann 2005). Nonetheless, the rapid rate of new discovery means that what we think we know today will probably change tomorrow. As Harvard historian Joyce Chapman remarked about the history of the Americas before Columbus, "No other field in American history has grown as fast" (Mann 2005). Recent discoveries about ancient civilizations in the Americas confirm her assessment.

CAHOKIA

Another advanced culture thrived in what is now the United States from around 950 A.D. to 1250 A.D. (Mann 2005). The location of Cahokia was on the confluence of the Illinois and Mississippi Rivers across from St. Louis—a site ideally suited for trade. Cahokia was a Mississippian culture and among those generally known as the Mound Builders. Mound builder cultures developed along the Mississippi watershed and extended as far north as northern New England. The oldest known mound builder site is at Watson Brake on the Ouachita River in Louisiana, which was occupied approximately 5,400 years ago and making it older than the pyramids of Egypt (Bonnicksen 2000a, Mann 2005).

Cahokia covered 13 square miles, and about 15,000 to 20,000 people occupied it. A total of 120 mounds dotted the landscape. The largest, Monks Mound, was 10 stories high, covered 15 acres and held the house of Cahokia's ruler (Bonnicksen 2000a, Mann 2005). Monks Mound, which is made of local clay that is prone to shrinking and swelling as it absorbs and loses moisture, was a major engineering feat (Mann 2005). The Cahokians were able to keep the mound stable by alternating layers of sand and clay in its construction. The clay held moisture in keeping the mound moist, and the sand allowed excess moisture to drain away, keeping the mound at a relatively constant moisture content.

A 15-foot-high wooden palisade 2 miles long and with guard towers spaced every 70 feet surrounded the area of the city containing Monks Mound. Nearby, there was a circular solar calendar composed of 48 perfectly spaced red cedar posts that archeologists have dubbed "Woodhenge."

Maize made feeding the population of Cahokia possible. Clearing the surrounding forests to plant crops made building the houses and public buildings of Cahokia more difficult because of the distances building materials had to be transported. To resolve the problem and provide a larger water supply for the inhabitants, Cahokians performed another engineering feat by diverting a small stream into another that flowed close to Monks Mound, increasing its flow. They used the widened stream to float logs into Cahokia, anticipating the river drives of American lumbermen of a later era. However, the area became more prone to the frequent flooding that occurs in the Mississippi River bottomland (Mann 2005).

Fossilized pollen samples indicate that elm trees became scarce at Cahokia somewhere around 1,000 years ago, while at the same time chestnut trees became more common. Apparently, the Cahokians were managing the nearby forests by replacing non-mast-producing trees with mast-producers (Bonnicksen 2000a, Mann 2005).

Occupation of Cahokia occurred during the Medieval Warm Period, contemporary with the Anasazi culture of the Four Corners. This was an era when cultures around the world flourished. The Vikings were crossing the Atlantic, settling Greenland and landing in Newfoundland. The Normans under William the Conqueror invaded Britain. In the Pacific, the Polynesians were in the midst of their great seafaring migrations that populated the islands of Polynesia, Hawaii and New Zealand.

CRADLES OF CIVILIZATION

Traditional world history texts frequently refer to four "cradles of civilization"—the Tigris and Euphrates River Valleys where ancient Sumer was located, the Nile Delta, the Indus Valley in Pakistan and the Huang He Valley in China (Mann 2005). Mann insists that two locales in the western hemisphere were every bit as important as wellsprings of civilization—Mesoamerica (Mexico and northern Central America) and the Peruvian littoral (the narrow Pacific coastline west of the Andes).

North of Lima four rivers carry the runoff from the Andes, providing water to the arid Norte Chico region of Peru's coastline. Between 3,200 and 2,500 B.C., a sophisticated culture inhabited this area and built twenty-five known cities with monumental buildings and irrigated fields. This civilization mummified their dead, providing clues that the people of Norte Chico subsisted on a diet consisting almost entirely of seafood. They planted their fields with cotton, which they used to make fish nets. To give a relative idea of the antiquity of the Norte Chico civilization, it was contemporary to ancient Sumer.

The most remarkable thing about the Norte Chico civilization is that explorers did not discover it until the twenty-first century, with the findings first published in 2004 (Mann 2005). Norte Chico would give rise to subsequent civilizations of the Andes, leading eventually to the Inca Empire.

The earliest of the great Mesoamerican civilizations was the Olmec, which originated around 1,800 B.C. Another Mesoamerican civilization, the Zapotec, had established writing around 500 B.C.. Mesoamericans also developed a 365-day calendar and the concept of the number zero—a mathematical concept requiring some sophistication.

The most remarkable contribution of Mesoamerican people to agriculture was the development of maize an estimated 6,000 years ago. Maize is a grain with no known genetic ancestor although some scientists believe it may have been teosinte, a mountain grass with similar genetics. Because of its thick husk, one must plant its seeds. The logical scenario for its creation was through breeding by Indian peoples of Mesoamerica. Mann (2005) quotes Nina V. Federoff, a geneticist at Pennsylvania State University: "'To get corn out of teosinte is so—you couldn't get a grant to do that now, because it would sound so crazy.' She added, 'Somebody who did that today would get a Nobel Prize! If their lab didn't get shut down by Greenpeace[6], I mean.'"

Mesoamericans also developed the milpa, an agricultural technique of planting maize, beans and squash together in the same field. The different plants each contribute nutrients to the soil, allowing for continuous growing in the same fields without either crop rotation or allowing the fields to lie fallow to restore the soil. Some milpas in Mexico have been under cultivation for a thousand years (Mann 2005). In addition, the combination of vegetables constitutes a balanced diet. The technique of the milpa had spread as far north as the Massachusetts coast before the time of the Pilgrims (Mann 2005, Philbrick 2006).

The people of the Americas made other numerous contributions to agriculture. Squash, pumpkins, peanuts, kidney and lima beans, manioc, peppers, tobacco, yams, potatoes and tomatoes all originated in the Americas and were cultivated by Indian people. They domesticated squash in Mesoamerica 10,000 years ago and raised maize in New Mexico as long ago as 4,500 years ago. Southwestern Indians used selective breeding techniques to develop a large-kernelled "Maiz de Ocho" approximately 3,000 years ago. The kidney bean came north from Mexico into New Mexico 3,000 years ago. Approximately 2,300 years ago, the Hohokam of southern Arizona migrated north from Mexico, developing sophisticated systems of irrigated fields at Snaketown to grow squash, maize and beans. The Hohokam built pueblos covering 500 to 1,000 acres, ball courts and canals. The agricultural cultures of the southwest— the Hohokam, Mogollon, and Anasazi—dominated the southwest for centuries. Agriculture probably reached the eastern woodlands 4,500 years ago.

Some of the most amazing examples of how knowledge about civilization in the Americas before Columbus has grown in the past several decades are in the Amazon basin. Scholars generally believed that this immense region is one of the last remaining pristine tropical rain forests on Earth. Environmental activists and the media frequently describe it in very alarming terms as an endangered wilderness. What Mann (2005) and Denevan (1992) describe in the next two chapters provides another example of how the pristine myth is being disproven even in the Amazon.

---

[7] Greenpeace is opposed to genetically modified organisms.

Homework

Name: _____ Date: _____

Visit the website for Chaco Culture National Historical Park, Mesa Verde National Park or Canyon de Chelly National Monument. Follow the link for "History and Culture" and list the three most interesting things you learned about the Anasazi from visiting the website.

Which website did you visit?_____

1.

2.

3.

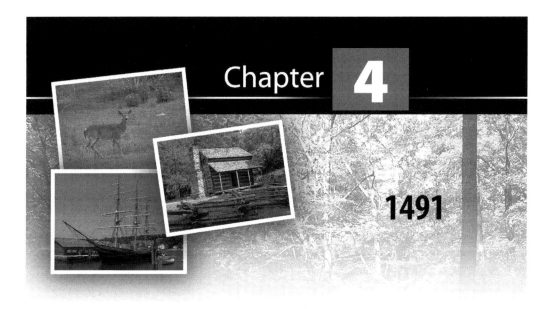

Chapter 4

1491

Before it became the New World, the Western Hemisphere was vastly more populous and sophisticated than has been thought—an altogether more salubrious place to live at the time than, say, Europe. New evidence of both the extent of the population and its agricultural advancement leads to a remarkable conjecture: the Amazon rain forest may be largely a human artifact.

BY CHARLES C. MANN

The plane took off in weather that was surprisingly cool for north-central Bolivia and flew east, toward the Brazilian border. In a few minutes the roads and houses disappeared, and the only evidence of human settlement was the cattle scattered over the savannah like jimmies on ice cream. Then they, too, disappeared. By that time the archaeologists had their cameras out and were clicking away in delight.

Below us was the Beni, a Bolivian province about the size of Illinois and Indiana put together, and nearly as flat. For almost half the year rain and snowmelt from the mountains to the south and west cover the land with an irregular, slowly moving skin of water that eventually ends up in the province's northern rivers, which are sub-subtributaries of the Amazon. The rest of the year the water dries up and the bright-green vastness turns into something that resembles a desert. This peculiar, remote, watery plain was what had drawn the researchers' attention, and not just because it was one of the few places on earth inhabited by people who might never have seen Westerners with cameras.

Clark Erickson and William Balée, the archaeologists, sat up front. Erickson is based at the University of Pennsylvania; he works in concert with a Bolivian archaeologist, whose seat in the plane I usurped that day. Balée is at Tulane University, in New Orleans. He is actually an anthropologist, but as native peoples have vanished, the distinction between anthropologists and archaeologists has blurred. The two men differ in build, temperament, and scholarly proclivity, but they pressed their faces to the windows with identical enthusiasm.

Dappled across the grasslands below was an archipelago of forest islands, many of them startlingly round and hundreds of acres across. Each island rose ten or thirty or sixty feet above the floodplain, allowing trees to grow that would otherwise never survive the water. The forests were linked by raised berms, as straight as a rifle shot and up to three miles long. It is Erickson's belief that this entire landscape—30,000 square miles of forest mounds surrounded by raised fields and linked by causeways—was constructed by a complex, populous society more than 2,000 years ago. Balée, newer to the Beni, leaned toward this view but was not yet ready to commit himself.

Erickson and Balée belong to a cohort of scholars that has radically challenged conventional notions of what the Western Hemisphere was like before Columbus. When I went to high school, in the 1970s, I was taught that Indians came to the Americas across the Bering Strait about 12,000 years ago, that they lived for the most part in small, isolated groups, and that they had so little impact on their environment that even after millennia of habitation it remained mostly wilderness. My son picked up the same ideas at his schools. One way to summarize the views of people like Erickson and Balée would be to say that in their opinion this picture of Indian life is wrong in almost every aspect. Indians were here far longer than previously thought, these researchers believe, and in much greater numbers. And they were so successful at imposing their will on the landscape that in 1492 Columbus set foot in a hemisphere thoroughly dominated by humankind.

Given the charged relations between white societies and native peoples, inquiry into Indian culture and history is inevitably contentious. But the recent scholarship is especially controversial. To begin with, some researchers—many but not all from an older generation—deride the new theories as fantasies arising from an almost willful misinterpretation of data and a perverse kind of political correctness. "I have seen no evidence that large numbers of people ever lived in the Beni," says Betty J. Meggers, of the Smithsonian Institution. "Claiming otherwise is just wishful thinking." Similar criticisms apply to many of the new scholarly claims about Indians, according to Dean R. Snow, an anthropologist at Pennsylvania State University. The problem is that "you can make the meager evidence from the ethnohistorical record tell you anything you want," he says. "It's really easy to kid yourself."

More important are the implications of the new theories for today's ecological battles. Much of the environmental movement is animated, consciously or not, by what William Denevan, a geographer at the University of Wisconsin, calls, polemically, "the pristine myth"—the belief that the Americas in 1491 were an almost unmarked, even Edenic land, "untrammeled by man," in the words of the Wilderness Act of 1964, one of the nation's first and most important environmental laws. As the University of Wisconsin historian William Cronon has written, restoring this long-ago, putatively natural state is, in the view of environmentalists, a task that society is morally bound to undertake. Yet if the new view is correct and the work of humankind was pervasive, where does that leave efforts to restore nature?

The Beni is a case in point. In addition to building up the Beni mounds for houses and gardens, Erickson says, the Indians trapped fish in the seasonally flooded grassland. Indeed, he says, they fashioned dense zigzagging networks of earthen fish weirs between the causeways. To keep the habitat clear of unwanted trees and undergrowth, they regularly set huge areas on fire. Over the centuries the burning created an intricate ecosystem of fire-adapted plant species dependent on native pyrophilia. The current inhabitants of the Beni still burn, although now it is to maintain the savannah for cattle. When we flew over the area, the dry season had just begun, but mile-long lines of flame were already on the march. In the charred areas behind the fires were the blackened spikes of trees—many of them, one assumes, of the varieties that activists fight to save in other parts of Amazonia.

After we landed, I asked Balée, Should we let people keep burning the Beni? Or should we let the trees invade and create a verdant tropical forest in the grasslands, even if one had not existed here for millennia?

Balée laughed. "You're trying to trap me, aren't you?" he said.

Like a Club Between the Eyes

According to family lore, my great-grandmother's great-grandmother's great-grandfather was the first white person hanged in America. His name was John Billington. He came on the *Mayflower*, which anchored off the coast of Massachusetts on November 9, 1620. Billington was not a Puritan; within six months of arrival he also became the first white person in America to be tried for complaining about the police. "He is a knave," William Bradford, the colony's governor, wrote of Billington, "and so will live and die." What one historian called Billington's "troublesome career" ended in 1630, when he was hanged for murder. My family has always said that he was framed—but we *would* say that, wouldn't we?

A few years ago it occurred to me that my ancestor and everyone else in the colony had voluntarily enlisted in a venture that brought them to New England without food or shelter six weeks before winter. Half the 102 people on the *Mayflower* made it through to spring, which to me was amazing. How, I wondered, did they survive?

In his history of Plymouth Colony, Bradford provided the answer: by robbing Indian houses and graves. The *Mayflower* first hove to at Cape Cod. An armed company staggered out. Eventually it found a recently deserted Indian settlement. The newcomers—hungry, cold, sick—dug up graves and ransacked houses, looking for underground stashes of corn. "And sure it was God's good providence that we found this corn," Bradford wrote, "for else we know not how we should have done." (He felt uneasy about the thievery, though.) When the colonists came to Plymouth, a month later, they set up shop in another deserted Indian village. All through the coastal forest the Indians had "died on heapes, as they lay in their houses," the English trader Thomas Morton noted. "And the bones and skulls upon the severall places of their habitations made such a spectacle" that to Morton the Massachusetts woods seemed to be "a new found Golgotha"—the hill of executions in Roman Jerusalem.

To the Pilgrims' astonishment, one of the corpses they exhumed on Cape Cod had blond hair. A French ship had been wrecked there several years earlier. The Patuxet Indians imprisoned a few survivors. One of them supposedly learned enough of the local language to inform his captors that God would destroy them for their misdeeds. The Patuxet scoffed at the threat. But the Europeans carried a disease, and they bequeathed it to their jailers. The epidemic (probably of viral hepatitis, according to a study by Arthur E. Spiess, an archaeologist at the Maine Historic Preservation Commission, and Bruce D. Spiess, the director of clinical research at the Medical College of Virginia) took years to exhaust itself and may have killed 90 percent of the people in coastal New England. It made a huge difference to American history. "The good hand of God favored our beginnings," Bradford mused, by "sweeping away great multitudes of the natives . . . that he might make room for us."

By the time my ancestor set sail on the *Mayflower*, Europeans had been visiting New England for more than a hundred years. English, French, Italian, Spanish, and

Portuguese mariners regularly plied the coastline, trading what they could, occasionally kidnapping the inhabitants for slaves. New England, the Europeans saw, was thickly settled and well defended. In 1605 and 1606 Samuel de Champlain visited Cape Cod, hoping to establish a French base. He abandoned the idea. Too many people already lived there. A year later Sir Ferdinando Gorges—British despite his name—tried to establish an English community in southern Maine. It had more founders than Plymouth and seems to have been better organized. Confronted by numerous well-armed local Indians, the settlers abandoned the project within months. The Indians at Plymouth would surely have been an equal obstacle to my ancestor and his ramshackle expedition had disease not intervened.

Faced with such stories, historians have long wondered how many people lived in the Americas at the time of contact. "Debated since Columbus attempted a partial census on Hispaniola in 1496," William Denevan has written, this "remains one of the great inquiries of history." (In 1976 Denevan assembled and edited an entire book on the subject, *The Native Population of the Americas in 1492*.) The first scholarly estimate of the indigenous population was made in 1910 by James Mooney, a distinguished ethnographer at the Smithsonian Institution. Combing through old documents, he concluded that in 1491 North America had 1.15 million inhabitants. Mooney's glittering reputation ensured that most subsequent researchers accepted his figure uncritically.

That changed in 1966, when Henry F. Dobyns published "Estimating Aboriginal American Population: An Appraisal of Techniques With a New Hemispheric Estimate," in the journal *Current Anthropology*. Despite the carefully neutral title, his argument was thunderous, its impact long-lasting. In the view of James Wilson, the author of *The Earth Shall Weep* (1998), a history of indigenous Americans, Dobyns's colleagues "are still struggling to get out of the crater that paper left in anthropology." Not only anthropologists were affected. Dobyns's estimate proved to be one of the opening rounds in today's culture wars.

Dobyns began his exploration of pre-Columbian Indian demography in the early 1950s, when he was a graduate student. At the invitation of a friend, he spent a few months in northern Mexico, which is full of Spanish-era missions. There he poked through the crumbling leather-bound ledgers in which Jesuits recorded local births and deaths. Right away he noticed how many more deaths there were. The Spaniards arrived, and then Indians died—in huge numbers, at incredible rates. It hit him, Dobyns told me recently, "like a club right between the eyes."

It took Dobyns eleven years to obtain his Ph.D. Along the way he joined a rural-development project in Peru, which until colonial times was the seat of the Incan empire. Remembering what he had seen at the northern fringe of the Spanish conquest, Dobyns decided to compare it with figures for the south. He burrowed into the papers of the Lima cathedral and read apologetic Spanish histories. The Indians in Peru, Dobyns concluded, had faced plagues from the day the conquistadors showed up—in fact, before then: smallpox arrived around 1525, seven years ahead of the Spanish. Brought to Mexico apparently by a single sick Spaniard, it swept south and eliminated more than half the population of the Incan empire. Smallpox claimed the Incan dictator Huayna Capac and much of his family, setting off a calamitous war of succession. So complete was the chaos that Francisco Pizarro was able to seize an empire the size of Spain and Italy combined with a force of 168 men.

Smallpox was only the first epidemic. Typhus (probably) in 1546, influenza and smallpox together in 1558, smallpox again in 1589, diphtheria in 1614, measles in 1618—

all ravaged the remains of Incan culture. Dobyns was the first social scientist to piece together this awful picture, and he naturally rushed his findings into print. Hardly anyone paid attention. But Dobyns was already working on a second, related question: If all those people died, how many had been living there to begin with? Before Columbus, Dobyns calculated, the Western Hemisphere held ninety to 112 million people. Another way of saying this is that in 1491 more people lived in the Americas than in Europe.

His argument was simple but horrific. It is well known that Native Americans had no experience with many European diseases and were therefore immunologically unprepared—"virgin soil," in the metaphor of epidemiologists. What Dobyns realized was that such diseases could have swept from the coastlines initially visited by Europeans to inland areas controlled by Indians who had never seen a white person. The first whites to explore many parts of the Americas may therefore have encountered places that were already depopulated. Indeed, Dobyns argued, they must have done so.

Peru was one example, the Pacific Northwest another. In 1792 the British navigator George Vancouver led the first European expedition to survey Puget Sound. He found a vast charnel house: human remains "promiscuously scattered about the beach, in great numbers." Smallpox, Vancouver's crew discovered, had preceded them. Its few survivors, second lieutenant Peter Puget noted, were "most terribly pitted . . . indeed many have lost their Eyes." In *Pox Americana* (2001), Elizabeth Fenn, a historian at George Washington University, contends that the disaster on the northwest coast was but a small part of a continental pandemic that erupted near Boston in 1774 and cut down Indians from Mexico to Alaska.

Because smallpox was not endemic in the Americas, colonials, too, had not acquired any immunity. The virus, an equal-opportunity killer, swept through the Continental Army and stopped the drive into Quebec. The American Revolution would be lost, Washington and other rebel leaders feared, if the contagion did to the colonists what it had done to the Indians. "The small Pox! The small Pox!" John Adams wrote to his wife, Abigail. "What shall We do with it?" In retrospect, Fenn says, "One of George Washington's most brilliant moves was to inoculate the army against smallpox during the Valley Forge winter of '78." Without inoculation smallpox could easily have given the United States back to the British.

So many epidemics occurred in the Americas, Dobyns argued, that the old data used by Mooney and his successors represented population nadirs. From the few cases in which before-and-after totals are known with relative certainty, Dobyns estimated that in the first 130 years of contact about 95 percent of the people in the Americas died—the worst demographic calamity in recorded history.

Dobyns's ideas were quickly attacked as politically motivated, a push from the hate-America crowd to inflate the toll of imperialism. The attacks continue to this day. "No question about it, some people want those higher numbers," says Shepard Krech III, a Brown University anthropologist who is the author of *The Ecological Indian* (1999). These people, he says, were thrilled when Dobyns revisited the subject in a book, *Their Numbers Become Thinned* (1983)—and revised his own estimates upward. Perhaps Dobyns's most vehement critic is David Henige, a bibliographer of Africana at the University of Wisconsin, whose *Numbers From Nowhere* (1998) is a landmark in the literature of demographic fulmination. "Suspect in 1966, it is no less suspect nowadays," Henige wrote of Dobyns's work. "If anything, it is worse."

When Henige wrote *Numbers From Nowhere*, the fight about pre-Columbian populations had already consumed forests' worth of trees; his bibliography is ninety pages long. And the dispute shows no sign of abating. More and more people have jumped in. This is partly because the subject is inherently fascinating. But more likely the increased interest in the debate is due to the growing realization of the high political and ecological stakes.

INVENTING BY THE MILLIONS

On May 30, 1539, Hernando de Soto landed his private army near Tampa Bay, in Florida. Soto, as he was called, was a novel figure: half warrior, half venture capitalist. He had grown very rich very young by becoming a market leader in the nascent trade for Indian slaves. The profits had helped to fund Pizarro's seizure of the Incan empire, which had made Soto wealthier still. Looking quite literally for new worlds to conquer, he persuaded the Spanish Crown to let him loose in North America. He spent one fortune to make another. He came to Florida with 200 horses, 600 soldiers, and 300 pigs.

From today's perspective, it is difficult to imagine the ethical system that would justify Soto's actions. For four years his force, looking for gold, wandered through what is now Florida, Georgia, North and South Carolina, Tennessee, Alabama, Mississippi, Arkansas, and Texas, wrecking almost everything it touched. The inhabitants often fought back vigorously, but they had never before encountered an army with horses and guns. Soto died of fever with his expedition in ruins; along the way his men had managed to rape, torture, enslave, and kill countless Indians. But the worst thing the Spaniards did, some researchers say, was entirely without malice—bring the pigs.

According to Charles Hudson, an anthropologist at the University of Georgia who spent fifteen years reconstructing the path of the expedition, Soto crossed the Mississippi a few miles downstream from the present site of Memphis. It was a nervous passage: the Spaniards were watched by several thousand Indian warriors. Utterly without fear, Soto brushed past the Indian force into what is now eastern Arkansas, through thickly settled land—"very well peopled with large towns," one of his men later recalled, "two or three of which were to be seen from one town." Eventually the Spaniards approached a cluster of small cities, each protected by earthen walls, sizeable moats, and deadeye archers. In his usual fashion, Soto brazenly marched in, stole food, and marched out.

After Soto left, no Europeans visited this part of the Mississippi Valley for more than a century. Early in 1682 whites appeared again, this time Frenchmen in canoes. One of them was Réné-Robert Cavelier, Sieur de la Salle. The French passed through the area where Soto had found cities cheek by jowl. It was deserted—La Salle didn't see an Indian village for 200 miles. About fifty settlements existed in this strip of the Mississippi when Soto showed up, according to Anne Ramenofsky, an anthropologist at the University of New Mexico. By La Salle's time the number had shrunk to perhaps ten, some probably inhabited by recent immigrants. Soto "had a privileged glimpse" of an Indian world, Hudson says. "The window opened and slammed shut. When the French came in and the record opened up again, it was a transformed reality. A civilization crumbled. The question is, how did this happen?"

The question is even more complex than it may seem. Disaster of this magnitude suggests epidemic disease. In the view of Ramenofsky and Patricia Galloway, an anthropologist at the University of Texas, the source of the contagion was very likely not Soto's army but its ambulatory meat locker: his 300 pigs. Soto's force itself was too small to be an effective biological weapon. Sicknesses like measles and smallpox would have burned through his 600 soldiers long before they reached the Mississippi. But the same would not have held true for the pigs, which multiplied rapidly and were able to transmit their diseases to wildlife in the surrounding forest. When human beings and domesticated animals live close together, they trade microbes with abandon. Over time mutation spawns new diseases: avian influenza becomes human influenza, bovine rinderpest becomes measles. Unlike Europeans, Indians did not live in close quarters with animals—they domesticated only the dog, the llama, the alpaca, the guinea pig, and, here and there, the turkey and the Muscovy duck. In some ways this is not surprising: the New World had fewer animal candidates for taming than the Old. Moreover, few Indians carry the gene that permits adults to digest lactose, a form of sugar abundant in milk. Non-milk-drinkers, one imagines, would be less likely to work at domesticating milk-giving animals. But this is guesswork. The fact is that what scientists call zoonotic disease was little known in the Americas. Swine alone can disseminate anthrax, brucellosis, leptospirosis, taeniasis, trichinosis, and tuberculosis. Pigs breed exuberantly and can transmit diseases to deer and turkeys. Only a few of Soto's pigs would have had to wander off to infect the forest.

Indeed, the calamity wrought by Soto apparently extended across the whole Southeast. The Coosa city-states, in western Georgia, and the Caddoan-speaking civilization, centered on the Texas-Arkansas border, disintegrated soon after Soto appeared. The Caddo had had a taste for monumental architecture: public plazas, ceremonial platforms, mausoleums. After Soto's army left, notes Timothy K. Perttula, an archaeological consultant in Austin, Texas, the Caddo stopped building community centers and began digging community cemeteries. Between Soto's and La Salle's visits, Perttula believes, the Caddoan population fell from about 200,000 to about 8,500—a drop of nearly 96 percent. In the eighteenth century the tally shrank further, to 1,400. An equivalent loss today in the population of New York City would reduce it to 56,000—not enough to fill Yankee Stadium. "That's one reason whites think of Indians as nomadic hunters," says Russell Thornton, an anthropologist at the University of California at Los Angeles. "Everything else—all the heavily populated urbanized societies—was wiped out."

Could a few pigs truly wreak this much destruction? Such apocalyptic scenarios invite skepticism. As a rule, viruses, microbes, and parasites are rarely lethal on so wide a scale—a pest that wipes out its host species does not have a bright evolutionary future. In its worst outbreak, from 1347 to 1351, the European Black Death claimed only a third of its victims. (The rest survived, though they were often disfigured or crippled by its effects.) The Indians in Soto's path, if Dobyns, Ramenofsky, and Perttula are correct, endured losses that were incomprehensibly greater.

One reason is that Indians were fresh territory for many plagues, not just one. Smallpox, typhoid, bubonic plague, influenza, mumps, measles, whooping cough—all rained down on the Americas in the century after Columbus. (Cholera, malaria, and scarlet fever came later.) Having little experience with epidemic diseases, Indians had no knowledge of how to combat them. In contrast, Europeans were well versed in the brutal logic of quarantine. They boarded up houses in which plague appeared and fled to the countryside. In Indian New England, Neal Salisbury, a historian at Smith College, wrote in *Manitou and Providence* (1982), family and friends gathered with the shaman at the sufferer's bedside to wait out the illness—a practice that "could only have served to spread the disease more rapidly."

Indigenous biochemistry may also have played a role. The immune system constantly scans the body for molecules that it can recognize as foreign—molecules belonging to an invading virus, for instance. No one's immune system can identify all foreign presences. Roughly speaking, an individual's set of defensive tools is known as his MHC type. Because many bacteria and viruses mutate easily, they usually attack in the form of several slightly different strains. Pathogens win when MHC types miss some of the strains and the immune system is not stimulated to act. Most human groups contain many MHC types; a strain that slips by one person's defenses will be nailed by the defenses of the next. But, according to Francis L. Black, an epidemiologist at Yale University, Indians are characterized by unusually homogenous MHC types. One out of three South American Indians have similar MHC types; among Africans the corresponding figure is one in 200. The cause is a matter for Darwinian speculation, the effects less so.

In 1966 Dobyns's insistence on the role of disease was a shock to his colleagues. Today the impact of European pathogens on the New World is almost undisputed. Nonetheless, the fight over Indian numbers continues with undiminished fervor. Estimates of the population of North America in 1491 disagree by an order of magnitude—from 18 million, Dobyns's revised figure, to 1.8 million, calculated by Douglas H. Ubelaker, an anthropologist at the Smithsonian. To some "high counters," as David Henige calls them, the low counters' refusal to relinquish the vision of an empty continent is irrational or worse. "Non-Indian 'experts' always want to minimize the size of aboriginal populations," says Lenore Stiffarm, a Native American-education specialist at the University of Saskatchewan. The smaller the numbers of Indians, she believes, the easier it is to regard the continent as having been up for grabs. "It's perfectly acceptable to move into unoccupied land," Stiffarm says. "And land with only a few 'savages' is the next best thing."

"Most of the arguments for the very large numbers have been theoretical," Ubelaker says in defense of low counters. "When you try to marry the theoretical arguments to the data that are available on individual groups in different regions, it's hard to find support for those numbers." Archaeologists, he says, keep searching for the settlements in which those millions of people supposedly lived, with little success. "As more and more excavation is done, one would expect to see more evidence for dense populations than has thus far emerged." Dean Snow, the Pennsylvania State anthropologist, examined Colonial-era Mohawk Iroquois sites and found "no support for the notion that ubiquitous pandemics swept the region." In his view, asserting that the continent was filled with people who left no trace is like looking at an empty bank account and claiming that it must once have held millions of dollars.

The low counters are also troubled by the Dobynsian procedure for recovering original population numbers: applying an assumed death rate, usually 95 percent, to the observed population nadir. Ubelaker believes that the lowest point for Indians in North America was around 1900, when their numbers fell to about half a million. Assuming a 95 percent death rate, the pre-contact population would have been 10 million. Go up one percent, to a 96 percent death rate, and the figure jumps to 12.5 million—arithmetically creating more than two million people from a tiny increase in mortality rates. At 98 percent the number bounds to 25 million. Minute changes in baseline assumptions produce wildly different results.

"It's an absolutely unanswerable question on which tens of thousands of words have been spent to no purpose," Henige says. In 1976 he sat in on a seminar by William Denevan, the Wisconsin geographer. An "epiphanic moment" occurred when he read shortly afterward that scholars had "uncovered" the existence of eight million people in Hispaniola. *Can you just invent millions of people?* he wondered. "We can make of the historical record that there was depopulation and movement of people from internecine warfare and diseases," he says. "But as for how much, who knows? When we start putting numbers to something like that—applying large figures like ninety-five percent—we're saying things we shouldn't say. The number implies a level of knowledge that's impossible."

Nonetheless, one must try—or so Denevan believes. In his estimation the high counters (though not the highest counters) seem to be winning the argument, at least for now. No definitive data exist, he says, but the majority of the extant evidentiary scraps support their side. Even Henige is no low counter. When I asked him what he thought the population of the Americas was before Columbus, he insisted that any answer would be speculation and made me promise not to print what he was going to say next. Then he named a figure that forty years ago would have caused a commotion.

To Elizabeth Fenn, the smallpox historian, the squabble over numbers obscures a central fact. Whether one million or 10 million or 100 million died, she believes, the pall of sorrow that engulfed the hemisphere was immeasurable. Languages, prayers, hopes, habits, and dreams—entire ways of life hissed away like steam. The Spanish and the Portuguese lacked the germ theory of disease and could not explain what was happening (let alone stop it). Nor can we explain it; the ruin was too long ago and too all-encompassing. In the long run, Fenn says, the consequential finding is not that many people died but that many people once lived. The Americas were filled with a stunningly diverse assortment of peoples who had knocked about the continents for millennia. "You have to wonder," Fenn says. "What were all those people *up* to in all that time?"

BUFFALO FARM

In 1810 Henry Brackenridge came to Cahokia, in what is now southwest Illinois, just across the Mississippi from St. Louis. Born close to the frontier, Brackenridge was a budding adventure writer; his *Views of Louisiana*, published three years later, was a kind of nineteenth-century *Into Thin Air*, with terrific adventure but without tragedy. Brackenridge had an eye for archaeology, and he had heard that Cahokia was worth a visit. When he got there, trudging along the desolate Cahokia River, he was "struck with a degree of astonishment." Rising from the muddy bottomland was a "stupendous pile of earth," vaster than the Great Pyramid at Giza. Around it were more than a hundred smaller mounds, covering an area of five square miles. At the time, the area was almost uninhabited. One can only imagine what passed through Brackenridge's mind as he walked alone to the ruins of the biggest Indian city north of the Rio Grande.

To Brackenridge, it seemed clear that Cahokia and the many other ruins in the Midwest had been constructed by Indians. It was not so clear to everyone else. Nineteenth-century writers attributed them to, among others, the Vikings, the Chinese, the "Hindoos," the ancient Greeks, the ancient Egyptians, lost tribes of Israelites, and even straying bands of Welsh. (This last claim was surprisingly widespread; when Lewis and Clark surveyed the Missouri, Jefferson told them to keep an eye out for errant bands of Welsh-speaking white Indians.) The historian George Bancroft, dean of his profession, was a dissenter: the earthworks, he wrote in 1840, were purely natural formations.

Bancroft changed his mind about Cahokia, but not about Indians. To the end of his days he regarded them as "feeble barbarians, destitute of commerce and of political connection." His characterization lasted, largely unchanged, for more than a century. Samuel Eliot Morison, the winner of two Pulitzer Prizes, closed his monumental *European Discovery of America* (1974) with the observation that Native Americans expected only "short and brutish lives, void of hope for any future." As late as 1987 *American History: A Survey,* a standard high school textbook by three well-known historians, described the Americas before Columbus as "empty of mankind and its works." The story of Europeans in the New World, the book explained, "is the story of the creation of a civilization where none existed."

Alfred Crosby, a historian at the University of Texas, came to other conclusions. Crosby's *The Columbian Exchange: Biological Consequences of 1492* caused almost as much of a stir when it was published, in 1972, as Henry Dobyns's calculation of Indian numbers six years earlier, though in different circles. Crosby was a standard names-and-battles historian who became frustrated by the random contingency of political events. "Some trivial thing happens and you have this guy winning the presidency instead of that guy," he says. He decided to go deeper. After he finished his manuscript, it sat on his shelf—he couldn't find a publisher willing to be associated with his new ideas. It took him three years to persuade a small editorial house to put it out. *The Columbian Exchange* has been in print ever since; a companion, *Ecological Imperialism: The Biological Expansion of Europe, 900–1900,* appeared in 1986.

Human history, in Crosby's interpretation, is marked by two world-altering centers of invention: the Middle East and central Mexico, where Indian groups independently created nearly all of the Neolithic innovations, writing included. The Neolithic Revolution began in the Middle East about 10,000 years ago. In the next few millennia humankind invented the wheel, the metal tool, and agriculture. The Sumerians eventually put these inventions together, added writing, and became the world's first civilization. Afterward Sumeria's heirs in Europe and Asia frantically copied one another's happiest discoveries; innovations ricocheted from one corner of Eurasia to another, stimulating technological progress. Native Americans, who had crossed to Alaska before Sumeria, missed out on the bounty. "They had to do everything on their own," Crosby says. Remarkably, they succeeded.

When Columbus appeared in the Caribbean, the descendants of the world's two Neolithic civilizations collided, with overwhelming consequences for both. American Neolithic development occurred later than that of the Middle East, possibly because the Indians needed more time to build up the requisite population density. Without beasts of burden they could not capitalize on the wheel (for individual workers on uneven terrain skids are nearly as effective as carts for hauling), and they never developed steel. But in agriculture they handily outstripped the children of Sumeria. Every tomato in Italy, every potato in Ireland, and every hot pepper in Thailand came from this hemisphere. Worldwide, more than half the crops grown today were initially developed in the Americas.

Maize, as corn is called in the rest of the world, was a triumph with global implications. Indians developed an extraordinary number of maize varieties for different growing conditions, which meant that the crop could and did spread throughout the planet. Central and Southern Europeans became particularly dependent on it; maize was the staple of Serbia, Romania, and Moldavia by the nineteenth century. Indian crops dramatically reduced hunger, Crosby says, which led to an Old World population boom.

Along with peanuts and manioc, maize came to Africa and transformed agriculture there, too. "The probability is that the population of Africa was greatly increased because of maize and other American Indian crops," Crosby says. "Those extra people helped make the slave trade possible." Maize conquered Africa at the time when introduced diseases were leveling Indian societies. The Spanish, the Portuguese, and the British were alarmed by the death rate among Indians, because they wanted to exploit them as workers. Faced with a labor shortage, the Europeans turned their eyes to Africa. The continent's quarrelsome societies helped slave traders to siphon off millions of people. The maize-fed population boom, Crosby believes, let the awful trade continue without pumping the well dry.

Back home in the Americas, Indian agriculture long sustained some of the world's largest cities. The Aztec capital of Tenochtitlán dazzled Hernán Cortés in 1519; it was bigger than Paris, Europe's greatest metropolis. The Spaniards gawped like hayseeds at the wide streets, ornately carved buildings, and markets bright with goods from hundreds of miles away. They had never before seen a city with botanical gardens, for the excellent reason that none existed in Europe. The same novelty attended the force of a thousand men that kept the crowded streets immaculate. (Streets that weren't ankle-deep in sewage! The conquistadors had never heard of such a thing.) Central America was not the only locus of prosperity. Thousands of miles north, John Smith, of Pocahontas fame, visited Massachusetts in 1614, before it was emptied by disease, and declared that the land was "so planted with Gardens and Corne fields, and so well inhabited with a goodly, strong and well proportioned people . . . [that] I would rather live here than any where."

Smith was promoting colonization, and so had reason to exaggerate. But he also knew the hunger, sickness, and oppression of European life. France—"by any standards a privileged country," according to its great historian, Fernand Braudel—experienced seven nationwide famines in the fifteenth century and thirteen in the sixteenth. Disease was hunger's constant companion. During epidemics in London the dead were heaped onto carts "like common dung" (the simile is Daniel Defoe's) and trundled through the streets. The infant death rate in London orphanages, according to one contemporary source, was 88 percent. Governments were harsh, the rule of law arbitrary. The gibbets poking up in the background of so many old paintings were, Braudel observed, "merely a realistic detail."

The Earth Shall Weep, James Wilson's history of Indian America, puts the comparison bluntly: "the western hemisphere was larger, richer, and more populous than Europe." Much of it was freer, too. Europeans, accustomed to the serfdom that thrived from Naples to the Baltic Sea, were puzzled and alarmed by the democratic spirit and respect for human rights in many Indian societies, especially those in North America. In theory, the sachems of New England Indian groups were absolute monarchs. In practice, the colonial leader Roger Williams wrote, "they will not conclude of ought . . . unto which the people are averse."

Pre-1492 America wasn't a disease-free paradise, Dobyns says, although in his "exuberance as a writer," he told me recently, he once made that claim. Indians had ailments of their own, notably parasites, tuberculosis, and anemia. The daily grind was wearing; life-spans in America were only as long as or a little longer than those in Europe, if the evidence of indigenous graveyards is to be believed. Nor was it a political utopia—the Inca, for instance, invented refinements to totalitarian rule that would have intrigued Stalin. Inveterate practitioners of what the historian Francis Jennings described as "state terrorism practiced horrifically on a huge scale," the Inca ruled so cruelly that one can speculate that their surviving subjects might actually have been better off under Spanish rule.

I asked seven anthropologists, archaeologists, and historians if they would rather have been a typical Indian or a typical European in 1491. None was delighted by the question, because it required judging the past by the standards of today—a fallacy disparaged as "presentism" by social scientists. But every one chose to be an Indian. Some early colonists gave the same answer. Horrifying the leaders of Jamestown and

Plymouth, scores of English ran off to live with the Indians. My ancestor shared their desire, which is what led to the trumped-up murder charges against him—or that's what my grandfather told me, anyway.

As for the Indians, evidence suggests that they often viewed Europeans with disdain. The Hurons, a chagrined missionary reported, thought the French possessed "little intelligence in comparison to themselves." Europeans, Indians said, were physically weak, sexually untrustworthy, atrociously ugly, and just plain dirty. (Spaniards, who seldom if ever bathed, were amazed by the Aztec desire for personal cleanliness.) A Jesuit reported that the "Savages" were disgusted by handkerchiefs: "They say, we place what is unclean in a fine white piece of linen, and put it away in our pockets as something very precious, while they throw it upon the ground." The Micmac scoffed at the notion of French superiority. If Christian civilization was so wonderful, why were its inhabitants leaving?

Like people everywhere, Indians survived by cleverly exploiting their environment. Europeans tended to manage land by breaking it into fragments for farmers and herders. Indians often worked on such a grand scale that the scope of their ambition can be hard to grasp. They created small plots, as Europeans did (about 1.5 million acres of terraces still exist in the Peruvian Andes), but they also reshaped entire land-scapes to suit their purposes. A principal tool was fire, used to keep down under-brush and create the open, grassy conditions favorable for game. Rather than domesticating animals for meat, Indians retooled whole ecosystems to grow bumper crops of elk, deer, and bison. The first white settlers in Ohio found forests as open as English parks—they could drive carriages through the woods. Along the Hudson River the annual fall burning lit up the banks for miles on end; so flashy was the show that the Dutch in New Amsterdam boated upriver to goggle at the blaze like children at fireworks. In North America, Indian torches had their biggest impact on the Midwestern prairie, much or most of which was created and maintained by fire. Millennia of exuberant burning shaped the plains into vast buffalo farms. When Indian societies disintegrated, forest invaded savannah in Wisconsin, Illinois, Kansas, Nebraska, and the Texas Hill Country. Is it possible that the Indians changed the Americas more than the invading Europeans did? "The answer is probably yes for most regions for the next 250 years or so" after Columbus, William Denevan wrote, "and for some regions right up to the present time."

When scholars first began increasing their estimates of the ecological impact of Indian civilization, they met with considerable resistance from anthropologists and archaeologists. Over time the consensus in the human sciences changed. Under Denevan's direction, Oxford University Press has just issued the third volume of a huge catalogue of the "cultivated landscapes" of the Americas. This sort of phrase still provokes vehement objection—but the main dissenters are now ecologists and environmentalists. The disagreement is encapsulated by Amazonia, which has become *the* emblem of vanishing wilderness—an admonitory image of untouched Nature. Yet recently a growing number of researchers have come to believe that Indian societies had an enormous environmental impact on the jungle. Indeed, some anthropologists have called the Amazon forest itself a cultural artifact that is, an artificial object.

GREEN PRISONS

Northern visitors' first reaction to the storied Amazon rain forest is often disappointment. Ecotourist brochures evoke the immensity of Amazonia but rarely dwell on its extreme flatness. In the river's first 2,900 miles the vertical drop is only 500 feet. The river oozes like a huge runnel of dirty metal through a landscape utterly devoid of the romantic crags, arroyos, and heights that signify wildness and natural spectacle to most North Americans. Even the animals are invisible, although sometimes one can hear the bellow of monkey choruses. To the untutored eye—mine, for instance—the forest seems to stretch out in a monstrous green tangle as flat and incomprehensible as a printed circuit board.

The area east of the lower-Amazon town of Santarém is an exception. A series of sandstone ridges several hundred feet high reach down from the north, halting almost at the water's edge. Their tops stand drunkenly above the jungle like old tombstones. Many of the caves in the buttes are splattered with ancient petroglyphs—renditions of hands, stars, frogs, and human figures, all reminiscent of Miró, in overlapping red and yellow and brown. In recent years one of these caves, La Caverna da Pedra Pintada (Painted Rock Cave), has drawn attention in archaeological circles.

Wide and shallow and well lit, Painted Rock Cave is less thronged with bats than some of the other caves. The arched entrance is twenty feet high and lined with rock paintings. Out front is a sunny natural patio suitable for picnicking, edged by a few big rocks. People lived in this cave more than 11,000 years ago. They had no agriculture yet, and instead ate fish and fruit and built fires. During a recent visit I ate a sandwich atop a particularly inviting rock and looked over the forest below. The first Amazonians, I thought, must have done more or less the same thing.

In college I took an introductory anthropology class in which I read *Amazonia: Man and Culture in a Counterfeit Paradise* (1971), perhaps the most influential book ever written about the Amazon, and one that deeply impressed me at the time. Written by Betty J. Meggers, the Smithsonian archaeologist, *Amazonia* says that the apparent lushness of the rain forest is a sham. The soils are poor and can't hold nutrients—the jungle flora exists only because it snatches up everything worthwhile before it leaches away in the rain. Agriculture, which depends on extracting the wealth of the soil, therefore faces inherent ecological limitations in the wet desert of Amazonia.

As a result, Meggers argued, Indian villages were forced to remain small—any report of "more than a few hundred" people in permanent settlements, she told me recently, "makes my alarm bells go off." Bigger, more complex societies would inevitably over-tax the forest soils, laying waste to their own foundations. Beginning in 1948 Meggers and her late husband, Clifford Evans, excavated a chiefdom on Marajó, an island twice the size of New Jersey that sits like a gigantic stopper in the mouth of the Amazon. The Marajóara, they concluded, were failed offshoots of a sophisticated culture in the Andes. Transplanted to the lush trap of the Amazon, the culture choked and died.

Green activists saw the implication: development in tropical forests destroys both the forests and their developers. Meggers's account had enonnous public impact—*Amazonia* is one of the wellsprings of the campaign to save rain forests.

Then Anna C. Roosevelt , the curator of archaeology at Chicago's Field Museum of Natural History , re-excavated Marajó. Her complete report, *Moundbuilders of the Amazon* (1991), was like the anti-matter version of *Amazonia*. Marajó, she argued, was "one of the outstanding indigenous cultural achievements of the New World," a powerhouse that lasted for more than a thousand years, had "possibly well over 100,000" inhabitants, and covered thousands of square miles. Rather than damaging the forest, Marajó's "earth construction" and "large, dense populations" had improved it: the most luxuriant and diverse growth was on the mounds formerly occupied by the Marajóara. "If you listened to Meggers's theory, these places should have been ruined," Roosevelt says.

Meggers scoffed at Roosevelt's "extravagant claims," "polemical tone," and "defamatory remarks." Roosevelt, Meggers argued, had committed the beginner's error of mistaking a site that had been occupied many times by small, unstable groups for a single, long-lasting society. "[Archaeological remains] build up on areas of half a kilometer or so," she told me, "because [shifting Indian groups] don't land exactly on the same spot. The decorated types of pottery don't change much over time, so you can pick up a bunch of chips and say, 'Oh, look, it was all one big site!' Unless you know what you're doing, of course." Centuries after the conquistadors, "the myth of El Dorado is being revived by archaeologists," Meggers wrote last fall in the journal *Latin American Antiquity,* referring to the persistent Spanish delusion that cities of gold existed in the jungle.

The dispute grew bitter and personal; inevitable in a contemporary academic context, it has featured vituperative references to colonialism, elitism, and employment by the CIA. Meanwhile, Roosevelt's team investigated Painted Rock Cave. On the floor of the cave what looked to me like nothing in particular turned out to be an ancient midden: a refuse heap. The archaeologists slowly scraped away sediment, traveling backward in time with every inch. When the traces of human occupation vanished, they kept digging. ("You always go a meter past sterile," Roosevelt says.) A few inches below they struck the charcoal-rich dirt that signifies human habitation—a culture, Roosevelt said later, that wasn't supposed to be there.

For many millennia the cave's inhabitants hunted and gathered for food. But by about 4,000 years ago they were growing crops—perhaps as many as 140 of them, according to Charles R. Clement, an anthropological botanist at the Brazilian National Institute for Amazonian Research. Unlike Europeans, who planted mainly annual crops, the Indians, he says, centered their agriculture on the Amazon's unbelievably diverse assortment of trees: fruits, nuts, and palms. "It's tremendously difficult to clear fields with stone tools," Clement says. "If you can plant trees, you get twenty years of productivity out of your work instead of two or three."

Planting their orchards, the first Amazonians transformed large swaths of the river basin into something more pleasing to human beings. In a widely cited article from 1989, William Balée, the Tulane anthropologist, cautiously estimated that about 12 percent of the nonflooded Amazon forest was of anthropogenic origin—directly or indirectly created by human beings. In some circles this is now seen as a conservative position. "I basically think it's all human-created," Clement told me in Brazil. He argues that Indians changed the assortment and density of species throughout the region. So does Clark Erickson, the University of Pennsylvania archaeologist, who told me in Bolivia that the lowland tropical forests of South America are among the finest works of art on the planet. "Some of my colleagues would say that's pretty radical," he said, smiling mischievously. According to Peter Stahl, an anthropologist at the State University of New York at Binghamton, "lots" of botanists believe that "what the eco-imagery would like to picture as a pristine, untouched Urwelt [primeval world] in fact has been managed by people for millennia." The phrase "built environment," Erickson says, "applies to most, if not all, Neotropical landscapes."

"Landscape" in this case is meant exactly—Amazonian Indians literally created the ground beneath their feet. According to William I. Woods, a soil geographer at Southern Illinois University, ecologists' claims about terrible Amazonian land were based on very little data. In the late 1990s Woods and others began careful measurements in the lower Amazon. They indeed found lots of inhospitable terrain. But they also discovered swaths of *terra preta*—rich, fertile "black earth" that anthropologists increasingly believe was created by human beings.

Terra preta, Woods guesses, covers at least 10 percent of Amazonia, an area the size of France. It has amazing properties, he says. Tropical rain doesn't leach nutrients from *terra preta* fields; instead the soil, so to speak, fights back. Not far from Painted Rock Cave is a 300-acre area with a two-foot layer of *terra preta* quarried by locals for potting soil. The bottom third of the layer is never removed, workers there explain, because over time it will re-create the original soil layer in its initial thickness. The reason, scientists suspect, is that *terra preta* is generated by a special suite of micro-organisms that resists depletion. "Apparently," Woods and the Wisconsin geographer Joseph M. McCann argued in a presentation last summer, "at some threshold level . . . dark earth attains the capacity to perpetuate—even regenerate itself—thus behaving more like a living 'super'-organism than an inert material."

In as yet unpublished research the archaeologists Eduardo Neves, of the University of São Paulo; Michael Heckenberger, of the University of Florida; and their colleagues examined *terra preta* in the upper Xingu, a huge southern tributary of the Amazon. Not all Xingu cultures left behind this living earth, they discovered. But the ones that did generated it rapidly—suggesting to Woods that *terra preta* was created deliberately. In a process reminiscent of dropping microorganism-rich starter into plain dough to create sourdough bread, Amazonian peoples, he believes, inoculated bad soil with a transforming bacterial charge. Not every group of Indians there did this, but quite a few did, and over an extended period of time.

When Woods told me this, I was so amazed that I almost dropped the phone. I ceased to be articulate for a moment and said things like "wow" and "gosh." Woods chuckled at my reaction, probably because he understood what was passing through my mind. Faced with an ecological problem, I was thinking, the Indians *fixed* it. They were in the process of terraforming the Amazon when Columbus showed up and ruined everything.

Scientists should study the microorganisms in *terra preta*, Woods told me, to find out how they work. If that could be learned, maybe some version of Amazonian dark earth could be used to improve the vast expanses of bad soil that cripple agriculture in Africa—a final gift from the people who brought us tomatoes, corn, and the immense grasslands of the Great Plains.

"Betty Meggers would just die if she heard me saying this," Woods told me. "Deep down her fear is that this data will be misused." Indeed, Meggers's recent *Latin American Antiquity* article charged that archaeologists who say the Amazon can support agriculture are effectively telling "developers [that they] are entitled to operate without restraint." Resuscitating the myth of El Dorado, in her view, "makes us accomplices in the accelerating pace of environmental degradation." Doubtless there is something to this—although, as some of her critics responded in the same issue of the journal, it is difficult to imagine greedy plutocrats "perusing the pages of *Latin American Antiquity* before deciding to rev up the chain saws." But the new picture doesn't automatically legitimize paving the forest. Instead it suggests that for a long time big chunks of Amazonia were used nondestructively by clever people who knew tricks we have yet to learn.

I visited Painted Rock Cave during the river's annual flood, when it wells up over its banks and creeps inland for miles. Farmers in the floodplain build houses and barns on stilts and watch pink dolphins sport from their doorsteps. Ecotourists take short-cuts by driving motorboats through the drowned forest. Guys in dories chase after them, trying to sell sacks of incredibly good fruit.

All of this is described as "wilderness" in the tourist brochures. It's not, if researchers like Roosevelt are correct. Indeed, they believe that fewer people may be living there now than in 1491. Yet when my boat glided into the trees, the forest shut out the sky like the closing of an umbrella. Within a few hundred yards the human presence seemed to vanish. I felt alone and small, but in a way that was curiously like feeling exalted. If that place was not wilderness, how should I think of it? Since the fate of the forest is in our hands, what should be our goal for its future?

NOVEL SHORES

Fernando de Soto's expedition stomped through the Southeast for four years and apparently never saw bison. More than a century later, when French explorers came down the Mississippi, they saw "a solitude unrelieved by the faintest trace of man," the nineteenth-century historian Francis Parkman wrote. Instead the French encountered bison, "grazing in herds on the great prairies which then bordered the river."

To Charles Kay, the reason for the buffalo's sudden emergence is obvious. Kay is a wildlife ecologist in the political-science department at Utah State University. In ecological terms, he says, the Indians were the "keystone species" of American ecosystems. A keystone species, according to the Harvard biologist Edward O. Wilson, is a species "that affects the survival and abundance of many other species." Keystone species have a disproportionate impact on their ecosystems. Removing them, Wilson adds, "results in a relatively significant shift in the composition of the [ecological] community."

When disease swept Indians from the land, Kay says, what happened was exactly that. The ecological ancien régime collapsed, and strange new phenomena emerged. In a way this is unsurprising; for better or worse, humankind is a keystone species everywhere. Among these phenomena was a population explosion in the species that the Indians had kept down by hunting. After disease killed off the Indians, Kay believes, buffalo vastly extended their range. Their numbers more than sextupled. The same occurred with elk and mule deer. "If the elk were here in great numbers all this time, the archaeological sites should be chock-full of elk bones," Kay says. "But the archaeologists will tell you the elk weren't there." On the evidence of middens the number of elk jumped about 500 years ago.

Passenger pigeons may be another example. The epitome of natural American abundance, they flew in such great masses that the first colonists were stupefied by the sight. As a boy, the explorer Henry Brackenridge saw flocks "ten miles in width, by one hundred and twenty in length." For hours the birds darkened the sky from horizon to horizon. According to Thomas Neumann, a consulting archaeologist in Lilburn, Georgia, passenger pigeons "were incredibly dumb and always roosted in vast hordes, so they were very easy to harvest." Because they were readily caught and good to eat, Neumann says, archaeological digs should find many pigeon bones in the pre-Columbian strata of Indian middens. But they aren't there. The mobs of birds in the history books, he says, were "outbreak populations—always a symptom of an extraordinarily disrupted ecological system."

Throughout eastern North America the open landscape seen by the first Europeans quickly filled in with forest. According to William Cronon, of the University of Wisconsin, later colonists began complaining about how hard it was to get around. (Eventually, of course, they stripped New England almost bare of trees.) When Europeans moved west, they were preceded by two waves: one of disease, the other of ecological disturbance. The former crested with fearsome rapidity; the latter some-times took more than a century to quiet down. Far from destroying pristine wilder-ness, European settlers bloodily created it. By 1800 the hemisphere was chockablock with new wilderness. If "forest primeval" means a woodland unsullied by the human presence, William Denevan has written, there was much more of it in the late eigh-teenth century than in the early sixteenth.

Cronon's *Changes in the Land: Indians, Colonists, and the Ecology of New England* (1983) belongs on the same shelf as works by Crosby and Dobyns. But it was not until one of his articles was excerpted in *The New York Times* in 1995 that people outside the social sciences began to understand the implications of this view of Indian his-tory. Environmentalists and ecologists vigorously attacked the anti-wilderness sce-nario, which they described as infected by postmodern philosophy. A small academic brouhaha ensued, complete with hundreds of footnotes. It precipitated *Reinventing Nature?* (1995), one of the few academic critiques of postmodernist philosophy writ-ten largely by biologists. *The Great New Wilderness Debate* (1998), another lengthy book on the subject, was edited by two philosophers who earnestly identified them-selves as "Euro-American men [whose] cultural legacy is patriarchal Western civi-lization in its current postcolonial, globally hegemonic form."

It is easy to tweak academics for opaque, self-protective language like this. Nonethe-less, their concerns were quite justified. Crediting Indians with the role of keystone species has implications for the way the current Euro-American members of that keystone species manage the forests, watersheds, and endangered species of America. Because a third of the United States is owned by the federal government, the issue inevitably has political ramifications. In Amazonia, fabled storehouse of biodiversity, the stakes are global.

Guided by the pristine myth, mainstream environmentalists want to preserve as much of the world's land as possible in a putatively intact state. But "intact," if the new research is correct, means "run by human beings for human purposes." Environmentalists dis-like this, because it seems to mean that anything goes. In a sense they are correct. Native Americans managed the continent as they saw fit. Modern nations must do the same. If they want to return as much of the landscape as possible to its 1491 state, they will have to find it within themselves to create the world's largest garden.

Homework

Name: _____ Date: _____

1. According to Charles Mann's sources, the people of the Amazon basin were raising crops approximately 4,000 years ago. What is unusual about the crops they raised and the soil they raised them in?

2. Why does Mann state that "When the Europeans moved west, they were preceded by . . . ecological disturbance"?

Chapter 5

The Pristine Myth: The Landscape of the Americas in 1492

WILLIAM M. DENEVAN

Department of Geography, University of Wisconsin, Madison, WI 53706

ABSTRACT. The myth persists that in 1492 the Americas were a sparsely populated wilderness, "a world of barely perceptible human disturbance." There is substantial evidence, however, that the Native American landscape of the early sixteenth century was a humanized landscape almost everywhere. Populations were large. Forest composition had been modified, grasslands had been created, wild-life disrupted, and erosion was severe in places. Earthworks, roads, fields, and settlements were ubiquitous. With Indian depopulation in the wake of Old World disease, the environment recovered in many areas. A good argument can be made that the human presence was less visible in 1750 than it was in 1492.

KEY WORDS: Pristine myth, 1492, Columbus, Native American settlement and demography, prehistoric New World, vegetation change, earthworks.

"This is the forest primeval . . ."

Evangeline: A Tale of Acadia
(Longfellow, 1847).

What was the New World like at the time of Columbus?—"Geography as it was," in the words of Carl Sauer (1971, x).[1] The Admiral himself spoke of a "Terrestrial Paradise," beautiful and green and fertile, teeming with birds, with naked people living there whom he called "Indians." But was the landscape encountered in the sixteenth century primarily pristine, virgin, a wilderness, nearly empty of people, or was it a humanized landscape, with the imprint of native Americans being dramatic and persistent? The former still seems to be the more common view, but the latter may he more accurate.

---

[1] Sauer had a life-long interest in this topic (1963, 1966, 1971, 1980).

The pristine view is to a large extent an invention of nineteenth-century romanticist and primitivist writers such as W.H. Hudson, Cooper, Thoreau, Longfellow, and Parkman, and painters such as Catlin and Church.[2] The wilderness image has since become part of the American heritage, associated "with a heroic pioneer past in need of preservation" (Pyne 1982, 17; also see Bowden 1992, 22). The pristine view was restated clearly in 1950 by John Bakeless in his book *The Eyes of Discovery:*

> There were not really very many of these redmen . . . the land seemed empty to invaders who came from settled Europe . . . that ancient, primeval, undisturbed wilderness . . . the streams simply boiled with fish . . . so much game . . . that one hunter counted a thousand animals near a single salt lick . . . the virgin wilderness of Kentucky . . . the forested glory of primitive America (13, 201, 223, 314, 407).

But then he mentions that Indian "prairie fires . . . cause the often-mentioned oak openings . . . Great fields of corn spread in all directions . . . the Barrens . . . without forest," and that "Early Ohio settlers found that they could drive about through the forests with sleds and horses" (31, 304, 308, 314). A contradiction?

In the ensuing forty years, scholarship has shown that Indian populations in the Americas were substantial, that the forests had indeed been altered, that landscape change was commonplace. This message, however, seems not to have reached the public through texts, essays, or talks by both academics and popularizers who have a responsibility to know better.[3]

Kirkpatrick Sale in 1990, in his widely reported *Conquest of Paradise,* maintains that it was the Europeans who transformed nature, following a pattern set by Columbus. Although Sale's book has some merit and he is aware of large Indian numbers and their impacts, he nonetheless champions the widely-held dichotomy of the benign Indian landscape and the devastated Colonial landscape. He overstates both.

Similarly, *Seeds of Change: Christopher Columbus and the Colombian Legacy,* the popular book published by the Smithsonian Institution, continues the litany of Native American passivity:

> pre-Columbian America was still the First Eden, a pristine natural kingdom. The native people were transparent in the landscape, living as natural elements of the ecosphere. Their world, the New World of Columbus, was a world of barely perceptible human disturbance (Sheller 1991, 226).

To the contrary, the Indian impact was neither benign nor localized and ephemeral, nor were resources always used in a sound ecological way. The concern here is with the form and magnitude of environmental modification rather than with whether or not Indians lived in harmony with nature with sustainable systems of resource management. Sometimes they did; sometimes they didn't. What they did was to change their landscape nearly everywhere, not to the extent of post-Colonial Europeans but in important ways that merit attention.

The evidence is convincing. By 1492 Indian activity throughout the Americas had modified forest extent and composition, created and expanded grasslands, and rearranged microrelief via countless artificial earthworks. Agricultural fields were

---

[2] See Nash (1967) on the "romantic wilderness" of America; Bowden (1992, 9–12) on the "invented tradition" of the "primeval forest" of New England; and Manthorne (1989, 10–21) on artists' images of the tropical "Eden" of South America. Day (1953, 329) provides numerous quotations from Parkman on "wilderness" and "vast," "virgin," and "continuous" forest.

[3] For example, a 1991 advertisement for a Time-Life video refers to "the unspoiled beaches, forests, and mountains of an earlier America" and "the pristine shores of Chesapeake Bay in 1607."

common, as were houses and towns and roads and trails. All of these had local impacts on soil, microclimate, hydrology, and wildlife. This is a large topic, for which this essay offers but an introduction to the issues, misconceptions, and residual problems. The evidence, pieced together from vague ethnohistorical accounts, field surveys, and archaeology, supports the hypothesis that the Indian landscape of 1492 had largely vanished by the mid-eighteenth century, not through a European superimposition, but because of the demise of the native population. The landscape of 1750 was more "pristine" (less humanized) than that of 1492.

INDIAN NUMBERS

The size of the native population at contact is critical to our argument. The prevailing position, a recent one, is that the Americas were well-populated rather than relatively empty lands in 1492. In the words of the sixteenth-century Spanish priest, Bartolomé de las Casas, who knew the Indies well:

> All that has been discovered up to the year forty-nine [1549] is full of people, like a hive of bees, so that it seems as though God had placed all, or the greater part of the entire human race in these countries (Las Casas, in MacNutt 1909, 314).

Las Casas believed that more than 40 million Indians had died by the year 1560. Did he exaggerate? In the 1930s and 1940s, Alfred Kroeber, Angel Rosenhlat, and Julian Steward believed that he had. The best counts then available indicated a population of between 8–15 million Indians in the Americas. Subsequently, Carl Sauer, Woodrow Borah, Sherburne F. Cook, Henry Dobyns, George Lovell, N. David Cook, myself, and others have argued for larger estimates. Many scholars now believe that there were between 40–100 million Indians in the hemisphere (Denevan 1992). This conclusion is primarily based on evidence of rapid early declines from epidemic disease prior to the first population counts (Lovell, this volume).

I have recently suggested a New World total of 53.9 million (Denevan 1992, xxvii). This divides into 3.8 million for North America, 17.2 million for Mexico, 5.6 million for Central America, 3.0 million for the Caribbean, 15.7 million for the Andes, and 8.6 million for low-land South America. These figures are based on my judgment as to the most reasonable recent tribal and regional estimates. Accepting a margin of error of about 20 percent, the New World population would lie between 43–65 million. Future regional revisions are likely to maintain the hemispheric total within this range. Other recent estimates, none based on totaling regional figures, include 43 million by Whitmore (1991, 483), 40 million by Lord and Burke (1991), 40–50 million by Cowley (1991), and 80 million for just Latin America by Schwerin (1991, 40). In any event, a population between 40–80 million is sufficient to dispel any notion of "empty lands." Moreover, the native impact on the landscape of 1492 reflected not only the population then but the cumulative effects of a growing population over the previous 15,000 years or more.

European entry into the New World abruptly reversed this trend. The decline of native American populations was rapid and severe, probably the greatest demographic disaster ever (Lovell, this volume). Old World diseases were the primary killer. In many regions, particularly the tropical lowlands, populations fell by 90 percent or more in the first century after contact. Indian populations (estimated) declined in Hispaniola from 1 million in 1492 to a few hundred 50 years later, or by more than 99 percent; in Peru from 9 million in 1520 to 670,000 in 1620 (92 percent); in the Basin of Mexico from 1.6 million in 1519 to 180,000 in 1607 (89 percent); and in North

America from 3.8 million in 1492 to 1 million in 1800 (74 percent). An overall drop from 53.9 million in 1492 to 5.6 million in 1650 amounts to an 89 percent reduction (Denevan 1992, xvii–xxix). The human landscape was affected accordingly, although there is not always a direct relationship between population density and human impact (Whitmore, et al. 1990, 37).

The replacement of Indians by Europeans and Africans was initially a slow process. By 1638 there were only about 30,000 English in North America (Sale 1990, 388), and by 1750 there were only 1.3 million Europeans and slaves (Meinig 1986, 247). For Latin America in 1750, Sánchez-Albornoz (1974, 7) gives a total (including Indians) of 12 million. For the hemisphere in 1750, the *Atlas of World Population History* reports 16 million (McEvedy and Jones 1978, 270). Thus the overall hemispheric population in 1750 was about 30 percent of what it may have been in 1492. The 1750 population, however, was very unevenly distributed, mainly located in certain coastal and highland areas with little Europeanization elsewhere. In North America in 1750, there were only small pockets of settlement beyond the coastal belt, stretching from New England to northern Florida (see maps in Meinig 1986, 209, 245). Elsewhere, combined Indian and European populations were sparse, and environmental impact was relatively minor.

Indigenous imprints on landscapes at the time of initial European contact varied regionally in form and intensity. Following are examples for vegetation and wildlife, agriculture, and the built landscape.

VEGETATION

The Eastern Forests

The forests of New England, the Midwest, and the Southeast had been disturbed to varying degrees by Indian activity prior to European occupation. Agricultural clearing and burning had converted much of the forest into successional (fallow) growth and into semi-permanent grassy openings (meadows, barrens, plains, glades, savannas, prairies), often of considerable size.[4] Much of the mature forest was characterized by an open, herbaceous understory, reflecting frequent ground fires. The de Soto expedition, consisting of many people, a large horse herd, and many swine, passed through ten states without difficulty of movement" (Sauer 1971, 283). The situation has been described in detail by Michael Williams in his recent history of American forests: "Much of the 'natural' forest remained, but the forest was not the vast, silent, unbroken, impenetrable and dense tangle of trees beloved by many writers in their romantic accounts of the forest wilderness" (1989, 33).[5] "The result was a forest of large, widely spaced trees, few shrubs, and much grass and herbage . . . Selective Indian burning thus promoted the mosaic quality of New England ecosystems, creating forests in many different states of ecological succession" (Cronon 1983, 49–51).

---

[4] On the other hand, the ability of Indians to clear large trees with inefficient stone axes, assisted by girdling and deadening by fire, may have been overestimated (Denevan forthcoming). Silver (1990, 51) notes that the upland forests of Carolina were largely uninhabited for this reason.

[5] Similar conclusions were reached by foresters Maxwell (1910) and Day (1953); by geographers Sauer (1963), Brown (1948, 11–19), Rostlund (1957), and Bowden (1992); and by environmental historians Pyne (1982, 45–51), Cronon (1983, 49–51), and Silver (1990, 59–66).

The extent, frequency, and impact of Indian burning is not without controversy. Raup (1937) argued that climatic change rather than Indian burning could account for certain vegetation changes. Emily Russell (1983, 86), assessing pre-1700 information for the Northeast, concluded that: "There is no strong evidence that Indians purposely burned large areas," but Indians did "increase the frequency of fires above the low numbers caused by lightning," creating an open forest. But then Russell adds: "In most areas climate and soil probably played the major role in determining the precolonial forests." She regards Indian fires as mainly accidental and "merely" augmental to natural fires, and she discounts the reliability of many early accounts of burning.

Forman and Russell (1983, 5) expand the argument to North America in general: "regular and widespread Indian burning (Day 1953) [is] an unlikely hypothesis that regretfully has been accepted in the popular literature and consciousness." This conclusion, I believe, is unwarranted given reports of the extent of prehistoric human burning in North America and Australia (Lewis 1982), and Europe (Patterson and Sassaman 1988, 130), and by my own and other observations on current Indian and peasant burning in Central America and South America; when unrestrained, people burn frequently and for many reasons. For the Northeast, Patterson and Sassaman (1988, 129) found that sedimentary charcoal accumulations were greatest where Indian populations were greatest.

Elsewhere in North America, the Southeast is much more fire prone than is the Northeast, with human ignitions being especially important in winter (Taylor 1981). The Berkeley geographer and Indianist Erhard Rostlund (1957, 1960) argued that Indian clearing and burning created many grasslands within mostly open forest in the so-called "prairie belt" of Alabama. As improbable as it may seem, Lewis (1982) found Indian burning in the subarctic, and Dobyns (1981) in the Sonoran desert. The characteristics and impacts of fires set by Indians varied regionally and locally with demography, resource management techniques, and environment, but such fires clearly had different vegetation impacts than did natural fires owing to differences in frequency, regularity, and seasonality.

Forest Composition

In North America, burning not only maintained open forest and small meadows but also encouraged fire-tolerant and sun-loving species. "Fire created conditions favorable to strawberries, blackberries, raspberries, and other gatherable foods" (Cronon 1983, 51). Other useful plants were saved, protected, planted, and transplanted, such as American chestnut, Canada plum, Kentucky coffee tree, groundnut, and leek (Day 1953, 339–40). Gilmore (1931) described the dispersal of several native plants by Indians. Mixed stands were converted to single species dominants, including various pines and oaks, sequoia, Douglas fir, spruce, and aspen (M. Williams 1989, 47–48). The longleaf, slash pine, and scrub oak forests of the Southeast are almost certainly an anthropogenic subclimax created originally by Indian burning, replaced in early Colonial times by mixed hardwoods, and maintained in part by fires set by subsequent farmers and woodlot owners (Garren 1943). Lightning fires can account for some fire-climax vegetation, but Indian burning would have extended and maintained such vegetation (Silver 1990, 17–19, 59–64).

Even in the humid tropics, where natural fires are rare, human fires can dramatically influence forest composition. A good example is the pine forests of Nicaragua (Denevan 1961). Open pine stands occur both in the northern highlands (below 5,000 feet) and in the eastern (Miskito) lowlands, where warm temperatures and heavy rainfall generally favor mixed tropical montane forest or rainforest. The extensive pine forests of Guatemala and Mexico primarily grow in cooler and drier, higher elevations, where they are in large part natural and prehuman (Watts and Bradbury 1982, 59). Pine forests were definitely present in Nicaragua when Europeans arrived. They were found in areas where Indian settlement was substantial, but not in the eastern mountains where Indian densities were sparse. The eastern boundary of the highland pines seems to have moved with an eastern settlement frontier that has fluctuated back and forth since prehistory. The pines occur today where there has been clearing followed by regular burning and the same is likely in the past. The Nicaraguan pines are fire tolerant once mature, and large numbers of seedlings survive to maturity if they can escape fire during their first three to seven years (Denevan 1961, 280). Where settlement has been abandoned and fire ceases, mixed hardwoods gradually replace pines. This succession is likely similar where pines occur elsewhere at low elevations in tropical Central America, the Caribbean, and Mexico.

Midwest Prairies and Tropical Savannas

Sauer (1950, 1958, 1975) argued early and often that the great grasslands and savannas of the New World were of anthropogenic rather than climatic origin, that rainfall was generally sufficient to support trees. Even nonagricultural Indians expanded what may have been pockets of natural, edaphic grasslands at the expense of forest. A fire burning to the edge of a grass/forest boundary will penetrate the drier forest margin and push back the edge, even if the forest itself is not consumed (Mueller-Dombois 1981, 164). Grassland can therefore advance significantly in the wake of hundreds of years of annual fires. Lightning-set fires can have a similar impact, but more slowly if less frequent than human fires, as in the wet tropics.

The thesis of prairies as fire induced, primarily by Indians, has its critics (Borchert 1950; Wedel 1957), but the recent review of the topic by Anderson (1990, 14), a biologist, concludes that most ecologists now believe that the eastern prairies "would have mostly disappeared if it had not been for the nearly annual burning of these grasslands by the North American Indians," during the last 5,000 years. A case in point is the nineteenth-century invasion of many grasslands by forests after fire had been suppressed in Wisconsin, Illinois, Kansas, Nebraska, and elsewhere (M. Williams 1989, 46).

The large savannas of South America are also controversial as to origin. Much, if not most of the open vegetation of the Orinoco Llanos, the Llanos de Mojos of Bolivia, the Pantanal of Mato Grosso, the Bolívar savannas of Colombia, the Guayas savannas of coastal Ecuador, the *campo cerrado* of central Brazil, and the coastal savannas north of the Amazon, is of natural origin. The vast *campos cerrados* occupy extremely senile, often toxic oxisols. The seasonally inundated savannas of Bolivia, Brazil, Guayas, and the Orinoco owe their existence to the intolerance of woody species to the extreme alternation of lengthy flooding or waterlogging and severe desiccation during a long dry season. These savannas, however, were and are burned by Indians and ranchers, and such fires have expanded the savannas into the forests to an unknown extent. It is now very difficult to determine where a natural forest/savanna boundary once was located (Hills and Randall 1968; Medina 1980).

Other small savannas have been cut out of the rainforest by Indian farmers and then maintained by burning. An example is the Gran Pajonal in the Andean foothills in east-central Peru, where dozens of small grasslands (*pajonales*) have been created by Campa Indians—a process clearly documented by air photos (Scott 1978). *Pajonales* were in existence when the region was first penetrated by Franciscan missionary explorers in 1733.

The impact of human activity is nicely illustrated by vegetational changes in the basins of the San Jorge, Cauca, and Sinú rivers of northern Colombia. The southern sector, which was mainly savanna when first observed in the sixteenth century, had reverted to rainforest by about 1750 following Indian decline, and had been reconverted to savanna for pasture by 1950 (Gordon 1957, map p. 69). Sauer (1966, 285–88; 1976, 8) and Bennett (1968, 53–55) cite early descriptions of numerous savannas in Panama in the sixteenth century. Balboa's first view of the Pacific was from a "treeless ridge," now probably forested. Indian settlement and agricultural fields were common at the time, and with their decline the rainforest returned.

Anthropogenic Tropical Rain Forest

The tropical rain forest has long had a reputation for being pristine, whether in 1492 or 1992. There is, however, increasing evidence that the forests of Amazonia and elsewhere are largely anthropogenic in form and composition. Sauer (1958, 105) said as much at the Ninth Pacific Science Congress in 1957 when he challenged the statement of tropical botanist Paul Richards that, until recently, the tropical forests have been largely uninhabited, and that prehistoric people had "no more influence on the vegetation than any of the other animal inhabitants." Sauer countered that Indian burning, swiddens, and manipulation of composition had extensively modified the tropical forest.

"Indeed, in much of Amazonia, it is difficult to find soils that are not studded with charcoal" (Uhl, et al. 1990, 30). The question is, to what extent does this evidence reflect Indian burning in contrast to natural (lightning) fires, and when did these fires occur? The role of fire in tropical forest ecosystems has received considerable attention in recent years, partly as result of major wild fires in East Kalimantan in 1982–83 and small forest fires in the Venezuelan Amazon in 1980–84 (Goldammer 1990). Lightning fires, though rare in moist tropical forest, do occur in drier tropical woodlands (Mueller-Dombois 1981, 149). Thunderstorms with lightning are much more common in the Amazon, compared to North America, but in the tropics lightning is usually associated with heavy rain and noncombustible, verdant vegetation. Hence Indian fires undoubtedly account for most fires in prehistory, with their impact varying with the degree of aridity.

In the Río Negro region of the Colombian-Venezuelan Amazon, soil charcoal is very common in upland forests. C-14 dates range from 6260–250 B.P., well within human times (Saldarriaga and West 1986). Most of the charcoal probably reflects local swidden burns; however, there are some indications of forest fires at intervals of several hundred years, most likely ignited by swidden fires. Recent wild fires in the upper Río Negro region were in a normally moist tropical forest (3530 mm annual rainfall) that had experienced several years of severe drought. Such infrequent wild fires in prehistory, along with the more frequent ground fires, could have had significant impacts on forest succession, structure, and composition. Examples are the pine forests of Nicaragua, mentioned above, the oak forests of Central America, and the babassu palm forests of eastern Brazil. Widespread and frequent burning may have brought about the extinction of some endemic species.

The Amazon forest is a mosaic of different ages, structure, and composition resulting from local habitat conditions and disturbance dynamics (Haffer 1991). Natural disturbances (tree falls, landslides, river activity) have been considerably augmented by human activity, particularly by shifting cultivation. Even a small number of swidden farmers can have a widespread impact in a relatively short period of time. In the Río Negro region, species-diversity recovery takes 60–80 years and biomass recovery

140–200 years (Saldarriaga and Uhl 1991, 312). Brown and Lugo (1990, 4) estimate that today about forty percent of the tropical forest in Latin America is secondary as a result of human clearing and that most of the remainder has had some modification despite current low population densities. The species composition of early stages of swidden fallows differs from that of natural gaps and may "alter the species composition of the mature forest on a long-term scale" (Walschburger and Von Hildebrand 1991, 262). While human environmental destruction in Amazonia currently is concentrated along roads, in prehistoric times Indian activity in the upland (interfluve) forests was much less intense but more widespread (Denevan forthcoming).

Indian modification of tropical forests is not limited to clearing and burning. Large expanses of Latin American forests are humanized forests in which the kinds, numbers, and distributions of useful species are managed by human populations. Doubtless, this applies to the past as well. One important mechanism in forest management is manipulation of swidden fallows (sequential agroforestry) to increase useful species. The planting, transplanting, sparing, and protection of useful wild, fallow plants eliminates clear distinctions between field and fallow (Denevan and Padoch 1988). Abandonment is a slow process, not an event. Gordon (1982, 79–98) describes managed regrowth vegetation in eastern Panama, which he believes extended from Yucatán to northern Colombia in pre-European times. The Huastec of eastern Mexico and the Yucatec Maya have similar forms of forest gardens or forest management (Alcorn 1981; Gómez-Pompa 1987). The Kayapó of the Brazilian Amazon introduce and/or protect useful plants in activity areas ("nomadic agriculture") adjacent to villages or camp sites, in foraging areas, along trails, near fields, and in artificial forest-mounds in savanna (Posey 1985). In managed forests, both annuals and perennials are planted or transplanted, while wild fruit trees are particularly common in early successional growth. Weeding by hand was potentially more selective than indiscriminate weeding by machete (Gordon 1982, 57–61). Much dispersal of edible plant seeds is unintentional via defecation and spitting out.

The economic botanist William Balée (1987, 1989) speaks of "cultural" or "anthropogenic" forests in Amazonia in which species have been manipulated, often without a reduction in natural diversity. These include specialized forests (babassu, Brazil nuts, lianas, palms, bamboo), which currently make up at least 11.8 percent (measured) of the total upland forest in the Brazilian Amazon (Bake 1989, 14). Clear indications of past disturbance are the extensive zones of terra preta (black earth), which occur along the edges of the large floodplains as well as in the uplands (Balée 1989, 10–12; Smith 1980). These soils, with depths to 50 cm or more, contain charcoal and cultural waste from prehistoric burning and settlement. Given high carbon, nitrogen, calcium, and phosphorus content, *terra preta* soils have a distinctive vegetation and are attractive to farmers. Balée (1989, 14) concludes that "large portions of Amazonian forests appear to exhibit the continuing effects of past human interference." The same argument has been made for the Maya lowlands (Gómez-Pompa, et al. 1987) and Panama (Gordon 1982). There are no virgin tropical forests today, nor were there in 1492.

WILDLIFE

The indigenous impact on wildlife is equivocal. The thesis that "overkill" hunting caused the extinction of some large mammals in North America during the late Pleistocene, as well as subsequent local and regional depletions (Martin 1978, 167–721, remains controversial. By the time of the arrival of Cortéz in 1519, the dense populations of Central Mexico apparently had greatly reduced the number of large game, given reports that "they eat any living thing" (Cook and Borah 1971–79, (3) 135, 140). In Amazonia, local game depletion apparently increases with village size and duration (Good 1987). Hunting procedures in many regions seem, however, to have allowed for recovery because of the "resting" of hunting zones intentionally or as a result of shifting of village sites.

On the other hand, forest disturbance increased herbaceous forage and edge effect, and hence the numbers of some animals (Thompson and Smith 1970, 261–64). "Indians created ideal habitats for a host of wildlife species . . . exactly those species whose abundance so impressed English colonists: elk, deer, beaver, hare, porcupine, turkey, quail, ruffed grouse, and so on" (Cronon 1983, 51). White-tailed deer, peccary, birds, and other game increases in swiddens and fallows in Yucatán and Panama (Greenberg 1991; Gordon 1982, 96–112; Bennett 1968). Rostlund (1960, 407) believed that the creation of grassy openings east of the Mississippi extended the range of the bison, whose numbers increased with Indian depopulation and reduced hunting pressure between 1540–1700, and subsequently declined under White pressure.

AGRICULTURE

Fields and Associated Features

To observers in the sixteenth century, the most visible manifestation of the Native American landscape must have been the cultivated fields, which were concentrated around villages and houses. Most fields are ephemeral, their presence quickly erased when farmers migrate or die, but there are many eye-witness accounts of the great extent of Indian fields. On Hispaniola, Las Casas and Oviedo reported individual fields with thousands of *montones* (Sturtevant 1961, 73). These were manioc and sweet potato mounds 3–4 m in circumference, of which apparently none have survived. In the Llanos de Mojos in Bolivia, the first explorers mentioned *percheles,* or corn cribs on pilings, numbering up to 700 in a single field, each holding 30–45 bushels of food (Denevan 1966, 98). In northern Florida in 1539, Hernando de Soto's army passed through numerous fields of maize, beans, and squash, their main source of provisions; in one sector, "great fields . . . were spread out as far as the eye could see across two leagues of the plain" (Garcilaso de la Vega 1980, (2) 182; also see Dobyns 1983, 135–46).

It is difficult to obtain a reliable overview from such descriptions. Aside from possible exaggeration, Europeans tended not to write about field size, production, or technology. More useful are various forms of relict fields and field features that persist for centuries and can still be recognized, measured, and excavated today. These extant features, including terraces, irrigation works, raised fields, sunken fields, drainage ditches, dams, reservoirs, diversion walls, and field borders number in the millions and are distributed throughout the Americas (Denevan 1960; see also Doolittle and Whitmore and Turner, this volume). For example, about 500,000 ha of abandoned raised fields survive in the San Jorge Basin of northern Colombia (Plazas and Falchetti 1987, 485), and at least 600,000 ha of terracing, mostly of prehistoric origin, occur in the Peruvian Andes (Denevan 1988, 20). There are 19,000 ha of visible raised fields in just the sustaining area of Tiwanaku at Lake Titicaca (Kolata 1991, 109) and there were about 12,000 ha of *chinampas* (raised fields) around the Aztec capital of Tenochtitlán (Sanders, et al. 1979, 390). Complex canal systems on the north coast of Peru and in the Salt River Valley in Arizona irrigated more land in prehistory than is cultivated today. About 175 sites of Indian garden beds, up to several hundred acres each, have been reported in Wisconsin (Gartner 1992). These various remnant fields probably represent less than 25 percent of what once existed, most being buried under sediment or destroyed by erosion, urbanization, plowing, and bulldozing. On the other hand, an inadequate effort has been made to search for ancient fields.

Erosion

The size of native populations, associated deforestation, and prolonged intensive agriculture led to severe land degradation in some regions. Such a landscape was that of Central Mexico, where by 1519 food production pressures may have brought the Aztec civilization to the verge of collapse even without Spanish intervention (Cook and Borah 1971–79 (3), 129-76).[6] There is good evidence that severe soil erosion was already widespread, rather than just the result of subsequent European plowing, livestock, and deforestation. Cook examined the association between erosional severity (gullies, barrancas, sand and silt deposits, and sheet erosion) and pre-Spanish population density or proximity to prehistoric Indian towns. He concluded that "an important cycle of erosion and deposition therefore accompanied intensive land use by huge primitive populations in central Mexico, and had gone far toward the devastation of the country before the white man arrived" (Cook 1949, 86).

Barbara Williams (1972, 618) describes widespread *tepetate,* an indurated substrate formation exposed by sheet erosion resulting from prehistoric agriculture, as "one of the dominant surface materials in the Valley of Mexico." On the other hand, anthropologist Melville (1990, 27) argues that soil erosion in the Valle de Mezquital, just north of the Valley of Mexico, was the result of overgrazing by Spanish livestock starting before 1600: "there is an almost total lack of evidence of environmental degradation before the last three decades of the sixteenth century." The Butzers, however, in an examination of Spanish land grants, grazing patterns, and soil and vegetation ecology, found that there was only light intrusion of Spanish livestock (sheep and cattle were moved frequently) into the southeastern Bajío near Mezquital until after 1590 and that any degradation in 1590 was "as much a matter of long-term Indian land use as it was of Spanish intrusion" (Butzer and Butzer forthcoming). The relative roles of Indian and early Spanish impacts in Mexico still need resolution; both were clearly significant but varied in time and place. Under the Spaniards, however, even with a greatly reduced population, the landscape in Mexico generally did not recover due to accelerating impacts from introduced sheep and cattle.[7]

THE BUILT LANDSCAPE

Settlement

The Spaniards and other Europeans were impressed by large flourishing Indian cities such as Tenochtitlán, Quito, and Cuzco, and they took note of the extensive ruins of

---

[6] B. Williams (1989, 730) finds strong evidence of rural overpopulation (66 percent in poor crop years, 11 percent in average years) in the Basin of Mexico village of Asunción, ca. a.d. 1540, which was probably "not unique but a widespread phenomenon." For a contrary conclusion, that the Aztecs did not exceed carrying capacity, see Ortiz de Montellano (1990, 119).

[7] Highland Guatemala provides another prehistoric example of "severe human disturbance" involving deforestation and "massive" soil erosion (slopes) and deposition (valleys) (Murdy 1990, 186). For the central Andes there is some evidence that much of the *puna* zone (3200–4500 m), now grass and scrub, was deforested in prehistoric times (White 1985).

older, abandoned cities such as Cahokia, Teotihuacán, Tikal, Chan Chan, and Tiwanaku (Hardoy 1968). Most of these cities contained more than 50,000 people. Less notable, or possibly more taken for granted, was rural settlement—small villages of a few thousand or a few hundred people, hamlets of a few families, and dispersed farmsteads. The numbers and locations of much of this settlement will never be known. With the rapid decline of native populations, the abandonment of houses and entire villages and the decay of perishable materials quickly obscured sites, especially in the tropical low-lands.

We do have some early listings of villages, especially for Mexico and Peru. Elsewhere, archaeology is telling us more than ethnohistory. After initially focusing on large temple and administrative centers, archaeologists are now examining rural sustaining areas, with remarkable results. See, for example, Sanders et al. (1979) on the Basin of Mexico, Culbert and Rice (1991) on the Maya lowlands, and Fowler (1989) on Cahokia in Illinois. Evidence of human occupation for the artistic Santarém Culture phase (Tapajós chiefdom) on the lower Amazon extends over thousands of square kilometers, with large nucleated settlements (Roosevelt 1991, 101–02).

Much of the rural precontact settlement was semi-dispersed (*rancherías*), particularly in densely populated regions of Mexico and the Andes, probably reflecting poor food transport efficiency. Houses were both single-family and communal (pueblos, Huron long houses, Amazon malocas). Construction was of stone, earth, adobe, daub and wattle, grass, hides, brush, and bark. Much of the dispersed settlement not destroyed by depopulation was concentrated by the Spaniards into compact grid/plaza style new towns (*congregaciones, reducciones*) for administrative purposes.

Mounds

James Parsons (1985, 161) has suggested that: "An apparent 'mania for earth moving, landscape engineering on a grand scale runs as a thread through much of New World prehistory." Large quantities of both earth and stone were transferred to create various raised and sunken features, such as agricultural land-forms, settlement and ritual mounds, and causeways,

Mounds of different shapes and sizes were constructed throughout the Americas for temples, burials, settlement, and as effigies. The stone pyramids of Mexico and the Andes are well known, but equal monuments of earth were built in the Amazon, the Midwest U.S., and elsewhere. The Mississippian period complex of 104 mounds at Cahokia near East St. Louis supported 30,000 people; the largest, Monk's Mound, is currently 30.5 m high and covers 6.9 ha (Fowler 1989, 90, 192). Cahokia was the largest settlement north of the Río Grande until surpassed by New York City in 1775. An early survey estimated "at least 20,000 conical, linear, and effigy mounds" in Wisconsin (Stout 1911, 24). Overall, there must have been several hundred thousand artificial mounds in the Midwest and South. De Soto described such features still in use in 1539 (Silverberg 1968, 7). Thousands of settlement and other mounds dot the savanna landscape of Mojos in Bolivia (Denevan 1966). At the mouth of the Amazon on Marajó Island, one complex of forty habitation mounds contained more than 10,000 people; one of these mounds is 20 m high while another is 90 ha in area (Roosevelt 1991, 31, 38).

Not all of the various earthworks scattered over the Americas were in use in 1492. Many had been long abandoned, but they constituted a conspicuous element of the landscape of 1492 and some are still prominent. Doubtless, many remain to be discovered, and others remain unrecognized as human or prehistoric features.

Roads, Causeways, and Trails

Large numbers of people and settlements necessitated extensive systems of overland travel routes to facilitate administration, trade, warfare, and social interaction (Hyslop 1984; Trombold 1991). Only hints of their former prominence survive. Many were simple traces across deserts or narrow paths cut into forests. A suggestion as to the importance of Amazon forest trails is the existence of more than 500 km of trail maintained by a single Kayapó village today (Posey 1985, 149). Some prehistoric footpaths were so intensively used for so long that they were incised into the ground and are still detectable, as has recently been described in Costa Rica (Sheets and Sever 1991).

Improved roads, at times stone-lined and drained, were constructed over great distances in the realms of the high civilizations. The Inca road network is estimated to have measured about 40,000 km, extending from southern Colombia to central Chile (Hyslop 1984, 224). Prehistoric causeways (raked roads) were built in the tropical lowlands (Denevan 1991); one Maya causeway is 100 km long, and there are more than 1,600 km of causeways in the Llanos de Mojos. Humboldt reported large prehistoric causeways in the Orinoco Llanos. Ferdinand Columbus described roads on Puerto Rico in 1493. Gaspar de Carvajal, traveling down the Amazon with Orellana in 1541, reported "highways" penetrating the forest from river bank villages. Joseph de Acosta (1880, (1) 171) in 1590 said that between Peru and Brazil, there were "wales as much beaten as those betwixt Salamanca and Valladolid." Prehistoric roads in Chaco Canyon, New Mexico are described in Trombold (1991). Some routes were so well established and located that they have remained roads to this day.

RECOVERY

A strong case can be made for significant environmental recovery and reduction of cultural features by the late eighteenth century as a result of Indian population decline. Henry Thoreau (1949, 132–37) believed, based on his reading of William Wood, that the New England forests of 1633 were more open, more park-like, with more berries and more wildlife, than Thoreau observed in 1855. Cronon (1983, 108), Pyne (1982, 51), Silver (1990, 104), Martin (1978, 181–82), and Williams (1989, 49) all maintain that the eastern forests recovered and filled in as a result of Indian depopulation, field abandonment, and reduction in burning. While probably correct, these writers give few specific examples, so further research is needed. The sixteenth-century fields and savannas of Colombia and Central America also had reverted to forest within 150 years after abandonment (Parsons 1975, 30–31; Bennett 1968, 54). On his fourth voyage in 1502–03, Columbus sailed along the north coast of Panama (Veragua). His son Ferdinand described lands which were well-peopled, full of houses, with many fields, and open with few trees. In contrast, in 1681 Lionel Wafer found most of the Caribbean coast of Panama forest covered and unpopulated. On the Pacific side in the eighteenth century, savannas were seldom mentioned; the main economic activity was the logging of tropical cedar, a tree that grows on the sites of abandoned fields and other disturbances (Sauer 1966, 132–33, 287–88). An earlier oscillation from forest destruction to recovery in the Yucatán is instructive. Whitmore, et al. (1990, 35) estimate that the Maya had modified 75 percent of the environment by A.D. 800, and that following the Mayan collapse, forest recovery in the central lowlands was nearly complete when the Spaniards arrived.

The pace of forest regeneration, however, varied across the New World. Much of the southeastern U.S. remained treeless in the 1750s according to Rostlund (1957, 408, 409). He notes that the tangled brush that ensnarled the "Wilderness Campaign of

1864 in Virginia occupied the same land as did Captain John Smith's 'open groves with much good ground between without any shrubs'" in 1624; vegetation had only partially recovered over 240 years. The Kentucky barrens in contrast were largely reforested by the early nineteenth century (Sauer 1963, 30). The Alabama Black Belt vegetation was described by William Bartram in the 1770s as a mixture of forest and grassy plains, but by the nineteenth century, there was only 10 percent prairie and even less in some counties (Rostlund 1957, 393, 401–03). Sections of coastal forests never recovered, given colonist pressures, but Sale's (1990, 291) claim that "the English were well along in the process of eliminating the ancient Eastern woodlands from Maine to the Mississippi" in the first one hundred years, is an exaggeration.

Wildlife also partially recovered in eastern North America with reduced hunting pressure from Indians; however, this is also a story yet to be worked out. The white-tailed deer apparently declined in numbers, probably reflecting reforestation plus competition from livestock. Commercial hunting was a factor on the coast, with 80,000 deer skins being shipped out yearly from Charleston by 1730 (Silver 1990, 92). Massachusetts enacted a closed season on deer as early as 1694, and in 1718 there was a three-year moratorium on deer hunting (Cronon 1983, 100). Sale (1990, 290) believes that beaver were depleted in the Northeast by 1640. Other fur bearers, game birds, elk, buffalo, and carnivores were also targeted by white hunters, but much game probably was in the process of recovery in many eastern areas until a general reversal after 1700–50.

As agricultural fields changed to scrub and forest, earthworks were grown over. All the raised fields in Yucatán and South America were abandoned. A large portion of the agricultural terraces in the Americas were abandoned in the early colonial period (Donkin 1979, 35–38). In the Colca Valley of Peru, measurement on air photos indicates 61 percent terrace abandonment (Denevan 1988, 28). Societies vanished or declined everywhere and whole villages with them. The degree to which settlement features were swallowed up by vegetation, sediment, and erosion is indicated by the difficulty of finding them today. Machu Picchu, a late prehistoric site, was not rediscovered until 1911.

The renewal of human impact also varied regionally, coming with the Revolutionary War in North America, with the rubber boom in Amazonia, and with the expansion of coffee in southern Brazil (1840–1930). The swamp lands of Gulf Coast Mexico and the Guayas Basin of Ecuador remained hostile environments to Europeans until well into the nineteenth century or later (Siemens 1990; Mathewson 1987). On the other hand, Highland Mexico-Guatemala and the Andes, with greater Indian survival and with the establishment of haciendas and intensive mining, show less evidence of environmental recovery. Similarly, Indian fields in the Caribbean were rapidly replaced by European livestock and sugar plantation systems, inhibiting any sufficient recovery. The same is true of the sugar zone of coastal Brazil.

CONCLUSIONS

By 1492, Indian activity had modified vegetation and wildlife, caused erosion, and created earthworks, roads, and settlements throughout the Americas. This may be obvious, but the human imprint was much more ubiquitous and enduring than is usually realized. The historical evidence is ample, as are data from surviving earthworks and archaeology. And much can be inferred from present human impacts. The weight of evidence suggests that Indian populations were large, not only in Mexico and the Andes, but also in seemingly unattractive habitats such as the rainforests of Amazonia, the swamps of Mojos, and the deserts of Arizona.

Clearly, the most humanized landscapes of the Americas existed in those highland regions where people were the most numerous. Here were the large states, characterized by urban centers, road systems, intensive agriculture, a dispersed but relatively dense rural settlement pattern of hamlets and farmsteads, and widespread vegetation and soil modification and wildlife depletion. There were other, smaller regions that shared some of these characteristics, such as the Pueblo lands in the southwestern U.S., the Sabana de Bogotá in highland Colombia, and the central Amazon floodplain, where built landscapes were locally dramatic and are still observable. Finally, there were the immense grasslands, deserts, mountains, and forests elsewhere, with populations that were sparse or moderate, with landscape impacts that mostly were ephemeral or not obvious but nevertheless significant, particularly for vegetation and wildlife, as in Amazonia and the northeastern U.S. In addition, landscapes from the more distant past survived to 1492 and even to 1992, such as those of the irrigation states of north coast Peru, the Classic Maya, the Mississippian mound builders, and the Tiwanaku Empire of Lake Titicaca.

This essay has ranged over the hemisphere, an enormous area, making generalizations about and providing examples of Indian landscape transformation as of 1492. Examples of some of the surviving cultural features are shown in Figure 1. Ideally, a series of hemispheric maps should be provided to portray the spatial patterns of the different types of impacts and cultural features, but such maps are not feasible nor would they be accurate given present knowledge. There are a few relevant regional maps, however, that can be referred to. For example, see Butzer (1990, 33, 45) for Indian settlement structures/mounds and subsistence patterns in the U.S.; Donkin (1979, 23) for agricultural terracing; Doolittle (1990, 109) for canal irrigation in Mexico; Parsons and Denevan (1967) for raised fields in South America; Trombold (1991) for various road networks; Hyslop (1984, 4) for the Inca roads; Hardoy (1968, 49) for the most intense urbanization in Latin America; and Gordon (1957, 69) for anthropogenic savannas in northern Colombia.

The pristine myth cannot be laid at the feet of Columbus. While he spoke of "Paradise," his was clearly a humanized paradise. He described Hispaniola and Tortuga as densely populated and "completely cultivated like the countryside around Cordoba" (Colón 1976, 165). He also noted that "the islands are not so thickly wooded as to he impassable," suggesting openings from clearing and burning (Columbus 1961, 5).

The roots of the pristine myth lie in part with early observers unaware of human impacts that may be obvious to scholars today, particularly for vegetation and wildlife.[8] But even many earthworks such as raised fields have only recently been discovered (Denevan 1966; 1980). Equally important, most of our eyewitness descriptions of wilderness and empty lands come from a later time, particularly 1750–1850 when interior lands began to be explored and occupied by Europeans. By 1650, Indian populations in the hemisphere had been reduced by about 90 percent, while by 1750 European numbers were not yet substantial and settlement had only begun to expand. As a result, fields had been abandoned, while settlements vanished, forests recovered, and savannas retreated. The landscape did appear to be a sparsely populated wilderness. This is the image conveyed by Parkman in the nineteenth century, Bakeless in 1950, and Shetler as recently as 1991. There was some European impact, of course, but it was localized. After 1750 and especially after 1850, populations greatly expanded, resources were more intensively exploited, and European modification of the environment accelerated, continuing to the present.

---

[8] The English colonists in part justified their occupation of Indian land on the basis that such land had not been "subdued" and therefore was "land free to be taken" (Wilson 1992, 16).

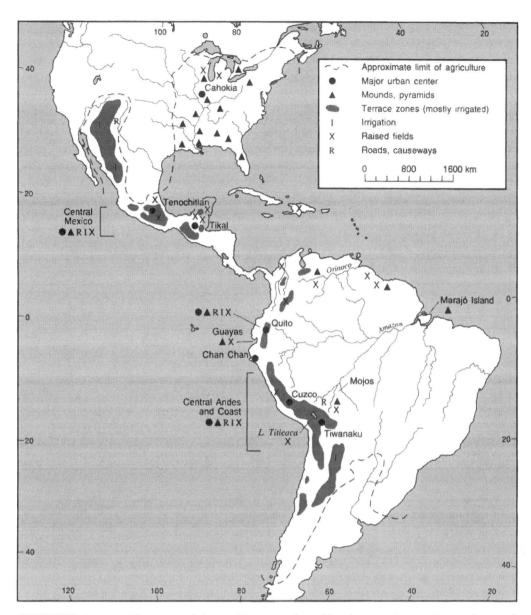

Figure 5.1 Selected features of the prehistoric cultural landscape. *Some cities and agricultural works had been abandoned by 1492. The approximate limit of agriculture and the distribution of terraces is based on Donkin (1979, 23); other features were mapped by the author.*

It is possible to conclude not only that "the virgin forest was not encountered in the sixteenth and seventeenth centuries; [but that] it was invented in the late eighteenth and early nineteenth centuries" (Pyne 1982, 46). However, "paradoxical as it may seem, there was undoubtedly much more 'forest primeval' in 1850 than in 1650" (Rostlund 1957, 409). Thus the "invention" of an earlier wilderness is in part understandable and is not simply a deliberate creation which ennobled the American enterprise, as suggested by Bowden (1992, 20–23). In any event, while pre-European landscape alteration has been demonstrated previously, including by several geographers, the case has mainly been made for vegetation and mainly for eastern North America. As shown here, the argument is also applicable to most of the rest of the New World, including the humid tropics, and involves much more than vegetation.

The human impact on environment is not simply a process of increasing change or degradation in response to linear population growth and economic expansion. It is instead interrupted by periods of reversal and ecological rehabilitation as cultures collapse, populations decline, wars occur, and habitats are abandoned. Impacts may be constructive, benign, or degenerative (all subjective concepts), but change is continual at variable rates and in different directions. Even mild impacts and slow changes are cumulative, and the long-term effects can be dramatic. Is it possible that the thousands of years of human activity before Columbus created more change in the visible landscape than has occurred subsequently with European settlement and resource exploitation? The answer is probably yes for most regions for the next 250 years or so, and for some regions right up to the present time. American flora, fauna, and landscape were slowly Europeanized after 1492, but before that they had already been Indianized. "It is upon this imprint that the more familiar Euro-American landscape was grafted, rather than created anew" (Butzer 1990, 28). What does all this mean for protectionist tendencies today? Much of what is protected or proposed to be protected from human disturbance had native people present, and environmental modification occurred accordingly and in part is still detectable.

The pristine image of 1492 seems to be a myth, then, an image more applicable to 1750, following Indian decline, although recovery had only been partial by that date. There is some substance to this argument, and it should hold up under the scrutiny of further investigation of the considerable evidence available, both written and in the ground.

References

Acosta, Joseph [José] de. 1880 [1590]. *The natural and moral history of the Indies.* Trans. E. Gimston, Hakluyt Society, vols. 60, 61. London.

Alcorn, J. B. 1981, Huastec noncrop resource management: Implications for prehistoric rain forest management. *Human Ecology* 9:395–417.

Anderson, R. C. 1990. The historic role of fire in the North American grassland. In *Fire in North American tallgrass prairies,* ed. S. L. Collins and L. L. Wallace, pp. 8–18. Norman: University of Oklahoma Press.

Bakeless, J. 1950. *The eyes of discovery: The pageant of North America as seen by the first explorers.* New York; J. B. Lippincott.

Balée, W. 1987. Cultural forests of the Amazon. *Garden* 11:12-14, 32.

———. 1989. The culture of Amazonian forests. In *Advances in Economic Botany,* vol. 7, pp. 1–21. New York: New York Botanical Garden.

Bennett, C. F. 1968. *Human influences on the zoogeography of Panama.* Ibero-Americana 51. Berkeley: University of California Press.

Borchert, J. 1950. Climate of the central North American grassland. *Annals of the Association of American Geographers* 40:1–39.

Bowden, M. J. 1992. The invention of American tradition. *Journal of Historical Geography* 18:3–26.

Brown, R. H. 1948. *Historical geography of the United States.* New York; Harcourt, Brace.

Brown, S., and Lugo, A. 1990. Tropical secondary forests. *Journal of Tropical Ecology* 6: 1–32.

Butzer, K. W. 1990. The Indian legacy in the American landscape. In *The making of the American landscape,* ed. M. P. Cowen, pp. 27–50. Boston: Unwin Hyman.

———, **and Butzer, E. K.** Forthcoming. The sixteenth-century environment of the central Mexican Bajío: Archival reconstruction from Spanish land grants. In *Culture, form, and place,* ed. K. Mathewson. Baton Rouge, LA: Geoscience and Man.

Colón, C. 1976. *Diario del descubrimiento,* vol. 1, ed. M. Alvar. Madrid: Editorial La Muralla.

Columbus, C. 1961. *Four voyages to the New World: Letters and selected documents,* ed. R. H. Major. New York: Corinth Books.

Cook, S. F. 1949. *Soil erosion and population in Central Mexico.* Ibero-Americana 34. Berkeley: University of California Press.

———, and Borah, W. 1971–79. *Essays in population history.* 3 vols. Berkeley: University of California Press.

Cowley, G. 1991. The great disease migration. In 1492–1992, *When worlds collide: How Columbus's voyages transformed both East and West. Newsweek,* Special Issue, Fall/Winter, pp. 54–56.

Cronon, W. 1983. *Changes in the land: Indians, colonists, and the ecology of New England.* New York: Hill and Wang.

Culbert, T. P., and Rice, D. S., eds. 1990. *Precolumbian population history in the Maya lowlands.* Albuquerque: University of New Mexico Press.

Day, G. M. 1953. The Indian as an ecological factor in the northeastern forest. *Ecology* 34:329–46.

Denevan, W. M. 1961. The upland pine forests of Nicaragua. *University of California Publications in Geography* 12:251–320.

———. 1966. *The aboriginal cultural geography of the Llanos de Mojos of Bolivia.* Ibero-Americana 48. Berkeley: University of California Press.

———. 1980. Tipología de configuraciones agrícolas prehispánicas. *América Indígena* 40:619–52.

———. 1988. Measurement of abandoned terracing from air photos: Colca Valley, Peru. *Yearbook, Conference of Latin Americanist Geographers* 14:20–30.

———. 1991. Prehistoric roads and causeways of lowland tropical America. In *Ancient road networks and settlement hierarchies in the New World,* ed. C. D. Trombold, pp. 230–42. Cambridge: Cambridge University Press.

———, ed. 1992 [1976]. *The native population of the Americas in 1492,* 2nd ed. Madison: University of Wisconsin Press.

———. Forthcoming. Stone vs. metal axes: The ambiguity of shifting cultivation in prehistoric Amazonia. *Journal of the Steward Anthropological Society.*

———, and Padoch, C., eds. 1988. *Swidden-fallow agroforestry in the Peruvian Amazon. Advances in Economic Botany,* vol. 5. New York: New York Botanical Garden.

Dobyns, H. F. 1981. *From fire to flood: Historic human destruction of Sonoran Desert riverine oases.* Socorro, NM: Ballena Press.

———. 1983. *Their number become thinned: Native American population dynamics in eastern North America.* Knoxville: University of Tennessee Press.

Donkin, R. A. 1979. *Agricultural terracing in the aboriginal New World.* Viking Fund Publications in Anthropology 56. Tucson: University of Arizona Press.

Doolittle, W. E. 1990. *Canal irrigation in prehistoric Mexico: The sequence of technological change.* Austin: University of Texas Press.

Forman, R. T. T., and Russell, E. W. B. 198.3. Evaluation of historical data in ecology. *Bulletin of the Ecological Society of America* 64:5–7.

Fowler, M. 1989. *The Cahokia atlas: A historical atlas of Cahokia archaeology.* Studies in Illinois Archaeology 6. Springfield: Illinois Historic Preservation Agency.

Garren, K. H. 1943. Effects of fire on vegetation of the southeastern United States. *The Botanical Review* 9:617–54.

Gartner, W. G. 1992. The Hulbert Creek ridged fields: Pre-Columbian agriculture near the Dells, Wisconsin. Master's thesis, Department of Geography, University of Wisconsin, Madison.

Garcilaso de la Vega, The Inca. 1980 [1605]. *The Florida of the Inca: A history of the Adelantado, Hernando de Soto.* 2 vols. Trans. and ed. J. G. Varner and J. J. Varner. Austin: University of Texas Press.

Gilmore, M. R. 1931. Dispersal by Indians a factor in the extension of discontinuous distribution of certain species of native plants. *Papers of the Michigan Academy of Science, Arts and Letters* 13:89–94.

Goldammer, J. G., ed. 1990. Fire in the tropical biota: Ecosystem processes and global challenges. *Ecological Studies,* vol. 84. Berlin: Springer-Verlag.

Gómez-Pompa, A. 1987. On Maya silviculture. *Mexican Studies* 3:1–17.

———; Salvador Flores, J.; and Sosa, V. 1987. The "pet kot": A man-made forest of the Maya. *Interciencia* 12:10–15.

Good, K. R. 1987. Limiting factors in Amazonian ecology. In *Food and evolution: Toward a theory of human food habitats,* ed. M. Harris and E. B. Ross, pp. 407–21. Philadelphia: Temple University Press.

Gordon, B. L. 1957. *Human geography and ecology in the Sinú country of Colombia.* Ibero-Americana 39. Berkeley: University of California Press.

——. 1982. *A Panama forest and shore: Natural history and Amerindian culture in Bocas del Toro.* Pacific Grove: Boxwood Press.

Greenberg, L. S. C. 1991. Garden-hunting among the Yucatec Maya. *Etnoecológica* 1:30–36.

Haffer, J. 1991. Mosaic distribution patterns of neotropical forest birds and underlying cyclic disturbance processes. In *The mosaic-cycle concept of ecosystems,* ed. H. Remmert, pp. 83–105. Ecological Studies, vol. 85. Berlin: Springer-Verlag.

Hardoy, J. 1968. *Urban planning in pre-Columbian America.* New York: George Braziler.

Hills, T. L., and Randall, R. E., eds. 1968. *The ecology of the forest/savanna boundary.* Savanna Research Series 13. Montreal: McGill University.

Hyslop, J. 1984. *The Inka road system.* New York: Academic Press.

Kolata, A. L. 1991. The technology and organization of agricultural production in the Tiwanaku state. *Latin American Antiquity* 2:99–125.

Lewis, H. T. 1982. Fire technology and resource management in aboriginal North America and Australia. In *Resource managers: North American and Australian hunter-gatherers,* ed. N. M. Williams and E. S. Bunn, pp. 45–67. AAAS Selected Symposia 67. Boulder, CO: Westview Press.

Lord, L., and Burke, S. 1991. America before Columbus. *U.S. News and World Report,* July 8, pp. 22–37.

McEvedy, C., and Jones, R. 1978. *Atlas of world population history.* New York: Penguin Books.

MacNutt, F. A. 1909. *Bartholomew de las Casas: His life, his apostolate, and his writings.* New York: Putnam's.

Manthome, K. E. 1989. *Tropical renaissance: North American artists exploring Latin America, 1839–1879.* Washington: Smithsonian Institution Press.

Martin, C. 1978. *Keepers of the game: Indian-animal relationships and the fur trade.* Berkeley: University of California Press.

Mathewson, K. 1987. Landscape change and cultural persistence in the Guayas wetlands, Ecuador. Ph. D. dissertation, Department of Geography, University of Wisconsin, Madison.

Maxwell, H. 1910. The use and abuse of forests by the Virginia Indians. *William and Mary College Quarterly Historical Magazine* 19:73–103.

Medina, E. 1980. Ecology of tropical American savannas: An ecophysiological approach. In *Human ecology in savanna environments,* ed. D. R. Harris, pp. 297–319. London: Academic Press.

Meinig, D. W. 1986. *The shaping of America. A geographical perspective on 500 years of history,* vol. 1, *Atlantic America, 1492–1800.* New Haven: Yale University Press.

Melville, E. G. K. 1990. Environmental and social change in the Valle del Mezquital, Mexico, 1521–1600. *Comparative Studies in Society and History* 32:24–53.

Mueller-Dombois, D. 1981. Fire in tropical ecosystems. In *Fire regimes and ecosystem properties: Proceedings of the Conference,* Honolulu, 1978, pp. 137–76. General Technical Report WO-26. Washington: U.S. Forest Service.

Murdy, C. N. 1990. Prehispanic agriculture and its effects in the valley of Guatemala. *Forest and Conservation History* 34:179–90.

Nash, R. 1967. *Wilderness and the American mind.* New Haven, CT: Yale University Press.

Ortiz de Montellano, B. R. 1990. *Aztec medicine, health, and nutrition.* New Brunswick, NJ: Rutgers University Press.

Parsons, J. J. 1975. The changing nature of New World tropical forests since European colonization. In *The use of Ecological guidelines for development in the American humid tropics,* pp. 28–38. International Union for Conservation of Nature and Natural Resources Publications, n.s., 31. Morges.

———. 1985. Raised field farmers as pre-Columbian landscape engineers: Looking north from the San Jorge (Colombia). In *Prehistoric intensive agriculture in the tropics,* ed. I. S. Farrington, pp. 149–65. International Series 232. Oxford: British Archaeological Reports.

———, **and Denevan, W. M.** 1967. Pre-Columbian ridged fields. *Scientfic American* 217 (1): 92–100.

Patterson, W. A., III, and Sassaman, K. E. 1988. Indian fires in the prehistory of New England. In *Holocene human ecology in northeastern North America,* ed. G, P. Nicholas, pp. 107–35. New York: Plenum.

Plazas, C., and Falchetti, A. M. 1987. Poblamiento y adecuación hidráulica en el bajo Río San Jorge, Costa Atlantica, Colombia. In *Prehistoric agricultural fields in the Andean region,* ed. W. M. Denevan, K. Mathewson, and G. Knapp, pp. 483–503. International Series 359. Oxford: British Archaeological Reports.

Posey, D. A. 1985. Indigenous management of tropical forest ecosystems: The case of the Kayapó Indians of the Brazilian Amazon. *Agroforestry Systems* 3:139–58.

Pyne, S. J. 1982. *Fire in America: A cultural history of wild/and and rural fire.* Princeton, NJ: Princeton University Press.

Raup, H. M. 1937. Recent changes in climate and vegetation in southern New England and adjacent New York. *Journal of the Arnold Arboretum* 18:79–117.

Roosevelt, A. C. 1991. *Moundbuilders of the Amazon: Geophysical archaeology on Marajó Island, Brazil.* San Diego: Academic Press.

Rostlund, E. 1957. The myth of a natural prairie belt in Alabama: An interpretation of historical records. *Annals of the Association of American Geographers* 47:392–411.

———. 1960. The geographic range of the historic bison in the southeast. *Annals of the Association of American Geographers* 50:395–407.

Russell, E. W. B. 1983. Indian-set fires in the forests of the northeastern United States. *Ecology* 64:78–88.

Saldarriaga, J. G., and West, D. C. 1986. Holocene fires in the northern Amazon Basin. *Quaternary Research* 26:358–66.

———, **and Uhl, C.** 1991. Recovery of forest vegetation following slash-and-burn agriculture in the upper Río Negro. In *Rainforest regeneration and management,* ed. A. Gómez-Pompa, T. C. Whitmore, and M. Hadley, pp. 303–12. Paris: UNESCO.

Sale, K. 1990. *The conquest of paradise: Christopher Columbus and the Columbian legacy.* New York: Alfred A. Knopf.

Sánchez-Albornoz, N. 1974. *The population of Latin America: A history.* Berkeley: University of California Press.

Sanders, W. T.; Parsons, J. R.; and Santley, R. S. 1979. *The Basin of Mexico: Ecological processes in the evolution of a civilization.* New York: Academic Press.

Sauer, C. O. 1950. Grassland climax, fire, and man. *Journal of Range Management* 3:16–21.

———. 1958. Man in the ecology of tropical America. *Proceedings of the Ninth Pacific Science Congress, 1957* 20:104–10.

———. 1963 [1927]. The barrens of Kentucky. In *Land and life: A selection from the writings of Carl Ortwin Sauer,* ed. J. Leighly, pp. 23–31. Berkeley: University of California Press.

———. 1966. *The early Spanish Main.* Berkeley: University of California Press.

———. 1971. *Sixteenth-century North America: The land and the people as seen by the Europeans.* Berkeley: University of California Press.

———. 1975. Man's dominance by use of fire. *Geoscience and Man* 10:1–13.

———. 1980. *Seventeenth-century North America.* Berkeley: Turtle Island Press.

Schwerin, K. H. 1991. The Indian populations of Latin America. In *Latin America, its problems and its promise: A multidisciplinary introduction,* ed. J. K. Black, 2nd ed., pp. 39–53. Boulder, CO: Westview Press.

Scott, G. A. J. 1978. *Grassland development in the Gran Pajonal of eastern Peru.* Hawaii Monographs in Geography 1. Honolulu: University of Hawaii.

Sheets, P., and Sever, T. L. 1991. Prehistoric footpaths in Costa Rica: Transportation and communication in a tropical rainforest. In *Ancient road networks and settlement hierarchies in the New World,* ed. C. D. Trombold, pp. 53–65. Cambridge: Cambridge University Press.

Shetler, S. 1991. Three faces of Eden. In *Seeds of change: A quincentennial commemoration,* ed. H. J. Viola and C. Margolis, pp. 225–47. Washington: Smithsonian Institution Press.

Siemens, A. H. 1990. *Between the summit and the sea: Central Veracruz in the nineteenth century.* Vancouver: University of British Columbia Press.

Silver, T. 1990. *A new face on the countryside: Indians, colonists, and slaves in South Atlantic forests, 1500–1800.* Cambridge: Cambridge University Press.

Silverberg, R. 1968. *Mound builders of ancient America: The archaeology of a myth.* Greenwich, CT: New York Graphic Society.

Smith, N. J. H. 1980. Anthrosols and human carrying capacity in Amazonia. *Annals of the Association of American Geographers* 70:553–66.

Stout, A. B. 1911. Prehistoric earthworks in Wisconsin. *Ohio Archaeological and Historical Publications* 20:1–31.

Sturtevant, W. C. 1961. Taino agriculture. In *The evolution of horticultural systems in native South America, causes and consequences: A symposium,* ed. J. Wilbert, pp. 69–82. Caracas: Sociedad de Ciencias Naturales La Salle.

Taylor, D. L. 1981. Fire history and fire records for Everglades National Park. Everglades National Park Report T-619. Washington: National Park Service, U.S. Department of the Interior.

Thompson, O. Q., and Smith, R. H. 1970. The forest primeval in the Northeast—a great myth? *Proceedings, Tall Timbers Fire Ecology Conference* 10:255–65.

Thoreau, H. D. 1949. *The journal of Henry D. Thoreau,* vol. 7, *September 1, 1854–October 30, 1855,* ed. B. Torrey and F. H. Allen. Boston: Houghton Mifflin.

Trombold, C. D., ed. 1991. *Ancient road networks and settlement hierarchies in the New World.* Cambridge: Cambridge University Press.

Uhl, C.; Nepstad, D.; Buschbacher, R.; Clark, K.; Kauffman, B.; and Subler, S. 1990. Studies of ecosystem response to natural and anthropogenic disturbances provide guidelines for designing sustainable land-use systems in Amazonia. In *Alternatives to deforestation: Steps toward sustainable use of the Amazon rain forest,* ed. A. B. Anderson, pp. 24–42. New York: Columbia University Press.

Walschburger, T., and von Hildebrand, P. 1991. The first 26 years of forest regeneration in natural and man-made gaps in the Colombian Amazon. In *Rain forest regeneration and management,* ed. A. Gómez-Pompa, T. C. Whitmore, and M. Hadley, pp. 257–63. Paris: UNESCO.

Watts, W. A., and Bradbury, J. P. 1982. Paleoecological studies at Lake Patzcuaro on the west-central Mexican plateau and at Chalco in the Basin of Mexico. *Quaternary Research* 17:56–70.

Wedel, W. R. 1957. The central North American grassland: Man-made or natural? *Social Science Monographs* 3:39–69. Washington: Pan American Union.

White, S. 1985. Relations of subsistence to the vegetation mosaic of Vilcabamba, southern Peruvian Andes. *Yearbook, Conference of Latin Americanist Geographers* 11:3–10.

Whitmore, T. M. 1991. A simulation of the sixteenth-century population collapse in the Basin of Mexico. *Annals of the Association of American Geographers* 81:464–87.

———; **Turner, B. L. II; Johnson, D. L.; Kates, R. W.; and Gotlschang, T. R.** 1990. Long-term population change. In *The earth as transformed by human action,* ed. B. L. Turner II, et al., pp. 25–39. Cambridge: Cambridge University Press.

Williams, B. J. 1972. Tepetate in the Valley of Mexico. *Annals of the Association of American Geographers* 62:618–26.

———. 1989. Contact period rural overpopulation in the Basin of Mexico: Carrying-capacity models tested with documentary data. *American Antiquity* 54:715–32.

Williams, M. 1989. *Americans and their forests: A historical geography.* Cambridge: Cambridge University Press.

Wilson, S. M. 1992. "That unmanned wild countrey": Native Americans both conserved and transformed New World environments. *Natural History,* May: 16–17.

Wood, W. 1977 [1635]. *New England's prospect,* ed. A. T. Vaughan. Amherst: University of Massachusetts Press.

Homework

Name: _____ Date: _____

Give two examples of Denevan's reasoning when he claims that the "pristine myth" is that the Americas were a vast wilderness prior to the arrival of Europeans.

1.

2.

Chapter 6

Shaping the American Landscape

Bonnicksen (2000a) aptly titles a chapter in his book "Enhancing Nature's Bounty"; and Charles C. Mann (2002) calls the Americas "the world's largest garden" when describing the impact of Indians on the continent's landscape in his *Atlantic Monthly* article "1491." However, scholars ranging from historians to ecologists have often overlooked the impact of Indians in shaping the American forest (Denevan 1992, Krech 1999, Mann 2005, Williams 2001). Through thousands of years of observation and experience, American Indians became adept users of the resources around them, and they learned to shape and manage the environment to meet their needs.

KEEPERS OF THE FLAME: STEWARDS OF THE LAND

Arguably the most powerful tool used by humans is fire. It is the predominant force for providing energy and is a component in the manufacture of nearly all necessities of our existence. It is also the most basic tool used by humans to modify vegetative cover and to manage their natural surroundings. Certainly, it was the most useful and powerful tool available to American Indians. Bonnicksen (2000a) estimates that humans have used fire for 25,000 generations and had already modified the vegetation of Africa, Europe, Asia and Australia through the use of fire before their arrival in the Americas. It is doubtful that Paleoindians could have survived in the Arctic without the mastery of fire. They and their descendants used fire to cook, keep warm, provide light at night, communicate and eliminate brush and vermin around their villages and campsites (Chase 1986).

Fire historian Stephen Pyne (1982) said it best: "It was as keeper of the flame that man became steward of the land."

People around the world have used and still do use fire to clear land for agriculture. At Cahokia, Indians burned to clear forest for massive fields planted with maize to support a population of 15,000 to 20,000 people (Mann 2005). In southern New England, the Narragansetts cleared land for eight to ten miles along the coast to plant crops (Williams 1989). Roger Williams[1] left this record of their burning practices, ". . . this burning of the Wood to them they count a Benefit, both for destroying of vermin, and keeping downe the weeds and thickets" (Cronon 1983). John Smith reported similar burning to create fields near Jamestown, Virginia (Williams 1989). The Haudenosaunee[2] and other tribes of the eastern woodlands employed fire to create fields. Fire opened up the woods, making travel easier, and created meadows where game and forage were plentiful (Bonnicksen 2000a).

By employing frequent fires, Indians could eliminate built up debris and fuel, lessening the risk of catastrophic fire. A catastrophic fire can reach temperatures as high as 2,000°F, killing anything in its path. The frequent fires were low intensity and generally confined themselves to the ground. Today, we would call this practice a "prescribed burn."

By burning a spot where Indians wanted to locate a campsite or a village they were able to "fireproof" the area to some extent. In 1949, a U.S. Forest Service smokejumper named Wagner Dodge survived a catastrophic fire in Mann Gulch in the Helena National Forest of Montana by employing a similar tactic to create a refuge in a burned patch of grass. Thirteen of Dodge's fellow smokejumpers perished in Mann Gulch (Turner 1999).

Indians used fire to promote habitat for game. Early successional species such as grasses, nuts, berries and forbs provide food for both humans and game (Bonnicksen 2000a, Chase 1986, Pyne 1982, Williams 1989). Grasslands and fire-disturbed sites within forests provided more food for animals than did mature forests.

Williams (1989) describes Indians as "careful users of fire." Others (Krech 1999, Pyne 1982, Chase 1986) point out that they were sometimes careless and, in some situations, such as war, intentionally destructive in setting fires. However, there is evidence that their use of fire was often methodical, well-managed and based upon many generations of observation and experience. "Cereal grasses were fired annually, basket grasses and nuts about every three years, brush and undergrowth in the forest every 7 to 10 years, large timber . . . every 15 to 30 years or more . . ." (Williams 1989).

Nonetheless, Indian use of fire was more frequent and widespread than early foresters and many twentieth century environmentalists realized or were willing to admit. European seamen reported that they knew they were approaching the shores of North America because they could smell smoke in the air (Krech 1999). In 1637, Thomas Morton reported

Figure 6.1 Burned Over White Spruce Forest. *Alaska.*

---

[1] Roger Williams was a founder of the colony of Rhode Island and Providence Plantations in 1644.

[2] Iroquois.

that the Indians of Massachusetts Bay set fires in the woods every spring and fall to clear undergrowth and make travel through the forest easier (Cronon 1983, Krech 1999). Mann (2005) tells of Adrien van der Donck, a Dutch lawyer with the Dutch West India Company in New Amsterdam, now New York City. Van der Donck wrote of sailing up the Hudson River in the fall while the woods on both sides of the river were ablaze from fires set by the Haudenosaunee. The Haudenosaunee set fire to "the woods, plains, and meadows," creating a spectacular site from the river at night. Travelers on the Great Plains attested to the difficulty of riding through tall, tangled grass and often planned their travels for the fall when they knew the Indians had burned the prairies and the travel was easy and game was easier to find (Bonnicksen 2000a). Accounts of Indian burning practices, although anecdotal, are too numerous to consider less than overwhelming.

FIRE HUNTING

Pyne (1982) claims that the "most widespread (and) probably the most ancient" use of fire was for hunting. The most common application of fire was to drive game toward hunters, a practice that humans used ten to twenty thousand years ago (Chase 1986). They hunted deer, elk, moose, bison, alligators and small mammals by using fire drives. The use of fire drives in hunting was universal among American Indians.

Indians used torches to draw fish to the surface of lakes and ponds and to spotlight deer. They baited traps and snares by burning grass and waiting for new grass to draw grazers and small mammals. They also used fire to smoke bears out of their dens and to drive bees away from their hives so they could collect the honey.

Cabeza de Vaca noted Indian fire hunting in Texas in the early sixteenth century; John Smith noted it at Jamestown in the early seventeenth century; John Lawson noted it in the Carolinas in the late seventeenth century; LaSalle made note of it along the Gulf plains and the Mississippi Valley; and Lewis and Clark reported it along the upper Missouri River (Pyne 1982). Discussion of fire hunting practices by local Indians appears in the personal correspondence between Thomas Jefferson and John Adams in 1813.

Mann (2005) poses an interesting theory. "Rather than domesticate animals for meat, Indians retooled ecosystems to encourage elk, deer, and bear. Constant burning of undergrowth increased the number of herbivores, the predators that fed on them, and the people that ate them both. Rather than the thick, unbroken, monumental snarl of trees imagined by Thoreau, the great eastern forest was an ecological kaleidoscope of garden plots, blackberry rambles, pine barrens, and spacious groves of chestnut, hickory, and oak."

FIRE AS A WEAPON

Indians, like other people throughout the world, used fire in warfare (Pyne 1982). They used fire to flush enemies out of hiding, to harass a superior enemy force, to deny them cover and to open up fields of fire. And they used it as a weapon of "total war" to destroy the homes, possessions, food stores, crops and hunting grounds of their enemies.

Pyne (1982) describes an incident observed by the Long Expedition of 1819–1820 in which a band of Sioux flushed some enemies out of hiding by setting the high grass on fire. Later military expeditions reported being harassed by Indians who set fire to the grass upwind from their encampments at night.

Indians burned the woods around their encampments to clear underbrush that could cover the approach of enemies and open up clear fields of fire in the event of attack. Burning also deprived enemies of fuel that they could use to set fires intended to destroy the encampment or create smoke to hide an attacking force.

A painting by the western artist, Charles Marion Russell, entitled "Blackfeet Burning the Crow Buffalo Range," sold at auction in 2007 for almost three million dollars. The painting, completed in 1905, illustrates Blackfeet warriors employing a "scorched-earth" policy to deprive an enemy of hunting grounds. This was a common strategy that they may have employed as a form of economic extortion or that they simply may have used to keep Crow hunting parties away from Blackfeet villages.

FIRE ECOLOGY IN AMERICA'S ANCIENT FORESTS

In the previous chapter, Denevan (1992) acknowledges that discussion of Indian burning practices is sometimes controversial. However, evidence that widespread use of fire by Indians was a dominant factor in shaping America's ancient forests is well documented and overwhelming (Bonnicksen 2000, Chase 1986, Denevan 1992, Krech 1999, MacCleery 1994a, Mann 2005, Pyne 1982, Williams 1989, Williams 2001).

Fire ecology played an important role in the characteristics and composition of America's ancient forests. Bonnicksen uses remarkably similar words to describe the various forest types that dominated American forests at the time of the first European contact. They were open, park-like, patchy mosaics of forest going through all stages of succession. Dominant tree species in most regions were pioneer species and many are well adapted to frequent, low intensity fire. In the southeast, southern pines—loblolly pine, shortleaf pine and longleaf pine—were thriving on sites that would have reverted to hardwoods in late-successional forests. Dominant western conifers such as Sequoia, redwood, Douglas-fir, western white pine, lodgepole pine and ponderosa pine require recent disturbance from fire or logging to regenerate (Bonnicksen 2000a, Harlow and Harrar 1969). Eastern white pine, red pine and the oaks in the east are also pioneer species that favor frequent, low intensity fire to regenerate (Bonnicksen 2000a). The great and ancient California redwoods tend to thrive when subjected to a regime of low-intensity surface fire every few years (Bonnicksen 2000a).

Throughout North America, Indian fire practices were an integral part of the composition of the forest. Repeated burning eliminated the understory, leaving the forest open or in a park-like state. Frequent and hot burning on dry sites eliminated sprouts and seedlings, leaving only older trees. When those trees died, grassland or prairie became established. On wetter sites, fire changed the composition of the forest, favoring fire tolerant species such as oaks and pines (Bonnicksen 2000a, Chase 1986, Mann 2005, Pyne 1982, Williams 1989).

The prevalence of fire allowed few forested areas to reach the self-replacing stage of forest succession. Widespread and repeated burning resulted in a forest that was patchy open, and park-like. Pioneer species dominated pre-settlement forests. Although the extent of America's forests may have been shrinking, the fire ecology imposed by Indians led to a degree of stability of forest ecosystems that has not been experienced since European settlement (Bonnicksen, 2000a).

CREATION OF GRASSLANDS

Some scholars believe that Indian fire practices had caused significant replacement of forest by grassland at the time of European discovery in 1492 (Denevan 1992, Pyne 1982, Williams 1989). Repeated ground fires in the forest eliminated vegetation in the forest understory. This included settler tree species. The large, older pioneers were able to withstand the low intensity burning. However, when they reached the end of their lives, continued frequent burning prevented trees from re-establishing themselves. Grasslands took over the landscape in those areas.

The Great Valley extends from the Delaware River in Pennsylvania westward across the Susquehanna and south through Maryland into Virginia. East of the Susquehanna it is known as the Lebanon Valley. To the west, it is the Cumberland Valley. Its southern portion is the Shenandoah Valley of Virginia (Stevens 1964). When Europeans first encountered the Great Valley, grasslands and savannas dominated it.[3] Grasslands also extended along the Rappahannock River in Virginia and along the Potomac, connecting with the Great Valley in the northern Shenandoah Valley. Known as the "barrens," this area was also dominated by grassland. Scientific evidence indicates that Indians repeatedly burned this area for at least a thousand years (Williams 1989).

The Kentucky bluegrass country was also the site of a prairie region. Early travelers in the Ohio Valley recorded meadows taken over by clover and even-aged stands of timber of approximately fifty years of age, indicating evidence of previous clearing. There were probably more grasslands further west between the Alleghenies and the Ohio River, but European disease and frequent raiding by the Haudenosaunee of upstate New York in the late seventeenth century caused the Indians that had once inhabited the region to abandon this area, as well as northern West Virginia. By the time the first Europeans reached the region in the middle of the eighteenth century, forests had reclaimed the land. George Washington offered 22,000 acres of land for sale along the Kanawha River, describing "excellent meadows" that may have been fields cleared by Indians at one time (Williams 1989).

Mann (2005) and Pyne (1982) report that the greatest impact of burning occurred in the Great Plains where frequent burning was increasing the extent of grassland. Mann calls the practice a transformation of the middle of the continent into a "prodigious game farm" where herds of bison, elk and other herbivores thrived. Fire established grasslands through the western fringes of the forest from Texas through Missouri, Iowa, Illinois and Wisconsin. The only forests existed in peninsulas that followed the wetter river bottom sites. Williams (1989) reports that archeological evidence of Indian burning in this area dates back to the times when the Pleistocene forest was breaking up at the end of the last ice age.

In the Pacific Northwest, "archeological, ethnological, and historical evidence suggests" that fire was extensive as long as 15,000 years ago (Chase 1995). Wildfire in the area was frequent and the extent of grassland, savanna, and "forest cover—and indeed the extent of old growth—fluctuated wildly" over time. Extensive burning established savannas and fields in California and promoted growth of oaks along the north coast (Bonnicksen 2000, Chase 1995). The Great Central Valley of California was a "vast grassland" when first observed by Europeans (Bonnicksen 2000a).

The cessation of fire results in the reclamation of grasslands by forest. In Wisconsin, 60 percent of the grassland disappeared between 1829 and 1854. As Mann (2002)

---

[3] A savanna is grassland containing scattered trees or small groves of trees.

shows in his description of the very different observations of the Soto and LaSalle explorations of the Arkansas country, the elimination of Indians by European disease and later conquest resulted in forests taking over grasslands. Without the frequent fires started by Indians, forest succession could progress. Oak-hickory forest encroached on grassland in northern Illinois, Wisconsin, eastern Nebraska and Kansas in the early to mid-1800s. In the words of Alston Chase (1986), "without fire, succession progresses and the number of species of plants—and animals that feed on these plants—declines." The net result of the conversion of grasslands to forests and farms is that most endangered species are grassland species (Pyne 1982).

AGRICULTURE AND WILDLIFE MANAGEMENT

As described in previous chapters, Indian contributions to agriculture were profound and long-lasting. The impact of those practices on forests and the landscape are still in evidence in many places in the Americas. Williams (1989) compares Indian practices of burning and conversion of land to agriculture to the "slash and burn" agricultural practices of modern people in the tropics.

One may still see remnants of Indian terracing of the land and irrigation systems in Peru, Mesoamerica and the southwestern United States (Mann 2005). Indian mounds attract twenty-first century tourists throughout the Mississippi watershed and in Florida and New England.

Indians often gathered and managed plants in a manner "that bordered on true agriculture" (Bonnicksen 2000a). They pruned trees and shrubs to promote the production of fruit and nuts. They weeded and transplanted wild plants to increase food production. Western tribes did not harvest camas bulbs until the plants had dropped their seeds. New England Indians cut back shrubs and vines that interfered with wild grape vines. California Indians pulled up cottonwood seedlings from the borders of meadows in order to prevent hot fires from burning into oak groves. Indians often pruned branches to stimulate growth of new straight shoots for arrows. Southwestern Indians carefully tended mesquite since they derived many useful products from this plant. Indians also spread seeds of useful plants. Chestnut and other mast-producing trees often surrounded village sites in the eastern woodlands.

Many tribes made bows by cutting strips of wood from living trees, thus ensuring that the tree would continue to live. This was a response to the scarcity of straight-grained trees of non-abundant species (osage-orange, juniper, etc.) that make the best bows.

West Virginians with a vegetable or flower garden know that frequently their hard work becomes an easy meal for the state's large deer population. To Indians dependent upon agriculture or gathering, animals and birds that fed on crops and mast were "ecological competitors" (Mann 2005). For Indians, it made sense to keep animals that would devour their crops as far away from them as possible. Some of their hunting practices would alarm modern hunters and animal lovers. Archeological evidence reveals that they hunted pregnant does and killed wild turkeys before they could lay their eggs. Mann (2005) describes these practices as "so consistent" that they must have been intended to maintain their populations at some perceived optimum. It also made sense to maintain game populations for hunting, but to manage populations by keeping them "at arm's length . . . a couple days' journey away" (Mann 2005).

Mann (2005) suggests that researchers often grossly overestimate wildlife populations at the time of European contact. Indians, in effect, reduced and controlled populations of species that were ecological competitors. Once European diseases reduced the competition by decimating Indian populations, deer, elk, turkey, raccoon, bison and passenger pigeon populations exploded as they occupied the vacated ecological niches.

INDIAN USE OF FOREST RESOURCES

Indians' use of forest resources was no less inventive and skillful than their shaping of vegetation and habitat. The forests of North America provided abundant resources for sustaining the lives of its aboriginal people. Trees were the source of medicines, food, shelter, decorative art, canoes and fuel.

The sap, needles or bark of many trees acted as laxatives. Indians used bark and leaves as poultices for burns. "Trees also provided drops for earaches and remedies for coughs, heartburn, toothaches, and headaches." They often ate tree bark during starving times. Northwest Indians made "cakes" of hemlock bark, which they considered a delicacy. Forests also provided fruits, berries, roots, nuts, acorns, maple syrup and honey (Bonnicksen 2000a).

"Most American Indians framed their homes with logs or branches and then covered them with earth, grass, hides, matting, brush, or bark" (Bonnicksen 2000a). The Pueblo built villages of stone and adobe but used logs and branches to support the roofs, much like their ancestors did in Chaco Canyon. Plains Indians built hide-covered tepees supported by poles—typically lodgepole pine—as early as 10,000 years ago. They used poles as travois[4] when camps moved or were discarded and cut new poles when arriving at the next camp. Eastern woodland tribes lived in lodges or wigwams supported by poles or willow branches and covered by grass mats, hides or bark.

Woodlands tribes cleared a patch of forest each time they relocated a village or set up a camp. They cleared trees near a village to make room for fields and to provide firewood. They also stripped bark from trees to cover lodgings and canoes, killing the trees. A village would create a large opening in the forest. When the band moved on, the abandoned clearing was an excellent site for young pioneer trees to establish themselves. Bonnicksen (2000a) notes that abandoned village sites were disturbances that helped create shifting mosaics of patches at different stages of succession throughout the forest landscape.

Eastern woodland tribes lived in villages surrounded by fields of tobacco, sweet potatoes, tomatoes, squash, watermelons, kidney beans, sunflowers and maize (Williams 1989). An estimated six square miles of fields planted with maize would surround the typical Haudenosaunee village (Mann 2005). Conrad Heidenreich estimated that a typical Haudenosaunee or Huron village of 1,000 people required 36 longhouses constructed of 16,000 3 to 4 inch diameter poles 10 to 30 feet long; 250 10 inch diameter interior poles 10 to 30 feet long; and 162,000 square yards of American elm or eastern red cedar bark. A palisade constructed of 3,600 5 inch diameter, 15 to 30 foot long stakes would surround the village (Williams 1989).

The Indians obtained the construction materials from second growth forest, probably originating with reclaimed agricultural fields. The village typically occupied a clearing of 150 to 600 acres (Williams 1989). Clearing practices in eastern woodlands

---

[4] A travois is a sled constructed by lashing two lodgepoles together on one end. The Indians lashed the other ends to the sides of a horse so they could drag the travois along behind it. They stretched hides across the travois to carry possessions or people. Before the Spanish introduced the horse to North America, dogs pulled the travois.

included the girdling of trees, fire and felling trees with stone axes (although as we will discuss below, the practicality of clearing land with stone tools is in doubt). Villages tended to relocate every 10 to 20 years because of depleted soils, infestation of pests and vermin, accumulation of filth and refuse and the need to travel too far to obtain fuel wood and game. Researchers know that between 1610 and 1780 the Haudenosaunee village of Onondaga occupied nine different sites (Williams 1989). Indians of New England also moved villages to best take advantage of resources (Cronon 1983). The Soto expedition (1538–1541) through Florida, Georgia, South Carolina, North Carolina, Tennessee, Alabama, Mississippi, Arkansas and Louisiana observed large fields, plains and open forest (Mann 2002, 2005). The Jamestown settlers 400 years ago observed large Powhatan villages occupied by a powerful Indian confederacy, and a people thriving on agriculture, abundant game and fish (Deans 2007). European settlers came to recognize the value of Indian fields and often sought abandoned fields for settlement.

Along the Pacific coast from the Columbia River Basin north into Alaska, Indians built plank houses. The plank houses were rectangular and supported by log frames and were as large as 50 × 200 feet. Supporting logs were as large as 6½ feet in diameter and, sometimes had to be rafted down rivers to villages. Planks were split and could be as wide as 5½ feet and 2 inches thick to cover the walls and roof. Northwest Indians used western redcedar while the Yurok and Hipa of northern California used redwood to construct the plank houses. Bonnicksen (2000a) describes the plank houses as "the most sophisticated wooden structures ever built in prehistoric North America."

Native Americans also used wood in their decorative art. Perhaps the best known examples are the ubiquitous totem poles of the Pacific coast tribes. The coastal tribes used totem poles to record clan and family histories, to describe an event or legend of the tribe or clan or to memorialize an individual (Borneman 2004). The totem poles could be enormous—up to six or seven feet in diameter and as much as 65 feet tall (Bonnicksen 2000a). The Hopi and other Pueblo tribes carved their kachinas from basswood. The Haudenosaunee of the eastern woodlands carved ceremonial "funny face" masks.

Lewis and Clark first described the ornately carved dugout canoes of the Columbia River basin tribes. The canoes were 15 to 50 feet long, and the largest could be 6½ feet wide. Frequently, the canoes had ornate carving in bow and stern. Tribes in the east also made dugout canoes. Florida tribes made canoes of baldcypress as large as those of the Pacific Northwest. Northeastern and Great Lakes tribes built birch bark canoes framed with white cedar. California Indians built plank canoes. Native Hawaiians, being the exceptional seafarers that they were, added outriggers to add stability to ocean-going canoes.

Simply keeping fires burning in campsites and villages consumed massive quantities of wood. European immigrants were sometimes shocked by the large amount of fuel wood consumed by Indians (Pyne 1982). They sometimes ritualized fuel gathering as in puberty rites. In the eastern woodlands, villagers traveled as far as three miles to gather firewood. They often resorted to felling live trees nearer to villages, encroaching into the surrounding forest. Cronon (1983) reports that Indians of southern New England migrated from their villages along the coastline during winter because the fuel supplies for the fires they needed to keep warm in winter were inadequate and the wood they required was only available in the forests of the interior. One can imagine that fuel was indeed a precious resource from the fact that Roger Williams recorded that Indians often asked him if Englishmen had come to New England to find firewood (Cronon 1983).[5]

RESTORATION FORESTRY

You may be wondering what relevance these discussions of the pre-Columbian forests have to forest management in the twenty-first century. The condition of many of our forests is not good, particularly on public land and in the west. Stands are densely packed and littered with dead timber and other combustibles. Catastrophic wildfire consumes millions of acres of coniferous forest in the west every year. Insect infestation and disease threaten stands and contribute to the fire hazard. Exotic plant and animal species are replacing native species in many forest ecosystems. However, Americans may be able to improve the conditions of our forests using the template of what we know about the forests of the past (Alvarez 2007, MacCleery 1994b).

Thomas Bonnicksen (2006) believes the answer lies in "restoration forestry." His proposal stems from the ideas of the forester and conservationist Aldo Leopold to restore forests to pre-settlement conditions. Granting that we cannot restore forests to the identical conditions and species composition that existed years ago, he believes that the health of modern forests will require restoring the character of those forests— open, park-like and dominated by big trees and pioneer species. The restored forest would contain patches in all stages of succession, including clearings.

While many subscribe to the idea of restoring forests, there is much disagreement on how to do it and what the forest should look like when it is done. Some people advocate creating large expanses of "old growth" forest, a condition that Bonnicksen and other scientists believe never existed until European diseases decimated Indian populations.[6] Some environmental organizations and government agencies advocate the reintroduction of widespread, frequent fire (prescribed burning) to restore forests. This would mimic Indian burning practices, but the smoke and other air pollution produced from widespread burning may not be acceptable in today's society (Bonnicksen 2006). In addition, fuel loads are so great in many of these forests that any fire, intentionally set or not, would become catastrophic.

Bonnicksen (2006) believes that the only practical way to restore forests is through mechanical thinning—cutting trees to thin overcrowded stands. Like thinning a garden, this would allow remaining trees to grow and would improve their health. In other words, what Bonnicksen recommends is forest management on these public lands. Unfortunately, the greatest obstacles to implementing Bonnicksen's vision for restoration forestry are public perceptions and attitudes stemming from the pristine myth (Bonnicksen 2002, 2006, MacCleery 1994b, Moore 2000). Specifically, a number of environmentalists oppose mechanical thinning on public lands because they view timber harvest as destructive. A blitzkrieg of lawsuits brought by these organizations in the federal courts have effectively blocked attempts to do much about the problem other than fight fires once they start.

---

[5] Perhaps Williams was the first to note an "energy crisis" in what is now the United States. As in his time, wood has great potential to be a partial solution to our current needs for sustainable, "green" energy sources.

[6] The term "old growth" has many definitions. In addition to disagreements over what constitutes old growth forest, disagreements over the extent of old growth complicate resolution of the issue.

In the meantime, devastating fires that alter forest ecosystems in unintended and undesirable ways continue to plague western forests. This author agrees with Thomas Bonnicksen that a full understanding of the history and characteristics of America's ancient forests are prerequisites to making rational, science-based decisions that will shape and sustain our forests for future generations—as Indians shaped theirs.

Homework

Name: _____   **Date:** _____

Define the following terms:

Crown fire:

Surface fire:

Fuel load:

Forest understory:

Herbivore:

Kachina:

SECTION II

The New Nation: America Was Built with Wood

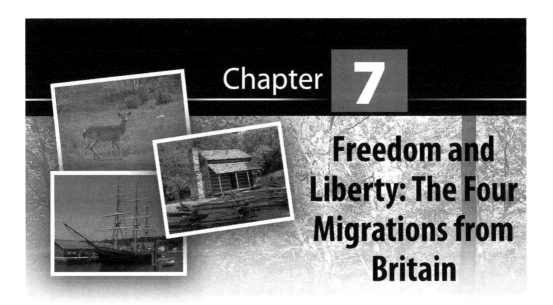

Chapter 7

Freedom and Liberty: The Four Migrations from Britain

Initial European settlement occurred in the Southwest with the arrival of the Spanish from Mexico and on the Atlantic seaboard. While Americans on the coast maintained close ties to Europe, others turned their eyes westward to the great American frontier. An example of the latter was the Virginian, George Washington, who spent much of his life as a young man west of the Alleghenies. As the new nation's first president, Washington's foreign policy was as focused upon the interior of the continent and its indigenous people as it was upon the great powers of Europe (Ellis 2004).

European immigrants came from cultures emerging from feudalism. Those societies restricted land ownership to the nobility and to the wealthy elite. The societies they established here were mostly agrarian. At the time of the first U.S. census in 1790, approximately 95 percent of American families were farmers. Land was a means to wealth and a family's security. Through much of Europe, its inhabitants had removed forests. European immigrants sought to own land and recreate a pastoral landscape like the one they left behind in their homelands. Most of all, they sought to survive, and survival meant clearing the land and planting crops.

THE FOUR COLONIAL MIGRATIONS

According to Census Bureau statistics, fewer than 20 percent of America's citizens trace their ancestry to Britain (Fischer 1989). Nevertheless, the United States owes its government, laws, language and much of its culture to immigrants from the British Isles who migrated to the thirteen British colonies prior to the American Revolution. However, to consider the British colonies a homogenous group originating from a homogenous culture is erroneous. Historian David Hackett Fischer (1989) attributes the origins of America's prevalent regional cultures to four migrations from the British Isles during the period of 1629 to 1775. These groups had different attitudes toward the land and brought their own distinctive cultural uses of the forest and forest products. Although the cultural differences are fading, their impact is still visible in American life. They brought with them building styles, the ways they laid out towns and farms and their attitudes toward the land. The regional cultures of the United States reveal evidence of their folkways today.

The migrations described by Fischer were the Puritans who came from East Anglia to New England from 1629 to 1640, the Cavaliers who immigrated from the south and west of England to the Virginia Tidewater from 1642 to 1675, the Quakers who arrived in the Delaware Valley from England's North Midlands from 1675 to 1725 and the people of the border region between England and Scotland and from Northern Ireland who came to the American backcountry from 1717 to 1775.

THE PURITANS: 1629–1640

The "Great Migration" of the Puritans from England in the 1630s was the result of religious and political upheaval after the death of Elizabeth I. Much of England had been swept up in the Protestant Reformation and the Puritans represented a diverse movement within the Church of England that believed that the Reformation in England was incomplete. Elizabeth's death ended the rule of the House of Tudor and began the short reign of the Stuarts. The Puritans' truce with the "high church" Stuarts collapsed when Charles I ascended to the throne in 1625. Charles was married to the Roman Catholic princess of France and set about restoring many of the church ceremonies opposed by the Puritans and dismissing Puritan clergy who opposed the theological leadership of his Archbishop of Canterbury. In 1629, the crisis intensified when Charles dissolved Parliament and assumed sole rule over the kingdom.

The first migration to Massachusetts began in 1620 with the Pilgrims landing at Plymouth. By 1630, approximately 1,500 colonists lived in the Bay Colony (Taylor 2001). The Great Migration began with the seventeen ships of the Winthrop Fleet of 1630, named for its leader and organizer, the Puritan clergyman John Winthrop. The majority of immigrants were of the "middling sorts" (Taylor 2001)—"yeomen, husbandmen, artisans, craftsmen, merchants, and traders" (Fischer 1989). A majority came from East Anglia—the densely populated eastern counties of England: Norfolk, Suffolk, Essex and Kent. This region was a stronghold of the Germanic Angle and Saxon tribes beginning in the fifth and sixth centuries, and it still retained Anglo-Saxon cultural and societal influences in 1630. The migration to New England was more urban than other migrations with many of the Puritans originating from small and moderately sized towns.

An estimated 21,000 people migrated from England to New England between 1629 and 1640. In the following decades, the immigrant tide dwindled to a trickle. But the hospitable climate of New England allowed the population to flourish so that by 1700 the population had increased to 100,000. Within a few years, Puritans were migrating into southern New England, eastern New Jersey and northern New York. Their descendents migrated to Maine, Canada and across the northern tier of States to the Pacific during the nineteenth century. Descendents of the Puritans founded the cities of Buffalo, Cleveland, Chicago, St. Paul, Denver, Salt Lake City, San Francisco and Seattle (Fischer 1989).

THE CAVALIERS' MIGRATION: 1642–1675

The settlement of Virginia and Maryland involved a much different group of people and resulted in a much different society from that of the Puritans who settled New England. A slow flow of immigrants followed the first settlement of Jamestown in 1607, increasing the population from 350 in 1616 to about 8,000 in 1642 (Taylor 2001, Fischer 1989). In 1641, Charles I appointed Sir William Berkeley the Royal Governor of Virginia. Berkeley was from a wealthy and aristocratic Gloucestershire family from the West Country of England. Fiercely loyal to Charles I, Berkeley set out to recruit immigrants to Virginia who matched his own social class and political leanings.

The immigration to the Chesapeake was different from the Puritan migration in several significant ways. Unlike the "middling sorts" who populated New England, two distinct social classes populated the Chesapeake: the aristocracy and an underclass of unskilled laborers and farmers imported to support the elite. More than 75 percent of Virginia's immigrants arrived as indentured servants (Fischer 1989). The majority of elites and indentured servants came from the south and west of England in what were once the kingdoms of the West Saxons: the counties of Devonshire, Somerset, Hampshire, Berkshire, Surrey, Middlesex and Kent. The aristocracy of this region traced its roots to the Norman invasion of 1066. The Normans and their descendants subjugated the tribal societies of Britain and established feudalism as the dominant government and social structure of British Isles. At the bottom of the social strata were African slaves and their descendants. Slavery existed in Virginia early in the history of the Jamestown Colony and was an established practice in the Tidewater several decades before the larger wave of migration to Virginia began in 1642 (Deans 2007).

The leading families of Virginia were Cavaliers, royalists loyal to the Stuart kings. In 1649, Oliver Cromwell and his Puritan "Roundheads" deposed and executed Charles I in the English Civil War. Virginia became a refuge for Cavalier families. By Berkeley's death in 1676, Virginia's population had grown to 40,000 (Fischer 1989). In subsequent years, Cavaliers settled the Carolina and Georgia Tidewater region and established the plantation-based economies of the Deep South.

THE FRIENDS' MIGRATION: 1675–1725

A third migration led by the Society of Friends or "Quakers" populated the Delaware Valley of Pennsylvania, New Jersey and Delaware. The Quakers were a Protestant sect that emerged in the English Midlands that sought simplicity in both religion and culture. The theology of the Friends' religion evolved through different phases during the seventeenth and eighteenth century transforming from a "radical, primitive, militant, aggressive, evangelical, and messianic" sect in its earliest form to an "increasingly institutional, rational, progressive, optimistic, enlightened, liberal, moderate, political . . . without losing its piety and godly purposes" in the mid seventeenth to mid eighteenth centuries (Fischer 1989). The Quakers have gone through several subsequent transformations, but they came to the New World during the second phase.

Although persecuted in England, a more important factor driving the Quaker migration was their refusal to pay taxes to support the Church of England (Fischer 1989). Neither the Puritans of New England nor the Anglicans of Virginia welcomed the Quakers. In the 1680s, William Penn, a wealthy son of the British aristocracy and a former soldier who had converted to the Quaker religion, was granted the proprietorship of a new colony on the west bank of the Delaware. Previously, Swedes, Dutch who had migrated from New York and New England Yankees had settled the Delaware Valley. Penn adopted a tolerant and welcoming philosophy of immigration that accepted previous occupants, including Indians, and invited people of other faiths, including Jews and Catholics. The most numerous of Penn's immigrants were Quakers and German Pietists.

The north Midlands of England were the hotbed of English Quakerism, and many of Penn's immigrants originated from this region. This region includes the counties of Cumbria, Lancashire, Yorkshire, Cheshire and Greater Manchester. The North

Midlands were the site of Viking settlements approximately 1,000 to 1,200 years ago, and the culture of this region of England retained Viking influences at the time of the Quaker migration. The folkways they brought to the Delaware Valley were the folkways of this British region.

THE BORDERERS' MIGRATION: 1717–1775

In 1286, Alexander III, the last Gaelic king of Scotland, died, leaving only an infant daughter to inherit the throne (Moffatt 2008, Sadler 2006). The daughter died shortly afterwards, throwing the Scottish succession into chaos. Into this void stepped one of the most ambitious and ruthless monarchs of the Middle Ages, Edward I, King of England. He appointed a new king he believed would serve as vassal to the English monarchy. The Scots quickly rebuffed Edward's attempts to rule Scotland, igniting several decades of brutal warfare known as the Scottish Wars of Independence. In 1314, Robert the Bruce defeated the English at Bannockburn, securing Scottish independence. But troubles along the Anglo-Scottish border would continue until several years after England and Scotland united in 1603.

For more than three hundred years, the Anglo-Scottish border was the front line of brutal warfare and chaotic violence. It is difficult to comprehend the turmoil and unpredictability of border history. To this author—a descendant of a border family—it appears that the violence along the border occurred in a bewildering mix instigated by all social classes and that it often had little to do with the broader conflict between England and Scotland. At the top of the societal food chain were the monarchs and royal courts of the two nations. In addition to the wars between the two nations, there were numerous rebellions and several civil wars on either side of the border that affected the people of the border no less severely than the wars between Scot and English. Border nobles also engaged in private wars and clans—regardless of their place in society—engaged in their own bloody feuds. These conflicts rarely spared civilians. Murder, rape, theft, arson, kidnapping, extortion, and countless other crimes occurred under the pretext of war and feud. People adapted by becoming a mobile society, able to flee at a moment's notice from the paths of invaders. Borderers shifted from a crop-based economy to one based on livestock. Passing armies can burn, trample or easily seize crops. A fleeing populace can drive livestock along (Fischer 1989, Fraser 2008, Sadler 2006).

Commoners of the border were the pawns in the politics of monarchs and nobles. During the Middle Ages, able-bodied men had to serve as soldiers at the call of king and noble. On both sides of the border, men most commonly served as mounted warriors, acting in the role of light cavalry. They were expected to serve as scouts, a mobile defensive force and as raiders who could disrupt enemy supply lines while tying up a portion of the enemy's strength defending towns, fortifications and supply lines. Borderers learned the arts of war at an early age. They learned how to protect themselves, their families and their meager possessions (Stephenson 1989).

A culture emerged amidst the violence and poverty of the border where people found protection in extended families or clans. The intrigues and shifting loyalties of the ruling class resulted in borderers becoming more loyal to their surname than to their noble lords or nations. The practice of mounted raiding became a means of survival. It was called "reiving" and the border clans became known as "reivers" or the "riding names." The term "reive" is an old English term that means "steal" (Fischer 1989). But to consider reivers common thieves or petty criminals does them an injustice. Men of the borders were warriors with few skills adaptable to times of peace (Sadler 2006).

Theft was often necessary to keep a man's family alive in starving times, which were frequent. Violence was ingrained. All levels of border society—Scottish and English—carried out and accepted the practice of reiving. Nobles and commoners frequently rode together to steal livestock, plunder homes and seek revenge for past wrongs. Kings alternately encouraged and punished reivers. Although England and Scotland were often at war, families frequently forged alliances with neighbors on the opposite side of the border that were stronger than allegiances to king and country.

In 1603, the border came to an end with the death of Queen Elizabeth I of England. Succession to the throne went to her cousin's son, then King James VI of Scotland. As James the VI was crowned James I of a united Scotland and England, the two nations became one under the name Great Britain (Armstrong 1986, Moffatt 2008, Sadler 2006, Stephenson 1989). The ascension of James I was not universally accepted. His royal line had remained Roman Catholic while England had become Protestant. He had also made numerous enemies on both sides of the border. English and Scottish nationalism fueled resistance to his ascension. To consolidate his power, he had to pacify the border. He accomplished the task in the manner his Stuart ancestors had long used to deal with the problem of the border. He turned nobles against commoners in a bloody campaign against the reiving surnames.

Those who resisted were killed in battle or executed. Military press gangs gathered up others and sent them to war in Europe or Ireland. Whole families were exiled to the English estates of Northern Ireland where they intermingled with the native Irish. Two families in particular received particularly brutal treatment. The English Grahams lost their lands and were driven into exile (Fraser 2008). On the Scottish side, the Armstrongs received particularly brutal treatment. Many of the most prominent of the Armstrongs were murdered, killed in battle or executed. The rest were forcibly deported to County Fermanagh in Northern Ireland. Today, few Armstrongs remain in their ancestral lands along the border (Armstrong 1986, Stephenson 1989).

Thus, Northern Ireland became one of the principal sources of migration for the people of the borders. Scottish highlanders also found their way into the ranks of the forcibly deported following the Scottish insurrection of 1745. During the years following the ascension of James I, a common culture developed among the diverse people of the Anglo-Scottish border, the Scottish coastline and Northern Ireland consisting of several distinct ethnic groups: the Scots-Irish, the Anglo-Irish and the Saxon-Scots. It was this culture, brought together in violence and grinding poverty, which constituted the fourth, the longest and the largest major migration to the British colonies of North America (Fischer 1989).

An estimated 250,000 borderers came to the United States prior to the Revolution. Peak migration years coincided with famine years in north Britain and Northern Ireland. America was a place where a landless immigrant could acquire land. And to eighteenth century Britons, land represented wealth. Note that there was no single leader of the migration of borderers to America—a John Winthrop, a Sir William Berkeley or a William Penn. Families and small groups of families migrated separately, usually under the leadership of one respected individual who in older times would have been recognized as a clan chief (Fischer 1989).

The borderers found the coast of America occupied by previous immigrants who were largely unwilling to accept a group against whom they held long-standing prejudices. The borderers migrated to the backcountry—the Berkshires of Massachusetts, the coast of Maine from Casco Bay to Boothbay, the Appalachians from western Pennsylvania to north Georgia, the coastal tidewater of South Carolina and the northwestern highlands of New Jersey. The early heritage of West Virginia consists largely of this immigrant group. The borderers were no strangers to migration, and their descendants settled much of the Ohio Valley, Kentucky, Tennessee, Missouri, much of the Mississippi Valley and Texas. Although historians credit them with settling Pennsylvania's Lancaster County and the Cumberland Valley, many families migrated to western Pennsylvania, and from there into Kentucky. The pattern of migration continued into the twentieth century as the descendents of borderers followed the "hillbilly highways" from the Appalachians to the industrial cities of the north in search of jobs and "Okies" fled the Depression-era dustbowl of the southern Great Plains to California.

These tribal people were quick to assimilate others whom they could trust to support the good of the community. And they were quick to lose a sense of their ethnic identity after arriving in America. As such, when asked to identify their ethnic background, they tend to respond "American." And their culturally assimilated neighbors with surnames originating in England, Germany, Italy or Eastern Europe are just as likely to reflect the community's values (Webb 2004).

VISIONS OF LIBERTY

Each of the four immigrant groups brought their own concepts of liberty to America. These reflected the attitudes and beliefs of the regions of Britain they came from.

The New England colonists brought a vision of "ordered liberty" from East Anglia to the New World. In this view, communities possessed the right to determine their form of government and their laws. However, order demanded conformity to those laws. Hence, the Salem witch trials and the persecution of religious minorities in colonial New England fit this view of liberty and freedom (Fischer 1989, 2004). Yet the first written constitution of the British colonies was the Fundamental Orders of Connecticut in 1639. Establishing a representative republic deriving its powers from the people, the Fundamental Orders anticipated the Constitution of the United States by 148 years (Skousen 1981). In New England society, intellectual elites were the most influential citizens, beginning with Winthrop and the Puritan clergy. By the time of the Revolution, attorneys and academics had joined the clergy among the power elite of New England. Even today, one sees this trend in the areas settled by New Englanders where journalists, academics, attorneys and other intellectuals are the elite and influential (Fischer 1989, 2004).

As we have seen, the Cavaliers brought a vision of "hierarchical liberty" where those born into the highest social class enjoyed the greatest freedom while those kidnapped or born into the lowest class were kept in bondage. The elites were the wealthy and the aristocratic. The feudalistic social structure of the Cavaliers began to collapse in the bloodshed of the Civil War.

In this light, it is ironic that Virginia contributed so many of the most notable proponents of freedom and liberty during the Revolution and the founding of the nation, most notably George Washington, Thomas Jefferson, James Madison and Patrick Henry (Ferling 2003, Fischer 1989, 2004).

The Quakers adopted a vision of "spiritual liberty" where they considered religious piety and introspection the path to true freedom. The ideals of William Penn made Pennsylvania a colony where religious and social tolerance was the accepted practices. In fact, Pennsylvania's Quakers led the movement that made Pennsylvania the first state in the new nation to abolish slavery.

The borderers brought a fierce belief in "individual liberty." People so often betrayed and abused by government learned to trust themselves. Unlike the other immigrant groups who originated in the feudal societies of England, the border regions remained more tribalistic in their culture. Hence the elites tended to come from among military leaders analogous to the clan chieftains of the border. As with New Englanders, the influences of the Anglo-Scottish border have deep roots in America's frontier heritage and culture. At least eighteen U.S. presidents were descendents of borderers—a larger number than any other ethnic group, including New England Yankees and Virginia Cavaliers (Fischer 1989).

THE COMMON VISION

By the time of the American Revolution, visions of liberty had coalesced around a set of core principles and beliefs (Bowen 1966, Levin 2009, Skousen 1981, Srodes 2002). The men who framed the Declaration of Independence and the Constitution of the United States came from diverse backgrounds. Some were wealthy merchants and planters. Others were tradesmen and impoverished backwoodsmen. They included lawyers, physicians and clergymen. Some like John Adams, Samuel Adams, John Hancock, James Madison and Thomas Jefferson were college graduates. Others like Benjamin Franklin and George Washington were self-taught (Bowen 1986, Ferling 2003, Skousen 1981). What they held in common was that they were literate and had educated themselves by reading a remarkably similar list of books on history, politics, law, philosophy and human nature. These included the writings of Shakespeare, Cervantes, Jean Jacques Rousseau, Sir Edward Coke, John Locke, David Hume, Charles Montesquieu, William Blackstone, Edmund Burke, Henry St. John Bolingbroke, Adam Smith, Plato, Thucydides and the Bible (Langguth 1989, Levin 2009, McCullough 2001, Skousen 1981).

One of the most influential writers on the framers of America's government was the Roman politician and statesman Marcus Tullius Cicero (McCullough 2001, Skousen 1981). He wrote, that humans are "endowed with foresight and quick intelligence, complex, keen, possessing memory, full of reason and prudence" (Skousen 1981). Cicero believed that the ability of rational thought was unique among all animals and that it was a gift from the Creator. Flowing from this gift was the concept of God-given rights (Levin 2009, Skousen 1981). Because these basic rights came from God, government could not alter them. The English jurist William Blackstone and the philosopher John Locke elaborated upon this concept as "Natural Law."

Thomas Jefferson articulated this belief in The Declaration of Independence: "We hold these truths to be self-evident, that all men are created equal, that they are endowed by their Creator with certain unalienable Rights, that among these are Life, Liberty and the pursuit of Happiness." The Bill of Rights further defines those "unalienable rights"—freedom of speech, freedom to assemble, freedom of the press, freedom of religion, freedom to keep and bear arms, freedom from illegal search and seizure, freedom to acquire and keep property and the right to due process under law.

The framers viewed government through a different political prism than we do today. Today, when Americans consider the terms "right" and "left," we generally think of conservative and liberal or Republican and Democrat. This concept is recent, originating in European parliaments of the twentieth century where communists sat on the far left side of the aisle and fascists sat on the far right (Skousen 1981). The other political parties filled in the middle seats of the legislative chambers. However, when one looks objectively at communism and fascism there is little difference. Both forms of government are tyrannies. The framers of the government of the United States considered the political spectrum in terms of law (Levin 2009, Skousen 1981). On the right of their political spectrum was a system of law where a monarch or ruler made law. When such law is subject to change at the whim of the ruler and the government—whether it is feudalism, communism, fascism, militarism, statism or a theocracy—it is tyranny. On the opposite or left end of the spectrum is the absence of law—anarchy. One need only study the history of the Anglo-Scottish border to understand the dangers and injustice inherent in both.

The founders sought to create a government "of the people" that struck a balance between a ruler's law and anarchy (Skousen 1981). The trick was to achieve a balance between individual liberty and the authority of the state (Levin 2009). The founders drew on two historical models in establishing the government under the Constitution of the United States: the Anglo-Saxon tribes of Britain and the Israelites of the Old Testament (Skousen 1981). In both societies, the essential unit of governance was the family. Both societies relied on small units of governance that consisted of approximately ten families where every adult had a voice in decision making and a vote in the outcome. The small units were organized into slightly larger units that were in turn organized into larger units. People or representatives of the next smaller unit elected leaders at each level. Disputes were resolved at the lowest level of government, and it was only when issues could not be resolved that they were referred to a larger unit. In both cases, the government was tribal, resembling many American Indian societies. Power flowed up from the people rather than down from a tyrant or from the mob rule of an anarchy. The New England states had a long tradition of power flowing up from the people in the form of strong local governments, town meetings and citizen participation in the affairs of government.

The Constitution established a federal government with powers limited to matters of national defense, regulation of trade and other matters of national import. All other powers were to remain in the hands of the people or the individual states in accordance to the Ninth and Tenth Amendments to the Constitution. The Ninth Amendment reads: "The enumeration in the Constitution, of certain rights, shall not be construed to deny or disparage others retained by the people." The Tenth Amendment to the Constitution reads: "The powers not delegated to the United States by the Constitution, nor prohibited by it to the states, are reserved to the states respectively, or to the people."

The framers feared a tyranny by the majority (what they called "mob rule") as much as they feared tyranny by a ruler or ruling elite. Thus, they established a representative republic where citizens elected members of the House of Representatives, the legislatures of the individual states elected members of the Senate,[1] and an Electoral College chosen according to methods specified by the state legislatures elected the President.[2] Justices of the Supreme Court are selected by the President and confirmed by the Senate under the Advise and Consent Clause of the Constitution (Article II, Section 2). The framers established this system of checks and balances to maintain three autonomous but interdependent branches of government that would protect the individual rights of the people.

---

[1] Ratification of the Seventeenth Amendment in 1913 changed the election of senators to general election by the voters of each state.

[2] All states currently select electors by popular vote.

Interpretation of the Constitution as first drafted has changed appreciably over the past two centuries. These changes have affected the ownership, management, regulation and use of America's forest resources. For more than two centuries, we find advocates of private, local, state and federal control of forest resources adding their voices to the debate. It is important to understand how attitudes and beliefs toward the Constitution and the government have changed while never forgetting the intent of the Framers of our government.

Homework

Name: _____   **Date:** _____

Although this chapter focuses on British colonization, Spain, France, the Netherlands and Russia also established colonies in North America. Where did these European powers establish colonies in what is now the United States?

Chapter 8

Wooden Ships

The immigrants from Europe described in the previous chapter crossed the Atlantic in wooden sailing ships. When they arrived in North America, they found themselves isolated from their homelands and from immigrants in other colonies. For those colonists, communication, import of goods, mutual defense and perhaps survival itself depended upon travel by sea. In fact, until the building of the railroads in the nineteenth century, the fastest, safest and least expensive way to travel was by water.

It didn't take long for the British colonies to develop a shipbuilding industry that would shape the destiny of a new nation. At the time of the American Revolution, American shipbuilders had developed the new nation's first great industry and created a revolutionary ship design that made thriving merchant, fishing and whaling industries possible. They also left a mark on the American economy and culture that remains long after the wooden ship became a historical curiosity or a plaything of the wealthy. It is doubtful that this could have happened had it not been for the diversity and quality of timber found along the eastern seaboard of North America.

> **Recommended Reading**
>
> Williams, Michael. 1989. *Americans and Their Forests: A Historical Geography.*
>
> Unfortunately, Williams' meticulously researched work is out of print. However, it is filled with information about the history of America's forests and was one of my favorite references while preparing this textbook. It is worth looking for in a used/out of print bookshop or a nearby library.

THE ROYAL NAVY IN AMERICA

The defeat of the Spanish Armada in 1588 made England the world's dominant sea power. However, England lacked the resources—particularly timber—to sustain its shipbuilding industry. Centuries of agricultural expansion, timber harvesting and fuel wood gathering had reduced its forests. As a result, England turned to the Baltic States—Prussia, Sweden, Denmark and Russia—for raw materials. However, this source of supply was precarious. England's war with Holland in 1652 closed the entrance to the Baltic. Other European wars involving the Baltic States forced them to

Figure 8.1 Re-creation of the Seventeenth Century Warship, *The Golden Hinde. Beaufort NC (1990).*

reserve raw materials for use by their own navies. On occasion, the Baltic States levied customs duties on exports, driving up costs of materials for Britain (Williams 1989).

The earliest English explorers recognized the potential of North American forests as a source of raw materials for shipbuilding. The Navigation and Trade Acts of the seventeenth century protected raw materials, particularly eastern white pines that were the best species for masts, spars and planking. In 1698, Britain sent a fact-finding commission to the colonies to investigate the potential for obtaining naval stores. As a result, the Naval Stores Act of 1705 established bounties for masts, spars, hemp, pitch, tar, turpentine and resins. Colonial governments also provided incentives for the production of goods for the Royal Navy.

Emergence of a local shipbuilding industry in New England, which grew rapidly in the 1660s, was a source of conflict with the Mother Country over supplies. In a way, England's desire to control Colonial commerce in forest products predated many of the economic issues that caused the American Revolution.

NAVAL STORES

Originally, the term "naval stores" included masts, spars, timbers and planking for shipbuilding. Later, the term came to mean pitch, tar, resins, turpentine, hemp for rope making and flax for sail making. Pitch, tar, resins, and turpentine derive from trees. "Whereas the Colonial hemp system was a failure—the special culture and techniques for hemp were never mastered—the production of tar and pitch was a success" (Williams 1989).

Pitch, tar, resins and turpentine are made from the class of chemicals in wood known as "extractives." *Extractives* are organic byproducts of the tree's metabolism. This group of chemicals received the name extractives because people can chemically extract them from wood using a solvent. These waste products are deposited in the center of the woody tissue of the stem, branches and roots, as well as in the bark. Biologists call the extractive-filled center of the stem the "*heartwood*." There are literally thousands of extractives found in trees. Many are volatile. Extractives lend wood color and odor, as well as decay and insect resistance (Panshin and deZeeuw 1980).

Shipbuilders used *pitch* to caulk ship's timbers. They soaked hemp rope in pitch to make "oakum," a rope caulk used between ship planks and used *tar* to preserve ropes and timbers. They used *resins* as an adhesive and distilled *turpentine* into thin, clear resins used as a paint carrier and thinner (Williams 1989).

North Carolina supplied approximately 60 percent of the naval stores because longleaf pine was the best species for their production. South Carolina was the other main producer and exporter of naval stores. The builders shipped some of the naval stores directly to Britain and others to New England where they were transshipped to Britain. Some was exported (illegally) to other European markets or consumed by Yankee shipbuilders.

The production of resin and turpentine was a difficult, dirty job, and, as such, usually relegated to slaves. To produce resin and turpentine, builders stripped bark on the sunny side of the tree and cut a notch near the ground. They periodically cut a V-shaped incision in the bark—the "box"—to stimulate resin flow. A cup at the base of the box collected resins that workers periodically ladled into barrels. One slave could collect two and a half barrels a day from approximately 1,000 trees. They periodically scraped the exposed xylem (wood) to collect heavier resins. Thinner, crude resins were distilled in copper vats—the clear, thinner distillates were turpentine. The thick residue and "scrapes" were the resin (rosin) used as glue.

Freshly split, fire-deadened, pine wood got burned—particularly the dried out old "boxed" trees—to produce tar and pitch. Workers piled logs in a cone-shaped heap over a sloping floor of clay, which had a wooden pipe or channel leading from the pile to barrels or pits where the tar was collected. Sometimes clay covered the pile as in charcoal production, and the fire started at a hole at the top of the pile. This would drive the tar down with it. A cord of wood (a stack of roundwood 4 × 4 feet on the ends and 8 feet long) produces between 40 and 50 gallons of tar. Pitch was boiled down in vats or kettles to remove volatiles. The extra processing resulted in pitch being twice as expensive as tar (Williams 1989).

MASTS AND SPARS

Masts were of much greater strategic importance than pitch and tar. Any sailing ship needed 23 timbers for masts, cross yards (spars) and a bowsprit. A ship of the line[1] (the eighteenth century equivalent of a battleship) needed a main mast at least 40 inches in diameter and up to 120 feet long. The eastern white pine of New England was ideal—tall, straight-grained and strong. As early as 1652, the Royal Navy sent ships to Portsmouth, New Hampshire to replace masts. By 1727, Falmouth, Maine was the center of trade in masts to England (Williams 1989). The charter of the Massachusetts Bay Company (Plymouth and Maine) of 1691 reserved all white pines over 25 inches for the navy. A surveyor of pines and timbers would mark trees reserved for masts with three cuts of a hatchet in the shape of an arrow. These were the famous "arrow trees" of New England folklore. With passage of the White Pine Act of 1722, Britain reserved all white pines on the northeastern coast for use by the navy. English efforts to reserve the white pines were the first efforts to regulate the use of the North American forests, and it met resistance from the New Englanders who wished to use the white pine for their own growing shipbuilding as well as for construction (Carlsen 2008, Williams 1989).

Figure 8.2 Model of a Full-rigged Sailing Ship. *Whaling Museum, New Bedford, MA.*

Nonetheless trade in masts and spars never amounted to much due to the distance and expense of finding quality raw material. Many of the trees of sufficient size were

---

[1] The term "ship of the line" comes from European naval tactics of the era. Opposing fleets would form lines of battle and sail past each other with cannons blazing. It was bloody work with the victory usually going to the side that was able to throw the most iron shot into the hulls, masts and sailors of their opponent. Because of this style of naval warfare, ships of the line tended to be large floating gun platforms with two gun decks. Ships of the line sacrificed speed and maneuverability for firepower.

hollow and unsuitable for masts although one could saw them into planks or boards. Felling such tall timber required great care by clearing a path for the tree, then preparing a bed of snow to cushion the fall. Logs had to be transported to a nearby river either by dragging or slinging them under axles connecting large wheels 16 to 18 feet in diameter and dragged by dozens of oxen. Masts lashed together into huge rafts were floated downriver to seaports and loaded on ships bound for England.

The system of resource acquisition for the Royal Navy was rife with corruption. Crown agents, local merchants, poachers and smugglers were able to turn a quick profit in a flourishing black market in masts and timbers. New England smugglers carried on a brisk trade in timbers with Spain and Portugal (Williams 1989). Disputes with the Mother Country over resources necessary to competing American and British shipbuilding were inevitable and often bitter. It is not surprising that the first sea skirmish of the Revolution took place over shipbuilding supplies. In May 1775 the townspeople of Machias, Maine chased and captured a British ship that had commandeered the shipment of pine lumber[2] (Youngquist and Fleischer 1977).

AMERICAN SHIPBUILDING

As early as 1629, fishing vessels were constructed in Salem, Massachusetts. During the seventeenth century, they were relatively small fishing and merchant vessels that plied the coastal trade with other colonies and the West Indies. During this era, New Englander ship owners tended to avoid the danger of trans-Atlantic crossings. Just four Massachusetts seaport towns—Boston, Charlestown, Salem and Scituate—accounted for three quarters of American vessels constructed in the late seventeenth century (Williams 1989, Van Oosterhaut 2008, Youngquist and Fleischer 1977).

In the early eighteenth century, Philadelphia, Charleston and Savannah emerged as additional centers of shipbuilding (Williams 1989). By 1793, Philadelphia claimed the largest and busiest shipyards in the United States (Toll 2006). Southern shipyards built fewer ships, but many thought that the ships they produced were superior in design and quality to those built farther north. The reason lies partly in superior design but also in the availability of superior timber to construct the frames and hulls of southern ships. Baltimore became famous for shipyards that built the fast Baltimore Clippers of the nineteenth century. Still, Boston, Newport, Portsmouth and other New England cities accounted for half the American tonnage built just prior to the Revolution (Youngquist and Fleischer 1977).

Figure 8.3 The Sailing Vessel *Charles W. Morgan* in Dry Dock for Repairs and Restoration. *Mystic Seaport, CT (July 2009).*

White oak was the preferred species for ship ribs and planking in the north

---

[2] Throughout this book, I use the term "lumber" to refer to wood products sawed into boards, planks or other solid wood products. The distinction between lumber and other wood products is how it is produced: by sawing.

while builders in the south preferred live oak. White oak is a widespread species through the eastern states (Harlow and Harrar 1969). It has large, curving branches that make it ideal for shaping into ship ribs, and builders could dig up the roots from the ground to make ship "knees."[3] It is tough, strong and able to take the shock and pounding of heavy seas and groundings. Its high extractive content makes it resistant to decay and marine organisms.[4]

Figure 8.4 Oak "Knees." *Mystic Seaport, CT.*

Live oak was so well suited for ship frames and planking that it was the preferred species used by the U.S. Navy. The live oak is a southern species that cannot tolerate lengthy exposure to sub-freezing temperatures. Therefore, it does not grow in northern forests farther north than Virginia (Harlow and Harrar 1969). Like white oak, it has wide, spreading branches whose curves make it ideal for the ribs of a ship (Ball 2003). It is denser, tougher and stronger than white oak, and it is also resistant to decay and degradation by marine organisms (Youngquist and Fleischer 1977). The nickname of the frigate *U.S.S. Constitution,*[5] launched in 1797, was "Old Ironsides" because its live oak hull and frame were so tough that they deflected cannonballs from British ships during the War of 1812 (Carlsen 2008). The

Figure 8.5 Live Oak Trees.

United States purchased groves of live oak in Georgia in 1789 and 1800 to provide timber for the navy. Perhaps the earliest forest plantation in the United States was one established by the navy in 1828 near Pensacola, Florida to cultivate live oak[6] (Anderson 2004, Toll 2006).

Shipbuilders used eastern white pine for decking and deckhouses in the north. Eastern white pine is lightweight but strong. It is easy to work with and was ideal for woodwork in the interior of the ship and above decks. Eastern white pine does not grow in

---

[3] A "knee" is a brace in the framing shaped to fit in a 90-degree angle but curved to give a concave appearance from inside the hull. The grain curvature of root and stem makes the knee a very strong supporting member.

[4] Decay is degradation by fungi and commonly referred to as rot. The marine organisms in question are the various shipworms and teredo that eat away at the base of coastal pilings on piers and wharves.

[5] The *U.S.S. Constitution* is still a fully commissioned ship of the U.S. Navy now serving as a museum ship open to the public in Charlestown, Massachusetts.

[6] The plantation still exists on Santa Rosa Island as part of the Gulf Islands National Seashore.

Figure 8.6 Boat Builder. *Plymouth Plantation, MA.*

Figure 8.7 The Schooner, *L.A. Dunton. Mystic Seaport, CT.*

the south so southern shipyards used southern pine[7] for decking. It is denser, harder and more resistant to wear and decay than white pine, so it was a superior material for this use. White pine, because of its superior workability, was better suited for intricately shaped parts of the ship. The superiority of these two woods for different uses encouraged trade in lumber between New England and the South that went hand in hand with the naval stores trade.

At first, American shipbuilders worked entirely with hand tools, sawing, chopping, carving and shaping the wood into the various pieces that would be painstakingly assembled to make a seaworthy vessel. The lack of mechanization partly explains why the earliest American vessels were small and limited to sailing close to shore. The introduction of water-powered sawmills in New England through the late seventeenth and early eighteenth centuries allowed shipbuilders to save time, labor and cost. This encouraged the building of larger, more seaworthy vessels in American shipyards.

An estimated 40 percent of all British tonnage and one third of all the ships in the British merchant marine were built in American shipyards on the eve of the Revolution (Williams 1989, Youngquist and Fleischer 1977). After the Revolution, the American shipbuilding industry experienced its heyday from approximately 1830 to the Civil War, primarily because of superior ship design (Sechrest 1998).

Americans built smaller ships than Europeans and developed the *"schooner,"* a sleek, narrow-hulled craft with a sharp bow and a stern that skimmed the water with great speed and maneuverability. The schooner has two or more masts.[8] Individual builders refined and improved their designs, adding their personal touches. Shipbuilders worked without plans but often built carefully carved scale models before building the ships. Different schooner designs sometimes went by different names, including the famous clippers (Van Osterhout 2008, Youngquist and Fleischer 1997).

---

[7] "Southern pine" is not a single tree species, but a group of closely related species that includes loblolly pine, shortleaf pine, longleaf pine and other species. Eastern white pine, on the other hand is a single species.

[8] The steel-hulled schooner *Thomas L. Lawson* (built in 1902) carried seven masts (Von Oosterhout 2008).

The schooner enabled American privateers to contend with the powerful British Royal Navy during the Revolution and the War of 1812. American captains commanded ships that had the speed to outrun the British when outnumbered or outgunned, thus living to fight another day. However, when confronting a single British warship or merchant, the American captains would employ the speed and maneuverability of the schooner to avoid a broadside of cannon shot by the British while maneuvering into a position to bear all guns on one side of the ship (a "broadside") on the enemy. An estimated 55,000 Americans served on privateers during the Revolution, doing great damage to the British and including taking approximately16,000 prisoners of war. In comparison, Washington's Continental Army captured approximately 15,000 British and mercenary soldiers in British service (American Merchant Marine at War 2009).

Following the Civil War, iron ships began to replace the wooden hull. Steamships began to replace sails but at a slower pace. Sechrest (1998) reports that by the 1870s, a large percentage of goods imported and exported by the United States were shipped on foreign vessels. He attributes this to prohibitive import tariffs on iron and hemp, the decline of the whaling industry, losses of merchant vessels to Confederate raiders during the Civil War and the inability of ship owners to purchase insurance for their vessels during the war along with the decline of the cotton trade during and after the Civil War.

LEGACY OF THE WOODEN SHIPS

The wooden ships are an important part of American history and have left their permanent mark on American culture. New England and other shipbuilding regions developed a network of interlocked industries that included lumbering, fishing, whaling and the merchant trade. These linked industries fueled the American entrepreneurial spirit and harnessed the creativity of a free people. Fortunes made in seafaring became reinvested in lumbering, mining, oil, banks, steel and railroads. Workers moved from the wooden ships into other industries, and nautical terms such as "spars," "rigging" and "ballast" found their way into lumbering and railroading.

Those of us whose ancestors came to America from Europe, Africa or Asia prior to the late nineteenth century are descendents of people who made the voyage across the Atlantic under sail on wooden ships. For more than three centuries of European settlement in the Americas, wooden ships provided the sole link with the rest of the world. Americans were able to build an economy by exporting raw materials—including naval stores, timbers, furs, tobacco, cotton and rum—to the Old World. Tools, furniture, books and other items imported from Europe made life in the New World easier. Later generations of American seafarers opened trade to the Orient, the Indies, the Spice Islands and Africa to bring back silks, pottery, art and spices. They also brought human beings in chains in the stinking holds of overcrowded slave ships. American fishermen worked the rich fisheries from Nova Scotia to the Gulf of Mexico, and American whaling ships chased their prey across the oceans of the world thanks to the skill and industriousness of American shipbuilders. The wooden ships helped the new United States win a Revolution and project itself as a growing world power, economically and militarily. Warships, blockade-runners and commerce raiders played an integral part in the Civil War.

The era of wooden sailing ships lives on in American folklore, art, music, literature and film. Sea captains and sailors were America's "worldliest" citizens at a time when many people never ventured very far from the family farm during their lifetimes.

Sailors had been to places that most Americans could only imagine. They sang chanteys of exotic places, of the perils of rounding Cape Horn and of the "Ladies of Spain" and the girls of "Old Mow-ee." Authors, from Herman Melville to Jack London, immortalized sailors and life on the wooden ships in literature. American artists from Winslow Homer to Mort Kunstler have portrayed nautical scenes. Numerous films, including the recent Master and Commander, have focused on life at sea. Ship carving, especially figureheads, is one of the best-known examples of folk art associated with the era of wooden ships.

This chapter ends with a travelogue. Mystic Seaport,[9] located in the old seaport town of Mystic, Connecticut, is the site of a restored seafaring village of the 1830s. It is a special place where visitors may experience what life was like in the past. Visitors may tour fishing vessels, pleasure boats, the training ship *Joseph Conrad* and the whaler *Charles W. Morgan,* the last surviving ship of its kind. The Seaport also has a working shipyard, a sail loft, a ropewalk, a cooperage, a ship carver, a ship smith, a ship chandlery, a sail loft, a shipyard and other examples of industries that supported the seafaring industry. Mystic Seaport is located at Exit 90 on Interstate 95 in southeastern Connecticut. It is well worth a visit.

Figure 8.8 H. B. DuPont Preservation Shipyard. *Mystic Seaport, CT.*

---

[8] The website for Mystic Seaport is *http://www.mysticseaport.org.*

Homework

Name: _____   Date: _____

1. Who was Andrew Robinson?

2. Who was Joshua Humphreys?

3. Visit the Mystic Seaport website (*http://www.mysticseaport.org*). What is remarkable about the *Charles W. Morgan?*

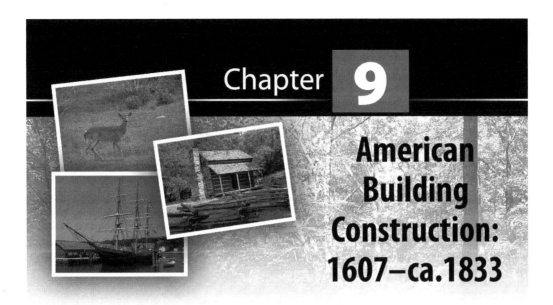

American Building Construction: 1607–ca.1833

America was built with wood. It was and remains an abundant raw material and is relatively easy to shape into useful form. One of its main uses is in building construction.

One of the primary reasons for the widespread use of wood is energy. Formation of wood in the living tree results from photosynthesis, a process driven by solar energy. Therefore, humans do not need to provide energy to formulate the chemical structure of wood. Energy, however, must be provided for sawing, cutting and shaping wood into useful products. Muscle power—human or animal—and water produced energy prior to the development of steam engines. Thus, labor was a critical issue in early American construction. Iron, steel, masonry and other materials that one could use instead of wood required significantly more energy to produce and use than wood. Stone and brick were in common use as we shall see, but generally only wealthier Americans used those materials.

Building construction in early America followed distinct regional styles in design, construction techniques and material use. Immigrants modeled regional practices on the regions of Europe they came from. The Dutch settlers of New York brought with them a distinctive architectural style patterned after the buildings of the Netherlands. One may find the styles of Spain in the American Southwest. The British immigrants of the eastern seaboard followed the regional styles of Britain (Fischer 1989).

TOWNS, FARMS AND LAND OWNERSHIP

Before we get into the specifics of construction, let us look at the patterns of how towns, villages and farms spread across the landscape following regional patterns of the British Isles.

Webb (2005) describes the Great Migration into New England as "well planned, carefully structured, and organized from [its] beginning to create townships and the advantages of urban infrastructure." The establishment of towns, farms and fields in New England followed the patterns of East Anglia. New Englanders formed corporations[1] to found well planned and laid-out villages and towns. Typically, they laid the town out around a "commons" or a "green" for pasturing livestock, conducting public markets and drilling the militia. They typically built public buildings—a church, town hall and tavern—adjacent to the green. Fields and pastures surrounded the town. Climate and terrain limited the size of the typical New England farm. However, East Anglians were comfortable with a pastoral landscape, and they sought to re-create it in New England (Fischer 1989). Settlement proceeded with expansion from the coast to new villages divided into surveyed lots in town and outlying farming lots. Northern New England developed on a township model with settlements more scattered than those in southern New England (Williams 1989).

The most striking difference between the land use practices of the British colonists and the Indians was the permanent settlement patterns that individual land ownership brought with it (Cronon 1983). The idea that an individual could own a plot of land with well-defined boundaries was an alien concept to tribal people. Indians of New England rarely occupied the same village site for more that a couple of decades before moving to a new site. This gave time for the land to recover and forests to regenerate, although they often reoccupied old village sites decades later. The British colonists were coming from a culture emerging from feudalism. Land ownership was, for the most part, limited to the nobility and the wealthy. In America, immigrants could lay title to land of their own. As a result, families of British colonists frequently occupied the same land and even the same house for generations. The concept of land ownership and the building of permanent structures gave rise to permanent settlements, a condition that was uncommon in North America prior to Columbus.

The plantation system, with estates of 250 to 1,000 acres, dominated the Southern landscape. Towns, per se, were not as common in the Tidewater as in New England or the Middle Colonies (Deans 2007, Williams 1989). Property owners maintained woodlands as parks for the sport of gentlemen in both England and Virginia. (One of Virginia's elite sons, George Washington, was an excellent horseman who honed his skills in the foxhunts of his youth.) Tobacco depleted the soil, requiring clearing of new fields while others lay fallow, typically reverting to forest unless burned (Williams 1989).

William Penn envisioned the Quaker ideal of "loving neighborhoods" consisting of clusters of farms with a group of adjacent farmhouses grouped on ten acre lots. This was a pattern of settlement of the North Midlands of England "equally distinct from the town life of East Anglia and the manorial villages of Wessex" (Fischer 1989). Instead, the people of the Delaware Valley built their farms in clusters, but they located their houses on the farms and did not build them in tight clusters as Penn wished.

As Penn's colony expanded into the ridge and valley district of central Pennsylvania, settlement followed the pattern of developing valleys into prosperous farmlands while leaving the ridges unoccupied. This pattern exists today in the ridge and valley country of central Pennsylvania. Different valleys often attracted distinctly different cultures. Fischer (1989) describes Big Valley near the center of the state as Pennsylvania Dutch Country. "The names on the mailboxes are Zook and Peachey and Hostetler." To the north, on the other side of Stone Mountain, lies the Nittany Valley. The settlers of the Nittany Valley were "Presbyterians and Anglicans who came mainly from the borderlands of North Britain." Fischer notes that the speech patterns of residents of these two adjacent valleys are distinctly different. (Note that neither sounds

---

[1] In the case of early New Englanders, corporations formed as a means of government. It is not surprising that business corporations as we know them today were strongest in New England in the early years of the nation.

remotely like the high nasal Brooklyn Italian accent of the Nittany Valley's most famous resident, a certain Mr. Joe Paterno.) However, the pattern of settlement by the two different cultural groups of the Big and Nittany Valleys follows the Quaker pattern established by the followers of William Penn.

Along the frontier of New York, Pennsylvania, Virginia, Kentucky and Tennessee settlement was by "tomahawk right"—blazing a tree to stake a claim (Williams 1989). The borderers initially favored isolated settlements and cleared small farms in the backcountry. This immigrant group had suffered under government oppression for centuries and desired nothing more than to be left alone.

THE TIMBER FRAME

The colonists who settled on the Eastern Seaboard—New England, Virginia and the Delaware Valley—constructed houses, barns, shops and other buildings based upon the prevalent styles of the regions of England from which they emigrated. In these cases they constructed the building framework of heavy timbers. For two thousand years, people constructed buildings using heavy timber frames. In the technical terms of a wood scientist, a timber is a wood structural component with cross-sectional dimensions of at least 5 by 5 inches. The frame was assembled in a post-and-beam style of architecture (Carlsen 2008, Fischer 1989).

The colonists squared the framing members by hand from logs using a process known as *hewing*. They used a broad-bladed axe to cut notches in the bark and outer wood every 12 to 18 inches apart. They split the slabs between each notch from the log with the axe. If the timber was going to be exposed, it might have been smoothed either with a hand axe or an adze—a tool with a blade that curves away from the handle. Unlike an axe where the edge of the blade is parallel to the handle, the blade of an adze is perpendicular. Builders in England had used oak for centuries for timber construction. Early British

Figure 9.1 Hewing a Timber. *Old Sturbridge Village, MA.*

colonists preferred to carry on this practice although they used other species as well. Because of the labor required to square the timbers, they smoothed or "finished" the sides of timbers exposed to view with an adze. They left the sides hidden from view in rough-hewn condition (Green 2006).

Early Americans hewed timbers because sawing technologies of the period were either by hand or employed a water-powered sawmill. Sawing by hand was a time-consuming, arduous process generally requiring two men. The water-powered sawmill was faster but required an investment in funds and technology that made hand hewing a better alternative for most Americans.

The connections of the timber posts, beams and cross bracing involved a complex array of hand-carved joints, including mortise and tenon and other joints. The mortise is a rectangular-sided hole carved and chiseled into the side of a timber. The hole may extend all the way through the timber or only part way. The tenon is a tongue

Figure 9.2 Timber Frame House with Mud Walls. *Jamestown, VA.*

carved out of the end of another timber. The builder shapes the tenon to fit snugly into the mortise. One may pin it in place by drilling through the assembled joint and securing it with one or two wooden pegs (Baylor 2006).

By the time of European settlement, timber framing had evolved into a sophisticated craft that employed a number of woodworking, engineering and architectural skills. In England, carpenters belonged to craft guilds. Colonial promoters recruiting colonists for their North American ventures sought carpenters highly. It is likely that the first carpenters to cross the Atlantic were generalists, making everything from timber frames to clapboards to furniture. As settlements became towns and towns grew to become cities, English-style carpenter guilds became established with carpenters becoming more and more specialized. Within a single business, one might find framers, hewers, sawyers, joiners and other specialized craftsmen. This pattern followed frontier settlement well into the nineteenth century. At the time of the Revolution, a number of American carpenters had served apprenticeships in England and returned with the skills learned in the mother country (Crews 2003a).

The forests of England had been cut back to an estimated 7.7 percent of the total land area by the seventeenth century. The lack of wood for building required filling spaces between the timber framework with stone, brick or mud and straw (Green 2006). In the colonies where timber was abundant, builders also used masonry, but wood siding was more common. English colonists typically clad buildings with ***riven*** (hand-split) clapboards.

Builders typically covered interior walls with plaster and lath although they sometimes employed wood paneling, perhaps as a wainscoting in combination with plaster. A typical American timber frame house often contained smaller vertical members known as studs between the timber columns used as nailing surfaces for the lath. An early timber frame house required more nails just to nail the laths to the studs than does a modern house. Blacksmiths had to manufacture nails by hand until the invention of a nail making machine circa 1800.

Floors were sawn or hand-hewn planks. Unpaved roads and streets (with a significant quantity of manure mixed in with mud) made maintenance of floors a practical challenge. Paint or sealant seldom protected floors, which were bare wood that the inhabitants could scrub by sweeping sand across the surface.

The common practice for sawing planks was with a ***pit saw***. The saw was a long-bladed, two-man saw. The builders either dug a pit in the ground or erected a scaffold so one man could stand underneath the log with a second man above. The man beneath the log would pull the saw during the cutting stroke, while the top man would pull the saw up for the next stroke. It was a difficult and inefficient process. Two men could saw only 100 to 200 lineal feet per day (Williams 1989). As a result, they employed labor saving devices such as the use of hand-split ***clapboards*** for siding and ***shingles*** for roof covering. Eventually, sawn siding would replace clapboards in American building construction.

Interior and exterior walls and places where building surfaces joined, such as a roof and wall or a floor and wall, were imperfect and prone to separate or crack. Thus decorative and functional mouldings—strips of wood carved or planed in a pattern—covered seams. Carpenters made all windows, doors, and window and door frames by hand until the early stages of the Industrial Revolution; the first few decades of the nineteenth century. They covered roofs with hand-split shingles.

Figure 9.3 Pit Saw at the Carpenters' Yard. *Colonial Williamsburg, VA.*

The carpenter had to know the properties of a number of species of wood and how to use them in construction. Oak was the preferred species for timber framing in England, and this preference carried over to America. Carpenters also employed other species, as long as they were strong and from trees that were large enough, straight enough and not too difficult to hew. They preferred rot resistant species in applications where the wood would be exposed to moisture.[2] They used weather-resistant woods, such as white oak, baldcypress, and cedar, for exposed siding, mouldings and shingles. Lightweight, workable woods such as eastern white pine and yellow-poplar were used for studs, interior paneling and mouldings. They made floors from wood that stood up to constant wear, such as maple, oak, southern pine and beech. The beautiful wood of the black walnut was often used as interior paneling. Builders used chestnut widely for house and barn framing and siding. Preferences in wood use depended upon the availability of species within a given region. This meant that houses constructed in Massachusetts and the Carolinas would likely have different groups of species used in their construction (Panshin and deZeeuw 1980, Youngquist and Fleischer 1977).

The building of a timber frame house required a great deal of skill, labor and material. By the 1830s, the cost of building a timber frame house became prohibitive for many Americans, resulting in the development of light framing. But many of the timber houses built in the Colonial era and in the early years of the nation still stand as a testimony to the quality and craftsmanship of the construction.

CONSTRUCTION IN NEW ENGLAND

New England building styles followed the practices and designs common in East Anglia (Fischer 1988). In particular, New England houses were, and still are, built with wood. Prior to the nineteenth century, heavy timber frames of oak supported houses. The framing details were those practiced by the carpenters of East Anglia. Floors were white pine and siding was of weather-resistant cedar clapboards.

The best known style for New England houses of the Colonial period was the "salt box." The salt box originated in East Anglia as a two-story house with a pitched gable

---

[2] Wood will not rot if kept dry. However, at moisture contents greater than 20 percent on a dry-basis (weight of water in the wood divided by the oven-dry weight of the wood), decay fungi will attack the wood.

Figure 9.4 New England Farmhouse. *Salisbury, NH.*

roof. As families grew, they added a single-story shed to the back of the house, making the back side of the roof a continuous plane. Another housing style of Colonial New England was the "Cape Cod." The Cape Cod is a small box-like structure of one and a half stories. This style also originated in the eastern counties of England as people expanded cottages by adding sleeping quarters on the second floor. They added windows to the upper story by adding gabled dormers. More elaborate styles such as houses with several gabled roofs also exist in both East Anglia and New England.

CONSTRUCTION STYLES OF THE VIRGINIA TIDEWATER

Building styles of the Virginia Tidewater reflected the practices of the English West Country. The elite built their Great Houses in the prevailing style of the manor houses of English elites. Houses were one and a half to two stories high, framed with timbers and clad in brick. The architectural style was symmetrical with a great hall running through the house from front to back. Large, high-ceilinged living spaces flanked the great hall. A back staircase led to living quarters on the second floor. Kitchens were in separate buildings, partly to keep the great house cool in summer, but largely to protect the great hall from fire (Fischer 1989).

Most houses in the Chesapeake were more modest "hall and parlor" houses. They were two story structures with two rooms downstairs and a corner staircase leading to the upstairs sleeping quarters. Two stone or brick fireplaces stood at either end of the house. Typically, these houses were 16 by 20 feet in size. Like the great houses, kitchens existed in separate buildings. The creators of the smaller houses of the

Figure 9.5 Blennerhasset. *An Example of a "Great House," Parkersburg, WV.*

Chesapeake built them mostly with wood, like New England houses. However, the construction details and style were different. Houses were raised on posts or blocks and lacked foundations or cellars. The carpentry was simple in this region where labor costs were high. Slaves and the poorest whites lived in one-room shacks or shanties constructed of crudely split timbers (Fischer 1989).

Figure 9.6 Hall and Parlor House. *Williamsburg, VA.*

THE QUAKER HOUSE

The preferred building material of Pennsylvania and the Delaware Valley was "the beautiful gray-brown fieldstone which gave the vernacular architecture of this region its special character and enduring charm" (Fischer 1989). Like the houses of New England and Virginia, the style of the Delaware Valley was common in the North Midlands of Britain. American builders replaced stone lintels and sills[3] with wood. Small pent roofs supported by wooden posts typically painted white covered doorways and windows.

"Quaker" houses characteristically were two stories. A typical floor plan included three rooms downstairs with a corner stairway leading to a "full second story." Another floor plan was the "four over four." Quaker houses were generally larger and more spacious than the houses of New England or among the lower classes in Virginia. Quakers had more bedrooms and placed greater importance on privacy than the other major immigrant groups. The Quakers kept the interiors bright and clean but lacking in decoration because of their aversion to ostentation. Furniture

Figure 9.7 Pottsgrove Manor. *An example of a "Quaker house," Pottstown, PA.*

was simple and functional. Wooden pegs on the walls were for hanging clothing instead of the armoires or chests used by other immigrant groups (Fischer 1989).

The other ethnic groups that settled in Pennsylvania added their own cultural influences. German Pietists introduced a style of barn building with heavy, braced timbers and massive floor joists. The house plans of the German immigrants were also distinctive. Large kitchens that spanned the length of the house characterized the Pennsylvania German style. By the time of the Revolution, Philadelphia had become the largest and most cosmopolitan city in North America. Philadelphians adopted house styles that

---

[3] A lintel is the horizontal structural component that supports the wall system over a window or door opening. A sill is the horizontal component underneath a window or that forms the base of a wall system at the top of the foundation wall.

copied the styles of cities of the British Isles, especially Bristol, London and Dublin. Raised entryways and brick fronts characterized Philadelphia's houses.

THE LOG CABIN OF THE BACKCOUNTRY

The most famous symbol of the backcountry is the log cabin. Laying logs horizontally is an ancient construction practice with its highest forms found in Scandinavia. Swedes in the Delaware Valley constructed the first log structures built by Europeans in what is now the United States (Carlsen 2008, Green 2006). Log cabins were rare in southern New England, Tidewater Virginia and among the British and German immigrants of the Delaware Valley. The "cabbin" is a word and a building style imported from the Anglo-Scottish border. Its original meaning was any rude hut or shack made of cheap and easily obtained materials. Along the border, builders used stone and thatch. In Northern Ireland cabins were built with turf and mud. In North America, logs and clay became the building materials of choice (Fischer 1989).

Figure 9.8 Log Cabin. *Great Smoky Mountains National Park, TN.*

The cabin was particularly suited to the dangers of the Anglo-Scottish border. One could construct it easily, abandon it with little regret and attract less attention from invaders or reivers than would occur with a larger building. In North America, the cabin was ideally suited to the dangerous and migratory nature of frontier settlement.

The construction of the frontier cabin consisted of logs, notched on both ends with cracks chinked with clay. The typical cabin was a one room structure, perhaps with a sleeping loft overhead. Cabins were typically between sixteen and seventeen feet long, a standard dimension—the rod—brought over from Britain. As families grew and circumstances changed, additions took place by adding an adjacent cabin. A covered, open breezeway connecting the adjacent cabins was known as a "dog-trot" (Fischer 1989, Campbell 2003). This too was a practice known in the border regions of Britain.

American culture has romanticized the log cabin, and it remains a popular building style (now referred to as a "log home"). But its early history was born in deep poverty and its early associations were with the poorest members of American society (Carlsen 2008, Fischer 1989, Williams 1989). Farm families took pains to camouflage their original log cabins with siding and plaster walls as they gained wealth and added on timber frame additions to the homesteads.

RELIANCE ON WOOD

America was built with wood. The twentieth century American architect Frank Lloyd Wright wrote, "We may use wood with intelligence only if we understand wood." American carpenters possessed a keen understanding of this group of materials.

Timber framing nearly disappeared in the United States following the development of light frame construction using nailed connections in the 1830s. However, in the 1970s, a revival of timber construction took place as people sought to replicate the old style of construction and rekindled appreciation for the beauty of exposed timber beams and columns. Today we can find timber framers throughout the United States.

Homework

Name: _____ Date: _____

Look up and write down the definitions of the following terms:

Adze:

Clapboard:

Dormer:

Gable:

Joinery:

Lath:

Moulding:

Shingle:

Post and beam:

Wainscoting:

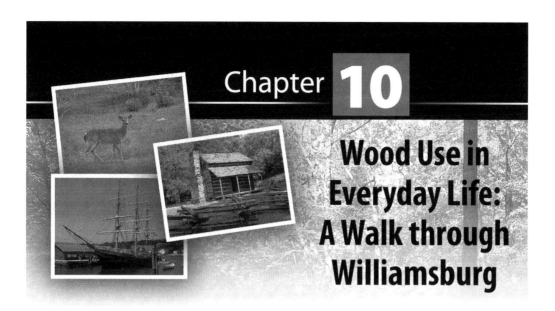

Chapter 10

Wood Use in Everyday Life: A Walk through Williamsburg

Williamsburg, Virginia, is located on Interstate 64 on the James River Peninsula between Richmond and Norfolk. In 1699, the capital of colonial Virginia moved here from Jamestown. For the next eighty-one years it remained the governmental and cultural hub of America's largest colony and, later, state. The Royal Governors erected a "palace" worthy of representing the power, wealth and authority of the British Empire in America. A representative democracy, modeled after Parliament, met in the Capital. Young men studied divinity and law at the College of William and Mary. Shops, tradesmen, merchants and taverns thrived in one of America's most vibrant communities.

In 1780, the capital moved up the James to Richmond and Williamsburg languished as a sleepy tidewater village. A year later, Washington and Rochambeau made the town their headquarters during the Yorktown Campaign. Over time, the memories of the thriving colonial capital would fade. Williamsburg gained public attention for a brief period in 1862 when Confederate forces commanded by General Joseph Johnston held off the over-cautious George B. McClellan and the Army of the Potomac during the Peninsular Campaign.

Figure 10.1 Governor's Palace.

The history of Williamsburg changed again in the 1920s with the vision of Dr. William Archer Rutherford Goodwin, rector of the historic Bruton Parish Church and later a professor at the College of William and Mary. Goodwin had a keen interest in the history of Williamsburg and advocated the restoration of the town to its colonial appearance as a "window" offering "unparalleled vistas . . . into the nation's past" (Yetter 1988). In 1926, he found the financial backing required to make his dream a reality when John D. Rockefeller, Jr. visited restorations Goodwin had supervised at Bruton Parish Church and the George Wythe house.

Today Williamsburg is the home of the Colonial Williamsburg[1] restoration. It is one of those special places where American history comes to life on a daily basis. Colonial Williamsburg provides visitors with a view of how Virginians lived in 1774. "Living history" is a major attraction. Visitors may run into such notable figures as "Patrick Henry" or "Thomas Jefferson" or speak to craftspeople, artisans, merchants, slaves and citizens who act the part of eighteenth century Americans.

However, for someone interested in the history of America's forests and the use of wood products, Williamsburg is an eye opener. Everywhere one looks wood products fill the everyday needs of Americans. Whether for construction, fuel, containers, furniture, fences or thousands of other uses, wood was an essential resource in creating an economy that provided Americans the highest standard of living in the world by the time of the American Revolution (Carlsen 2008, McCullough 2005, Youngquist and Fleischer 1977).

Recommended Reading

Carlsen, Spike. 2008. *A splintered history of wood: Belt sander races, blind wood-workers and baseball bats.*

How can a book about the history of wood be fun to read? Pick up Spike Carlsen's "A splintered history" and you will learn how. This is a fast-paced compilation of stories that are humorous, fascinating, off-beat, and surprising. From my perspective, a student who reads this book will better understand wood and its vital role in our existence as human beings.

THE GOVERNOR'S PALACE

The centerpiece of Colonial Williamsburg is the reconstructed Governor's Palace. Fire destroyed the original Palace in 1781 when Colonial troops wounded in the Siege of Yorktown used it as a hospital. Excavations of the Palace's basement, a floor plan drawn by Thomas Jefferson, and other historic documents helped architects determine what the mansion and surrounding outbuildings must have looked like before it burned (Yetter 1988).

Tour groups enter the mansion through the same door that visitors to the Governor would have entered in the eighteenth century. The entrance hall is paneled with solid black walnut; one of the most valuable American wood species that is prized for its rich, chocolate brown color. Weapons and battle flags of His Majesty's regiments deployed in Virginia line the walls. It is here that the might of the British Empire was on display to impress visitors to the Royal Governor. Visitors deemed worthy of an audience with the Governor would be escorted to the second floor reception room. Here the intention was to convey the wealth of the Empire through the elaborate hand-tooled leather wall coverings and exquisitely crafted walnut furniture (imported from England, of course).

Figure 10.2 Entrance Hall of the Governor's Palace.

---

[1] The official website for Colonial Williamsburg is http://www.history.org.

But Williamsburg is not about Royal Governors or Revolutionary governors Patrick Henry and Thomas Jefferson. It is about ordinary Americans in a small, but important, Colonial town. Visitors may see how these ordinary folk, as well as Virginia's elites, lived. How did these people live, and how much did they depend upon the forests of Virginia to support their way of life?

Figure 10.3 Reception Room on Second Floor of the Governor's Palace.

FENCES

Fences were one of the major uses of wood on frontier farms. They were also commonplace in the small towns and villages of early America as well. Estimates are that 3.4 million miles of fence existed in America in 1850 (Williams 1989). On the frontier, people intended fences to keep livestock out of cultivated fields. Only the "cowpens" of the backcountry—corrals brought to America from the border country of Britain—were intended to keep animals in.

The most common fence in early America, comprising an estimated 79 percent of all fences, was the snake rail—also called a zigzag or a Virginia fence. The snake rail was built by simply laying rails across each other in a zigzag pattern. This fence required more wood than other types of wood fences, but it was easy to erect, dismantle and move as farmers expanded their cultivated fields. Fences were typically seven to eight feet tall. They did not require decay-resistant wood and were constructed of what was available as farmers cleared land: black locust, eastern redcedar, chestnut, black walnut and hickory. A man could cut and split between 50 and 100 rails a day. A strong man could split 175 to 200 rails. In the South, slave masters often required slaves to split 100 rails in a day. A 10 rail high, zigzag fence sur-

Figure 10.4 Zigzag or Virginia Fence.

rounding a 160 acre field required 15,000 10-foot rails; a post and rail fence required 8,800 rails. Four miles of fence required an estimated 26,500 rails (Williams 1989).

Another common fence type was the post and rail fence. An estimated 14 percent of early fences were this type. The post and rail required less wood, but it was more permanent and required more labor to erect than the snake rail fence. These fences also required decay-resistant wood—eastern redcedar, white oak, chestnut, or black locust—for fence posts, which had to be mortised for inserting the rails. Post holes had to be dug two to three feet deep, which also increased the time required to erect the fence. The split auger—developed after 1800—made post hole digging easier and led to greater adoption of the post and rail fence. One would probably have found the post and rail fence more frequently in towns where wood was scarcer and labor more readily available than in the hinterlands (Williams 1989).

Seven percent of the fences in early America were stone fences. In New England and into eastern Pennsylvania, clearing rocky ground led to use of stone fences—the greater population density required containing livestock within fenced pasture. Another fence type was the plank fence, which was common in England and found in the earliest settlements like Plymouth. "As early as 1750 Peter Kalm made the dire prediction that the forest in Pennsylvania would last only another 40 to 50 years if the zigzag fence continued to be built" (Williams 1989). This is the earliest prediction of a timber famine in North America that this author has found—a prediction that would reappear frequently over the subsequent years.

FUEL

On a cold day in the late fall, the scent of wood smoke hangs in the air over Colonial Williamsburg. In many of the shops, taverns and houses, the people burn wood in open fireplaces as occurred throughout much of the United States until the twentieth century. Like the Indians they were displacing, the British colonists relied on wood for domestic cooking and heating. Wood was also a primary source of heat for industrial purposes such as blacksmithing and metalworking. Williams (1989) estimates that people consumed more wood for fuel over the course of American history than for any other use. Even today, it is estimated that 55 percent of the wood consumed world-wide is used for fuel (Moore 2000).

Firewood was readily available and the natural byproduct of clearing land for agriculture. Cutting, splitting and gathering firewood was labor intensive, so farmers typically cut wood in the winter when they could not do other farm work. Typically, they cut small trees for fuel—avoiding knotty or twisted stems. Hardwoods are generally denser than softwoods, producing more heat and burning longer. Softwoods also produce sparks and form creosote in the chimney, creating a fire hazard. They preferred hickory because of its density, which made it a slow burning wood that threw off a lot of heat. Oak, beech, birch, black locust and maple were also good firewood species. Farmers avoided elm because it is nearly impossible to split and difficult to dry.

How much firewood was cut? A skilled axman can cut, split and stack one to one and a half cords[2] per day. One estimate is that a typical rural homestead produced 20 to 30 cords per year. The homestead consumed at least half and sold the rest. Another estimate was that the homestead consumed 4.5 cords of fuel wood per capita per year (Williams 1989).

Urban areas experienced wood shortages. As a result, fuel wood brokers became common in cities like New York and Philadelphia. Producing firewood became a cash business for farmers (Williams 1989). For example, in the late 1850s William Tecumseh Sherman spotted a small man in a shabby army overcoat selling firewood on a street corner in St. Louis. Sherman recognized the man from their days together at West Point—a down-on-his-luck former infantry captain, U. S. Grant (Lewis 1950).

As wood prices rose, coal became competitive. In Anderson's Blacksmith Shop in Williamsburg, coal fuels the forge the same way it did during the American Revolution,

---

[2] A *cord* is a stack of roundwood measuring $4 \times 4 \times 8$ feet.

reflecting a scarcity of firewood on the James River Peninsula in the late eighteenth century.

THE COLONIAL CRAFTSMEN

Williamsburg is as notable for its living history portrayal of shopkeepers and small businesses as it is for portraying the leading historical figures of eighteenth century Virginia. Among the businesses are a number of trades and crafts that depended upon wood as their primary raw material.

Colonial Williamsburg maintains a staff of **carpenters** who are skilled in eighteenth century arts of building construction (Crews 2003a). The carpenters are more than just a living history demonstration of old fashioned tools and techniques. They are responsible for restoring and reconstructing buildings within Colonial Williamsburg. Within the past several decades they have built Anderson's Blacksmith Shop, restored the Peyton Randolph House and worked on the buildings at Great Hopes Plantation, a recreation of an eighteenth century Tidewater farm. Because of their active role in expanding and maintaining Colonial Williamsburg, their location within the restored area has changed over the years. Interested visitors should inquire at the Visitors Center to determine where the carpenters are working.

You can see the use of wood in transportation in early America in the streets of Colonial Williamsburg. Although Williamsburg does not have a carriage shop, you can see carriages, wagons and coaches throughout the restored city. The body of a carriage was typically ash, cherry and yellow-poplar. Its builders constructed the wheels and running gear of hickory and maple and paneled coaches and carriages with butternut, a lightweight wood with an attractive grain (Youngquist and Fleischer 1977).

Figure 10.5 Carriage.

There is a **wheelwright's shop** located on the grounds of the Governor's Palace. The selection of species was very important in order to keep wagons and coaches on the road. Builders typically made wheel hubs of elm. It is a species that possesses a characteristic known as "interlocking grain." *Interlocking grain* is a characteristic where the grain, or wood cells, spiral around the tree stem in opposing directions. This makes elm nearly impossible to split—an undesirable characteristic for a fuel wood but a distinct advantage for a wheel hub. Tupelo and hickory were also in use. Early wheelwrights preferred oak and ash for the spokes and wheels. These were the species used by English carriage makers, and the tradition carried to America. Later wheelwrights discovered the great usefulness of an American species, hickory, for wheels and spokes. By 1900, hickory and ash were the most expensive American hardwoods, primarily because of their use for wheels. The wheelwrights also made wheels of sycamore. Each of these species is tough, resilient and able to absorb the repeated shocks of rutted roads and heavy loads (Crews 2004).

Figure 10.6 Cooper.

Coopers, or barrel makers, were ubiquitous in early America. Visitors to Williamsburg, Old Sturbridge Village,[3] and Mystic Seaport will notice cooper's shops at each. Coopers produced barrels, casks, hogsheads, tubs, buckets, churns, firkins and pipes. Cooperage was either "slack" for containing solid material or "tight" for containing liquids. Staves for slack cooperage were red oak, maple, elm, ash, hickory, chestnut and pine. Barrel makers used white oak for tight cooperage because an encrusting substance known as "tyloses" blocks its pores (Carlsen 2008, Panshin and deZeeuw 1980).

Red oak does not generally have tyloses, making it unsuitable for tight cooperage. White oak is still used to make barrels for aging wine, brandy and whiskey. The makers char the insides of the barrels for aging bourbon (Carlsen 2008). Scotch whiskey is aged in barrels previously used to age wine or brandy. Barrel hoops could be iron or wood—oak, ash or hickory. The cooper's craft requires a high level of skill and patience. "The unglamorous yet versatile cask of the 1700s was as necessary, varied, and unremarkable as today's cardboard box" (Crews 2003b).

Basket making was a relatively common craft that required a modest amount of skill. The basket makers of colonial America commonly used ash splints and hickory.

Figure 10.7 Gunsmith.

The **gunsmith's shop** is one of the most popular trades on exhibit at Colonial Williamsburg. Gunsmiths were versatile craftsmen who were both skilled woodworkers and metal smiths. The famed rifled musket—the Kentucky or Pennsylvania rifle—was one of the most valued possessions of frontiersmen. In Williamsburg, the gunsmith operates an ingenious rifling machine that has both wood and metal components. Gunstocks used curly maple, black cherry and black walnut and stocks finished with "Nitrate of Iron"—one part nitric acid, three parts water and iron filings (Crews 2000).

The **cabinetmaker** is another of the highly talented craftsmen of Colonial Williamsburg. The furniture produced today at the Hay Cabinetmakers' Shop in Williamsburg using eighteenth century tools and techniques is superbly crafted and beautiful (Crews 2003c). Furniture makers in small towns were "generalists" who constructed plain furniture much like that constructed in the seventeenth century and often constructed houses and many other wood products. In cities, the crafts-

---

[3] Chapter 11 describes Old Sturbridge Village in Sturbridge, Massachusetts in more detail.

men were more specialized—joiners, turners, cabinetmakers, chair-makers, uphol-sterers, and carvers that were often organized along the line of the English guilds. American furniture makers copied European styles and created pieces that were not only functional but also artistically attractive (Youngquist and Fleischer 1977).

American furniture makers followed European styles and used familiar species—oak, elm, maple, pine and walnut—especially walnut (Crews 2003c). The more elegant furniture makers also used imported mahogany—a favorite in England. American species began to find favor in the eighteenth century: yellow-poplar and black cherry. Each ethnic group had distinctive styles, such as heavy Dutch furniture, brightly painted Pennsylvania German and Spanish mission. Local styles emerged as crafts-men added distinctive touches and flourishes to their work.

The twentieth century American architect Frank Lloyd Wright wrote, "We may use wood with intelligence only if we understand wood." Farmers, artisans, and crafts-men possessed a keen understanding of this group of materials. Different wood species have different properties. Some are strong, some lightweight, some springy, some easily carved or worked and some less prone to warp than others. Craftsmen, as well as farmers, learned to differentiate and specify different species for uses for which they are well suited (Youngquist and Fleischer 1977).

Youngquist and Fleischer (1977) cite the example of a rocking chair. Craftsmen may have used ten to fifteen species. They made pegs from a hard, dense wood. Softer woods cradled the load. Springy woods carried the weight. Rockers of black walnut would not creep forward like maple or hickory made slick by wear. No glue or nails were available so they inserted seasoned parts into parts of green wood so that the joint would tighten as the parts dried. Craftsmen learned to mix and match woods to overcome tendencies to warp or to take advantage of their different properties. It is a tribute to the skills of the cabinetmaker that a chair made two hundred and fifty years ago using the age-old arts of furniture making will not wobble when an average size person sits on it.

Other crafts and trades depended upon wood tools and wood machines. The weaver spun her wool on a wooden spinning wheel and wove her fabric on a wooden loom. She used tree roots and berries to make dyes for the yarn and cloth. The printer set type in a wooden printing press. The shoemaker used a wooden last to shape the leather and wooden shoe heels connected to the uppers with wooden pegs. The brick maker shaped bricks in a wooden mold before firing them in a wood-fired oven. All of the various trades used wooden tools or wood-handled tools.

A final craftsman housed at the Hay Cabinetmaker Shop deserves special mention. He is Peter Redstone, a harpsichord maker (Crews 2002). The harpsichord was one of the most complicated musical instruments made from wood, but it was not the only one. As visitors tour Colonial Williamsburg, they may see and hear mandolins, violins, fifes and drums, all made from wood. "In retrospect life in early America was not only made possible, but it was made beau-tiful by wood" (Youngquist and Fleischer 1977).

Figure 10.8 Harpsichord Maker.

Homework

Name: _____   **Date:** _____

Visit the website for Colonial Williamsburg (*http://www.history.org*) and read one of the articles on a Colonial trade. Write a one paragraph summary below about what you learned.

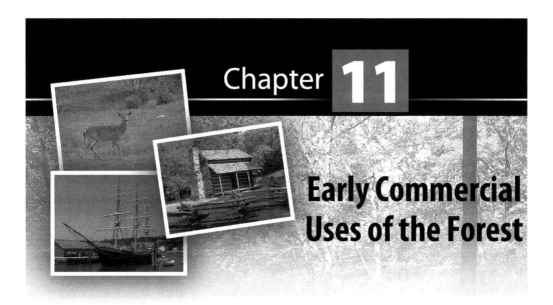

Chapter 11

Early Commercial Uses of the Forest

Even before the Revolution, cities of the Eastern Seaboard were beginning a transformation from an agrarian to a commercial society. But the Industrial Revolution that began in England in the eighteenth century did not take root in the United States until the beginning to middle of the nineteenth.

REGIONAL ECONOMIES IN BRITAIN AND NORTH AMERICA

Immigrants, with the unhappy exception of African slaves, came to America because they believed they would have the opportunity for a better life in the New World. The means to that end was land ownership and readily available resources. But what made opportunity possible was a level of personal freedom, especially the right to own and control property, unknown in Europe. As a result, the average colonist in the British colonies at the time of the Revolution had achieved a remarkable level of prosperity (Gordon 2004, McCullough 2005).

New Englanders established a manufacturing economy supported by coastal seaports and fishing villages much the same as East Anglia. The pattern of small villages, agriculture and commerce followed the pattern of the eastern counties of England. Farming practices also followed the patterns of eastern England. They used English ploughs rather than hoes as used elsewhere in British America (Fischer 1989). The beginning of industrialization in America took place in New England with the establishment of the textile industry in 1790.

The elite of Virginia created huge, self-sufficient plantations based upon the tobacco trade with England. Servants, laborers and artisans lived in quarters and operated small shops surrounding the "Great House" of each estate (Fischer 1989). The dominant crops were tobacco and, later, cotton; both were export products. Slaves became the predominant source of labor. The economy of the South remained largely based upon single-crop agriculture worked by slaves until the Civil War (Deans 2007, Ellis 2004). However, George Washington had converted his estate at Mount Vernon to a more diversified agriculture similar to the farm economy of Pennsylvania. At the end of his life Washington was unique among the prominent southerners of the American Revolution in freeing his slaves in his will (Ellis 2004). One must wonder how American history might have changed had other southern planters followed Washington's example.

Like New England, Pennsylvania and the Delaware Valley blended manufacturing, merchant and agricultural economies. German immigrants were largely responsible for developing the region west of Philadelphia into the nation's most productive farmland at the time of the Revolution. Likewise, the freedom and tolerance of Penn's Quaker philosophy allowed Philadelphia to develop into the cultural and economic "Athens of America."

The borderers tended to migrate to the frontiers. As such, they resorted to subsistence agriculture as the most common means of support. As more people ventured west, the trappings of civilization followed. Towns grew and rudimentary industry became established to support the farming communities. Typically, the first business established in a frontier community was a grist mill for grinding grain into flour (Williams 1989).

THE AGRARIAN ECONOMY AND ITS IMPACT ON FORESTS

The greatest loss of forest in the United States from the time of European discovery to the present resulted from the clearing of forest for agriculture. Much of the loss took place in the eastern United States, and nearly all took place prior to 1900. The U.S. Forest Service estimates that 1.03 billion acres of forest existed in the U.S. in 1630. In 2007, approximately 751 million acres of forest remained (two-thirds of the forest acreage of 1630). Forest cover has remained relatively constant since 1910 (Alvarez 2007, Kellogg 1909, Smith et al. 2009).

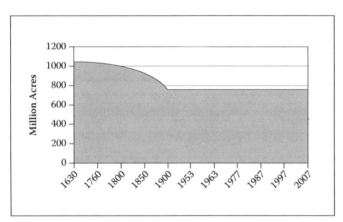

Figure 11.1 Forested Acres in the U.S.

Wood was the primary resource used to construct homes and farm buildings, to make furnishings and household implements and to make tools. The use of wood for the items of everyday life was ubiquitous. In spite of all the well-known and clever uses of wood on the pioneer farm, the volume of timber used for these items paled in comparison to the quantity of timber felled to clear fields, make fences and potash, to build farm structures and for use as fuel.

Europeans cleared the land more extensively than the Indians. They cleared bottomlands and hilltops and replaced the mosaic of forest, savannah and grassland established by Indian burning practices by a more or less open landscape. Europeans established permanent settlements rather than semi-permanent villages; they had domesticated animals and planted domesticated grasses and grains (Cronon 1983, Williams 1989).

Increasing population resulted in a greater demand for croplands and for forest products. Researchers estimate that it required three to four acres of farmland to feed each person in the United States in the nineteenth century (MacCleery 1994a). In 1700, the European population in the British colonies of what is now the U.S. was approximately 0.25 million. By 1760, the population had expanded to 1.6 million and by 1790 to 3.9 million. By 1810, the population had nearly doubled again to approximately seven million people.

Figure 11.2 Tools and Farm Implements. *Old Sturbridge Village, MA.*

European settlers first claimed abandoned Indian fields for their farmsteads. As Indian populations were pushed westward in advance of settlement, forests reclaimed areas cleared by indigenous burning. Pioneers quickly learned to place varying value upon forest land. They avoided low ground because of the prevalence of malaria. Sloping ground was more valuable than flat ground because it drained without effort by the farmer, and it was easier to clear forest since it was not as dense. Farmers judged soil fertility by the species of trees found on the land. They initially considered grassland infertile, later

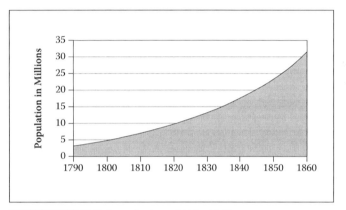

Figure 11.3 U.S. Population: 1790–1860.

calling it desert or barrens. They thought that larger trees, luxuriant growth and the presence of hardwoods indicated fertile soil and that pines indicated dry, sandy, infertile soil (Williams 1989).

Settlers cleared forest by two methods—chopping down trees or girdling them. Cutting was more common in New England and Pennsylvania and those regions settled by people from those two areas—Kentucky, Ohio, New York and Tennessee. The Germans of Pennsylvania were known to cut rather than to girdle trees. The Swedes who first settled the Delaware Valley were said to have completely cleared the trees and stumps. In New Netherlands, the Dutch cut the trees and burned the residue. In most cases, stumps were too difficult to remove so farmers planted between them (Williams 1989). Early American farmers frequently employed fire in much the same manner as Indians to prepare for a new rotation of crops and to dispose of slash in newly cleared fields (Pyne 1982).

Estimates are that the typical pioneer in western New York took 10 years to clear between 30 and 40 acres. Others estimate that a skilled axman could clear an acre a day, while others claimed 7 to 10 days (Williams 1989).

In the South, girdling was the more common way to clear forest. After branches fell from dead timber, the pioneer would pile it around the standing stems and set it ablaze. It was more economical in terms of labor.

Settlers permitted livestock to graze freely in the forest. The razorback hog, probably descended from those brought to America by De Soto, roamed freely throughout the eastern woodlands in great numbers and became the primary source of protein for pioneer families. It was not until the late nineteenth century that pork was surpassed as the most widely used meat in America. Pork was often salted and packed in barrels. A full pork barrel was a symbol of plenty. Scraping the bottom of the barrel meant hard times. Continuing Indian burning practices ensured a continuing supply of grasses for cattle and mast for swine.

POTASH

Potash—potassium carbonate—is the raw material used for making lye. It was produced by burning logs out in the open then collecting the ashes and sending them to an ashery that repeatedly leached them by pouring water over them and evaporating the water in a large iron pot. When potash was boiled, the residue was lye, a strong alkali used to make soap. Pioneers also used lye in glass making, tanning, bleaching and cleaning wool, as well as printing calico and making saltpeter for the production of gunpowder (Williams 1989).

Potash was a natural byproduct of clearing land for agriculture and a ready source of cash (one of the few) for farmers, allowing them to purchase goods they could not readily produce on their own. Researchers estimate that it required an acre of hardwood trees to produce a ton of potash. Settlers used potash domestically and also exported it to Britain.

THE LUMBER INDUSTRY PRIOR TO THE CIVIL WAR

The two-man, manual pit saw was no match for the mechanization provided by a water-powered sawmill. The first sawmill in America reportedly became established prior to 1633 on the falls of the Piscataqua River near York, Maine (Williams 1989, Youngquist and Fleischer 1977). Sawmills rapidly spread across the Eastern Seaboard to supply the lumber for construction of the growing settlements. It is an indication of the importance of wood in America that sawmills appeared in America before they did in England.

As settlement expanded, the first industries in frontier communities were grist mills and sawmills. The Census Bureau recorded statistics of manufacturing industries for the first time in 1850. At that time, lumber manufacturing ranked second only to flour and gristmills, accounting for 5.9 percent of all manufacturing in the United States. It is likely that its place among manufacturing industries was similar through previous decades of the eighteenth and nineteenth centuries. Sawmills in frontier communities typically operated as a part-time or seasonal business to supplement the income of a farmer. When other farmers cleared land, they would bring logs to the sawmill for conversion into planks and lumber for constructing barns, houses, sheds and furnishings. Payment was often "in kind" among the cash-strapped frontier farmers with the sawmiller keeping part of the lumber for his own use or sale. Sometimes they accepted crops or livestock in payment (Williams 1989).

A mill wheel powered early water-powered mills in an up-and-down motion. The blades were stationary with the logs either pushed or mechanically ratcheted into the blade. The sawmill was an ingenious machine consisting of a straight blade held in a frame or sash and moved by the waterwheel by means of a system of wooden wheels, cogs and cranks. Builders preferred hickory, a very tough, strong, shock-resistant wood, for use in the machinery of these early sawmills (Youngquist and Fleischer 1977). The technology was crude by today's standards but a vast improvement over the pit saw, increasing productivity from an estimated 100 to 200 lineal feet per day to 500 to 3,000 feet per day.

You may see a working, water-powered sawmill today at Old Sturbridge Village[1] in Massachusetts. Old Sturbridge Village is a living history museum that recreates a New England farming village of the 1830s. Like Williamsburg, Old Sturbridge impresses visitors with the widespread use and utility of wood in everyday American life.

Shipbuilding, the merchant trade and the growing textile industries of New England led to the development of a more permanent lumber industry. Until

Figure 11.4 Water-Powered Sawmill. *Old Sturbridge Village, MA.*

approximately 1850, Maine was the leading lumber manufacturing state in the nation. Settlers prized its forests of eastern white pine not only for shipbuilding but also for the construction of houses, businesses and factories. Sawmills were located on rivers because water was necessary to power the mills and to transport logs from the forest to the mill.

Winter was the season for logging. The frozen ground made it easy to "skid" or drag logs behind teams of horses or oxen to a log landing on the frozen rivers. Loggers, often living in logging camps in the woods, worked from sunrise to sunset chopping, sawing, limbing and skidding logs to the landings. In the spring, when melting snow and ice swelled the rivers, they floated the logs downriver to the sawmill. Logs often became jammed against rocks or along the banks of rivers. To clear the rivers and keep the logs floating toward the mills, loggers would engage in the dangerous task of river driving, leaping from log to log and prying apart jams with long poles or chopping logs to clear the more difficult jams.

Logging was—and remains—hard and dangerous work. Like sailors, and later railroad workers, loggers secured a permanent place in American folklore, particularly in the tall tales of Paul Bunyan (Schlosser 2008).

THE TIMBER TRADE

American involvement in the international timber trade began about 1640 at the end of the Puritans' Great Migration. The New England ports of Falmouth, Portsmouth, Salem, Marblehead, Boston, Fall River, Providence, New London and New Haven shipped their products to Britain, the West Indies, Spain, Portugal, and the Wine Islands of the Azores, Madeira and the Canaries. Return journeys brought back molasses, rum and cotton from the West Indies, wine from the Mediterranean and slaves from Africa. Cargoes also included tropical timber such as mahogany. "Only

---

[1] The website for Old Sturbridge Village is *http://www.osv.org/*.

premium-quality timber products were exported" due to the economics of transport (Williams 1989). The ports shipped masts, potash and naval stores to Britain and white oak barrels and pipe staves to the Wine Islands of the Azores. They sent white oak staves for rum casks and red oak for sugar and molasses barrels and hogsheads to the West Indies—every 100 acres of sugar cane required 80 1,000 pound hogsheads for sugar and 20 for molasses. As the settlers depleted the timber of the Indies in the mid-seventeenth century, exports of planks, boards, clapboards, and shingles from New England became common.

The New England merchant trade required a shipbuilding industry and sawmills to support it. Reportedly, 20 sawmills lined the Piscataqua inlet by 1665. The customs returns from 1768 to 1772 have survived, giving us an indication of the extent of the timber trade (Williams 1989). Piscataqua was the leading exporter of sawn lumber (two-thirds was white pine, one-third was oak). Philadelphia exported oak staves. Piscataqua shipped pine and oak shingles from New Hampshire and Maine; and the James River ports of Virginia shipped red cedar and cypress shingles. A number of American ports shipped naval stores and potash (Williams 1989).

CHARCOAL AND IRON-MAKING

The early American iron industry depended upon wood as its primary energy source. To generate sufficient heat, the industry converted wood to charcoal through a controlled process of incomplete combustion. It manufactured charcoal by stacking wood in a "hearth" and covering the pile with dirt before setting a fire to the pile. A chimney at the top of the heath let in enough air to permit the wood to smolder for up to two weeks. The resulting charcoal fueled the iron furnaces. The work of the charcoal makers, known as "colliers," was filthy, arduous labor that required round the clock tending of the hearths (Williams 1989).

Iron making required large quantities of charcoal. Making charcoal for one day's operation of an iron furnace required the consumption of an estimated 1 to 6 acres of hardwood forest. Williams (1989) estimates that every ton of pig iron produced consumed150 acres. Only 11 of 173 iron furnaces in England were using charcoal as fuel in 1806. The rest were using coal. In contrast, 439 of 560 American furnaces burned charcoal as late as 1856.

Each furnace had to own several thousand acres of forest to support its operations, and those forests were clear-cut every 20 to 30 years. Hardwoods were preferable over softwoods in charcoal production because hardwoods tend to be denser, burn longer and provide more heat per volume burned. By 1840, many eastern iron furnaces were abandoned due to a "scarcity of timber" (Hillstrom and Hillstrom 2005).

Figure 11.5 Covered Bridge. *Bedford County, PA.*

WOOD IN TRANSPORTATION

Wood was the primary material for building a transportation system in America's early years. Riverboats, ferries and barges were of wooden construction as were the ocean-going sailing ships. Wharves, docks and piers also were of wood.

Road systems also relied on wood. Bridges were constructed from timbers with plank decks. Oftentimes, roads were "corduroyed" by laying logs across the road to provide a dry, but very bumpy surface. Wheeled transportation—wagons, carriages, carts and shays—were primarily of wood construction. Bridges were of stone or wood. The covered bridge protected the deck from the weather, extending the service lives of timbers and decking.

Construction, however, remained one of the principal uses of wood. But local timber shortages, the high price of labor and westward expansion would radically change how Americans build houses.

Homework

Name: _____   Date: _____

Refer to the reference by Smith et al. 2009 (*http://nrs.fs.fed.us/pubs/gtr/gtr_wo78.pdf*). Look up the following information for your home state:

Home State: _____

What was the estimated forested acreage in your home state in each of the following years?

1630:

1907:

1963:

2002:

What are some of the causes of the trend from 1907 to 2002?

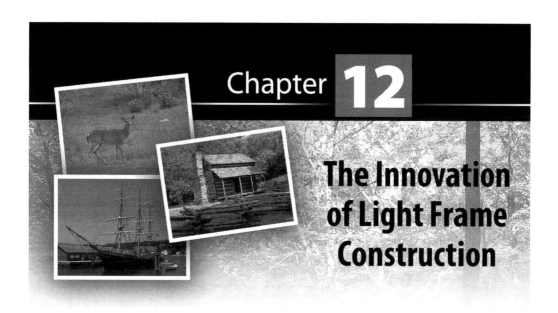

Chapter 12

The Innovation of Light Frame Construction

In Colonial America, houses were generally either framed with large timbers or were backcountry log cabins. In 1833, home building radically changed as increasing population, declining resources, westward expansion, technological advancement and American ingenuity converged. The result was a revolutionary new concept in building construction that Americans have used (with some modification) for more than 175 years.

POPULATION, WESTWARD EXPANSION AND FORESTS

The Treaty of Paris established the original boundaries of the United States in 1783. The treaty, which brought a formal end to the American Revolution, ceded approximately 890,000 square miles to the United States and included the original thirteen states plus what would become the states of Maine, Ohio, Michigan, Indiana, Illinois, Wisconsin, Kentucky, Tennessee and parts of Alabama, Mississippi and Minnesota. In 1803, President Thomas Jefferson purchased the Louisiana Territory from France for approximately fifteen million dollars. The Louisiana Purchase almost doubled the size of the United States by adding almost 830,000 square miles. Florida was annexed from Spain in 1819, adding another 70,000 square miles to the United States.

America's population grew rapidly in the era between the War of Independence and the Civil War. Expanding population and the concept of "manifest destiny" drove the westward expansion of the new nation to the Mississippi and beyond. At the time of the first census in 1790, 3,894,000 people populated sixteen states. In 1832, 12,786,000 Americans lived in

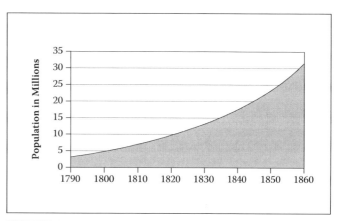

Figure 12.1 U.S. Population: 1790–1860.

twenty-four states. At the outbreak of the Civil War in 1861, 31,184,000 people lived in thirty-four states. Westward expansion had grown into the prairies of Illinois and Wisconsin.

Agrarian economies supported the new states, but the northeast was becoming more populous and more industrialized. Farms had replaced clearings and forests, and settlers had cut over forests near population centers. As a result, wood required transport over greater distances to get to the majority of American consumers. This resulted in increased harvests of timber to meet the needs for wood of a growing population. It also resulted in increasingly efficient means of harvest, lumber production, transportation and distribution of wood to the market.

As the nation grew, the growing lumber industry shifted its base of operations westward. In the late eighteenth and early nineteenth centuries, Maine was the primary lumber-producing state. The preference for eastern white pine as a construction material led to the diminishment of the timber supply in Maine. Northern New York had forests of old growth white pine and the center of lumber production shifted from Maine to New York in the early nineteenth century. By the time of the Civil War, Pennsylvania had taken New York's place as the leading lumber producing state.

A migratory pattern was emerging where the industry would move from a region where the timber was cut over to a region where it could find virgin timber. The Lake States, primarily Michigan, were growing as centers of the emerging lumber industry in the first half of the nineteenth century. They would become the leading wood-producing region until the twentieth century when the great stands of eastern white pine were finally cut over (Youngquist and Fleischer 1977, Williams 1989).

It is difficult for twenty-first century Americans to accept this practice, but prevailing values and attitudes among the American public were much different than they are today. America was a predominantly agricultural society. Settlers considered removing trees from the land beneficial as it made more cleared land available for farming. Much of the logging was on public land and clearing land of trees made it more attractive to homesteaders. The national priority of the era was to populate the continent, not to conserve its natural resources.

In addition, most Americans believed that the forests of the United States were inexhaustible. However, as regions of the country such as Maine were logged, it took decades for new forests to grow to replace those cut. As a result, the supply of timber was farther removed from the population centers of the Eastern Seaboard. Transportation systems would be constructed to get goods from the western farms and forests to the growing cities of the east.

IMPROVEMENTS IN TRANSPORTATION

Westward expansion went hand in hand with improvements in the American transportation system during the early eighteenth century. Pioneers built a number of canals to help transport goods from farms and forests ever farther removed from major population centers. In 1825, the Erie Canal opened, linking the Great Lakes to the Hudson River. Businesses could ship lumber from the sawmills of Michigan, Wisconsin and Minnesota to western New York via the Great Lakes, load it onto barges bound for Albany on the Erie Canal and then ship it downriver on the Hudson to New York City. The Erie Canal cut the cost of shipping a ton of goods from $100 to $10 (Burton 2007, Lienhard 1999). Subsequent canal systems opened the waterways of the interior of the continent to expanded trade.

Improvements in transportation led to the development of more efficient business methods for getting products to market. Lumber wholesale centers sprang to life in Albany, New York, at the eastern terminus of the Erie Canal, and at Buffalo and Tonawanda, New York, where the Erie Canal and Great Lakes waterways met (Williams 1989). To the west, another great transportation hub was emerging at Chicago, a site that linked the Great Lakes to the Mississippi Valley. Lumber was one of the most important products flowing through the wholesale markets of Chicago.[1]

IMPROVEMENTS IN LUMBER AND WOOD PRODUCTS PRODUCTION

The steam engine also revolutionized transportation in America. In 1807, Robert Fulton attempted to use steam to power the riverboat "Clermont." Within a few years, steamboats plied most major river systems from the Hudson to the Mississippi. In 1828, the Baltimore and Ohio Railroad began laying track. In 1830, the Baltimore & Ohio's "Tom Thumb" locomotive began pulling passengers between Baltimore and Ellicott City, a distance of 13.5 miles. In 1833, railroads and steam-powered riverboats were very new. By the start of the Civil War in 1861, railroads connected many eastern cities with the interior.

Concurrently, the lumber industry was harnessing steam power. The first steam-powered sawmill was developed in 1811. However, this innovation was slow to catch on as water power still dominated most production until the 1870s. Once steam replaced water, productivity increased to up to 40,000 board feet[2] per day.

Other innovations were revolutionizing the industry. The invention of the edger, capable of cutting lumber with parallel edges, occurred in 1825. William Wordsworth of Poughkeepsie, New York, invented the planer in 1828, which could mechanically smooth the surface of a board. Soon a planing mill industry emerged, capable of producing mouldings and trim that craftsmen previously had to carve or shape with hand planes. Mechanization of these processes enabled American entrepreneurs to create businesses that produced doors, windows, stairway parts and mouldings in factories at a lower cost to consumers (Williams 1989).

At the same time, furniture production and other wood products industries became more mechanized. Mechanization eliminated the need for highly skilled craftsmen and enabled mass production of similar products, thus reducing labor costs. Businesses were becoming more specialized, and companies that could afford better and faster equipment gained an advantage over their competition on the open market. Mechanization spurred invention and creativity as woodworkers constantly sought better ways to produce their products.

THE PROBLEM OF HOUSING ON THE GREAT PLAINS

Timber framing is a labor intensive way to build a house. In the early nineteenth century, the scarcity of local supplies of high quality timber was driving up housing costs on the Eastern Seaboard. Skilled labor was becoming scarce and increasingly

---

[1] Within a few decades, Chicago would become the principal railroad hub of the north central states. It maintained its importance as a lumber wholesale and transportation center well into the twentieth century.

[2] The board foot is the standard unit of measure for lumber in the United States and Canada. It is equivalent to a board 1-inch thick, 12-inches wide, and 12-inches long (144 cubic inches or 1/12 cubic foot).

expensive, particularly in the emerging towns and cities of the frontier. In the forested regions of the frontier, people were still building log cabins.[3] In the cities of the Eastern Seaboard, transportation costs were driving up the costs of timber frame houses. During this era, people were moving onto the Great Plains where wood was scarce. Sod houses were no solution. A serious housing problem was developing. Nowhere was this problem felt more acutely than in the growing transportation center of Chicago.

Industrialization was the key to solving the housing problem. In 1795, Jacob Perkins patented a nail-making machine that could cut nails from sheets of iron. This resulted in considerable increases in production efficiency when compared to forging nails in a blacksmith shop. Over the next few decades, nail production kept improving and prices dropped steadily.

Improved lumber production created other possibilities. In addition, improvements in transportation made it feasible to transport wood economically from greater distances. The solution to the housing problem was within reach and simply required the right touch of creative genius.

BALLOON FRAMING

In 1833, Augustine Taylor designed and built St. Mary's Church in Chicago using a revolutionary framing system. Instead of heavy timbers that required labor intensive mortise and tenon connections, Taylor used smaller, lighter framing members spaced 16 to 18 inches apart. Nails connected the **studs** (the vertical members that make up the wall frame), the **joists** (horizontal members that support the floor) and the **rafters** (roof framing). Construction of the 24 by 36-foot structure cost $400 (Lienhard 1993, Spence 1993).

Balloon framing starts with a 2 by 4-inch or wider **sill** connected flat on the top of the foundation wall with anchor bolts. Floor joists—typically 2 by 8-inch, 2 by 10-inch, or 2 by 12-inch members[4]—rested on and were nailed to the sills (or sometimes a large supporting beam for lengthier spans between foundation walls). The exterior wall studs—2 by 4-inch members as long as the height of the exterior wall—also rested on the sill and were nailed to the sill and joist. The studs were notched at the height of upper floors and ceiling and a 1 by 10-inch[5] horizontal **ribbon** was "let in" to the notches in the joists to support upper floor and ceiling joists. Nailing connected the ribbon to the studs and the joists to the ribbon and studs. A top **plate** consisting of two 2 by 4-inch members laid horizontally across the tops of the studs connected the top of the wall system together. The rafters that supported the roof—typically 2 by 8-inch or 2 by-10 inch members—were notched and nailed to the top plate. A ridge board connected the rafters at the peak of the roof (Anderson 1970).

Planks nailed diagonally across the floor joists formed a **subfloor**. The house frame was clad with solid wood **sheathing**—typically 1 by 6-inch to 1 by 10-inch boards nailed diagonally to the studs and rafters. The diagonal application of subfloor and sheathing braced the rectangular framing to form a rigid, triangular structure in the house.

---

[3] As late as 1855, 20 percent of all farm families in New York were living in log cabins.

[4] Framing lumber is manufactured in 2-inch incremental widths, i.e., 2 by 4, 2 by 6, 2 by 8, 2 by 10 and 2 by 12. Lengths are manufactured in 2-foot increments from 8 to as much as 24 feet.

[5] Later, builders found that 1 by 4-inch ribbons were adequate support for the floor joists and replaced the 1 by 10-inch boards.

Carpenters made fun of Taylor's design, calling it a "balloon frame" because they thought it was likely to blow away like a balloon in the first heavy wind. The name stuck, and so did the framing style. Balloon frame houses were, in fact, strong. "The multiple-member construction and nonweight-bearing walls anticipated the steel-framed skyscraper" (Youngquist and Fleischer 1977).

Builders could now construct houses using light framing elements, nails and semi-skilled labor at a fraction of the cost of heavy timber framing. They wasted less wood in sawing light framing from a log than in hewing or sawing timber framing.[6] They could easily cut framing to specific shapes and sizes on the construction site and eliminate the labor-intensive processes of mortising, tenoning, drilling and pegging connections.

Light framing was cheaper to transport to the marketplace because it is smaller, lighter and easier to handle than timbers or logs. Packaging it was easy. The lumber could be dried at the sawmill, reducing its shipping weight.

An American family could afford to build a modest balloon frame house for a few hundred dollars. Some say that Chicago and San Francisco could not have been built without light framing. Housing costs would otherwise have been prohibitive. Augustine Taylor's ingenuity enabled the United States to become a "nation of homeowners" (Youngquist and Fleischer 1977).

Creative marketing went hand in hand with innovative construction. Some companies sold pre-cut house "kits" through a catalog. They cut materials to shape in a factory and shipped them to a job site. Sears and Roebuck sold approximately 100,000 "catalog houses" between 1908 and 1940. By 1854, companies had emerged that specialized in making doors, windows and staircases.

Figure 12.2 Victorian House. *San Francisco, CA.*

Light framing also revolutionized housing design. Timber framing was limited geometrically to construction of "boxy" houses with rectangular plans and shapes. Log cabins were even more restrictive in design flexibility. Balloon framing and advances in automated woodworking allowed more angles, curves and embellishments typical of the Victorian-era house. Plaster and lath covering interior walls permitted high ceilings. Builders could place interior, non load-bearing partitions anywhere, permitting flexibility in interior design.

The great disadvantage of balloon framing was fire. The Chicago Fire of 1871 and the San Francisco earthquake and fire of 1906 revealed the fire hazard inherent in balloon frame construction in tragic fashion. The long stud cavities that ran the full height of the houses each served as a small chimney, allowing fire to spread rapidly up the walls of the houses. Fire also quickly consumed the light framing because of its high surface-to-volume ratio. By comparison, a heavy timber will develop a layer of char that insulates the core of

Figure 12.3 Victorian Houses. *San Francisco, CA.*

---

[6] The geometry of producing rectangular products from a cylindrical raw material.

Figure 12.4 Victorian House. *New Bedford, MA.*

wood, allowing a timber frame to retain some structural integrity during a fire. Municipalities began requiring "fire stops"—short pieces of 2 by 4s nailed horizontally between the studs at each floor. This increased the cost of balloon framing.

PLATFORM FRAMING

The fire hazard inherent in balloon framing, the safety concerns in erecting a two story wall system and the increasing scarcity and cost of longer, high quality 2 by 4s led to the modification of balloon framing. Construction practices changed with the emergence of platform framing after the First World War. A platform frame is still a light frame structure. The biggest difference between it and balloon framing is in the framing of the floors and the length of the studs.

Like balloon framing, the first floor joists rest on a sill connected to the foundation. Builders lay the headers, which are the same width as the joists, on edge around the perimeter of the house, resting on the outer side of the sills. They nail the subfloor directly to the joists and header and build the walls upon this platform floor system.

Figure 12.5 Platform Framing. *Note that the wall frame is one story in height.*

If they desire a second story, it rests on an upper platform that rests on the first floor wall system. The studs are a single story in length—most often eight feet.

Platform framing represented an improvement in safety and cost, but it made the angles, curves and embellishments of the Victorian houses more difficult and expensive to construct. As a result, designs have changed to the rectangular shapes reminiscent of the era of timber framing.

The platform frame house is the most common design used in the United States although materials have changed dramatically from the solid, sawn wood used a century ago. Plywood panels and later oriented strandboard (OSB) replaced solid wood sheathing and subfloor after World War II. Builders frequently use roof trusses constructed of cheaper 2 by 4s in place of wider rafters cut and erected into a roof system on the construction site. Houses built in the past two decades frequently have floor trusses or engineered wood I-joists instead of solid wood joists. However, the principals of platform construction remain the same.

Today, the construction of most American houses utilizes Augustine Taylor's concept of light framing with nailed joints. As such, they are simply a modification of balloon framing. But things are changing. Light framing is giving way to more complex engineered wood composites and panelized housing. The next era of transformation of residential construction is taking place today. And it is bringing new opportunities for innovation and creativity.

Homework

Name: _____ Date: _____

Look up and write down the definitions of the following terms:

Joist:

Stud:

Rafter:

Subfloor:

Sheathing:

Plywood:

Oriented Strandboard (OSB):

Truss:

The Industrial Revolution and the American Conservation Movement

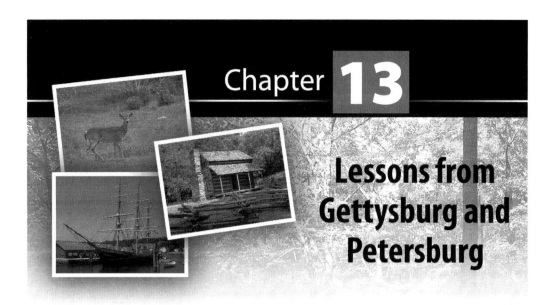

Chapter 13

Lessons from Gettysburg and Petersburg

The Civil War marks one of the most important turning points in American history. The war effort involved a massive mobilization of people, industrial might and national energy to fight the war. In the narrow view of a history of forest resources, it marks a dramatic upsurge in the pace of industrialization in the United States. The transformation occurred in its forests, sawmills, farms, shipyards and rail yards.

The Civil War transformed a nation and its character. People now viewed longstanding concepts of liberty such as states rights and property rights more skeptically as they had been used to justify secession, slavery and the subsequent legalized racial discrimination of the post-Reconstruction era. It also changed government. In order to fight the war, the power of the federal government was necessarily increased, and governments are historically reluctant to give up power once established.

The war offers examples of how changing landscapes affect our interpretation of historical events. Historical events also influence how people view and decide to manage the land. The Battle of Gettysburg provides several examples.

The hardship and tragedy of war changed people. Former soldiers and officers came out of the war to lead the United States into the twentieth century. Ordinary people who may have led ordinary lives in time of peace rose to prominence in post-war government, industry and public affairs.[1] Perhaps no one rose more dramatically from obscurity during the war than Ulysses S. Grant. Some historians consider Grant the first modern warrior. In terms of his understanding and use of the most up-to-date technological advances in warfare, he may very well be. As such, the Civil War story of this remarkable American serves to portray the industrial and technological changes taking place in the United States. The Petersburg Campaign of 1864–1865 offers an example of Grant's mastery of transportation, communication and supply.

---

[1] Several of these people, including Grenville Mellen Dodge, Wade Hampton and John Wesley Powell, would play prominent roles in the history of America's forest resources.

Gettysburg: July 1–3, 1863

On June 30, 1863, approximately 160,000 men of the Confederate Army of Northern Virginia and the Union Army of the Potomac were converging on the small town of Gettysburg in rural Adams County, Pennsylvania. For three days, the two armies would entangle in the bloodiest battle in American history. When the smoke cleared, approximately 45,400 men of the two armies were casualties[2] (Sears 2003).

The Confederacy was in a period of crisis in the spring of 1863, with U. S. Grant's Army of the Tennessee poised to cut the Confederacy in two at Vicksburg, Mississippi. When Vicksburg fell, Union armies would control the Mississippi River and most of the territory along its navigable tributaries. General Robert E. Lee received permission from Jefferson Davis to risk everything in an invasion of Pennsylvania (Bowden and Ward 2001). Lee won a tactical masterpiece at the Battle of Chancellorsville in early May and sought to end the war by winning a decisive victory over the Army of the Potomac north of Washington, D.C. General George Meade received promotion to command the Army of the Potomac three days before the opening shots of the Battle of Gettysburg. At this point in the war, Lee was recognized as one of the very best military commanders the United States had ever produced. Meade was a respected general but had never exercised independent command of an army.

Figure 13.1 Robert E. Lee.

Courtesy of the Library of Congress Prints and Photographs Division. Reproduction number: LC-USZ62-11452

The Stand of the 154th New York: July 1

Approximately 2,400 people lived in Gettysburg on July 1, 1863 (Trudeau 2002). The size of the town has grown to approximately 7,500 according to the 2000 Census. Expansion of the town resulted in areas of the battlefield that housing and other developments now obliterate. A case in point is a site on Coster Avenue in a residential neighborhood where 235 men of the 154th New York Infantry regiment made a stand against attacking Confederates. In 1863, this area was a brickyard surrounded by open fields and pasture lands northeast of the town.

On July 1, Confederate forces routed two divisions of the 11th Corps north of Gettysburg. Three regiments, including the 154th, were rushed into the fight to delay the Confederate advance. The brigade made a stand northeast of town, where the 154th formed a line behind a fence between two other regiments. As Confederates converged on the thin line of Federals, the regiments on either side of 154th broke and ran leaving the New Yorkers to face an overwhelming number of Confederates on their own. The 154th did their job, delaying the Confederates and buying time for their comrades to escape to the high ground south of town. But they did so at tremen-

---

[2] People often confuse the number of "casualties" with the number of dead. Casualty figures include wounded, missing and captured soldiers in addition to the dead. Reported Union casualties at Gettysburg were 22,813, including 3,149 dead. The Confederates lost an estimated 22,625 or 22,874 (depending upon the source) casualties, including 4,536 dead (Sears 2003, Trudeau 2002).

dous cost. Nearly surrounded, almost all of the regiment's officers and men were killed, wounded or captured (Trudeau 2002).

Today a monument stands on the site where the 154th fought. Behind it, a mural painted by Mark Dunkelman, a Providence, Rhode Island artist and a descendant of a soldier of the 154th, portrays the regiment's stand on what would otherwise be an ugly concrete-block wall of a warehouse (Dunkelman 2006). Because of its location in downtown Gettysburg, the site of the 154th New York Monument is off the beaten path for battlefield visitors. For those who do seek

Figure 13.2 154th New York Infantry Monument and Mural. *Gettysburg.*

out the site of the 154th's stand, it is nearly impossible to visualize the action that took place on July 1, 1863 except through Mr. Dunkelman's mural. We have largely forgotten the heroism of the men of the 154th.

LITTLE ROUND TOP: JULY 2

One of the best known sites on the Gettysburg battlefield is Little Round Top. Located at what was the southern end of the Union line, it was the scene of one of the bitterest struggles of the battle. The post-war writings of two officers who faced each other on the afternoon of July 2 bring the valor of the officers and men who fought on Little Round Top sharply into focus. Colonel Joshua Lawrence Chamberlain of the 20th Maine regiment had been a professor at Bowdoin College before the war and was perhaps the finest writer among all of the Civil War veterans to have penned his story

after the war. His writings remain compelling, and his descriptions of the actions of the 20th were one of the principal sources for Michael Shaara's Pulitzer Prize-winning novel *The Killer Angels* and the 1993 film *Gettysburg.* Chamberlain's Confederate counterpart, Colonel William C. Oates of the 15th Alabama, also wrote his recollections of the war and, although less well known than Chamberlain, his writings added to the tales of the heroism of the men who fought on the slopes of that hill.

On July 2, Lee ordered an attack on the Union left by General James Longstreet's corps. Success of Longstreet's attack was a near thing. The fight in Peach Orchard and Devil's Den nearly destroyed the Union 3rd Corps. Fighting in the Wheatfield was perhaps the bloodiest in the battle. But the struggle for Little Round Top eclipses the rest in terms of Americans' knowledge of the battle.

Figure 13.3 Joshua Lawrence Chamberlain.

Courtesy of the Library of Congress Prints and Photographs Division. Reproduction number: LC-B81/2-1859

One can make a compelling case that over time historians have exaggerated the importance of Little Round Top on the outcome of the battle (Bowden and Ward 2001, Harman 2003). In 1863, the west face of Little Round Top—the side facing the Confederate lines—had been cleared of trees (at it is today). It was steep and rocky, a difficult slope to assault as the Confederates did on July 2. Timber covered the east slope, which was not as steep as the west slope. This slope was not visible to Confederate troops and was the route used by Union infantry and artillery to reach the summit in order to defend the hill from the Confederate attack.

Figure 13.4 Little Round Top. *West slope of Little Round Top from the Devil's Den, Gettysburg.*

Perhaps the most commonly held myth is that if the Confederates had taken Little Round Top, their artillery would have been able to sweep the Union lines on Cemetery Ridge, leading to a likely Confederate victory. There are two problems with that myth. Visitors to Little Round Top would understand that there is little room to deploy more than a battery of six to eight cannons facing Cemetery Ridge. Union forces were able to bring a battery up the concealed eastern slope of the hill to support the infantry defending the hill. Had the Confederate infantry taken Little Round Top, they would have had to bring guns up the east slope, which was steeper, rocky and recently cleared of timber. They would have been in plain view of Union forces and within range of Union gunners on Cemetery Ridge and Cemetery Hill. In this scenario, the number of guns that they could effectively have put in place would have been limited. And it is not hard to imagine that numerous Union infantry held in reserve out of sight of the Confederates could have used the cover of the trees on the east slope to drive the Confederates from Little Round Top.

Study of the landscape of Little Round Top and understanding of the disposition of opposing forces on July 2 tend to reveal that there was an overestimation of the importance of Little Round Top, although certainly not of the courage of the soldiers who fought and died there.

ZEIGLER'S GROVE AND THE COPSE OF TREES: JULY 3

On July 3, 12,000 Confederates attacked the center of the Union lines in what history remembers as Pickett's Charge. One of the great puzzles of Gettysburg is why Lee, one of the best battlefield commanders in American history, would order a suicidal charge across three-quarters of a mile of open ground into the face of massed Union artillery and infantry on Cemetery Ridge. And why would he do so while the rest of his army stood by and did nothing to support the attackers?

Several recent books have re-examined Lee's battle plans and posed possible answers to these and other questions concerning Lee's objectives at Gettysburg and for his Pennsylvania Campaign (Bowden and Ward 2001, Carhart 2005, Harman 2003). Harman (2003) has challenged the traditional interpretation that Lee directed his attack toward a "copse of trees" behind The Angle[3] on Cemetery Ridge. Harman

---

[3] The Angle gets its name from a stone wall that turns at right angles near the Copse of Trees.

contends that Lee intended to attack Cemetery Hill, the key point in the Union line where it bends toward the east and Culp's Hill. Harman cites two reports written by Lee after the battle, reports by Longstreet and Pickett, and reports and articles written by Colonel Edward Porter Alexander, the officer directing the Confederate artillery that supported Pickett's Charge. These reports suggest that Cemetery Hill—not Cemetery Ridge—was the objective of the attack.

Figure 13.5 **Union Cannon.** *Union cannon at The Angle facing west toward Seminary Ridge, Gettysburg.*

Changes in the landscape on Cemetery Hill and at The Angle may have affected interpretations of Lee's objective. Harman (2003) cites and supports a theory first posed by Kathy Georg Harrison, a senior historian at Gettysburg National Military Park. A stand of timber known as Zeigler's Grove stood atop Cemetery Hill on July 3, 1863. The stand would have been clearly visible from Lee's position on Seminary Ridge and would clearly have stood at the vulnerable point where the Union line bends from south-to-north to west-to-east. In the late 1870s and early 1880s, Zeigler's Grove was cut down. In the late 1880s, John B. Bachelder, director of the Gettysburg Battlefield Memorial Association, met with Colonel Walter Harrison, formerly on General Pickett's staff at Gettysburg. While standing on Seminary Ridge, Bachelder pointed to the copse of trees at The Angle, south of Cemetery Hill, and asked if that stand of trees were Lee's objective. With Zeigler's Grove no longer there, Harrison concurred that they must represent the place. Bachelder erected an iron fence around the copse of trees, erected a sign explaining their supposed significance and coined a phrase that would describe this place on the Gettysburg battlefield: "the high water mark of the Confederacy." Harman contends that the trees were clearly visible from Seminary Ridge in 1887 or 1888 but were saplings in 1863 not visible or barely visible from Lee's position. Construction of the old National Military Park Visitor Center and Cyclorama Center on Cemetery Hill, as well as encroachment by commercial properties on the north side of the hill, further obstructed visitors' understanding of the importance of this key point on the battlefield.[4]

There is no doubt that the only Confederates to reach the Union line on July 3 did so at The Angle. But these were men of Pickett's Division who were on the right or the southern flank of the Confederate assault. The two divisions on Pickett's left that would have penetrated the Union lines to the north at Cemetery Hill never made it that far. Harman (2003) poses the possibility that Pickett's men changed the direction of their attack toward The Angle because of the heavy fire they were under from the Union forces.

As far as the outcome of the Battle of Gettysburg, it matters little whether Lee intended to break the Union lines at Cemetery Hill or farther south along Cemetery Ridge. The significance of the Zeigler's Grove vs. Copse of Trees controversy is that changes in the tree cover at points along the Union lines at Gettysburg have altered and perhaps confounded our understanding of the battle.

---

[4] The Park Service recently demolished the old Visitor Center and Cyclorama as part of the Service's battlefield restoration efforts.

BATTLEFIELD PRESERVATION AT GETTYSBURG

Efforts to preserve portions of the battlefield began only weeks after the battle when Gettysburg attorney David McConaughy purchased ground adjacent to the Evergreen Cemetery atop Cemetery Hill to serve as a burial place for Pennsylvania soldiers killed in the battle. By the end of the summer, the decision took place to use the site to establish the Gettysburg National Cemetery. By the time of its dedication in November, the remains of 3,152 Union dead from all states were reinterred from temporary graves scattered about the battlefield to the new cemetery. On the 19th of November, President Abraham Lincoln stood at a podium in the cemetery and delivered the greatest speech in American history, the Gettysburg Address. In 1872, the federal government took control of the National Cemetery (Sheldon 2003).

The first monument at Gettysburg was the Soldiers' National Monument erected in 1865 in the National Cemetery. Hundreds more would follow in the 1870s through the end of the century, most commemorating Union officers and regiments. States and the veterans themselves paid for them, and they remain a legacy to the importance this battle had to the men who had fought there. John Bachelder would lead many of the efforts to protect the battlefield, to erect monuments and to maintain the Gettysburg battlefield for several decades following the war.

McConaughy founded the Gettysburg Battlefield Memorial Association in 1864 with the support of Pennsylvania Governor Andrew Curtin and fellow Gettysburg attorney David Wills. Wills was one of the leading proponents of the Gettysburg National Cemetery. From 1864 to 1895, the Association purchased land on Little Round Top, Culp's Hill, and the site where Union General John Reynolds, a Pennsylvanian, had been killed on July 1.

Gettysburg became a tourist attraction in the decades following the battle. Local citizens hired themselves out as tour guides, and a trolley line constructed in 1893 connected portions of the battlefield. Several amusement parks were constructed along the trolley line on the battlefield.

Most of the battlefield remained in private ownership until 1915 when Congress passed a bill establishing the Gettysburg National Military Park. The War Department administered the park until 1933. It is now under the administration of the National Park Service. Gettysburg National Military Park encompasses approximately 6,000 acres. The Park Service remains engaged in efforts begun in 1863 to maintain the character of the battlefield by restoring it to the way it looked at the time of the battle (National Park Service 2009, Sheldon 2003).

THE PETERSBURG CAMPAIGN: 1864–1865

For nearly three years, the Army of the Potomac and the Army of Northern Virginia slugged it out in the Virginia Theater of the war. While the Union was winning victories in the west, most of the nation focused on Virginia. The capitol cities of both sides, Washington and Richmond, defined the northern and southern ends of the theater and experienced risk through the first three years of war. Virginia was the closest major battleground to the population centers of the North and South and thus drew more attention from the press. In addition, the Armies of the Potomac and Northern Virginia were the largest armies on each side. Folks back home were more likely to have loved ones fighting in Virginia than fighting elsewhere. Virginia was where the war would ultimately be won or lost.

In spite of Gettysburg, the war in Virginia was not going well for the North. Robert E. Lee had won an impressive series of battles leading up to Gettysburg, but the two armies were locked in a strategic stalemate. A predictable pattern had emerged. The two armies would meet in pitched battle resulting in thousands of casualties and then limp off to their respective camps to lick their wounds, reorganize and rebuild. Lincoln struggled to find a general who could defeat Lee. John Pope had experienced sound defeat at the Second Battle of Bull Run and was relieved of command. George B. McClellan had squandered an opportunity to destroy Lee's army at Antietam in September 1862. His intransigence led to his dismissal as commander of the Army of the Potomac. Ambrose Burnside and Joseph Hooker had proven themselves incompetent and been fired. George Meade defeated Lee at Gettysburg by fighting defensively, adroitly moving his troops to repulse each attack by Lee. But Meade lacked the aggressiveness that Lincoln thought necessary to bring the war to an end. After Antietam, Lee had occupied a defensive position on the south bank of the Rappahannock River centered in the town of Fredericksburg. The Northern army was encamped on the north side of the Rappahannock. The armies remained in the same relative positions as 1864 began.

However, the South was standing on its last legs. A Union naval blockade had strangled Confederate commerce and Union naval and land forces had taken many of the major seaports of the South. Militarily, the Confederacy was in serious jeopardy. Its manpower and industrial reserves were near exhaustion and a large portion of its territory was in Union hands. The Confederacy had one great chance to successfully secure its independence.

Lincoln was up for re-election in November, 1864. The American model of government, a representative republic, was still relatively rare. Most nations were either monarchies or empires. Lincoln believed that the breakup of the Union would shatter the fragile concept of democratically-elected government and convince the world that democracy would not work. Although he was determined to win the war or negotiate its conclusion contingent upon restoration of the seceded states to the Union, he was also determined to conduct the national elections in the middle of a brutal civil war. But what if Lincoln lost the election?

An anti-war movement in the North was gaining momentum. The futility of the war in Virginia was a source of frustration and growing outrage as citizens in the North read the casualty lists of the major battles in the East. Illness took a greater toll among the armies. More than two Union soldiers died of disease for every soldier who died in battle or from wounds received in battle.[5] Draft riots had broken out in New York and other cities of the North shortly after the Battle of Gettysburg.

The Democrats appeared ready to gamble that an anti-war platform would carry the election amidst the growing discontent with the Lincoln administration's handling of the war. There was also growing sentiment among Democrats to nominate a war hero as their candidate to counter Lincoln's perceived advantage as a war-time President. Major General George McClellan, a Democrat and still an army officer although on inactive duty, was rumored to be a leading candidate.[6] On August 23, Lincoln wrote of his chances, "It seems exceedingly probable that this administration will not be re-elected. Then it will be my duty to so co-operate with the President-elect as to save the Union between the election and the inauguration; as he will have secured his election on such ground that he cannot possibly save it afterwards" (Catton 1968).

---

[5] No one knows precisely how many Americans died in the Civil War. Estimates range from approximately 618,000 to 700,000, with many historians agreeing that 620,000 is the best estimate (Davis 1988).

[6] McClellan would indeed receive the nomination and would oppose Lincoln in November.

Lincoln was convinced that his re-election would depend upon the success of his generals in the campaigns of 1864. His most successful general was U. S. Grant, and Lincoln was ready to "stake everything on the bet that Grant was going to win the war" (Catton 1968). On December 7, 1863, Congressman Elihu Washburne introduced a resolution to Congress to restore the rank of Lieutenant General.[7] The laws governing the small, peacetime military prior to the Civil War permitted the appointment of general officers at two ranks: Brigadier General and the higher rank of Major General. No effort to change the law took place to accommodate the explosive expansion of the army during the war until Washburne's resolution became law. Promoting Grant to this rank made him the highest-ranking officer in the U.S. Army and elevated him to command of all other officers, regardless of seniority. The government issued his orders to report to Washington on March 3, 1864 (Catton 1968).

GRAND STRATEGY: THE CAMPAIGNS OF 1864

Grant's victories in the west had proven him the North's best military strategist. At the beginning of 1864, he was poised to begin operations in the west against Atlanta or Mobile. But now, he began to apply the concepts of grand strategy—moving numerous armies at different locations—in a coordinated effort to end the war. To win, Grant put unrelenting pressure on every Confederate army in the field. This would prevent the Confederates from reinforcing one army from another as they did during the Chattanooga Campaign of 1863 to meet the most immediate threat. Up to this point in the war, such coordinated efforts by separate commands did not take place. Sherman, who had replaced Grant as commander of the western armies, would move against Joe Johnston in north Georgia. Meanwhile, George Meade's Army of the Potomac was to make Robert E. Lee's Army of Northern Virginia its objective. Grant, wary of political interference in Washington, would establish his headquarters in the field with the Army of the Potomac.

Grant was acutely aware of the political situation. Either he or Sherman needed to give Lincoln victories on the battlefield and, if at all possible, end the war before the November elections. Inaction was not an option. In addition, he knew that he could replace his losses while Lee could not. The winter of 1863–1864 was particularly costly to the men of the Army of the Potomac. Grant knew it was better to lose men in battle accomplishing results than to lose men from disease while sitting idle in the camps. His strategy for the campaign of 1864 was to fight a war of attrition.

Grant had previously won battles through maneuver, managing to keep his own casualties relatively light. But Lee was not about to cooperate. The Confederate commander was an engineering officer during the Mexican War and had supervised construction of several coastal forts in the South during his military career. Lee was a brilliant tactician, but he was at his absolute best when preparing his men to fight defensively behind entrenchments. Knowing that he was outnumbered and that his battered army could ill afford to absorb heavy casualties by fighting in the open, Lee prepared to fight a defensive campaign. If he could prolong the war and inflict a high cost on his foes, perhaps Lincoln would be defeated in November and the Confederacy could negotiate its independence with the new administration.

In a series of deadly battles beginning at the Wilderness and Spotsylvania Courthouse in May and culminating with an ill-conceived assault at Cold Harbor in June, Grant

---

[7] George Washington was the only officer to have previously held the rank of Lieutenant General in the Regular Army of the United States.

hammered relentlessly at Lee. Grant's plan was to beat Lee's army in a race to the southeast, to get between Lee and Richmond to and force a battle on open ground. Grant could use his numerical superiority to better effect here. Always with an eye to his lines of supply,[8] Grant kept the Chesapeake Bay to his back while unsuccessfully attempting to draw the wily Lee out of his entrenchments.

On June 1, 1864, Grant was east of Richmond at the site of a small tavern known as Cold Harbor. Once again Lee had placed his army in well-designed entrenchments with open lines of fire that would rake an attacker with deadly crossfire. Here, Grant made what he would later call his greatest mistake of the war, ordering a frontal assault on June 3 against the entrenched Confederate veterans. The cost was horrible. It added an estimated 12,000 Union soldiers to the casualty lists while Lee suffered a relatively light 2,500 casualties. It is easy to be critical of Grant's generalship at Cold Harbor. But frontal assaults against well entrenched troops were all too common in the Civil War. Burnside had led his men into slaughter in a frontal assault at Fredericksburg, as had Lee himself at Gettysburg[9] (Catton 1968, Fuller 1991, Grant 1885–86).

Figure 13.6 **U.S. Grant at Cold Harbor (1864).**

Courtesy of the Library of Congress Prints and Photographs Division. Reproduction number: LC-USZ61-903

UNION ENGINEERS CROSS THE JAMES

Perhaps Grant's military genius lay in his unwillingness to accept defeat. His response to the disaster at Cold Harbor was to respond with his most brilliant maneuver of the war. Grant stole a march on Robert E. Lee. Grant (1885–86) would remember his next decision in his memoirs: "Lee's position was now so near Richmond, and the intervening swamps of the Chickahominy so great an obstacle to the movement of troops in the face of the enemy, that I determined to make my next flank move carry the Army of the Potomac south of the James River."

Grant moved his men out of their position at Cold Harbor under cover of darkness on June 15. His engineers had erected a pontoon bridge across the James. The pontoons were wood boats transported overland on wagons. The engineers placed the boats at anchor across the river, nailing wood stringers across the gunnels of the boats, and nailing planks to the stringers in order to construct a floating bridge for the army, its supply wagons and its artillery to cross a river that was 2,100 feet wide and 72 to 90 feet deep. The pontoon bridge consisted of 92 boats and was 13 feet wide. Three schooners anchored near the center of the bridge supported it against

---

[8] Grant's knowledge and appreciation for what it took to keep an army supplied developed while serving as a regimental quartermaster during and after the Mexican War.

[9] Sixty years later, the generals of World War I would lead troops against fortified entrenchments and suffer appalling losses. For example, 19,000 British soldiers—"the flower of a generation"—died in a suicidal attack on German trenches on the first day of the Battle of the Somme in 1916. It was not until the development of the tank that trench warfare would become obsolete.

Figure 13.7 **Pontoon Bridge.** *Across the James River (1864).*

Courtesy of the Library of Congress Prints and Photographs Division.
Reproduction number: LC-USZ62-92629

the current. It took the engineers ten hours to erect the bridge, and by midnight of the following day, more than half of the army of more than 100,000 men had marched 45 miles and safely crossed the river. To accomplish this in the face of an alert foe was incredible, but the engineers and the officers of Grant's and Meade's staffs handled the task brilliantly (Catton 1968, Fuller 1991, Porter 2000).

The important railroad junction of Petersburg, 25 miles south of Richmond, lay lightly defended before Grant's forces. Subordinate commanders delayed their attack, and Lee was able to shift forces in time to repel the attack when it came. So, as he had Vicksburg, Grant began siege operations. Lee's line of entrenchments protecting Richmond and Petersburg extended for 26 miles from the east of Richmond to the south of Petersburg. By November, Grant continued the flanking movements that began after the Wilderness, striking west four times, cutting railroads from the south into Lee's lines and forcing Lee to lengthen those lines an additional nine miles. Lee's defenses were becoming dangerously thin.

THE SUPPLY DEPOT AT CITY POINT

Grant would assemble 115,000 to 125,000 men along his lines at Petersburg in a siege that would last until April, 1865. The men had to be fed, clothed, sheltered, armed and equipped. The sick and wounded needed care. The army's horses had to be shoed, fed, and harnessed. Wagons and artillery pieces had to stay in a good state of repair. The logistics involved in keeping an army of this size in the field were unprecedented in American history (Catton 1968, Fuller 1991, Porter 2000).

The man in charge of supplying the armies in the trenches facing Petersburg was Brigadier General Rufus Ingalls. Ingalls was a West Point classmate of Grant who was chief quartermaster of the Army of the Potomac. Grant entrusted Ingalls to oversee the complex job of keeping his army well supplied and would later praise him in his memoirs (Grant 1885–86), "There has been no army in the history of the United states where the duties of Quartermaster have been so well performed."

On June 18, Grant ordered the creation of a supply depot at City Point (now Hopewell, Virginia), below the confluence of the Appomattox and James Rivers. The James at City Point was navigable by ship from the Chesapeake Bay, allowing the movement of troops and supplies by sea. The army took over Appomattox Plantation on the James as its headquarters. Ingalls converted the manor house into the offices for the quartermaster's staffs. Grant and his staff pitched tents on the lawn and later built cabins as their quarters and offices. The use of the more comfortable quarters for the quartermaster's officers is an indication of the importance Grant attached to Ingalls' operations.

Eight wharves and more than 280 buildings were constructed at City Point. Warehouses covered 100,000 square feet along the wharf. And it was all built within thirty days. At any point in time 150 to 200 ships anchored off City Point. Union gunboats patrolled the James, protecting the depot and ships from Confederate attack.

The North shipped food, except for bread. The army had to bring in provisions for the 125,000 men and 65,000 horses and mules. The depot stored nine million meals and 12,000 tons of hay and oats on any given day. A bakery it constructed produced 100,000 loaves per day.

A repair shop covered one wharf covering 190 feet along the waterfront where it repaired wagons and artillery caissons and cared for animals. Some 26,000 square feet of warehousing was dedicated to the repair shop. Six large buildings covering 17,000 square feet provided work space for 1,800 carpenters, wheelwrights, blacksmiths, saddlers, teamsters and corral hands.

General Horace Porter (2000), one of Grant's staff officers wrote, "A hospital had been established at City Point large enough to accommodate 6000 patients. The General manifested a deep interest in this hospital, frequently visited it, and constantly received verbal reports from the surgeons in charge." Eventually the army built seven hospitals that could care for 10,000 patients at City Point. At first it used 1,200 tents as the hospital facility. Later, it replaced the tents with 90 log buildings, 20 by 50-foot (Zinnen 1991). Civilian organizations such as the U.S. Sanitary Commission and the Christian Commission provided volunteer nurses and doctors and established relief stations for the soldiers.

THE U.S. MILITARY RAILROAD AND THE MILITARY TELEGRAPH

By July 2, 1864, the Union Army's railroad engineers had repaired five miles of damaged track from City Point to Petersburg. The U.S. Military Railroad immediately began laying track for 21 miles in the rear of the Union lines south of the city. The Military Railroad provided an efficient means for moving supplies—approximately 600,000 tons of supplies—from the supply depot to the front. Nine hundred personnel operated 24 locomotives behind the lines. The building of the Military Railroad at Petersburg reduced the need for wagons by 50 percent (Zinnen 1991).

The army extended the Military Telegraph on the south side of the James where it connected to a cable across Hampton Roads at the mouth of the Chesapeake Bay connecting Grant's headquarters with the War Department in Washington. Telegraph lines were set up behind the lines to keep Grant in constant communication with his subordinates (Porter 2000). Grant was one of the first generals of the Civil War to employ the telegraph effectively to communicate with his subordinates and superiors as early as the beginning of 1862 (Ross 2000).

Operation of the Military Railroad required the construction of supporting facilities. The army built a rail yard, a repair shop and a fueling

Figure 13.8 **U.S. Military Railroad Depot at City Point.**
Courtesy of the Library of Congress Prints and Photographs Division. Reproduction number: LC-DIG-ppmsca-08248

Figure 13.9 **Union Railroad Mortar at Petersburg.**

Courtesy of the Library of Congress Prints and Photographs Division.
Reproduction number: LC-DIG-ppmsca-08270

station at City Point, as well as way stations and numerous sidings along the length of the railroad. The crews of the U.S. Military Railroad constructed the 280 buildings of the City Point depot. Northern mills pre-cut the buildings and shipped them by sea for reassembling at the front.

The military railroad also served a deadly purpose. The army mounted cannon and mortars on flatcars and moved them along the lines to support attacking troops or to counter Confederate threats. They could also move the guns easily and concentrate them to bombard the Confederate works, wearing down the morale of the defenders of the city.

END GAME

The service of the quartermaster corps, the military railroad and the civilian volunteer organizations did much to keep Grant's men well clothed and fed. As a result, their morale remained high while the half-starved, poorly clothed and ill-equipped men of Lee's proud army became discouraged. Desertions among the Confederate forces reached unprecedented levels as the Petersburg Campaign drew to its inevitable conclusion. In spite of the heroic efforts of Lee and his surviving officers, Grant's object of fighting a war of attrition had taken brutal effect on the South's best army.

While Grant laid siege to Petersburg, Sherman advanced on Atlanta. On September 3, 1864, Sherman wired Washington, "Atlanta is ours, and fairly won." Not even McClellan's popularity could overcome the political advantage Sherman had given Lincoln. The President was re-elected.

Grant finally forced Lee to abandon the Petersburg defenses in April of 1865. The tattered remnants of the Army of Northern Virginia marched west, attempting to flee the overwhelming numbers of Grant's pursuing armies. On April 9, Grant's forces had surrounded the Army of Northern Virginia at the tiny Virginia village of Appomattox Courthouse forcing its surrender. When Sherman accepted the surrender of Joseph Johnston's army two weeks later, the war was over.

Homework

Name: _____   Date: _____

Sketch a map of the Gettysburg battlefield. Locate Seminary Ridge, Cemetery Hill, Cemetery Ridge, Little Round Top and Culp's Hill.

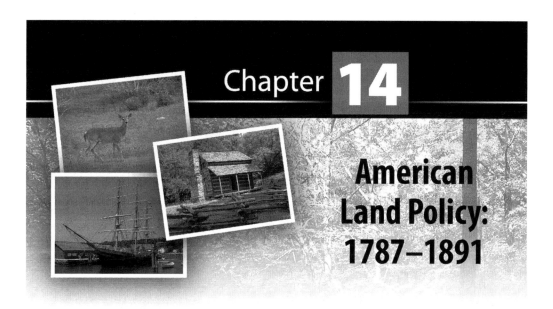

Chapter 14

American Land Policy: 1787–1891

To understand what has transpired in America's forests from the Civil War to the present era, it is necessary to have some background that reflects the current situation of forest distribution and composition. Although forests have changed over that time, the geographic regions containing hardwood and softwood forests have not. The most recent data published by the U.S. Forest Service indicate that 751 million acres of the United States are forest covered, accounting for approximately one third of the total land area of the nation. The location of approximately 52 percent of the forested land is in the east, and 48 percent is in the west, including Alaska and Hawaii (Alvarez 2007, Smith et al. 2009).

Softwood timber makes up 57 percent of the nation's forest growing stock while hardwoods make up the remainder. Of this total, the location of 67 percent of the nation's softwood growing stock is in the west and 90 percent of the hardwood growing stock

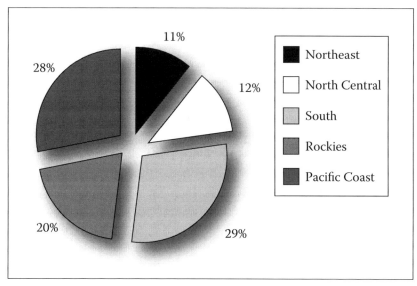

Figure 14.1 Forestland by Region: 2007.

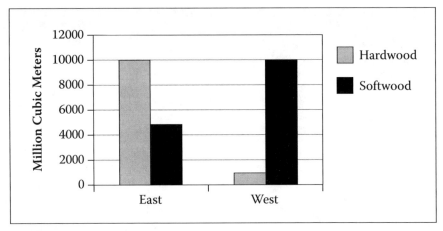

Figure 14.2 Hardwood and Softwood Growing Stock by Region.

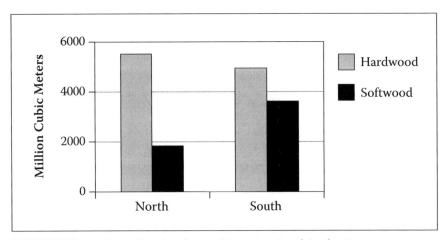

Figure 14.3 Hardwood and Softwood Growing Stock in the East.

is in the east. Looking at it another way, two-thirds of the eastern forest consists of hardwood growing stock while 90 percent of the western forest consists of softwood growing stock (Smith et al. 2009).

In the east, two-thirds of the softwoods are in the south, while the hardwood growing stock is evenly split between the north and south. Thus, the southern pine region is the primary location of softwood timber in the east (Alvarez 2007, Smith et al. 2009).

PREVAILING ATTITUDES TOWARD THE FOREST

In 1869, the prevailing attitude among Americans was that agriculture still represented the highest and best use of land. There was good reason to think this since most Americans still earned their living on farms and agricultural production was not nearly as efficient as it is today. People needed to eat and more land was cleared to feed the growing population.

Moses Austin,[1] a New England businessman traveling through the new state of Kentucky in 1798, encountered a number of distressingly poor families heading west

---

[1] Austin's objective was to survey potential investments in lead mines on the west side of the Mississippi. His experience with the land-poor pilgrims in Kentucky would plant a seed that led him into land speculation and the establishment of an American colony in the Spanish territory of Texas. Moses Austin died before bringing his dream to fruition. That was left to his son, Stephen F. Austin.

with their meager belongings. When asked what they expected to find in Kentucky, the answer was always "land." Americans of the eighteenth and nineteenth centuries placed a premium on land and considered it the key to opportunity and wealth (Brands 2005).

People considered forests inexhaustible. Those calling for a more cautious approach were uncommon. The United States did not yet recognize sustainability, a concept Europeans understood and practiced.

Frederick Jackson Turner (1921), an influential historian of the late nineteenth and early twentieth century, represented the prevailing view of the era, "The existence of an area of free land, its continuous recession, and the advance of American settlement westward explain American development." Prevailing attitudes toward the land shaped the land policies of the federal government in the early years of the republic. It encouraged settlement and agriculture, industrial development and territorial expansion. Those perceptions and attitudes would change in the latter decades of the nineteenth century.

MANIFEST DESTINY AND TERRITORIAL EXPANSION

During the War of 1812, a British fleet sailed up the Chesapeake and landed several thousand Redcoats and Royal Marines at Benedict, Maryland. The British marched overland to the new capital city of Washington. They burned government buildings, including the White House, the partially constructed Capital, and the Treasury, War and Navy buildings. Fleeing American Naval officers set the Washington Naval Yard, including two vessels under construction, to the torch rather than have it fall into the hands of the enemy. Sacking Washington, for all the panic and national embarrassment it caused, was nothing more than a destructive raid. British attempts to invade the United States from Canada had failed and their invasion of Louisiana ended in disaster at the Battle of New Orleans. But, the success of the British raid on Washington exposed the vulnerability of the United States to foreign invasion (Gaddis 2004, Toll 2006).

Manifest Destiny was the strategic vision of John Quincy Adams. At the time he articulated it as a national security policy he was James Monroe's Secretary of State.[2] Adams believed the experiences of the War of 1812 made it clear that territorial expansion was necessary to deprive foreign powers a base from which they could launch an invasion of the United States. His belief became enacted into policy with the acquisition of Florida from Spain in 1819. He would also author the Monroe Doctrine, declaring that the United States would not tolerate European powers attempting to establish new colonies in the Western Hemisphere (Gaddis 2004).

Expansionism continued through the nineteenth century with the Annexation of Texas in 1845, the acquisition of the Oregon territory through

Figure 14.4 **John Quincy Adams.**

Courtesy of the Library of Congress Prints and Photographs Division. Reproduction number: LC-USZ62-44523

---

[2] Adams succeeded Monroe as President of the United States.

a treaty with Great Britain in 1846, the Mexican War in 1848, the Gadsden Purchase of 1853, the purchase of Alaska from Russia in 1867 and the annexation of Hawaii in 1898.

Acquisition of new territories added new land to the public estate. At one time or another, the federal government held title to 82.5 percent of the total land area of the United States. Approximately 29 percent remains in public ownership. The government transferred the remaining 53.5 percent to the private sector or to the states (Cubbage et al. 1993).

LAND SALES AND GRANTS TO INDIVIDUALS

A corollary to the policy of Manifest Destiny required filling the continent with people because a hostile nation could easily seize empty territory. "Although the U.S. Government was eager to acquire all lands within its present borders, it was just as eager to sell or give those lands to private landowners or firms in order to spur development and generate revenues for the fledgling government" (Cubbage et al. 1993).

The Land Ordnance of 1785 established the legal mechanism for selling national lands. A Public Land Survey established "sections" of 640 acres. In 1812, the General Land Office became established in the Treasury Department to oversee federal lands. The fact that it was under Treasury is a clear indication that the intention of the Land Office was to sell land and generate revenues.

Land Acts passed by Congress in 1800 and 1820 established prices, terms of credit and minimum sizes of land purchases of federal lands. The Preemption Act of 1841 allowed squatters on public land to purchase a section of land at a very low price. To be eligible, purchasers had to have lived on that section for the previous fourteen months.

The Homestead Act of 1862 granted 270 million acres of federal land to private citizens (10 percent of the nation). Grants were for 160 acres, and the act was not repealed until 1976. A homesteader had to build a 12 by 14 cabin, "bring water" to the land, farm the land for five years and pay a fee (Cubbage et al. 1993).

The Timber Culture Act of 1873 offered 160 acres to anyone who would plant 40 acres with trees. The Timber and Stone Act of 1878 granted additional land to farmers who made improvements to the land.

LAND GRANTS TO THE STATES

The federal government granted a total of 328 million acres to the states under several programs established by Congress.

The Morrill Act of 1862 granted 30,000 acres each to the states still in the Union to sell to raise funds to establish a college dedicated to providing education in agriculture, the mechanical arts[3] and military science. Its author, Congressman Justin Smith Morrill of Vermont, first proposed the bill in 1857. It passed by a slim margin in 1859 (with many of the southern states opposed) but President James Buchanan vetoed it. At the time, a college education was a privilege of the elite and the Land Grant colleges made an education available to the children of farmers and the working class.

---

[3] "Mechanical arts" was the term used to describe engineering programs during the mid-nineteenth century.

The young State of West Virginia, added under the Morrill Act in 1864, established its land grant college, the West Virginia Agricultural College in Morgantown, in 1869.

Land grants to western states established public school trust lands under state ownership that required management with the proceeds from timber sales used to support the public schools. This was a compromise that compensated state and local governments for lost tax revenues as the federal government set aside land in perpetual federal ownership as forest reserves or other federal set-asides.

LAND GRANTS FOR PUBLIC WORKS

The government also granted land to states and to the private sector to subsidize public work projects. In 1827, Congress granted 1.8 million acres of land to Indiana

Figure 14.5 Justin Smith Morrill.
Courtesy of the Library of Congress Prints and Photographs Division. Reproduction number: LC-DIG-cwpbh-01804

and Illinois to build canals. Land grants for canal building took place in the following several decades to Ohio, Wisconsin and Michigan. By 1866, Congress had granted 4.6 million acres to the five states of the old Northwest. It also granted land to improve river systems by building locks and improving channels. Land grants also established wagon roads (Orfield 1915).

Land grants partly funded four of the first five transcontinental railroads.[4] The Pacific Railroad Acts of 1862 and 1864 provided 10 to 20 acres of land for every mile of track built. The government granted land in a pattern of "checkerboard" grants while retaining alternate sections or offering them to homesteaders (Cox 2009). It granted approximately 129 million acres—approximately 7 percent of the land area of the United States—to railroads between 1850 and 1870. It permitted railroads to use the land as their right-of-way or to sell it to raise funds (Cubbage et al. 1993).

The exception was James J. Hill's Great Northern Railroad. Hill was one of the Gilded Age's most successful industrial capitalists. After building railroads and a small fortune in the upper Midwest, he set out to build the Great Northern Railroad to the Pacific Northwest. Hill refused to accept federal land grants, preferring to raise funds on his own. He was so successful that he was able to acquire the rival Northern Pacific when that line went bankrupt in the mid-1890s.

LAND FRAUD AND CONFLICT

The system provided ample opportunities for profiteers to game the system to commit land fraud. The checkerboard grants allowed railroads and other large corporate owners to squeeze out homesteaders from in-holdings by denying access or water rights across company land. They often forced homesteaders to sell at a fraction of the value of the land. Basing land grants on the mileage of track built offered numerous

---

[4] These were the Union Pacific and the Central Pacific (the first transcontinental railroad), the Southern Pacific, the Northern Pacific and the Atchison, Topeka and Santa Fe.

opportunities for railroads to game the system by constructing unnecessary routes or double-charging the government for track hastily built at low cost and replaced with permanent track later. The Union Pacific, in particular, was guilty of these corrupt practices (Ambrose 2000, Cubbage et al. 1993).

Unscrupulous land speculators applied loose interpretations of the law to obtain a grant under the Homestead Act: They would build a 12 by 14 inch cabin (the law did not specify units of measure), "bring water" to the land by throwing a cupful of water on the ground, place a single shingle over a tent and drive a cabin on wheels from claim to claim. Companies would have their employees claim land then let the claim lapse after cutting the timber. Other companies would have their employees transfer homesteads to the company after six months (Cubbage et al. 1993, Youngquist and Fleischer 1977).

In 1906 the Roosevelt administration exposed fraudulent sales of Oregon and California Railroad and Coos Bay Wagon Road land grants. In 1915, Congress passed the Revestment Act, authorizing government purchase of the land. As a result of this scandal, nearly 64 percent of Oregon's forests are in public ownership. In contrast, only 55 percent of the forests of neighboring Washington and 58 percent of California are in public ownership. The impact of this land fraud and subsequent government intervention reverberates through the forests of Oregon into the twenty-first century (Williams 1989).

Acquisition of western territories placed huge tracts of land in federal ownership. Much of the land was inaccessible, arid and otherwise undesirable for homesteading or industrial use. Other tracts of land came under federal protection as national parks and forest reserves as the conservation movement blossomed in the late nineteenth century. The government seized other lands as land frauds became exposed.

Land use became an issue in the west more than in any other region because vast tracts of land remained in federal ownership. Ranchers had grown accustomed to grazing their cattle on public land. Homesteaders on that land built fences and deprived the cattlemen of the open range. Prospectors staked claims on public land and lumbermen harvested timber. Railroads added to the potential for conflict amongst the diverse interests clamoring for public land.

Figure 14.6 **The Grand Falls of the Yellowstone.** *Yellowstone National Park (Underwood & Underwood, New York, CA, 1911).*

Courtesy of the Library of Congress Prints and Photographs Division. Reproduction number: LC-USZ62-97306

ESTABLISHMENT OF NATIONAL PARKS

Government policy evolved in the last quarter of the nineteenth century. A conservation movement was taking root in the United States among the nation's elites. The movement grew out of concern that America's resources were being drained at an alarming rate. Discovery of scenic and natural wonders in the west prompted calls for government protection of certain public lands from exploitation.

Congress created the world's first national park, Yellowstone, in 1872. It created the park to preserve its natural wonders and to make them accessible to tourists (Reiger 1997). There was no overriding supervisory agency for the national parks until the creation of the National Park Service in 1916. The Department of the Interior technically administered the early national parks. However, from 1886 until 1916, the Army was in charge of Yellowstone. Yellowstone's first sixteen rangers were ex-cavalrymen and their primary responsibilities were in law enforcement. The dominance of the law enforcement arm of the Park Service within the agency's hierarchy confounded the management of wildlife and other resources for at least the next one hundred years of Yellowstone's history (Chase 1986).

Other national parks followed—Sequoia, Kings Canyon and Yosemite in 1890; Mt. Rainier in 1899; and Crater Lake in 1902. The government first set aside Grand Canyon as a forest reserve in 1893. It later became a national monument before becoming a national park in 1919. Congress also set aside a number of Civil War battlefields for the War Department to manage in the 1890s.

Figure 14.7 Cavalrymen at Drill in Yellowstone National Park. *(ca, 1904)*

Courtesy of the Library of Congress Prints and Photographs Division. Reproduction number:LC-USZ62-52424

Chase (1986) chronicles and harshly criticizes the policies that governed Yellowstone up to the book's publication in 1986. At the time of European contact, elk and bison were rare in the Yellowstone country. Beaver, wolves, white-tailed deer, antelope, bighorn sheep and cutthroat trout defined Yellowstone's terrestrial and aquatic ecosystems. To lure sportsmen to Yellowstone, the Army introduced non-native

species such as elk, bison and rainbow trout to Yellowstone between 1886 and 1912. Park rangers began a program to eradicate wolves and other carnivores from 1918 through the 1930s, largely at the request of local ranchers.

Large elk and bison were able to out-compete smaller species for food leading to the disappearance of the white-tailed deer and the dramatic population decline of antelope and bighorn sheep from 1912 to 1924. From 1920 through 1950, beaver populations declined. Again, the large elk herd was the cause as it devoured the willows and aspens that beaver depended upon along the streams and creek beds. Rainbow trout began to replace the native cutthroat.

Figure 14.8 Bears Near Lake Hotel. *Yellowstone National Park (Northern Pacific Railway photo).*

Courtesy of the Library of Congress Prints and Photographs Division. Reproduction number: LC-USZ62-100982

---

[5] The Yellowstone dumps were tourist attractions in the early 1900s. The Park Service provided transportation and bleachers at the dumps so tourists could watch the grizzlies feed.

Disposing of garbage from Yellowstone's lodges and campgrounds in open dumps led to another wildlife problem. Grizzly and black bear populations grew as bears thrived on the easy source of food.[5] In the 1960s, the Park Service closed the dumps because it didn't conform to the concept of the "balance of nature." But taking away a vital food source for the expanded bear population caused the "bear problem" of the 1970s and 1980s when hungry, unhealthy bears wandered into campgrounds and out of the park into nearby towns to find food, occasionally with tragic consequences (Chase 1986).

ESTABLISHMENT OF THE FOREST RESERVES

In 1891, Congress passed the Forest Reserve Act empowering the President to create "forest reserves" from the public domain. At the time, there was little public land remaining in the east that the government had not reserved for other purposes, such as military bases and ports. Therefore, the location of the new forest reserves was in the west. In 1905, Congress renamed the forest reserves, which became the national forests that we know today. It was not until 1911 that it authorized national forests in the eastern United States. This pattern of set asides established the predominant forest land ownership patterns that remain in place today.

The federal government owns one third or 248 million of the 751 million forested acres of the United States. The National Forest system contains nearly 147 million acres or 19.6 percent of the nation's forest land. National Parks, Bureau of Land Management (BLM) land, Indian reservations, the military and other federal installations make up the remaining 101 million acres of federal forest land. An additional 80 million acres are in state or local ownership, making a total of 43.6 percent of all forested land that is in public ownership. (Smith et al. 2009)

Approximately 86 percent of the federal forest acres are in the west. Forty-four percent of the federal forest is in the Pacific Coast region (including Alaska), and 42 percent is in the Rocky Mountain States. Approximately three quarters of the softwood forests of the west are under federal ownership. The preponderance of softwood timber on federal land in the west has a profound impact on our timber supply situation in the twenty-first century.

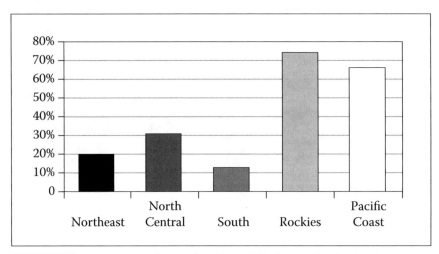

Figure 14.9 Percentage of Forestland in Public Ownership by Region: 2007.

There is a reverse trend in private ownership with 74 percent of the privately owned forests of the United States in the east. Approximately 44 percent of the privately-owned forest land in the U.S. is in the south. This regional pattern of private and public land ownership is a direct result of the pattern of westward expansion of settlement through American history and the determination by the government to begin setting aside forests in the federal estate in perpetuity long after the government had disposed of the public forests of the east (Cubbage et al. 1993, Smith et al. 2009).

Homework

Name: _____   Date: _____

Three significant land grant bills passed in 1862: the Homestead Act, the Pacific Railroad Act and the Morrill Act. Why had all of these legislative efforts suffered defeat earlier and what had changed to enable their passage in 1862?

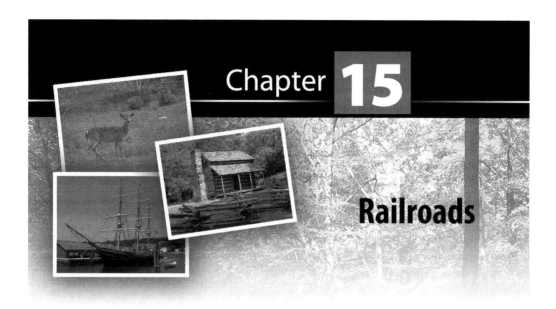

Chapter 15

Railroads

Railroads were a product of the development of the steam engine during the Industrial Revolution of the early nineteenth century. The first passenger train began operations in England in 1825. The Baltimore and Ohio was the first American railroad, opening a line seventeen miles long in 1830 (Van Ophem 2001). By 1850, there were fewer than 10,000 miles of railroad in the United States (MacCleery 1994a).

The industrial potential of the United States was mobilized to fight the Civil War. By war's end approximately five million men had worn the uniform of the Union or the Confederacy. These men were highly trained and toughened to the discipline and hardships of war. A cadre of highly motivated officers had developed under some of the most brilliant generals the nation has ever produced—Grant, Lee, Longstreet, Sherman, Jackson and Thomas. Above all, the nation's collective energy had focused on the war effort. The collective national energy and a spirit of restlessness unleashed by war would turn to the building of an industrialized society.

The building of the first transcontinental railroad led the way. The two railroad companies that accomplished the task of building the transcontinental railroad, the Union Pacific (U.P.) and the Central Pacific (C.P.), were the biggest corporations of their time and established the model for modern corporations—for better and for worse (Ambrose 2000).

THE CALIFORNIA GOLD RUSH

California was part of the territory ceded to the United States in 1848 in the treaty that ended the Mexican War. A few weeks before the signing of the treaty, the discovery of gold at Sutter's Mill on the American River near Sacramento started "one of the largest human migrations in history as a half-million people from around the world descended upon California in search of instant wealth" (California Resources Agency 2009). A number of business people looking to build their own fortunes by relieving successful miners of their riches accompanied prospectors (Ambrose 2000).

In 1849, when the Gold Rush was at its peak, the journey from the East Coast to California was long, arduous and dangerous. In 1850, 50,000 immigrants left Missouri for California traveling overland to reach the goldfields. Cholera alone claimed the lives of 5,000 on the overland journey (Ambrose 2000).

One of the many immigrants to California was Charles Crocker, a twenty-seven-year-old from Troy, New York. Crocker and four other men headed for California in 1850 traveling overland and following the Platte River across the Great Plains. It took Crocker's party almost half a year to reach the Gold Fields. Collis Huntington was also twenty-seven when the gold fever struck him. He sailed from New York to Panama, crossed the Isthmus and waited for a ship to San Francisco. It took Huntington five and a half months to reach San Francisco. Mark Hopkins was thirty-four when he sailed for California from New York around Cape Horn on a ship beset by storms, bad food, a lack of water and a tyrannical captain. It took Hopkins' ship 196 days to make the journey (Ambrose 2000).

Crocker, Huntington and Hopkins became three-fourths of the "Big Four," the principal owners of the Central Pacific Railroad. The fourth member of the Big Four was Leland Stanford who was in California prior to the Gold Rush. No doubt, their own experiences in crossing the continent by various routes was incentive to span the nation by rail.

The rapid growth of California's population and the economic importance of its newfound riches led to statehood in 1850. Maps of the United States in 1850 reveal California's isolation from the remainder of the nation. Its nearest neighboring state, Texas, was approximately four hundred miles away at the closest point. Communication with the remainder of the United States was difficult, as the experiences of Huntington, and Hopkins show.

NATIONAL SECURITY

The United States acquired California by conquest from Mexico. How would the U.S. defend the western territories from foreign aggression? In particular, how could the United States rapidly move troops and equipment west to respond to a threat when it took at least two months to reach California by the fastest route? The experiences of two of America's great military leaders illustrate the problem.

In 1846, during the Mexican War, Lieutenant William Tecumseh Sherman sailed around Cape Horn for California as a member of the 3rd Artillery. Sherman left a record of the sea journey in his memoirs. He described the voyage through the Straits of Magellan: "Here we experienced very rough buffeting about under storm stay-sails, and spending nearly a month before the wind favored our passage and enabled the course of the ship to be changed for Valparaiso." A navigational error that carried the ship too far north as it arrived off the California coast further delayed the voyage. The journey lasted 212 days. The length of that journey was simply too long for a response to an invasion by a foreign power (Ambrose 2000).

Captain Ulysses S. "Sam" Grant was deployed to California in 1852 with the 4th Infantry Regiment. The army transported the 4th by ship from Brooklyn to the Isthmus of Panama, then took it by boat and mule across the Isthmus, where it again boarded ship bound for San Francisco. Grant was the regimental quartermaster. As such he was responsible for arranging transport and supervising the movement of men, supplies and equipment across Panama. In addition Grant had to look after a small group of wives and children accompanying their husbands on the journey. Grant recalled the hardships of Panama in his memoirs (Grant 1885–1886). Heavy rains and flooding delayed their journey across the Isthmus. Cholera broke among the men and families of the 4th, killing one out of seven.

GRENVILLE MELLEN DODGE

On August 13, 1859, a former U.S. congressman and railroad attorney, Abraham Lincoln, gave a speech in Council Bluffs, Iowa. Lincoln was keenly interested in the idea of a railroad that would span the continent.

Lincoln's host introduced him to a young man named Grenville Mellen Dodge "and said that the young engineer knew more about railroads than any two men in the country" (Ambrose 2000). Dodge was a civil engineer and a railroad surveyor. He shared Lincoln's interest in a railroad to the Pacific and impressed the future president with his ideas on a possible route.[1]

Figure 15.1 Grenville Mellen Dodge.
Courtesy of the Library of Congress Prints and Photographs Division. Reproduction number: LC-DIG-cwpb-05485

Dodge enlisted in the Union army during the Civil War and rose to the rank of Major General. During the war, he served directly under both Grant and Sherman. He spent part of his wartime service overseeing the operations of the U.S. Military Railroad in the western theater of the war and rose to command a corps during Sherman's Atlanta Campaign. Dodge's personal relationship with arguably the two most powerful men in post-Civil War America would serve him well, for both shared his vision of a transcontinental railroad.

Dodge would become the chief engineer and guiding genius[2] of the Union Pacific Railroad. (Dodge City, Kansas, would be named in his honor.) As Dodge pushed the Union Pacific west, the Big Four began construction of the Central Pacific east (Ambrose 2000).

THE PACIFIC RAILROAD ACTS

Building the transcontinental railroad was a national priority. The Pacific Railroad Act of 1862—passed in the middle of the Civil War—established the Union Pacific (U.P.) Railroad. The U.P. was the first nationally chartered corporation since the Second National Bank of the United States.

The federal government encouraged and subsidized the development of infrastructure since the early days of the public. Since the treasury did not possess a lot of ready cash, selling grants of public lands to raise funds had supported public works projects. Land grants to railroad companies began with Midwestern railroads in the 1850s. The Pacific Railroad Act of 1862 granted the Union Pacific ten acres of land for every mile of track laid and gave loans to finance construction.

As the U.P. pushed west from St. Joseph, Missouri, the Central Pacific (C.P.) Railroad was building track east from Sacramento. Strong lobbying by the C.P. resulted in passage of the Pacific Railroad Act of 1864 that recognized the role of the C.P. in spanning the continent. The 1864 act raised the land grant from ten to twenty acres per

---

[1] While many historians (including Ambrose) cite this story, there are skeptics who doubt it happened (Farnham 1965).

[2] Farnham (1965) once again believes Dodge's role in shaping the routes of the U.P. is exaggerated, crediting U.P. Vice President Thomas C. Durant and Samuel B. Reed, the railroad's Superintendent of Construction.

mile of track laid for both companies. In addition, the two railroads received permission to sell bonds to finance construction.[3]

On July 3, 1866, Congress amended the Pacific Railroad Act to authorize the Central Pacific to construct their road until it joined with the U.P. With twenty acres of land at stake for each mile of track laid, the amended act sparked competition between the two companies to lay track and generate profit. "A race fit perfectly into the business climate of America. The businessmen spoke little and did much, while the politicians did as little as possible and spoke much." (Ambrose 2000) Financial difficulties delayed the start of construction of the Union Pacific until 1866 (Farnham 1965).

BUILDING THE FIRST TRANSCONTINENTAL RAILROAD[4]

The two railroads approached the problem of finding men to build the railroad in different ways. The Union Pacific found a dependable, highly disciplined workforce in the veterans leaving the armies at the end of the Civil War. The men were used to living in camps, to arduous toil and to the discipline necessary to work in well coordinated crews. Many of the young veterans were immigrants. As a result, the chatter of a U.P. crew was thick with the accents of Limerick and Dublin, Bavaria and Sweden. The men wore faded and worn parts of blue uniforms with an occasional gray and butternut coat of a former Rebel. The U.P. hired former officers and sergeants to supervise the crews. Higher ranking officers like the former major general, Grenville Dodge, filled the ranks of U.P. executives. These men brought the experience of military command to the task of organizing and directing a large workforce dedicated to completing a complex task. Men who helped keep armies supplied were eminently qualified to keep large work crews fed, sheltered, paid and supplied (Ambrose 2000).

California and the C.P. did not have a large cadre of veterans to draw upon. Instead, they turned to immigrant labor from China. The C.P. negotiated a contract with the Emperor to provide crews. The Chinese were hard working, willing to work from sunrise to sunset and not prone to violence or lawlessness—a problem with transient laborers and drifters hired by the railroad. Railroad foremen assigned the Chinese crews tasks, and the crews worked out the division of labor. The Chinese presented several cultural challenges to the management of the C.P. The contract with the Chinese required that the body of any worker who died while working for the railroad would be returned to China, the "Celestial Kingdom," for burial. The Chinese also were unwilling to eat the mess hall meals served to crews made up of Americans or European immigrants. The C.P. worked out a solution, providing the Chinese crews with an allowance. The crews would purchase their own foods, choose their own cooks and provide for their own nourishment. The problem of feeding the Chinese crews disappeared (Ambrose 2000).

Crews on both railroads lived in mobile camps that followed construction. The camps included the shops, yards, depots and sidings necessary to support the building of wood bridges and trestles, as well as the storage and handling of rails, ties, spikes,

---

[3] The U.P. was involved in one of the first large corporate scandals in U.S. history when it set up a dummy construction company, Crédit Mobilier of America, and awarded it bids at exorbitant costs. The scam nearly bankrupt the U.P. and its investors while the U.P. executives who invested in Crédit Mobilier lined their pockets. To make matters worse, Crédit Mobilier also sold stocks below cost to members of Congress who, in return, voted hefty subsidies to the U.P.

[4] You may find histories and collections of photographs of the building and operation of the U.P. and C.P. at the Union Pacific Railroad website (*http://www.uprr.com/aboutup/history/index.shtml*) and the Central Pacific Railroad Photographic History Museum (*http://cprr.org/*).

timbers, tools and supplies. The camps and depots were not unlike the operations constructed by Rufus Ingalls' quartermasters and the Military Railroad of the Army of the Potomac at City Point.

As with the army, profiteers and legitimate business people followed the railroad, each looking to relieve the workers of their hard earned pay. Boom towns sprung up with the railroad. Many disappeared as the camps and workers moved farther along the line. Others remain and thrive to this day. In 1868, the CP began selling lots in a new Nevada town they named after Civil War hero Jesse Reno. "... There was a rush of buyers, and choice twenty-five-foot lots sold for $1,200 apiece" (Ambrose 2000). Railroad towns catered to the vices of the workers. Saloons, gambling halls and brothels followed the rails in mobile communities nicknamed "Hell on Wheels." Four times as many U.P. workers were murdered in these lawless shanty towns than died in construction accidents (Van Ophem 2001).

Construction of bridges, trestles and tunnels through the Sierras and Rockies required engineering feats that challenged men like Grenville Dodge. The Howe Truss—a structure made up of structural triangles—made the spanning of rivers and canyons possible. The Chicago Howe Truss Bridge Company manufactured prefabricated sections for bridges for the U.P. They constructed the trusses of 12" × 12" sixteen-foot timbers (Ambrose 2000).

Constructing tunnels through the high mountains was dangerous and difficult. Dynamite, hand drills driven with sledges and reinforcing openings with timber made this the most time-consuming part of constructing the miles of track. The C.P. had the more difficult task of crossing the Sierra Nevada. The deep snows of winter closed the tracks and made construction nearly impossible. Chinese crews digging the tunnels through the mountains literally lived underground, in shelters buried in snow, walking to the tunnels through wood-covered walkways through the deep drifts, to spend their days in the mountain (Ambrose 2000).

One of the engineering marvels of the Central Pacific was the snow shed constructed to keep the tracks clear of snow and the railroad operating through the Sierras in the winter. The sheds, constructed of 75 million feet of timber and 900 tons of bolts and spikes, totaled 37 miles in length. Their cost was more than $2 million (Ambrose 2000).

Figure 15.2 Snow Sheds on the Central Pacific.
Courtesy of the Library of Congress Prints and Photographs Division. Reproduction number: LC-USZ62-27595

While the C.P. dug its way through the Sierras, the U.P. raced across the Great Plains, facing a different challenge. Where would the railroad obtain the material for ties in the vast, nearly treeless prairies? "By far the most significant railroad use of wood was for crossties. Each mile of track required over twenty-five hundred ties" (MacCleery 1994a). The only wood available locally to the Union Pacific was cottonwood, a tree that grew along the river bottoms. The wood of cottonwood is light, weak, susceptible to rot and not very resistant to the wear and tear of supporting the heavy and repeated loads of railroad traffic. But the U.P. used cottonwood. It could replace ties later. Winning the race with the C.P. and collecting the profits from the land grants came first (Ambrose 2000).

M. G. Kern of the U.S. Department of Agriculture's Forestry Division—the forerunner of today's Forest Service—described the problems that were becoming apparent in the late nineteenth century as a result of the railroads' insatiable appetite for wood. Kern predicted timber shortages that would result from the "reckless system of forest clearing" to obtain sufficient wood for crossties (Williams 1989). Preservative treatments for crossties did not appear until the twentieth century, so they had to replace ties every five to seven years. They replaced crossties on an estimated 50,000 miles of track annually by 1900, requiring an annual harvest of 15,000 to 20,000 acres of timber (MacCleery 1994a). Kern recommended treating crossties with chemical preservatives and the replanting of forests to alleviate the problems he foresaw (Williams 1989).

Methods developed of extending the life of railroad ties with chemical preservatives. The preservatives were fungicidal and insecticidal. The Burnett process injected zinc chloride into the wood with high pressure. The Bethel process also involved pressure treating but used the more effective creosote—made from coal tar—as the preservative. We still use creosote to treat ties, marine pilings and utility poles (Williams 1989).

The companies also constructed rolling stock primarily with wood. Wheels, chassis and locomotives were iron or steel. But the carriages, flat cars and box cars were mostly wood. They lavishly decorated the interiors of passenger cars and trolley cars with oak, walnut and butternut. The Pullman Company of Chicago became a household name for building light wood passenger rail cars. Pullman introduced sleepers for overnight travel in 1858 and dining cars after the Civil War. The Pullman cars were known to be "as luxurious as the interior of a Victorian mansion" (Youngquist and Fleischer 1977).

Figure 15.3 Print of Pacific Railroad. *Harper's Weekly print of the completion of the first transcontinental railroad, Promontory Point, Utah (1869).*

Courtesy of the Library of Congress Prints and Photographs Division.
Reproduction number: LC-USZ62-116354

REVOLUTIONIZING TRANSPORTATION

On May 10, 1869, the Central Pacific and Union Pacific Railroads joined their tracks with a golden spike at Promontory Point, Utah. One could now measure the journey across America in days instead of months. The C.P. and U.P. were soon advertising travel from New York to San Francisco in less than seven days—a far cry from the six months required before. Travel costs significantly reduced, allowing Americans to travel more extensively and to see the wonders of their great and beautiful country.

The railroad along with the telegraph led to the development of nationwide markets for a wide variety of goods as well as a national economy, including a national stock market. Railroads contributed to the melding of various regional cultures that existed before the Civil War into a national culture. Wholesale and distribution centers grew around railroad hubs as they had around major waterway junctions before the Civil War. Chicago remained an important wholesale and distribution center for the lumber industry as railroads replaced waterways as the primary mode of transportation (Ambrose 2000).

The railroads were pioneers in developing and promoting an American tourism industry by making it possible for people to travel rapidly and inexpensively for pleasure. Railroads lobbied Congress to establish national parks, built luxury hotels and established spur lines to make scenic places accessible. The Northern Pacific built the historic "Old Faithful Inn" and several other lodges in Yellowstone. It completed a spur line to the north entrance of the park in 1883 where one of the railroad's fleet of horse-drawn coaches transported visitors into the park. The Great Northern built a spur into Glacier National Park and constructed several hotels, including the luxurious Many Glacier Hotel. The Santa Fe was not to be outdone, running a line to the Grand Canyon and building its luxury hotel, El Tovar, and Hopi House, a replica of a Hopi Indian pueblo, to sell Indian arts and crafts to visitors. The Alaska Railroad, built by the Department of the Interior and completed in 1923, remains the most traveled link to Denali National Park in Alaska's remote interior[5] (Kraft and Chappell 1999).

Railroads advertised and sold hunting packages to the American west to American and European sportsmen. In 1866, a "cog railroad" was built to transport tourists to the top of New Hampshire's Mount Washington (elevation 6,288 feet), the highest point in the eastern United States. A railroad magnate built a grand hotel at the foot of the mountain in 1905. Railroads made it possible for Americans to travel rapidly and inexpensively for pleasure.

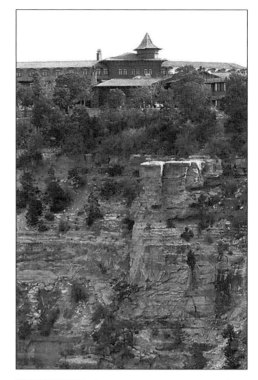

Figure 15.4 El Tovar. *Grand Canyon National Park.*

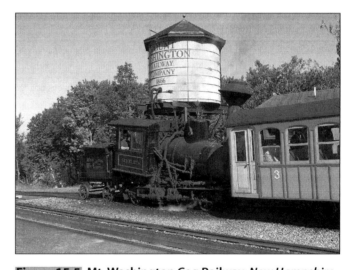

Figure 15.5 Mt. Washington Cog Railway. *New Hampshire.*

ENVIRONMENTAL IMPACTS OF THE RAILROADS

There was an estimated 350,000 miles of railroad in the United States in 1910. The construction and maintenance of railroads had a greater impact on America's forests of the late nineteenth and early twentieth centuries than any other industry. Historical records

---

[5] Princess Cruises, a transportation company, not a railroad, operates the largest lodging accommodations at Denali.

indicate that railroads consumed 20 to 25 percent of the total timber harvest during this era (MacCleery 1994a). Wood burning locomotives required fueling stations every 10 to 25 miles and consumed an estimated 4 to 5 million cords of firewood per year during the 1850s (Carlsen 2008).

Railroads not only consumed vast quantities of wood. They made formerly inaccessible stands of timber accessible to logging operations. The pattern of lumbering prior to the railroads was consistent in the mountainous terrain of the Appalachians, the Rockies, the Sierras and the Cascades, as well as in the swamps of the Deep South. Settlers had timbered valleys and gentle slopes, but ridges, mountainous terrain and swampy ground remained forested because they were inaccessible or because removing logs from inhospitable terrain was too difficult. The railroads changed the accessibility equation (Clarkson 1964, Williams 1989).

Logging railroads enabled fast and inexpensive transportation of logs out of the woods. Powerful locomotives, such as the Shay, Climax and Heisler engines, were specifically designed to operate on steep slopes and pull heavy loads.[6] Linked in tandem, the engines were capable of pulling astonishing amounts of wood out of the forest. Railroads made the industry more mobile. Logging camps on rails could move quickly and easily from a cut over area to new stands of timber. Boom towns sprung up in the woods as loggers and mills moved in and withered and died as they moved out. In many ways, the pattern of industrial migration was reminiscent of the building of the transcontinental railroad (Clarkson 1964, Williams 1989).

Figure 15.6 Train Pulled by Shay Engines. *Cass Scenic Railroad, Cass, WV.*

The railroads brought fire into the woods. Locomotives threw sparks, and the building of railroads chopped up forests and grasslands and enabled the establishment of fire-prone weeds along track beds. Railroads brought farmers, loggers and towns into the forests, contributing to the fuels that could ignite into a major grass or forest fire (Carlsen 2008, Pyne 1982, 2001).

Railroads impacted wildlife. Nowhere was this more apparent than on the Great Plains. The transcontinental railroad split the great bison herd into northern and southern herds because bison would not cross the tracks. Later railroads across the Plains further fragmented the herds.

The railroads brought bison hunters onto the Plains—wealthy sportsmen and men who made their livings killing the great beasts for their tongues, leaving the remainder of the carcass to rot. They sent the tongues to meat packing plants and exported them France where the buffalo tongues were considered a delicacy. Passengers on trains killed more bison, taking pot shots from moving trains. Railroads even advertised the

---

[6] Cass Scenic Railroad State Park in Cass, West Virginia, is the site of an old logging town where a logging railroad built in 1901 transports tourists to the top of Bald Knob behind original Shay locomotives. The website of the state park is *http://www.cassrailroad.com/index.html.*

chance to kill bison without leaving the train. The herds began to disappear and with them the way of life of the Indians of the Plains—the bison hunters whose culture flourished with the introduction of the horse and just as quickly declined with the coming of the railroad.

THE LEGACY OF THE TRANSCONTINENTAL RAILROAD

As the Civil War tore the United States apart, the transcontinental railroad helped bring the nation together as nothing before it. By 1900, five great railroads connected the east coast to the west coast. A sixth transcontinental railroad spanned the continent in Canada. In the twentieth century, sleeper cars and domed rail cars catered to the cross-country tourist trade.

Development of a paved U.S. and Interstate highway system and inexpensive, fast and convenient air travel after World War II caused the decline of passenger railroads. Today tourist railroads exist in every corner of America, keeping alive the technologies and spirit of rail travel. The railroads were an imperfect system and those who built them were imperfect men. But their vision and what they built was, as Stephen Ambrose describes it, "grand."

Figure 15.7 Budd "Vista Dome" Rail Car. *Built in the 1950s, this car is now operated by the Conway Scenic Railroad, Conway, NH.*

Homework

Name: _____ Date: _____

What were the major cities along the routes of the five major U.S. transcontinental railroads?

1. Atchison, Topeka ands Santa Fe

2. Central Pacific/Union Pacific

3. Great Northern

4. Northern Pacific

5. Southern Pacific

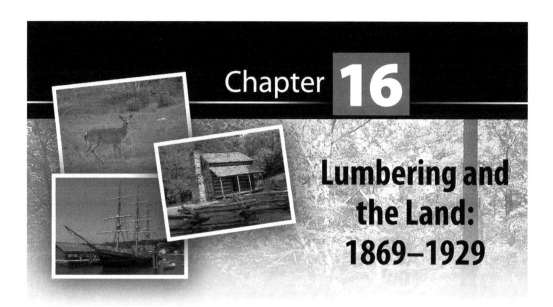

Chapter 16

Lumbering and the Land: 1869–1929

Between 1869 and 1929, the lumber industry experienced the same rapid industrialization and growth that occurred in other industries. Driven by the consumption of wood by the railroads, a growing population and the needs for housing, the rate of industrial timber harvesting increased. Commercial lumber production increased from eight billion board feet in 1860 to 45 billion board feet in 1906 (Williams 1989).

During this era, the lumber industry evolved into two distinct segments using different resources that centered in different regions and produced different products. The divergence into separate softwood and hardwood industries remains in place in the twenty-first century.

The softwood industry used coniferous trees in the northern tier of eastern states from Maine to Minnesota where white pine was the primary resource. In addition, it existed in the southeast where southern pines and, to a lesser extent, baldcypress were the primary resources, and in the west where the mixed conifer forests provided a variety of species, including Douglas-fir, ponderosa pine, redwood, larch, western hemlock, western spruces, incense-cedar and western redcedar. Softwoods were useful primarily in construction and were less expensive than hardwoods. This was a production-driven industry where profits depended on the volume of wood produced. It resulted in economies of scale that favored large mills owned by big corporations.

The hardwood industry remained an eastern industry. In general, many small mills dominated it, with its products intended for secondary manufacture. That is to say, sawmills shipped lumber to flooring, furniture, millwork and cabinet manufacturers where they converted it to final products. The industry valued the higher quality hardwoods for their appearance, and the uses made this a quality-driven industry in which small mills and single mill companies could thrive. Lower quality hardwood lumber and less desirable species found their way into timbers, crossties, fences and pallets. Today, the pallet industry consumes the greatest volume of hardwood lumber.

THE FORCES OF CHANGE

The population of the United States grew from 38 million in 1870 to 105 million in 1920. Twenty-seven million immigrants arrived between 1870 and 1915 to help swell the population. The growing population required a rapid increase of the rates of timber harvest. At the same time, economic prosperity increased the per capita consumption of wood. Steam power resulted in greater mechanization, but the high capital cost of boilers, steam engines and machinery favored larger companies.

Unrestricted capitalism with little regulation or interference from the federal government led to growth of corporations and monopolies. There was no income tax until 1913, so huge fortunes became amassed. This was the "Gilded Age"—the era of the "robber barons." Great industrialists created great corporations: Andrew Carnegie and U.S. Steel, John D. Rockefeller and Standard Oil and Cornelius Vanderbilt and the New York Central Railroad (Williams 1989).

It was an era of mechanized woodworking. Improvements in metallurgy led to better woodworking tools. A Shaker woman, Tabitha Babbitt,[1] invented the circular saw in 1810 in Massachusetts. Babbitt saw the need for a more efficient sawing technology after watching her brothers sawing lumber with a two-man pit saw and was inspired to invent a saw that operated on the same principal of rotary motion as a spinning wheel (Lienhard 2007, McClintock 2000).

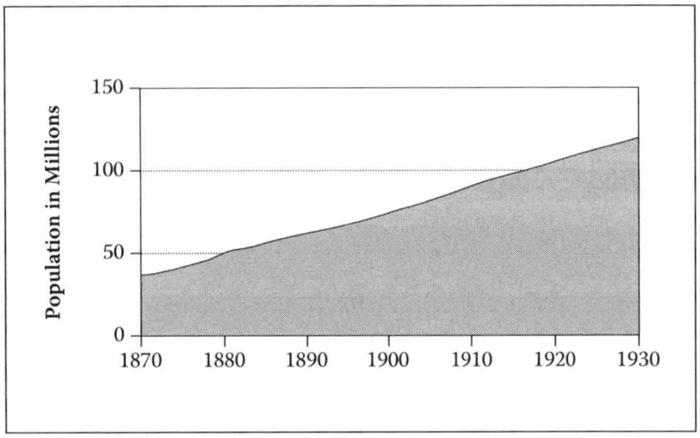

Steel and better welding technology enabled the invention of the high-speed bandsaw capable of cutting larger logs at greater rates of speed. "The band saw is an endless belt of steel, having teeth on one or both edges, traveling at great speed around an upper and lower pulley. The latter is attached by belts to a steam engine which drives the saw" (Clarkson 1964). The circular saw and bandsaw were more efficient than the older up-and-down sawmills in that they replaced reciprocal motion where the wood was cut only on the down stroke of the saw with rotary motion where the saw was constantly cutting wood.

Figure 16.1 U.S. Population: 1870–1930.

Industry became more specialized, producing fewer products at lower cost. Balloon framing led to "mass production of a standardized manufactured end product" (Williams 1989).

At the end of the era, Swiss inventor Andreas Stihl invented a workable chainsaw. The device was large, heavy and unwieldy to operate. A lighter, more manageable chainsaw was not developed until the 1950s (Lienhard 2007).

Lumber and other products had become commodities. In other words, their quality and characteristics changed little from manufacturer to manufacturer. Consumers would thus choose between products based upon price alone. Manufacturers able to keep production costs low held a competitive advantage in the marketplace.

---

[1] Tabitha Babbitt (sometimes spelled "Babbit") also invented cut nails.

Railroads provided fast, widespread and reliable transportation to get logs from the forest to the mills and lumber from the mills to the markets. The railroad transformed lumbering from local and regional industries into a national industry (Williams 1989).

The industry's practice was to cut timber in the winter, to drive it down rivers in the spring and to mill it in the summer. This tied up business capital for up to a year, giving another competitive advantage to larger, better capitalized companies. Lumber was like other industries of the Gilded Age in that it became a big business.

LUMBERING AS BIG BUSINESS

Companies vertically and horizontally integrated their operations. They vertically integrated by purchasing timberland and harvesting their timber as well as by owning logging railroads or other means of transporting logs to their own sawmills and distribution and retail lumber yards in order to market their products directly to consumers. They achieved horizontal integration by attempting to build competitive monopolies in certain regions or with certain product lines. For example, if you travel across the state of Washington today, you will find that large companies control certain regions. In many cases, this ownership pattern formed between 1869 and 1919 (Williams 1989).

Lumber barons (similar to Carnegie in steel and Rockefeller in oil) had their hands in many operations. Businessmen held joint ownership in companies that bought and sold from each other. For example, Albert Ames of Ames Tools was president of the Union Pacific. Of course, the Union Pacific needed tools to build and maintain track and Ames needed an inexpensive means to transport tools to markets (Ambrose 2000). Companies formed trade associations to fix prices and collectively force down costs in the era before the Sherman Anti-trust Act. Businessmen amassed unimaginable fortunes in an era with little regulation and no income tax.

LUMBER PRODUCTION AND PRICES

Prior to 1850, the record of land use and lumber production is largely compiled from anecdotal evidence. Beginning with the 1850 census, the government collected

Table 16.1 *Leading Manufacturing Industries in 1870 and 1920*

1870 Census of Manufacturers		1920 Census of Manufacturers	
1. Flour and Grist Mills	10.0 %	1. Slaughtering and Meat Packing	6.8 %
2. *Lumber*	6.0 %	2. Iron and Steel	4.5 %
3. Iron and Steel	5.0 %	3. Automobiles	3.8 %
4. Clothing	4.7 %	4. Foundry and Machinery	3.4 %
5. Boots and Shoes	4.3 %	5. Cotton Goods	3.4 %
6. Cotton Goods	4.0 %	6. Flour and Grist Mills	3.3 %
7. Woolen Goods	3.6 %	7. Petroleum	2.6 %
8. Carpentering	3.1 %	8. Shipbuilding	2.3 %
9. Foundry and Machinery	3.0 %	9. *Lumber*	2.2 %
10. Sugar and Molasses	2.8 %	10. Railroad Cars	2.1 %

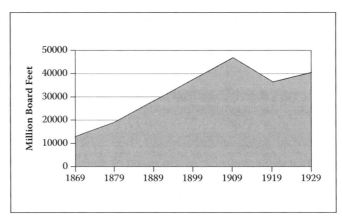

Figure 16.2 U.S. Lumber Production: 1869–1929.

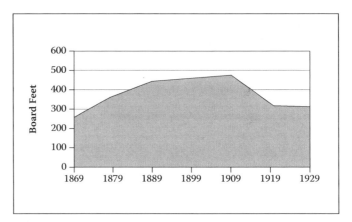

Figure 16.3 Per Capita Lumber Consumption: 1869–1929.

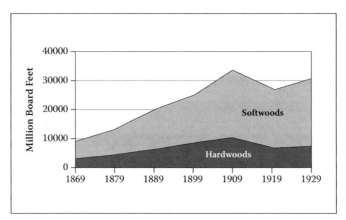

Figure 16.4 Softwood and Hardwood Lumber Production: 1869–1929.

industry data. The Census Bureau began collecting total lumber production data in 1869. The Forestry Division and, later, the Forest Service collected or estimated production by species and price data beginning in 1899.

In 1870, the U.S. Census indicated that the lumber industry ranked second to flour and gristmills among all manufacturing industries, accounting for 6 percent of all manufacturing. This ranking remained unchanged from the first census of manufacturers in 1850. However, by 1920 lumber production had fallen to ninth, accounting for 2.2 percent of manufacturing. Industries that had emerged during the Industrial Revolution had surpassed it, along with some older industries that had grown in importance as American society became more urbanized and less agrarian.

During the period from 1869 to 1919, lumber production tripled, growing from 12.7 billion board feet in 1869 and reaching a peak of 44.5 billion feet in 1909 (Steer 1948).

In 1869, softwood lumber production was an estimated 9.2 billion board feet. Hardwood production was an estimated 3.5 billion board feet, a little more than a third of the production of softwoods. Production of softwoods and hardwoods increased until the peak production year of 1909. That year produced approximately 33.9 billion board feet of softwoods and 10.6 billion board feet of hardwoods. During this forty year period, both softwood and hardwood production increased approximately threefold (Steer 1948).

The story of the lumber industry in the nineteenth century is a story of a migratory industry as lumbermen moved from cutover land to regions where virgin stands of timber were plentiful.

LUMBERING IN THE NORTHEAST

The lumber industry of New England led production during the early decades of the nineteenth century with Maine producing the largest quantity of lumber in the U.S. "The heavy cutting of early days, particularly for fuel, produced a shortage of wood as early as 1840 in many sections of New England" (U.S. Forest Service 1920). White pine made up almost the entire harvest of softwoods prior to 1840. As supplies of white pine dwindled, spruce took on a more prominent role. By 1870 logging had almost entirely removed the best old growth white pine, and by 1880 lumbering of second growth yielded "an annual cut of 200 to 300 million board feet."

By 1850, New York had overtaken Maine as the leading state for lumber production, contributing an estimated 29 percent of national production (U.S. Forest Service 1920). By 1920, the annual cut in New York had decreased to less than 350 million board feet from 1,300 million board feet in 1850.

In 1860, Pennsylvania led the nation in lumber production. As in Maine and New York, white pine was the most highly valued softwood species, and by 1870 lumbering had greatly diminished Pennsylvania's white pine stands. Hemlock became an increasingly significant part of Pennsylvania's production as the state had to import white pine from Michigan. In 1889, Pennsylvania experienced its peak production of the era. Since that time, Pennsylvania has become a hardwood producer.

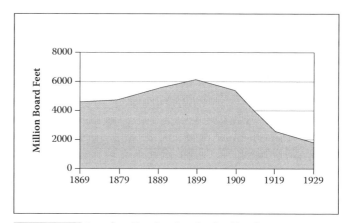

Figure 16.5 Lumber Production in the Northeast: 1869–1929.

A significant development occurred in this era as wood pulp became a cheap substitute for rags in papermaking. New England and New York became leading paper producers between 1890 and 1920 (U.S. Forest Service 1920). Later in the twentieth century Wisconsin emerged as the nation's leading paper producing state.

Lumbering in the Lake States

Lumber operations began in Michigan and Wisconsin as early as 1835. As the lumber industry declined in the northeast with the removal of the white pine, the industry began its migration to the Lake States. In 1876, Michigan had surpassed Pennsylvania as the leading lumber producing state. Pennsylvania was second followed by Wisconsin and New York (U.S. Forest Service 1920).

White pine in the northern regions of Michigan, Wisconsin and Minnesota was what drew the lumbermen to the Lake States, and white pine constituted a large portion of production through much of the era. In 1869, it constituted an estimated 45 percent of the nation's timber harvest and 76 percent of the harvest in the Lake States (Steer 1948). In the peak production year of 1889, the Lake States accounted for 76 percent of the white pine harvested nationwide. After 1889, white pine harvests declined rapidly as logging had cut the best stands over.

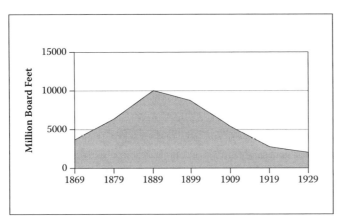

Figure 16.6 Lumber Production in the Lake States: 1869–1929.

A significant development in the Lake States was the concentration of the American furniture industry in Grand Rapids Michigan. Grand Rapids has a unique location between Michigan's hardwood forests to the south and softwood forests to the north. Previously the furniture industry had centered in New England, but, like lumbering, it followed resource supplies into the Lake States (Wisdom and Wisdom 1983).

In the mid 1800s, five factors enabled the development of a thriving center for the furniture industry in Grand Rapids: a plentiful, inexpensive and readily available supply of timber; an available source of skilled immigrant labor; the Grand River: a waterway for transportation and power; capital and Yankee experience of New England investors; and a ready market in the growing settlements of the Midwest. Companies built the Grand Rapids mills on the New England system of industrialization. In its heyday, approximately one third of the Grand Rapids workforce was under fourteen years of age.

The history of the Grand Rapids industry is also a story of the development of marketing institutions in the furniture industry that exist to this day. The Grand Rapids furniture industry began by manufacturing inexpensive pieces that settlers could afford. At the 1876 Centennial Exhibition in Philadelphia, Grand Rapids manufacturers were showing, large, heavy, ornately carved Victorian furniture. In 1878, the city held its first Furniture Trade Show to attract buyers from department stores around the country. Soon afterwards, it built a Furniture Exhibition Building to house exhibits by out-of-town manufacturers. Grand Rapids became an "industry cluster" where hardware and finish manufacturers located close to the furniture manufacturers.

By the 1890s, the local supply of hardwoods had disappeared and Grand Rapids manufacturers developed roller printing of hardwood grain patterns on pine. In 1891, the last log drive on the Grand River took place, and from the 1890s through the 1920s the industry of Grand Rapids was evolving into a high-end industry. In the '20s and

'30s Grand Rapids was becoming known for "museum quality reproductions." By the 1930s North Carolina was capturing markets largely for the same reasons that made Grand Rapids so successful seventy to eighty years earlier.

As eastern lumbermen led the timbering operations into the Lake States, lumbermen from the Lake States moved south and west as they depleted timber supplies. The cut and run timbering that took place in the Lake States in the late 1800s marked a transition in attitudes toward forests and industrial responsibility. The lumbermen came to the Great Lakes with the attitudes that predominated in the northeast. They thought that clearing the land of trees made the land more valuable for settlement by homesteaders who would farm the land, thus achieving what most Americans believed was the highest and best use of the land.

In the southern Lake States, the northeastern precedent held as the land was fertile and valuable for agriculture. Farther north, in the pineries, this was not true. Although timber companies sold land to farmers, the long winters and infertile soil led to the rapid abandonment of farms. Afterwards, timber companies abandoned land after harvesting and moved on.

Harvesting was by clear-cutting, with only the largest and best logs going to the mill. Tops and branches—slash—was left in the woods. *A lot* of slash was left in the woods. The slash was kindling, and some of the most tragic forest fires in the nation's history occurred in the late 1800s in the Lake States.

On October 8, 1871, the Great Peshtigo Fire in Wisconsin burned 2,400 square miles and killed 1,200 people. It was the worst forest fire disaster in American history. That same day to the south another fire consumed much of the city of Chicago. The Great Hinckley Fire in Minnesota killed 600 people and consumed 160,000 acres on September 1, 1894. Fires swept across Michigan's Upper Peninsula that same year and again in 1896, burning the town of Ontonagon. Metz, Michigan burned in 1908 (Pyne 1982).

The worst fire seasons were the result of a deadly combination of events. Drought and wind turned the slash from farming and logging operations into a tinderbox. Fires set by farmers, sparks set by steam engines and industrial fires set the forests ablaze. Towns and new construction added fuel to the infernos.

The industry "passed through" Michigan, Wisconsin and Minnesota, leaving cut-over lands as it moved west and south. Some of the land was sold to farmers who generally had trouble succeeding, especially in the northern regions of the Lake States. Local government reclaimed other timberland in lieu of delinquent taxes. Eventually the industry moved on to the Pacific Northwest and into the South. But people, including lumbermen, looked at the lessons of the Lake States and began to rethink the way the lumber industry would meet the nation's growing demand for wood.

LUMBERING IN THE SOUTH

As had occurred in other regions along the east coast, the inhabitants of Maryland, Virginia the Carolinas and Georgia had cleared the forests and used the timber of the coast since the time of the first European settlement. The longleaf pine forests of North Carolina became the primary source of naval stores. Some southern pine lumber from the tidewater of Virginia and Maryland's eastern shore got shipped north by schooner into the ports of Baltimore and Philadelphia prior to the Civil War. But, for the most part, lumber production in the South was used locally (U.S. Forest Service 1920).

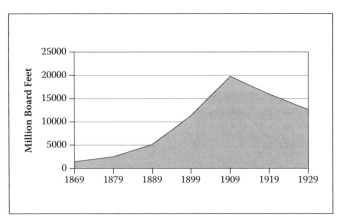

Figure 16.7 Lumber Production in the South: 1869–1929.

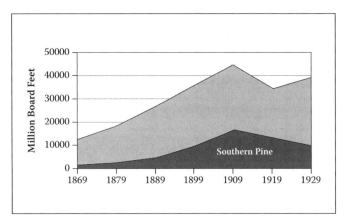

Figure 16.8 Southern Pines in Nationwide Production: 1869–1929.

The lumber industry of the southeast was, and is, a southern pine industry. In the 1870s, extensive lumber production began in Georgia and the Gulf States. Southern pine lumber began penetrating markets in the North around 1875 and grew rapidly in the 1890s as its low market price drove northern demand for southern pine. By 1909, southern pine accounted for approximately half of the nation's softwood lumber production. Although baldcypress brought the highest prices among southern softwoods between 1889 and 1919, southern pine accounted for 79 percent of the south's production and 36 percent of all lumber production in the U.S. in the peak year of 1909. Production declined afterwards, but the South's second growth pine forests once again became a primary source of resources in the last few decades of the twentieth century (U.S. Forest Service 1920, Steer 1948).

As production levels in the Lake States declined, lumbermen from that region moved operations into the South just as they had moved from the northeast into the Lake States earlier in the century. But there were indications that the lessons learned in the Lake States were taking hold. The stirrings of a conservation ethic were emerging in the South.

The idea of the reforestation of southern pine timberlands may have begun in the 1890s with the botanist Charles Mohr, who observed that shortleaf pine regenerated naturally on cutovers and abandoned fields in Mississippi. Henry Hardtner of the Urania Lumber Company of Urania, Louisiana, began experimenting with pine reforestation in 1904. Hardtner concluded that reforestation efforts would succeed if they controlled razorback hogs and fire (Williams 1989).

LUMBERING IN THE WEST

Lumbering in the West began at the time of settlement. The first sawmill on Puget Sound began operations in 1845 (U.S. Forest Service 1920). "Within a decade lumbering became

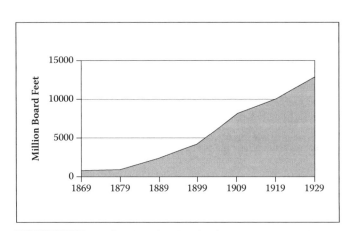

Figure 16.9 Lumber Production in the West: 1869–1929.

. . . the chief industry in western Washington." When the Northern Pacific Railroad was completed in 1882, production in the Pacific Northwest increased rapidly as Midwestern and eastern markets became more accessible to western sawmills. However, competition from southern pine was intense and West Coast mills had trouble competing because of the greater cost of shipping from the West.

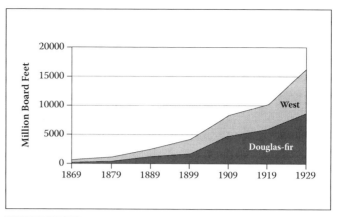

Figure 16.10 Production of Douglas-fir Lumber: 1869–1929.

Railroads promoted the western softwood industry by establishing "blanket" freight rates that set a single shipping charge (as opposed to a mileage-based rate) from certain regions of the West to any point in the Midwest or East. This was mutually beneficial to both western lumber companies and railroads. Each was able to boost the volume of its business by setting a uniform rate. The blanket rates helped western softwood producers compete successfully in eastern construction markets at least into the 1970s and '80s.

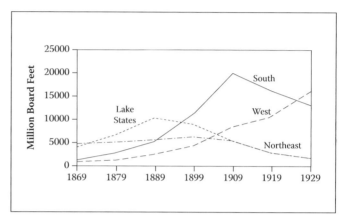

Figure 16.11 Lumber Production by Region: 1869–1929.

There was very little timber harvest and lumber production in California before the Gold Rush of 1849. Redwood production began about 1860. Mining also increased demand for lumber in the Rocky Mountains beginning in the early 1850s. It wasn't until after 1900 that the lumber industry in the Rockies expanded past local markets into the Midwest and East. (U.S. Forest Service 1920)

Western forests are a diverse mix of mostly coniferous species. Douglas-fir, hemlock, larch, spruce, fir, cedars and redwood are the dominant Pacific Coast timber species. Redwood is a California species. Ponderosa pine, Douglas-fir, western white pine, lodgepole pine, spruce and white fir are among the important species of the Rockies.

By 1919, Douglas-fir had become the leading western timber species when the industry produced 5.9 billion board feet, accounting for 58 percent of western production. Douglas-fir is still the dominant commercial species of the West although the industry has greatly reduced harvests since the spotted owl controversy of the 1990s curtailed harvest from national forests. Ponderosa pine (1.76 billion board feet; 17 percent) was second in importance.

Although the migratory nature of the industry characterized the era, lumbering continued throughout the forested regions of the United States. As the forests in one region diminished, another region rose in prominence. However, lumbering continued in the old region, although at a lower rate (Williams 1989).

THE DOMINANT COMMERCIAL SPECIES

As the industry moved to new regions, the production levels and value of different timber species rose and fell.

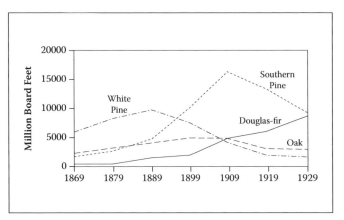

Figure 16.12 Production of Major Species: 1869–1929.

White pine was the dominant commercial timber species in the United States from 1869 to 1889. By 1899, southern pine surpassed white pine in volume produced and widened the gap with other species each succeeding decade. In 1899, Douglas-fir production began to rise rapidly. While white pine, southern pine and oak production fell between 1909 and 1919, Douglas-fir production continued to grow (Steer 1948).

Steer's data included information on lumber prices. From the figures below, you can see that softwood lumber prices rose from 1899—the first year Steer was able to quantify—to 1919. But the relative position of various species changed little over those twenty years with two notable exceptions. Eastern white pine was losing its position to western pines and southern pine was improving its price position (Steer 1948).

Oaks dominated hardwood production during this period. In 1869, the oaks constituted an estimated 57 percent of hardwood production. In 1909, oaks comprised 41 percent of hardwood production. Price data for hardwoods reveal greater volatility in markets than softwood prices. Prices of more valuable hardwoods were and still are significantly higher than softwood prices, reflecting the emphasis upon appearance uses and quality in the hardwood industry. In 1899, prices for black walnut were double that of any other species. Hickory and ash prices were second and third respectively because of the high demand for those species in the manufacture of wagon wheels.

The year 1919 reflected one of the remarkable trends in the history of the hardwood lumber industry as dogwood became the highest priced American wood by a large margin. Dogwood is a very hard, fine textured wood that was in high demand in this

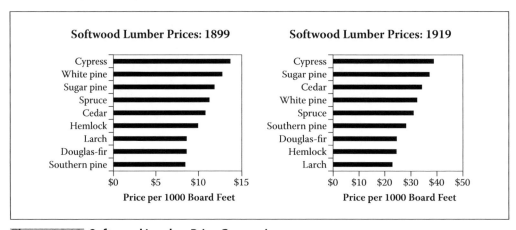

Figure 16.13 Softwood Lumber Price Comparison.

era for use for shuttles and other tools in the textile industry. The price of ash had surpassed hickory because logging had removed the best quality hickory from the forest. (It was during this era that white ash replaced hickory as the primary raw material for the manufacture of baseball bats for the same reason.)

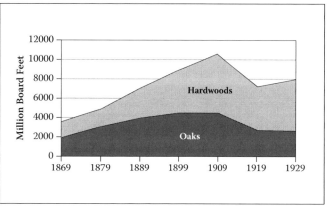

Figure 16.14 Oaks and Hardwood Production: 1869–1929.

It is surprising to someone familiar with the lumber industry in the twenty-first century that yellow-poplar commanded a higher price than oak. At the time, many of the historic uses for oak had disappeared—ship timbers and timber framing—and oak became a crosstie (a low value use) species. People valued yellow-poplar for furniture frames and core stock—the hidden parts or parts covered by a veneer of a more valuable species like walnut (Steer 1948).

The changes observed in hardwood prices reflect the volatility of hardwood markets. Primary uses of certain hardwoods tend to come and go. In other hardwood markets such as furniture and cabinets, species preferences change as styles change. Softwood markets, on the other hand, are commodity markets. Therefore, species preferences are less likely to change unless the availability of certain species diminishes.

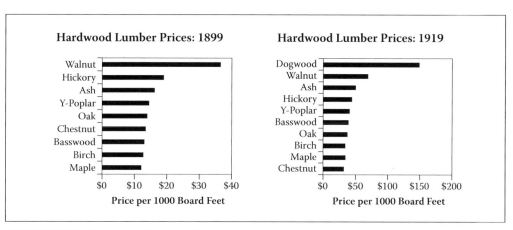

Figure 16.15 Hardwood Lumber Price Comparison.

Homework

Name: _____ Date: _____

Define the following logging and lumbering terms:

Cant hook:

Choker:

Edger:

Log loader:

Peavey:

Skidder:

Slash:

Trim saw:

Widow maker:

Yarding:

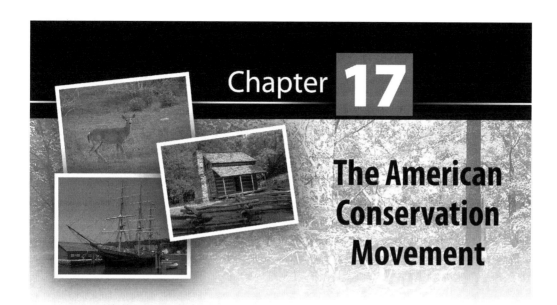

Chapter 17

The American Conservation Movement

The post-Civil War period was a time of rapid population increase driven, in large part, by immigration. During this era Ellis Island was built to process the millions of immigrants arriving from Italy, Austria-Hungary, Poland, Russia, Germany, Ireland and other countries. The nation was undergoing a transition from a rural, agrarian society to an industrialized, urban society. It was the "Gilded Age" when industrialists such as John D. Rockefeller, J. P. Morgan, Andrew Carnegie, Cornelius Vanderbilt, John Jacob Astor and other "robber barons" accumulated tremendous fortunes. It was not just the extremely wealthy who enjoyed this prosperity. The standard of living of most Americans was improving through the Victorian era.

Recommended Reading

Miller, Char. 2001. *Gifford Pinchot and the Making of Modern Environmentalism.*

Pinchot's story is the story of the maturation of the American conservation movement into a political reality. Miller's biography is a straightforward account that neither discredits Pinchot's contributions nor glosses over his shortcomings.

There was a growing mistrust—often, but not always, justified—of big business (Cubbage et al. 1993). The Peshtigo Fire and other catastrophic forest fires alarmed the public, particularly in fire prone regions of New England, the Lake States, and west. The country recognized the massacre of Big Foot and his band of Minneconjou Lakota by the 7th Cavalry at Wounded Knee in 1890 as the closing of the frontier in the continental United States. The long era of westward expansion had come to an end. Americans reacted with a sense of loss and nostalgia.

The excesses of the era led to numerous reform movements: business reform, the labor movement, women's suffrage and the temperance movement. Reform took place in the passage of anti-trust laws, child labor legislation and worker protection, which marked a significant change of attitude toward unrestricted capitalism. Reform marked an expansion of the government's role in regulating business and everyday life. Reform found its champion in the first decade of the twentieth century in the progressive politics of President Theodore Roosevelt.

The conservation movement emerged along with these other reform movements in response to the perceived ills of the Industrial Revolution. Pisani (1997) characterizes the conservation movement of the nineteenth century as afflicted with an overriding sense of pessimism. There was a growing sense of alarm over urban crowding, poverty, strikes, the economic depression of the 1890s, the rapid growth of cities, land monopolies and a relative decline of the rural population. Professional hunters and trappers along with the loss of habitat were causing the decimation of waterfowl, bison, beaver, white-tailed deer and other species. Agriculture, railroads and lumbering contributed to the loss of the great virgin forests of the northeast and Lake States. Progress was wonderful, but Americans learned that progress without prudence carried a great cost.

Early conservationists focused on four primary natural resource issues: wildlife, water, soil and forests. These issues intertwined, and conservationists found it necessary to become knowledgeable in a variety of subjects. The movement derived its inspiration from George Perkins Marsh's 1864 book, *Man and Nature,* and found its leaders in large part among the nation's intellectual and, ironically, wealthy industrial elite. The ideas promoted by the early conservationists were often in conflict with each other as people with differing interests and priorities contributed their various points of view to a growing debate over natural resources.

By the end of the nineteenth century, the primary division within the movement had coalesced around fundamental philosophical differences between advocates of conservation and the preservation of natural resources. Although utilitarian conservation was the dominant philosophy of the movement, its proponents were frequently at odds with adherents of the hands-off philosophy of preservation. The two divergent philosophies toward land management found their champions in Gifford Pinchot and John Muir. The two began as allies who, over time, became bitter antagonists. The policy battles they waged in the early twentieth century continue between their philosophical heirs of the twenty-first century.

Figure 17.1 George Perkins Marsh.

Courtesy of the Library of Congress Prints and Photographs Division. Reproduction number: LC-DIG-cwpbh-02223

GEORGE PERKINS MARSH

The man considered the father of the conservation movement was a New England Yankee, George Perkins Marsh (1801–1882). It is not surprising that the conservation movement of the nineteenth century had its roots in New England. It was the first region to lose most of its forest land to agriculture and the first to become industrialized. In addition, New England was the breeding ground for many social reform movements, including the abolition of slavery and public education.

Marsh was part of New England's intellectual elite. He was the son of a U.S. Senator, a graduate of Dartmouth College and a lawyer. Marsh was also a scholar who spoke several European languages, wrote several notable works on linguistics and was knowledgeable in a diversity of subjects. He served as a congressman from Vermont from 1843 until 1849 and later as a diplomat in Turkey, Greece, and Italy.

Like most of his generation, Marsh was from a rural background. In a letter to Asa Gray written in 1849, Marsh declared, "I spent my early life almost literally in the woods . . . personally engaged to a considerable extent in clearing lands, and manufacturing and dealing with lumber." Marsh was troubled by the rapid loss of forest that he had observed in his life and began speaking and writing about the "injudicious system of managing woodlands and the products of the forest."

His 1847 "Address to the Agricultural Society of Rutland County, Vermont"[1] was among the first public alarms to the sometimes deleterious impact humans have upon nature. In 1864, Marsh wrote "Man and Nature,"[2] which he later renamed "The Earth as Modified by Human Action: Man and Nature." His writings were not so much a prescription for conservation as they were a catalog of the excesses of agricultural clearing upon forests. But, his writings would influence the generation that would lead the conservation movement, including Gifford Pinchot, George Bird Grinnell and John Muir.

FREDERICK LAW OLMSTED AND THE PRESERVATION OF NIAGARA FALLS

One of the great natural and scenic wonders of the eastern United States is Niagara Falls. The area on the Niagara River by the Falls had become an unsightly complex of mills and factories by the end of the Civil War. The development had obscured the spectacular view of the Falls. In 1869, a group of citizens led by Frederick Law Olmsted (1822–1903) began efforts to preserve the area surrounding the Falls. Their efforts resulted in the establishment by the New York Legislature in 1885 of the Niagara Reservation (now Niagara Falls State Park), the first state park in the United States. Olmsted designed the park, planning for removal of the buildings, creating unobstructed views of the Falls and planting to block the view of the city to the east (Dahl and Molnar 2003, Miller 2001).

Olmsted, a native of Hartford, Connecticut, is best known as the "father of landscape architecture" in America and the designer of New York's Central Park. His role in the conservation movement would extend beyond Niagara Falls. He was one of the earliest advocates of preserving the wonders of Yosemite and would, later in life, have a significant impact upon the establishment of forestry in the United States.

Figure 17.2 Frederick Law Olmsted.

Courtesy of the Library of Congress Prints and Photographs Division. Reproduction number: LC-USZ62-36895

---

[1] *http://memory.loc.gov/cgi-bin/query/r?ammem/consrvbib:@FIELD(NUMBER(vg02))*

[2] *http://memory.loc.gov/cgi-bin/query/r?ammem/consrvbib:@FIELD(NUMBER(vg07))*

YOSEMITE STATE PARK AND THE ADIRONDACK RESERVE

The nation's wealthy elite may have had the strongest longing for frontier and wilderness. Millionaires and their families spent summers in the Adirondacks, the Catskills, the White Mountains, the Appalachians and in the west. Civil War veteran John Wesley Powell led a daring expedition down the Colorado River by boat. John Muir found his solace in the Sierra Nevada. New York politician Theodore Roosevelt became a part-time cowboy, woodsman and big game hunter. The forests and wild lands were becoming the recreational playground of America's most influential citizens. These were the people who could, and did, make the conservation movement possible.

As early as 1864, Congress granted 36,000 acres in the Yosemite Valley and the Mariposa Grove of giant sequoias to the State of California for creation of a state park. This was the first federal action to preserve one of the scenic and natural wonders of the United States. Not surprisingly, Frederick Law Olmsted was one of the most influential proponents of preserving Yosemite and the Mariposa Grove (Greene 1987).

The Adirondacks became a favorite playground of the Gilded Age's elite because of their proximity to New York City. Collis Huntington of the Central Pacific passed away in the Adirondacks. Mark Twain, J. P. Morgan and Woodrow Wilson were frequent visitors. In 1901, Vice President Teddy Roosevelt was hiking in the Adirondacks when a messenger delivered word that President McKinley had died from an assassin's bullet (Schneider 1998). Another New York businessman, James Pinchot, took his son, Gifford, to the Adirondacks where the youngster developed a keen love of nature and interest in wood lore (Miller 2001).

In the same year the New York Legislature created the Niagara Reservation, it created the first major state forest in the nation, the Adirondack Forest Preserve encompassing 750,000 acres (Williams 1989, Youngquist and Fleischer 1977). In 1892, the reserve was enlarged to three million acres to become the Adirondack State Park (Williams 1989). The primary mission of the newly-created state park was recreation, one of the first set-asides of land for this purpose in the United States. Names that would appear in the early history of forestry in America, Franklin B. Hough and Charles Sprague Sargent, were among those involved in the creation of the Adirondacks reserve.

GEORGE BIRD GRINNELL AND THE BOONE AND CROCKETT CLUB

During the nineteenth century, the bison herds became decimated by the fragmentation of habitat caused by the railroads and the professional hunters who slaughtered thousands of the beasts for their hides and tongues.[3] Trappers had pushed the beaver to the brink of extinction to provide pelts to make the stovepipe hats worn by gentlemen during the first half of the century.[4] Waterfowl populations were diminished to alarming levels because of the value of plumes to decorate ladies' hats. White-tailed deer were in danger because doeskin gloves and buckskin jackets and dresses were a

---

[3] Buffalo tongues were canned and exported to France where people considered them a delicacy.

[4] Silk top hats eventually replaced beaver hats in approximately 1850.

fashion rage in Europe and in the eastern cities of the U.S.

Patrician sportsmen were profoundly influenced by calls for conservation of habitat appearing in sporting periodicals—*American Sportsman, Forest and Stream* and *Field and Stream*—that began appearing in the 1870s (Reiger 1997). Charles Hallock, founder (1873) and editor of *Forest and Stream,* stated in the magazine's subtitle that it was "Devoted to . . . Preservation of Forests." Hallock was an advocate of what he called European-style forestry as a means of conserving habitat. In Europe, forestry had developed in the seventeenth and eighteenth centuries out of necessity. Agricultural development had drastically reduced European forests and those that remained had to be carefully managed and used to maintain a sufficient supply of wood to meet the needs of the people. European foresters learned to apply scientific principles in their efforts.

The most influential sportsman/writer was George Bird Grinnell (1849–1938), who became editor and owner of *Forest and Stream* in 1880. Grinnell was typical of the patrician-sportsmen of the era. However, he was very well educated for the time, having a Ph.D. from Yale in natural sciences in

Figure 17.3 George Bird Grinnell. *Accompanied by his wife on Grinnell Glacier (1925).*

Courtesy of the Library of Congress Prints and Photographs Division. Reproduction number: LC-USZ62-93186

1880. In 1882, Grinnell became a powerful advocate of forestry on the editorial page of *Forest and Stream.* He believed that forests should be treated as a "crop . . . which is slow in coming to harvest." Under his leadership, *Forest and Stream* reported the latest developments from Europe in sport, natural history and science. Like Hallock, he advocated scientific forestry as practiced in Europe. He also advocated the creation of a national forestry agency headed by "a competent forestry officer" (Reiger 1997).

The leading conservation organization of the era was the Boone and Crockett Club, established in 1887 by Theodore Roosevelt with Grinnell and Gifford Pinchot among its founding members (Borneman 2004, Reiger 1997). Its membership read like a who's who of patrician sportsmen-conservationists: Roosevelt, Grinnell, General William Tecumseh Sherman, geologist Arnold Hague, Supreme Court lawyer William Haslett Phillips and prominent politicians Henry L. Stimson, Henry Cabot Lodge, Wade Hampton and Elihu Root. Because of its influential membership, "the Boone and Crockett Club—and *not* the Sierra Club—was the first private organization to deal effectively with conservation issues of national scope" (Reiger 1997). Among the many accomplishments of the Boone and Crockett Club was convincing Congress to designate the area around Mount McKinley in remote Alaska as a national park in 1917 (Borneman 2004).

George Grinnell and the Boone and Crockett Club argued that the size of Yellowstone National Park provided insufficient habitat for the game species of the Yellowstone basin and called for expansion of the federally-protected lands around the park. In 1891, President Benjamin Harrison issued a Presidential proclamation creating the Yellowstone National Forest Reserve in Wyoming adjacent to Yellowstone National Park, the nation's first forest reserve (Williams 1989).

Grinnell's other significant contributions to the conservation movement include advocating the creation of Glacier National Park and helping found the Audubon Society and the New York Zoological Society. Another sportsman, William Temple Hornaday, published "The Extermination of the American Bison" in 1889. This report helped focus public attention on the plight of the species and helped generate support to save the species. Grinnell was there alongside Hornaday calling for measures to protect the remaining bison herds.

THE LUMBERMEN: FREDERICK WEYERHAEUSER AND HENRY HARDTNER

Figure 17.4 Mt. Rainier National Park, Washington.

Figure 17.5 Weyerhaeuser Company Timberlands. *In the Cascades, Washington (1997).*

Frederick Weyerhaeuser (1834–1914) was a Minnesota lumberman who, by the end of the nineteenth century, built his company into the largest in the United States. In 1900, Weyerhaeuser and his close friend and neighbor, James J. Hill of the Great Northern and Northern Pacific Railroads, transacted one of the largest land sales in American history. A land swap preceded it that would lead to the establishment of Mount Rainier National Park. Weyerhaeuser purchased 900,000 acres of prime timberland in Washington's Cascade Mountains from the Northern Pacific for $5,400,000.[5] Hill had acquired Mount Rainier when he purchased the Northern Pacific and its remaining land grants in the mid-1890s. When the federal government created Mount Rainier National Park in 1899, Hill arranged to exchange the land within the park boundaries for valuable timberland included in the sale to Weyerhaeuser[6] (Williams 1989).

The sale of land was mutually beneficial to both parties. Weyerhaeuser obtained high quality raw material to keep his mills operating for a number of years. He also probably anticipated that rapid creation of federal forest

---

[5] Ten years earlier, Weyerhaeuser purchased 212,722 acres in Minnesota from the Northern Pacific Railway. He would eventually acquire a total of 1.9 million acres of timberland in the Northwest as well as land in the Lake States and the South.

[6] Hill was more interested in promoting lumber and coal shipments for the Northern Pacific than promoting tourism to Mount Rainier.

reserves would leave little forestland for later purchase. Hill obviously received operating funds but also assured business from Weyerhaeuser's lumber shipments east and the shipment of goods west to support Weyerhaeuser's operations (Williams 1989).

Weyerhaeuser introduced sustainable forestry on his company lands. This made perfect business sense as well as environmental sense. Weyerhaeuser needed to maintain a sustainable supply of timber on company land to keep his mills operating. Paradoxically, the federal Bureau of Corporations was harsh in its criticism of Weyerhaeuser for "hoarding timber and neglecting manufacturing" (Williams 1989). Under the direction of general manager George Long, the Weyerhaeuser Company experimented with reforestation on its cutover Douglas-fir timberland in the Cascades. Nobel Peace Prize laureate Norman E. Borlaug put Weyerhaeuser's contributions to sustainable forestry in perspective when he said, "When Weyerhaeuser's management decided to hold and protect logged-off land for regeneration it was a radical concept" (Snyder 1999).

Figure 17.6 Frederick Weyerhaeuser.

Courtesy of the Library of Congress Prints and Photographs Division. Reproduction number: LC-DIG-ggbain-05198

Henry Hardtner (1870–1935) of the Urania Lumber Company of Urania, Louisiana, experimented with reforestation. Hardtner often cooperated with Yale University's School of Forestry and the U.S. Forest Service, experimenting with prescribed burning and commercial thinning of his timber. Yale forestry students traveled to Urania each spring to study and practice practical forestry on commercial land. Hardtner found that southern pines thrived when planted on cutover lands. His concept of commercial reforestation was the forerunner of the extensive forest plantations that one may find throughout the southeastern United States (Arnold and Justice 2003, Williams 1989).

While Weyerhaeuser and Hardtner pioneered sustainable forestry on commercial land, other lumber companies either refused or were too small to adopt sustainable forestry.

JOHN WESLEY POWELL

Another influential voice in the molding of early conservation policy was John Wesley Powell (1834–1902), Director of the U.S. Geological Survey from 1881 to 1894. Powell was an officer in the Union army who lost his right arm at Shiloh. In 1869 he led an expedition of ten men, traveling in wooden boats, down the thousand mile length of the Colorado River through the Grand Canyon. He led a second exploration of the Colorado River in 1871, producing the first maps and scientific publications on the geology of the great river.

In 1878 Powell published his *Report on the Lands of the Arid Region of the United States,* focusing on waters as well as on fire protection. He argued that climate controls forests and that forests have little effect upon western watersheds—an argument that ran counter to the beliefs of many of the early foresters, including Bernhard Fernow and Gifford Pinchot. He urged adoption of a policy of fire control, believing that fire was the most destructive threat to the forests of the west (Pyne 2001).

Figure 17.7 John Wesley Powell.

Courtesy of the Library of Congress Prints and Photographs Division. Reproduction number: LC-USZ62-3862

"Powell challenged much of the growing doctrine of forest conservation on the European model. He urged local, not national, control, thus questioning the premise behind carving vast federal forest reservations out of the public domain" (Pyne 2001).

One wonders how things might be different if the nation had adopted Powell's recommendation of local or state control of public forests.[7] Federal lands are "owned" by the citizens of the United States—all citizens. Thus all citizens, through their elected representatives in Congress, have a say in determining policies governing management of the public lands. But is this really fair? For example, more than 75 percent of the forestland in the states of Idaho, Wyoming and Nevada is in the federal domain (Smith et al. 2009). Yet New York City alone has more than three times the number of representatives in the House than the three western states combined. As a result, people who live near, work in and depend upon those forests have less political influence than a city on the other side of the continent. Conflict is inevitable.

BERNHARD FERNOW AND THE BEGINNINGS OF WOOD SCIENCE IN THE U.S.

The impact of railroads on forests led to many of the early forest conservation efforts in the U.S. The Division of Forestry was established in the U.S. Department of Agriculture in 1881. The Division had responsibility for gathering information and conducting research on forestry. It had no authority over public forests, which were under the management of the Department of the Interior. The noted botanist Franklin B. Hough was appointed the Division's first chief.

In 1886, Bernhard Eduard Fernow (1851–1923) was appointed head of the Division of Forestry. He was born in Germany where he received his education in forestry. When he immigrated to the United States in 1876, he became the first professional forester in the country. Fernow was soon an active and influential advocate of forest conservation.

Fernow made a number of significant contributions to American forestry. He helped found the American Forestry Association in 1887, an organization of like-minded citizens interested in conserving forest resources. After stepping down as chief of the Forestry Division, he founded the forestry school at Cornell University, and later he helped found several other forestry schools in the United States and Canada. He was very influential in the passage of the Forest Reserve Act of 1891 that authorized the creation of forest reserves from public domain.

Under his leadership, the Forestry Division dedicated two thirds of its budget to wood research. He was an advocate of the substitution of low value species of wood for more valuable but diminishing species. For example, his scientists discovered that

---

[7] This is the model adopted by Canada. The provinces own and control public forests, not the federal government.

chestnut oak was a suitable substitute for white oak and that all southern pines were very similar and could replace white pine for use as bridge timbers. The Forestry Division began an extensive research program to learn the comparative strength and durability of various wood species. Research was carried out to determine the best ways to dry and preserve crossties (Williams 1989).

As chief of the Division of Forestry, he instituted the first research program in what was called "timber science." (At the time there was not the degree of specialization within forest resource professions that there is today. Wood science and wildlife management were considered part of the broader profession of forestry. The creation of separate professions and educational disciplines did not occur until the mid-twentieth century.)

In 1910 the Forest Service consolidated all of its wood research at the new Forest Products Laboratory (FPL) located on the campus of the University of Wisconsin in Madison (Forest History Society 2009, Peterson 2003). FPL remains the focal point for the federal government's wood research programs as it celebrates its one hundredth anniversary in 2010.

Figure 17.8 Bernhard Fernow.

Courtesy of the Library of Congress Prints and Photographs Division. Reproduction number: LC-USZ62-49489

JOHN MUIR AND THE PRESERVATION ETHIC

John Muir (1838–1914) championed the preservation ethic, seeking to protect wilderness for wilderness' sake. Preservation represented a hands-off approach to public lands. Favoring aesthetic and recreational use of public lands, Muir grudgingly accepted some industrial or commercial use of public land, but he was opposed to widespread timber harvest, grazing, mineral extraction, or development.

Muir was born in Scotland and came to the United States as a boy. He studied natural sciences at the University of Wisconsin but never graduated. After being injured in an industrial accident, he set about wandering and wound up in California in 1868. Muir traveled much of the western United States, including Alaska, but his first love was California's High Sierras. He was instrumental in the establishment of Yosemite National Park.

Muir was a prolific nature writer. As such, he gained widespread influence over the perceptions and attitudes of the public. Among his accomplishments, he

Figure 17.9 John Muir.

Courtesy of the Library of Congress Prints and Photographs Division. Reproduction number: LC-USZ62-50012

was able to successfully convey the idea that wilderness had spiritual as well as economic value. In 1892, he and fellow Californians founded the Sierra Club, at the time an elite mountaineering club dedicated to organizing expeditions into the Sierras and other wild places in the west. The Sierra Club under Muir's leadership advocated preservation in the Sierras (Chase 1995, Miller 2001, Williams 1989).

GIFFORD PINCHOT AND THE CONSERVATION ETHIC

Gifford Pinchot (1865–1946) was the first American-born forester. He first coined the term "conservation," which he defined as "the wise use of the earth and its resources for the lasting good of men." Conservation is a utilitarian approach to resource management that sought to protect forest resources in perpetuity while still allowing for timber harvest and other uses of resources.

Pinchot was a product of the Gilded Age. His parents, James Pinchot and Mary Eno Pinchot, were part of the wealthy elite of New York City. After graduating from Yale, Pinchot studied forestry in France. He replaced Bernhard Fernow as Chief of the Division of Forestry in 1898, which he would shape, along with his political mentor and ally, Theodore Roosevelt, into the U.S. Forest Service. Pinchot's philosophy and policies shaped the administration and direction of the Forest Service and national forests until the end of the twentieth century. Pinchot is considered the father of forestry in America (Chase 1995, Miller 2001, Williams 1989).

Figure 17.10 President Theodore Roosevelt.

Courtesy of the Library of Congress Prints and Photographs Division.
Reproduction number: LC-USZ62-90405

THEODORE ROOSEVELT

Theodore Roosevelt (1858–1919) became President of the United States in 1901 following the assassination of William McKinley. Roosevelt's administration began the progressive era in American politics. He based his policies on a strong national defense, corporate reform, and conservation. Although Roosevelt had met John Muir and had spent four days in Yosemite with Muir in 1903, his philosophy was more in tune with the utilitarian conservationist and his close friend, Gifford Pinchot (Miller 2001, Morris 2001).

Roosevelt used the bully pulpit—a phrase he coined—of the presidency to promote conservation to the public and to the nation's political leadership. His administration organized three national commissions in an attempt to convince industry leaders to adopt the conservation ethic.

John Wesley Powell and others had been urging watershed protection and irrigation of arid lands since the 1870s. In 1902, Roosevelt pushed the National Reclamation Act through Congress, expanding the staff of the U.S. Geological Survey and authorizing the construction of dams, aqueducts and vast irrigation projects in the west. Twenty irrigation projects started under the National Reclamation Act during his administration (Morris 2001).

The 1906 Preservation of Antiquities Act authorized the creation of national monuments on federal land to protect historic sites and places of "scientific interest." Originally intended to protect Anasazi sites from destruction, Roosevelt interpreted the scientific interest clause in the law broadly to designate sites such as Devil's Tower in Wyoming, the Petrified Forest in Arizona and the Grand Canyon as national monuments. In all, Roosevelt placed eighteen national monuments under federal protection (Morris 2001).

The credit goes to Teddy Roosevelt for creating the first national wildlife refuge in 1903. Other wildlife preservation actions by the federal government had preceded this action, including the transfer of Yosemite to the state of California in 1864 and the establishment of a federal Commissioner of Fisheries in 1871 and the Division of Economic Ornithology and Mammalogy in 1886. The Game and Bird Preserves Protection Act passed in 1906, establishing what are now known as the national wildlife refuges. Under the authority of the new act, Roosevelt issued fifty-one executive orders establishing refuges in seventeen states and three territories (U.S. Fish and Wildlife Service 2008).

Roosevelt did not establish the national parks and forest reserves. But he did expand the number and extent of both. Roosevelt created five national parks during his presidency, doubling the number of parks designated when he took office. With the capable assistance of Pinchot, he created thirteen new forest reserves, reorganized their administration and implemented policies that would govern their management for most of the century.

Roosevelt, with Pinchot working as his right hand man, convened the Governors Conference on Conservation on May 8, 1908. The conference resulted in greater interagency cooperation and consolidation, and it increased the authority and budget of Pinchot's Forest Service. Although there was a striking agreement in principle among the participants, there were vastly divergent views on implementation. What was accomplished was a testament to Roosevelt's and Pinchot's political skills.

RECREATION AND WILDERNESS PRESERVATION IN THE NATIONAL FORESTS

Recreation did not become a high priority for the national forests until after World War II. In 1917, one year after creation of the National Park Service, the Forest Service released a report outlining a positive role for recreation in national forests. However, fear of a timber famine kept recreation from being a high priority of the Forest Service for a number of years. In addition, national park advocates feared that promoting recreation in the national forest system would divert funds and potentially hold back expansion of the national parks. As such, timber interests and national park advocates were often allies in resisting development of recreational opportunities in the national forests.

Interagency feuding between the Forest Service and the Department of the Interior also impeded creation of a coherent recreation policy for national forests as the two agencies competed for resources at the expense of each other. Conflict also existed within the ranks of the conservation movement and the organizations that sought to protect forests for its various amenities. Recreationists wanted access, roads and amenities in the national forests. Preservationists wanted untouched wilderness. Wildlife advocates and wilderness advocates also found themselves in disagreement over whether or not active management to create habitat should take place (Williams 1989).

The first formal set aside of public land for wilderness protection was in 1924 when the Gila Wilderness Preserve became established on the Gila National Forest in New Mexico at the urging of Aldo Leopold. Robert Marshall founded the Wilderness Society in 1935, which is an outspoken advocacy group for the protection and expansion of wilderness areas. Congress passed the Wilderness Act of 1964 and the Eastern Wilderness Act of 1975 to set aside permanent wilderness areas within public lands. The battle over where and how many wilderness areas they should protect goes on.

The conservation movement set the agenda that prompted the federal government to set aside public land for protection as national parks, forest reserves and grazing lands. A new profession would emerge from the clear-cuts and forest fires with the mission of conserving forest resources. It was the era of the birth of forestry in America.

Homework

Name: _____   Date: _____

1. What is the largest national park in the United States, how large is it, and where is it located?

    What are some of the unique scenic and natural features of this national park?

2. What is the nation's largest national forest, how large is it, and where is it located?

    What are some of the unique scenic and natural features of this national forest?

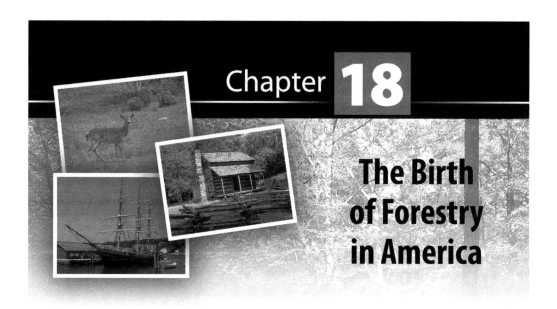

Chapter 18

The Birth of Forestry in America

Forestry is a relatively young profession in America. It developed as a part of the American conservation movement of the late nineteenth and early twentieth centuries as a means of rationally controlling the loss of forest to unsustainable timber harvest, fire and agricultural development. But forestry in America in its early years largely derived from the principles of forest management practiced in Europe, and in particular Germany.

Scientific inquiry into the nature of forests and trees dates back nearly two thousand years when the Roman Gaius Plinius Secundus, "Pliny the Elder," published *Natural History* in 77 A.D. In 1662, John Evelyn published *Silva: Discourse of Forest-trees and the Propagation of Timber,* "probably the first book published on silviculture" (Nix 2004a). The Royal Society had commissioned Evelyn to gather and catalog information on propagating timber in response to a shortage of wood at the end of the English Civil War that threatened England's ability to defend itself from European rivals.

European forestry had its roots in the Middle Ages as an outgrowth of forest clearing and feudalism. The Romans who conquered the south of Britain around the time of Christ described the island as heavily forested. As European populations grew, they cleared forests for agricultural development, for the growth of towns and cities and for fuel until only a few remained by the late medieval period. Under the feudal system monarchs owned land and granted it to lesser nobles to ensure their loyalty or to reward service to the monarch. Europe was embroiled in a state of near-continuous warfare as monarchs and the nobility struggled to expand their power and wealth. For example, very few of the kings of Scotland prior to James VI died of natural causes.

Monarchs and nobles valued the remaining forests as scarce resources for building ships and structures and began to restrict their use by peasants. But the most precious resource found in the European forest was game. It was more practical to feed knights and soldiers meat than to grow, store and transport crops to keep their armies fed, so kings and nobles set the priority of reserving game for their own purposes. The earliest foresters were law enforcers and game wardens.

Forestry began to evolve into a profession focused upon timber management in the seventeenth and eighteenth centuries. Henry Cotta founded one of the first forestry schools in Europe in Tharandt, Germany in 1811. European forestry was utilitarian by necessity. Scarcity of timber required the cultivation of forests to meet the demand for wood. For example, German foresters are said to "build" forests by planting hardwood trees that are not planned to be harvested for 300 years. As Cotta wrote, "There would be no physicians if there were no diseases, and no forestry science without deficiency in wood supplies" (Carlsen 2008, Nix 2004a).

EARLY REGULATION OF FORESTS IN AMERICA

As mentioned in the chapter on wooden ships, the first attempt to regulate American forests occurred when Parliament reserved the white pines of New England for masts and spars for the Royal Navy in 1691. This law met resistance from colonists who wished to use the pines in their own shipbuilding industries and for construction and proved very difficult to enforce.

After the Revolutionary War, the U.S. Navy reserved stands of live oak in the southeast for its use, and it undertook experimentation in cultivating live oak in Florida. In 1831, Congress passed a law making it illegal to harvest live oak for any purpose other than for the Navy.

Timber theft on public land was widespread and very difficult or impossible to stop. Timber agents were employed to try to apprehend timber trespassers. The "tragedy of the commons" was taking place on public land. Farmers and settlers were taking wood for their own use and commercial timber operations were also "rustling" timber illegally and without compensating the government. In 1852, the government adopted a policy of prosecuting only commercial trespassers. It required the trespassers simply to pay for the timber taken. In effect, this was the beginning of timber sales although there was no official authorization, planning or system of management in place to control harvest (Williams 1989).

The system of land grants to railroads and homesteaders also led to the abuse and exploitation of resources. The government gave millions of acres to railroads and homesteaders who were supposed to farm the land. Often the settlers cut and sold the timber and then moved on or sold the land. Fraud was a serious problem in the government's program of land grants.

In 1874, the Secretary of the Interior, Columbus Delano, said there was a "rapid destruction of timber," especially on public land, and declared that the government must take steps to protect the public interest. The depletion of timber, catastrophic fire and watershed protection were emerging issues of great concern to many Americans. New York State was the first to respond to calls for preserving forests by setting aside the Adirondack and Catskill Forest Preserves in 1885. Conservationists were talking about forestry (Pisani 1997, Reiger 1997). But, unlike Europe, the United States lacked a specialized forestry profession, organizations or agencies staffed by professional foresters and schools dedicated to the education of professional foresters (Williams 1989).

A lack of sound scientific background about forests hampered early efforts to preserve forests (Pisani 1997). Fernow complained that foresters in the United States needed to know the characteristics of several hundred tree species while Europeans needed to know only six to ten species (Williams 1989). Natural science was primitive; therefore, there was much speculation about the role of forests in the natural world. Early foresters believed that forests were "normal" while deserts and grasslands were "abnormal." They misunderstood the role of fire in shaping forest ecosystems. In 1891, no less an authority than Bernhard Fernow stated, "You must remember that the entire earth is a potential forest" (Pisani 1997).

Early foresters believed that forests affected climate by promoting rainfall and that forests were necessary to prepare soils for agriculture. They believed that forests were essential for maintaining watersheds and that destruction of forests led to desertification (using Chaco and other ancient civilizations as examples). They believed that nature would always return to a "balance" if left alone where forests would replace other vegetative cover (Pisani 1997).

The issue of forest conservation had come to the attention of the American public and the nation's political leaders. But forest conservation bills had become frustrated in Congress in the 1870s and 1880s (Miller 1997).

Setting aside public land in forest reserves required an increase in the role of the federal government in owning and regulating natural resources. There was disagreement over whether or not that should happen, with one side arguing that conservation of resources required federal government intervention and the other arguing that doing so would hurt local economic interests and was unconstitutional. Even those who favored federal set asides disagreed over how much land to set aside, what land to include, what activities to permit on that land, whether states or the federal government should control public forests and what agency should manage the land. An additional question was whether to permit the federal government to purchase land from the private sector or the states to incorporate into set-asides (Williams 1989).

PROBLEMS WITH THE FOREST RESERVE ACT OF 1891

In 1891, Congress passed the Forest Reserve Act enabling the President to set aside public forestlands for protection in perpetuity. The act placed forest reserves under the administration of the General Land Office[1] (GLO) in the Department of the Interior. Established in 1812 with the primary objective of disposing of federal lands, the GLO was ill equipped to manage forests designated for protection.

The Forest Reserve Act contained a significant flaw—it lacked any clear mission or policy for managing the forest reserves, a weakness that would later need correction. What would be permitted on the reserves? The set aside of public forest reserves quickly became fraught with controversy among timber companies, mining interests, ranchers, homesteaders, conservationists, citizens and politicians over their use and management. Industry advocated permitting timber harvest and mining. Ranchers advocated open grazing. Sportsmen advocated the creation and preservation of wildlife habitats. Preservationists, led by John Muir, advocated minimizing human activity. When President Grover Cleveland took office in 1893, he recognized the need to formulate a national policy before setting aside more land.

Bureaucratic barriers within the federal government impeded formulating policy for the forest reserves. The reserves were established within the Department of the Interior. However, the government's forestry expertise was housed in Bernhard Fernow's Forestry Division within the Department of Agriculture. The Division received responsibility for gathering information and conducting research on forestry, but it had no authority over management of the public forests.

---

[1] The General Land Office was the predecessor to the current Bureau of Land Management.

Fernow was a cautious man and too often self-conscious about being a "foreigner" (Williams 1989). It required a stronger personality than Fernow's to move the debates toward resolution.

GIFFORD PINCHOT (1865–1946)

Gifford Pinchot was born into wealth on August 11, 1865. His parents, James Pinchot and Mary Eno Pinchot, were among the social and economic elite of New York City and raised young Gifford in a life of privilege. He became educated at the exclusive Phillips Exeter Academy and Yale where he was a member of the Skull and Bones Society and played football for Walter Camp.

Figure 18.1 Gifford Pinchot.

Courtesy of the Library of Congress Prints and Photographs Division. Reproduction number: LC-DIG-ppmsca-19459

Pinchot developed a keen interest in nature and a love of the outdoors while on childhood trips to the Adirondacks. Like many educated Americans, he was influenced by George Perkins Marsh's *Man and Nature.* With the encouragement of his parents, Pinchot set out on a career in forestry. The Pinchots were well aware that forestry was not an established profession and that Gifford would be "breaking new ground." Encouragement came from a number of the era's conservationists, but it was Fernow who recommended that Pinchot pursue postgraduate study in Europe.

In 1889, Pinchot enrolled at *L'Ecole Nationale Forestière*—the French national forestry school—in Nancy.

L'Ecole was one of the first and most venerated forestry schools in Europe, established in 1824. While in Europe, Pinchot was introduced (probably through Fernow) to Sir Dietrich Brandis who had established the Forestry Service in British India. He traveled through Europe with Brandis and a group of British students in 1890, observing forestry practices throughout the continent. Although Brandis and his mentors at *L'Ecole* recommended further study, Pinchot was impatient to return home and begin practicing forestry in the United States. Pinchot, not lacking in ambition, was also eager to establish his reputation as the first American forester. He got his chance in the mountains of western North Carolina in 1892.

BILTMORE

The 1890s were the peak years of the Gilded Age in America and the Vanderbilts[2] were one of the nation's wealthiest and most influential families. George W. Vanderbilt was building his estate, Biltmore,[3] on 125,000 acres he had purchased near Asheville.

---

[2] The Vanderbilt family amassed a fortune in steamboats, steam ships and the New York Central Railroad.

[3] The website for Biltmore is http://www.biltmore.com/.

Vanderbilt was the grandson of Commodore Vanderbilt who had amassed the family fortune in the shipping industry. The Commodores' grandsons were railroad men, and George's older brother, Cornelius, Jr., had built the magnificently lavish Breakers as his summer home in Newport, Rhode Island. Sibling rivalry was a characteristic of this generation of Vanderbilts and George was determined to outdo his brothers in building his estate in the mountains of western North Carolina. To do this, George Vanderbilt contracted the finest design team in America to create a little "Eden" at Biltmore.

The prominent New York architect Richard Morris Hunt designed the home—a 250 room mansion covering four acres of floor space. Hunt designed the pedestal for the Statue of Liberty, the façade of the Metropolitan Museum of Art and the administration building for Chicago's Columbian Exposition of 1893. He designed several of the homes of the Vanderbilt family, including William K. Vanderbilt's lavish Fifth Avenue home in New York and Cornelius Vanderbilt's "The Breakers" in Newport, Rhode Island. He also designed James Pinchot's "Grey Towers" in Milford, Pennsylvania (Miller 2001).

The grounds of the estate, which had been cut over, were placed in the hands of landscape designer Frederick Law Olmstead, the father of landscape architecture in America. Olmstead's many accomplishments included the design of New York's Central Park, numerous parks in New York and other cities, college campuses and institutional grounds and private estates.[4] He was prominent in the conservation movement for having led conservation efforts at Niagara Falls.

Olmstead recommended reforesting the surrounding mountains and valleys and recommended Gifford Pinchot to Vanderbilt in 1892. There Pinchot was first able to put his ideas on sustainable forest management into practice. It also enabled him to rise to prominence in the conservation community and to attract the political attention he sought for his ideas. Biltmore also represented the first experience with professional foresters on private land in the United States (Miller 2001).

FORESTRY EDUCATION IN THE UNITED STATES

George Vanderbilt's influence on forestry extended beyond giving Gifford Pinchot a job. In 1895, he hired the German forester Carl Schenck to replace Pinchot, who was moving on to bigger things. In 1898, he had Schenck establish the Biltmore Forestry School to train foresters to manage his extensive estate. It was the first forestry school in America. The Biltmore Forestry School closed in 1913. Vanderbilt's forest is now the Pisgah National Forest, and a site on the Pisgah—"The Cradle of Forestry in America"—preserves the history of the Biltmore School[5] (Nix 2004b).

Schenck implemented a "practical forestry" curriculum, as opposed to the theory-based university curriculum established later by Fernow at Cornell and Pinchot at Yale. Schenck's philosophy lives on in the two-year forestry technician schools that continue to train practical field foresters. Pinchot was critical of both Schenck's and Fernow's approach to forestry education, which Jolley (1998) attributes to American "chauvinism." However, Pinchot was often critical of his perceived rivals, and there is no doubt that he saw Fernow, and perhaps Schenck, as such (Miller 2001).

---

[4] For example, Olmstead designed the courtyard in front of the downtown library at West Virginia University that a library addition replaced a few years ago.

[5] Website: *http://www.cradleofforestry.com/default.asp.*

Figure 18.2 Henry S. Graves.

Courtesy of the Library of Congress Prints and Photographs Division. Reproduction number: LC-USZ62-125775

Fernow established a second forestry school at Cornell University in 1898.[6] Yale established a School of Forestry in 1900 with the urging and support of Gifford Pinchot. Its first faculty member and dean was Henry S. Graves, a Yale graduate who had followed Pinchot to Europe to study forestry. Elers Koch, a student in the early days of the school, noted, "There were practically no American textbooks in forestry at that time, so we had to use European ones." This underscored how predominant European ideas and methods were in the early years of American forestry (Koch 1998).

Pinchot led the way in founding a national professional society, the Society of American Foresters (SAF), in 1900. Following conferences in 1909 and 1911, SAF issued a report on "The Standardization of Instruction in Forestry" in 1912, noting that there were twenty-four forestry schools in the country at the time (Laurie 1964). In 2009, SAF recognizes fifty forestry bachelors' degree programs in thirty-nine states through its accreditation process.[7]

The first wood technology program in the United States became established in 1929 with a rapid expansion of programs taking place during and immediately after World War II (Ellis 1964). The first bachelor's degree program in wildlife management was established in 1933 at the University of Wisconsin (The Wildlife Society 2005). University programs in recreation and parks programs evolved from landscape architecture (parks) and physical education (recreation). Recreation as a program within forestry schools began to emerge following World War II.

THE NATIONAL FORESTRY COMMISSION

Gifford Pinchot's next work was to promote forestry as a matter of national policy. Pinchot advocated the creation of a national forest policy that favored expansion of the forest reserves and a clearly defined policy for management of the reserves that included sustainable timber harvest to meet the needs of the people of the United States in perpetuity. This was very much in line with European forest policy and was much like the policies adopted in British India implemented by his mentor, Sir Dietrich Brandis.

He enlisted the support of the respected Charles Sprague Sargent, curator of Harvard's Arnold Arboretum, to create a national commission to study the forest reserves and their management. The National Academy of Sciences appointed the commission over Fernow's objections in 1896. Sargent chaired the commission with Pinchot serving as its secretary (Miller 2001).

Pinchot soon grew impatient with what he perceived as the chairman's foot dragging. When Sargent recommended to Cleveland the creation of more forest reserves before

---

[6] Cornell disbanded its forestry school in 1903 as a result of internal politics at Cornell and the failure of the state of New York to provide funds for its support (New York Times 1903). New York would re-establish a forestry school in 1911, this time in cooperation with Syracuse University (Lassoie et al. 1998).

[7] The forestry school at West Virginia University was founded in 1935.

creating a national forest policy, the split between Pinchot and Sargent widened. On Washington's birthday in 1897, Grover Cleveland created thirteen new reserves of 21.2 million acres in eight western states. Still, no policy existed outlining what was and was not allowed on the reserves. Western states became outraged by the "Washington's Birthday Reserves" (Miller 2001).

Finally, on May 1, 1897, Congress received the Forestry Commission Report, which concluded that the reserves perform "their part in the economy of the nation." Pinchot's ideas had carried the debate within the Commission. The political situation concerning the reserves had become untenable, forcing Congress to take action.

THE ORGANIC ACT OF 1897

The Forest Management Act of 1897—also known as the "Organic Act"—passed on June 4, 1897. The Organic Act clarified the role of the forest reserves in a manner that reflected the thinking of Pinchot—to protect the forests so that citizens may have a reliable supply of water and timber. Criteria for reserve designation would be water protection and timber production. It established a system of relative values for determining whether an area should become, or be retained within, a reserve—if the area's value as a forest resource was greater than its value for mineral extraction or agriculture, it should; otherwise, it should not. The Organic Act permitted mining and agriculture, including grazing, and continued the practice of allowing local residents to use the timber, stone and water on the reserves. Most importantly, it authorized the sale of dead and mature timber after appraisal, advertisement and sale.

Specifically, the Act established the mission of the forest reserves:

- "Improve and protect the forests,"
- "Secure favorable conditions of water flow" and
- "Furnish a continuous supply of timber for the use and necessities of the citizens of the United States."

This Act settled the question of whether the reserves should be preserved or managed forests. It clearly came down on the side of use and management. And its passage elevated Gifford Pinchot to prominence as the nation's leading authority on forests and forestry (Williams 1989).

THE CHIEF

Bernhard Fernow resigned as chief of the Division of Forestry in 1898 to found and become dean of the new College of Forestry at Cornell. Pinchot's appointment as his successor was a foregone conclusion. In fact, there were suggestions that Pinchot's skillful political maneuvering had prompted Fernow's exit. Pinchot was ambitious and impatient, and he tended to roll over real and perceived foes. He was also energetic, committed, politically astute and highly skilled at public relations.

Gifford Pinchot was the driving force and principal architect of the U.S. Forest Service and the present National Forest system. In 1898, the Forestry Division employed sixty people. Under Pinchot's leadership, the number had grown to five hundred in 1905. The young men who filled the Division of Forestry and later the Forest Service became known as "Pinchot's young men" or, more derisively, "Pinchot's boys."

Typical of this group was Elers Koch, a young man raised in Montana. Explaining in his autobiography, "I think I was born to be a forester," he went to Yale to study forestry after graduating from Montana State in 1900. Koch (1998) went on to say, "I have always been proud of being one of Gifford Pinchot's young men. It was as fine, enthusiastic, and inspired a group of public employees as was ever assembled."

THE TRANSFER ACT OF 1905

In 1901, President William McKinley was assassinated and his vice president, Theodore Roosevelt, sworn in as President of the United States. Pinchot had formed a friendship with the new president in 1899 when Roosevelt was governor of New York. Both men were reformers, conservationists and avid outdoorsmen. Pinchot soon became the new president's closest political advisor (Miller 2001).

By 1905, more than twenty government agencies had some jurisdiction over natural resources. Six had authority over federally-owned forestlands. There were more than 75 million acres set aside in eighty-three reserves. As Pinchot (1998) wrote in his autobiography, *Breaking New Ground*, "Instead of being, as we should have been, like a squadron of cavalry, all acting together for a single purpose, we were like loose horses in a field, each one following his own nose."

Pinchot seized the opportunity to consolidate the forest reserves and forestry expertise within the federal government under a single agency. He openly criticized the General Land Office in the Department of the Interior for its many abuses. He recommended expansion of the forest reserves and their transfer from GLO oversight to the Forestry Bureau (renamed in 1901) of the Department of Agriculture.

With Pinchot's urging, Roosevelt appointed a Public Lands Committee in 1903 to investigate that consisted of Pinchot and two political allies. The commission's findings were predictable. The rationale for reform of the forest reserve system was on the table (Miller 2001).

Pinchot continued to exercise formidable political skills in organizing the American Forestry Congress of 1905. The Congress took place from January 2 to 6 in Washington, D.C. to coincide with the introduction of a bill by Roosevelt to transfer the forest reserves to the Forestry Bureau. Pinchot enlisted support from Frederick Weyerhaeuser and James J. Hill, proclaiming the need for lumbermen and foresters to unite behind the proposal (Miller 2001).

Under the Transfer Act of 1905 the forest reserves transferred to the Forestry Bureau on February 1. Later that year the Forestry Bureau became the Forest Service. In 1907, the forest reserves became the national forests. The nation's 63 million acres of national forest were under Forest Service control (Miller 2001). "In the process, the Forest Bureau, run by bureaucrats, had become the Forest Service, run by foresters" (Morris 2001).

Now in charge, Pinchot developed guidelines for management of the national forests, including where to cut, how to cut and how much to cut. He put programs in place to monitor and control stream flow, to restrict livestock grazing and to lease mineral rights. The Forest Service also implemented a fire fighting program that evolved into fire suppression. At that time, Forest Service timber sales were often underpriced and revenues did not cover the agencies' expenses. This problem continued well into the twentieth century, an issue that sparked criticism of the Forest Service by organizations advocating a ban on timber harvest in the last decades of the century.

THE MIDNIGHT RESERVES

Designation of forest reserves hit the western states hardest. Homesteaders could no longer stake claims to public lands. Timber and mining interests now had to adhere to regulations they previously did not have to deal with. Most affected were the ranchers and stockmen, who voiced the strongest objections to the federal set-asides (Koch 1998).

Members of Congress representing the western states opposed setting aside additional land for forest reserves. They took action to stop further set asides by adding an amendment to the Agriculture Appropriation Bill of 1907. The Fulton Amendment, proposed by Senator Charles W. Fulton of Oregon, prohibited the President from creating new reserves in Oregon, Washington, Idaho, Montana, Colorado and Wyoming. If signed into law by Roosevelt, only Congress would have authority to designate future forest reserves in those states (Miller 2001, Morris 2001, Williams 1989).

The amendment handed Roosevelt a difficult choice. If he vetoed the bill, he would lose funding for conservation measures he had been pushing. If he signed, the restrictions on new national forests would bind him. And, he and Pinchot had planned on additional set asides.

With a week in which to sign the Bill, Roosevelt, Pinchot and their staffs prepared the paperwork to set aside the land Fulton had hoped to keep out of the forest reserve system. At the last minute before signing the Agricultural Appropriations

Figure 18.3 Theodore Roosevelt.

Courtesy of the Library of Congress Prints and Photographs Division. Reproduction number: LC-USZ62-23232

Bill, the president issued executive orders designating twenty-one new forest reserves encompassing 16 million acres and enlarging eleven other reserves in the six western states (Miller 2001, Morris 2001, Williams 1989).

Tempers reached the boiling point over what became known as the "Midnight Reserves." As was often the case, Roosevelt designated Pinchot as his public face in dealing with the controversy. Roosevelt trusted and relied on Pinchot to handle tough situations because he had the rare combination of "killer instinct" and integrity that made him "invulnerable to charges of corruption" (Morris 2001).

The conflict came to a head at the 1907 Public Lands Convention in Denver where Pinchot faced down the administration's opponents. Contemporaries described Pinchot, who was tall and lean, as "panther-like." One contemporary described his eyes as appearing "as if they gazed upon a cause." When he rose to take the podium, that gaze must have met the mostly hostile audience as Pinchot began, "If you fellows can stand me, I can stand you." Through adroit political skill, and promises to favor local input in managing the national forests, Pinchot was able to soften opposition to the administration's actions (Miller 2001, Morris 2001).

Pinchot was able to skillfully negotiate compromise without betraying his principles. In 1908, Congress enacted legislation ensuring that 25 percent of the money received from sales of timber on national forests would go to states for schools and roads in the county in which the timber sold. This defrayed the loss of property tax revenues that would have gone to states and counties if the land had been in the private sector[8] (Miller 2001, Morris 2001).

THE FALLING OUT WITH MUIR

Too many modern accounts of Pinchot's role in the American conservation movement focus on his disagreements with John Muir with too many ignoring or discrediting Pinchot's preeminent role in the American conservation movement. For example, some historians cite a public argument between the two that took place in a San Francisco hotel lobby in the late 1890s over Pinchot's support of grazing in the Sierras. Pinchot's biographer Char Miller (2000, 2001) presents very credible evidence that the incident never occurred. Nonetheless, Miller's scholarship does not stop Muir's admirers and Pinchot's detractors from continuing to cite the incident as if it was irrefutable fact.

The truth is the relationship between the two men with very different philosophies was complex. Early in their relationship, Pinchot and Muir were allies in establishing forest reserves and promoting conservation of resources. Muir considered Pinchot's views on forest management a vast improvement over the indiscriminate cutting of forests that occurred through most of the century. Pinchot understood that Muir's support was critical in implementing the policies that united the forest reserves under the supervision of the Forest Service. In fact, Muir praised Pinchot in some of his work stating that Pinchot "refused to deliver its forests to more or less speedy destruction by permitting them to pass into private ownership" (Miller 2001).

Disagreements over Pinchot's utilitarian approach to policy on the national forests led to a steady deterioration of their alliance. Muir, always an advocate of wilderness preservation, came to view forestry as incompatible (Miller 2001). When Teddy Roosevelt spent four days hiking in Yosemite National Park in 1903, Muir lectured the President over what he believed were the shortcomings of Pinchot and the forestry profession (Morris 2001).

The two men's disagreements hardened into outright enmity over plans to build a dam in the Hetch Hetchy Valley in Yosemite National Park. The growing city of San Francisco faced a water supply crisis and had petitioned the federal government to build a reservoir in Hetch Hetchy to supply the city. Roosevelt and Pinchot supported the project while Muir was outraged over the destruction of a part of his beloved Yosemite. Pinchot, ever the loyal subordinate to the President, served as the administration's front man, absorbing the anger of Muir and his allies. Ironically, the dam was not built until 1913 after Pinchot and Roosevelt had returned to private life (Miller 2001, Morris 2001).

Miller (2001) observes that the public disagreements between Pinchot and Muir caught the attention of the American people. Their debate over conservation and preservation carried over into the print and public. "In no other way could conservation so quickly have become a household word and an idea of considerable force in the politics of the Progressive Era."

For most of the twentieth century, Pinchot's philosophy of conservation would prevail among the public and with policymakers. In the latter half of the century, the

---

[8] The cessation of nearly all timber sales from western national forests as a result of court decisions involving the northern spotted owl in the 1980s and '90s shut off that source of revenue, worsening the economic distress in rural areas of the west that also suffered the severe loss of timber-related industries.

debates over forests and the environment would rise again. This time Muir's philosophy of preservation would achieve dominance and change the paradigms of natural resource management (Chase 1995).

PINCHOT LEAVES THE FOREST SERVICE

William Howard Taft replaced Roosevelt as president in 1908. Taft did not share Roosevelt's and Pinchot's commitment to conservation. His Secretary of the Interior, Richard Ballinger, was a westerner with anti-conservation sentiments. Pinchot had never shied away from public disputes with those he disagreed with, including Fernow, Sargent, western Senators and Muir. It was inevitable that he would disagree with Ballinger and make his disagreement public. It was his style.

When Taft sided with Ballinger, Pinchot became openly critical of Taft. The President dismissed Pinchot as Chief of the agency he had created in 1909. He named Henry S. Graves, Pinchot's protégé and dean of the Yale School of Forestry, the second Chief of the Forest Service. Graves and the young foresters that Pinchot brought into the agency would keep Pinchot's legacy and ideals alive within the Forest Service through most of the century.

The Forest Service won two cases before the U.S. Supreme Court in 1911—*U.S. vs. Grimaud* and *U.S. vs. Light.* Both upheld the right of the government to regulate grazing in national forests. Both were victories for the Roosevelt/Pinchot forest conservation program.

In 1910, the location of every national forest was in the western states. A bill that proposed the purchase of land for creating national forests in the east was stalled in Congress. The intention of the Weeks Act was to protect eastern watersheds by restoring forests on cut over or burned land. The fires of 1910 shocked the nation. Three million acres of virgin timber in Idaho and Montana burned, killing eighty-six people, mostly fire fighters. The severity of the fires moved fire suppression to the head of the Forest Service agenda and startled Congress into passage of the Weeks Act in 1911. Although Pinchot and Roosevelt were gone, the Weeks Act was a testimony to their leadership (Pyne 2001).

Figure 18.4 Gifford Pinchot.

Courtesy of the Library of Congress Prints and Photographs Division. Reproduction number: LC-DIG-hec-21097

Pinchot later joined his old friend Teddy Roosevelt in Bull Moose politics in Roosevelt's unsuccessful run for the presidency in 1912. He served two terms as Governor of Pennsylvania from 1923–27 and 1931–1935. Near the end of his life, he wrote his autobiography, *Breaking New Ground*.

Gifford Pinchot and Theodore Roosevelt were able to form a coherent and effective strategy for protecting the nation's forest resource. It was Pinchot who turned idealism into action and ideas into national policy. The national forest system, the Forest Service and, most importantly, forestry in the United States, are the lasting legacies of Gifford Pinchot (Williams 1989).

Homework

Name: _____   Date: _____

There are a lot of basic things an American forester must know. Try your hand at these:

1. How many tree species are native to the United States?

2. What is DBH?

3. Why don't foresters replant eastern hardwood forests after harvesting?

4. What is an "exotic invasive" tree species? Give an example.

Forest Resources of the United States at the Beginning of the Twenty-first Century

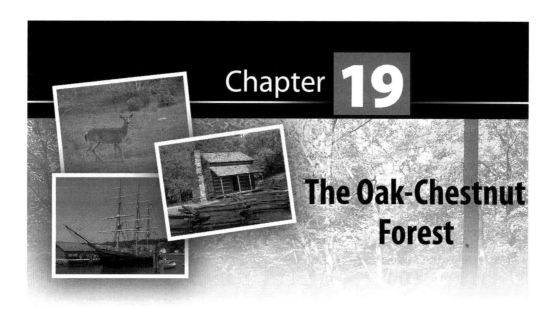

Chapter 19

The Oak-Chestnut Forest

This topic represents a break point in the progression of the history of forest resources in America. It is an opportunity to summarize by taking a closer look at one region—what was once the oak-chestnut forest. The oak-chestnut forest has a similar history to other forest types in America. It is a history of change.

The oak-chestnut forest describes a forest type that existed at the time of European settlement across 84,000,000 acres from southern New England extending west in a wide swath roughly defined by the Ohio River, Kentucky and Tennessee, and south through the Appalachians. The oaks and the American chestnut dominated the forests throughout the region and gave this particular forest type its name because of their abundance (Bonnicksen 2000a).

The oaks belong to the botanical genus *Quercus* and include possibly as many as 600 species worldwide. The wood of the oaks has such an important place in human history that Carlsen (2008) calls it "the breakfast of civilizations." An estimated 60 to 70 oak species exist in North America. Oaks are widespread across the continent with the greatest concentration of species found in the eastern United States in what was the oak-chestnut forest type. Botanists, foresters and wood scientists tend to separate North American oaks into two categories: white oaks and red oaks. This becomes a bit confusing as there are individual species bearing the same name: white oak (*Quercus alba*), Oregon white oak (*Quercus garryanna*), California white oak (*Quercus lobata*), southern red oak (*Quercus falcata*) and northern red oak (*Quercus rubra*). For clarity's sake, this chapter uses the plural terms white oaks and red oaks to refer to the broader classifications unless specified with the scientific name[1] (Harlow and Harrar 1969).

The average heights and diameters of the oaks vary from species to species.[2] Northern red oak, scarlet oak and pin oak—all members of the red oak group—attain heights of up to 80 feet and diameters of two to three feet. White oak (*Q. alba*) was typically the

---

[1] The listing of a scientific or Latin name for a species is always by genus followed by species. The genus is always capitalized and the species always in lower case. Scientific names often appear with the genus abbreviated, e.g., *Q. alba*.

[2] Virginia Tech has a very good online database of "Tree Fact Sheets" describing the characteristics of approximately 900 tree species. *http://www.fw.vt.edu/dendro/dendrology/factsheets.cfm.*

Figure 19.1 White Oak.

largest tree in the forest at the time of settlement, growing to 100 feet with diameters of three to four feet. Chestnut oak, one of the white oaks, can grow to 50 to 60 feet with diameters of up to two feet (Clarkson 1964, Harlow and Harrar 1969).

The American chestnut (*Castanea dentata*) was the other major component of the oak-chestnut forest type. Chestnut was generally a faster-growing tree than the oaks. Average heights at maturity ranged from 70 to 90 feet with diameters of three to five feet (Harlow and Harrar 1969).

FORMATION OF THE OAK-CHESTNUT FOREST

The oak-chestnut forest that existed at the time of European contact was a forest that had formed over thousands of years of climate fluctuations and frequent burning.

In the Pleistocene Epoch, the white spruce forest covered much of the region. Hardwoods, including the oaks and chestnut, existed in two narrow bands (refuges) on the higher ground on either side of the Mississippi Valley. As the glaciers began to recede and the Ice Age forests began to disintegrate approximately 17,000 years ago, the species that occupied the eastern forests spread at different rates to their present range (Bonnicksen 2000a).

Oaks, elms and maples appeared in New England approximately 10,000 years ago. Scientists believe that blue jays helped the spread of oaks by carrying acorns. Hickory arrived 5,000 years later. Eastern hemlock, occupying wet sites, arrived in southern Michigan about 7,000 years ago. The hemlock population crashed approximately 4,800 years ago—possibly due to a fungal disease—and did not recover until 2,000 years later. Chestnut was a late arrival. It did not become abundant in southern New England until approximately 2,000 years ago. White pine, believed to have been located on the exposed Continental Shelf during the Ice Age, had moved into the Shenandoah Valley by 12,700 years ago (Bonnicksen 2000a).

Oaks and chestnut share a number of characteristics. They are early successional species that can grow in light shade. They require disturbance to regenerate and neither is self-replacing. Fire was integral to the ecology of the oak chestnut forest. Frequent fire created disturbances required for oak and chestnut regeneration. Both regenerate primarily by sprouting from existing root systems more than by regenerating through a seed crop (Bonnicksen 2000a).

Indian fire was integral to forming and maintaining the oak-chestnut forest. As with other forest types subject to frequent Indian burning, the oak-chestnut forest was open, park-like, patchy and dominated by large trees. Without the disturbance of Indian fire, beech-maple or hemlock forests would have replaced much of the oak-chestnut forest (Bonnicksen 2000a).

THE OAK-CHESTNUT FOREST AT THE TIME OF EUROPEAN CONTACT

One of the first Europeans to record observations of the oak-chestnut forest was the English explorer Henry Hudson in 1609, who described "great store of goodly oakes and walnut-trees and Chestnut trees." The oak-chestnut forest type dominated the eastern United States, but other species and other forest types existed within the region. Different sites supported different species to form a diverse mixture of hardwoods with a number of softwood species adding to the richness of the forest. The distribution and existence of individual species also varied geographically from north to south and east to west within the general confines of the oak-chestnut forest (Bonnicksen 2000a).

The eastern ridge and valley country of the Alleghenies was oak-chestnut forest. Chestnut and chestnut oak occupied northern and southern slopes. Ridges also supported scarlet oak, black oak, eastern white pine and pitch pine. White oak dominated moist sites and along river bottoms. Pines existed on the thin soils of southern and eastern slopes. Coves contained chestnut, hemlock, black oak, beech, ash, northern red oak and some pine. Cool, wet ravines contained settler species such as hemlock, maple, beech, basswood and elm. Hickory and black walnut, pioneer species, also existed in the ravines. Red spruce dominated the highest elevations. A band of northern hardwoods such as yellow birch, red maple, beech and basswood existed in a strip at elevations below the red spruce (Bonnicksen 2000a, Clarkson 1964, Harlow and Harrar 1969).

Valleys were where Indians burned most frequently, and grassland and savanna dominated them. White oak (*Q. alba*) was scattered in small stands and savannas. These sites also contained black oak, hickory and some white pine (Bonnicksen 2000a).

Oak-chestnut forests dominated the slopes and ridges of the Allegheny plateau that characterizes the western hill country of the Appalachians. Cove hardwoods such as yellow-poplar, basswood, maple, buckeye, beech, chestnut, birch, ash, black cherry, northern red oak and white oak occupied cool, moist northern slopes along with hemlock. Northern hardwoods occupied higher elevations. Yellow-poplar, hickory, birch, ash and maple occupied better sites. Stands of white pine existed along the rivers and their tributaries. Sycamore located along the streams in the western part of the region (Bonnicksen 2000a, Clarkson 1964).

Northern red oak, now one of the most common species in the region, was widespread but limited in quantity. It is more sensitive to fire than other oaks so it could not survive in areas where Indians burned frequently (Bonnicksen 2000a).

Deer, turkey and black bear were plentiful in the region but their numbers were greatly reduced by the early twentieth century. Elk were common at one time, and there were occasional reports of them prior to the Civil War. Bison roamed the grasslands of the region.[3] Panthers and wolves once existed in the region but had disappeared in the late nineteenth and early twentieth century (Clarkson 1964).

---

[3] Conversion of grasslands to farmlands and hunting led to the disappearance of the "woodland" bison. For example, the last known bison in West Virginia was killed in Randolph County in 1825 (Clarkson 1964).

THE AMERICAN CHESTNUT

The American chestnut once comprised 25 to 40 percent of the trees within the oak-chestnut forest. There were patches of chestnut scattered throughout the forest. The largest chestnut trees could reach 10 feet in diameter and 130 feet in height. Most trees were in the four to five foot diameter range.

The story of the American chestnut provides examples of how human activity shapes forest ecology. It existed in abundance around Indian villages such as the Cahokia site in Illinois, suggesting that Indians may have cultivated chestnut. The many nuts that ripened every fall provided food for wildlife and Indians. It was a late arrival in the region it would dominate, arriving in southern New England approximately two thousand years ago. There is evidence that increased levels of Indian burning and clearing for agriculture aided the advance of the species (Bonnicksen 2000a).

European settlers found numerous uses for the wood of the chestnut. It is a light-weight, attractive wood with a distinctive grain. Like oak, a ring of large pores in the earlywood of each growth ring characterizes it anatomically. In the terminology of the wood anatomist, it is a "ring-porous hardwood." Its extractive content made it durable (decay resistant).

Settlers used chestnut in construction and for fence rails. Many of the older barns in the region are framed with chestnut timbers and sheathed with chestnut siding. It was not a species favored by cabinetmakers for furniture for sale to wealthier customers in the urban areas, but it was widely used for the rustic furniture of the frontier. Pioneers also crafted kitchenware from the wood of chestnut.

The oak-chestnut forest began to change drastically with the introduction of Japanese chestnut[4] to America prior to 1900. The exotic species carried a fungus, *Cryphonectria parasitica,* which causes the chestnut blight or chestnut bark disease (Anagnostakis 2000). The American chestnut was not immune to the disease and nearly all the native chestnut died off by 1930. Some American chestnut survives throughout its natural range because it readily regenerates through root sprouting.[5] Unfortunately, it is short-lived because of the blight (Harlow and Harrar 1969).

The demise of the chestnut has changed the character of the forest. Today, what was so recently the oak-chestnut forest is now the oak-hickory forest type. Efforts are under way to establish disease-resistant strains of chestnut in order to restore the character of the forest. However, it is unlikely that conservationists will ever regain the true character of the oak-chestnut.

Exotic species are one of the most difficult environmental challenges facing the eastern forests. Some, like the chestnut blight, have caused drastic and undesirable ecological changes. There are other exotics, including the gypsy moth, the emerald ash borer, Dutch elm disease, the Asian longhorned beetle and the hemlock woolly adelgid that threaten a number of the native trees of the eastern hardwood forest (U.S. Forest Service 2009). Scientists also consider invasive plants such as kudzu, multiflora rose, Tree-of-Heaven and Norway maple problematic (Huebner et al. 2007). But not all exotics are undesirable. Maize, beans, squash and other vegetable crops developed by Mesoamerican Indians, as well as Eastern Hemisphere crops such as wheat and rice, are also exotic species in the eastern United States (Moore 2002a).

---

[4] Until very recently, scientists believed that the Chinese chestnut was the source of *Cryphonectria parasitic.*

[5] Chestnut wood is now in high demand. Entrepreneurs have formed small businesses to tear down old structures, particularly abandoned barns, to salvage the chestnut and sell it at premium prices.

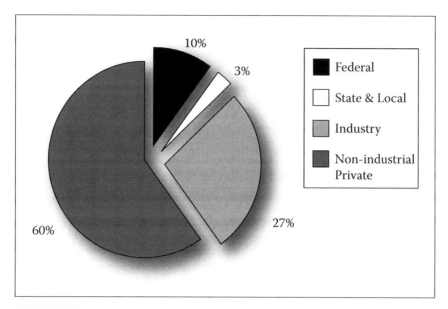

Figure 19.2 Forest Ownership in West Virginia.

LAND OWNERSHIP IN THE APPALACHIAN FOREST

The advance of the westward expansion of settlement through American history has shaped the forests of the east by establishing the dominance of private ownership. Non-industrial private landowners own approximately 60 percent of the forested land in West Virginia (Figure 19.2). These are ordinary citizens and families. Industry owns 27 percent, and only 13 percent is publicly owned. In contrast, 60 percent of the forested land in the Pacific Northwest states of Oregon and Washington is publicly owned. Industry owns 21 percent of the Northwest forest and 19 percent is in non-industrial private ownership (Smith et al. 2009).

European settlers acquired the land in the east and converted much of it from forest to farmland. They first cleared valleys and gentle slopes for agriculture, which may have remained cleared for as long as three hundred years. Steeper slopes and ridges were logged later in the era of the logging railroad.

HARDWOOD MARKET ERAS

From 1870 to the present, the hardwood forests of the northeast and the Appalachians have undergone four "market eras" defined by differing rates and types of human activity. Available resources characterize each market era, along with the changing demand for various wood products and the predominant strategies for removing timber from the woods (silviculture). Each era affected the forest composition of today (Luppold 2003a).

The Era of Heavy Cutting (approximately 1870 to 1929)

Luppold (2003a) characterizes the era that began after the Civil War and continued until the start of the Great Depression in 1929 as the "era of heavy cutting." "Widespread, large scale and somewhat indiscriminant removal" of timber marked this era where loggers heavily cut over the forest not already cleared for agriculture.

Logging railroads and steam-powered yarders made timber on steeper slopes of the Appalachians accessible. Steam-powered sawmills permitted the rapid conversion of logs to lumber. Large bandsaw mills were capable of handling the large timber that came out of the virgin stands. In the peak harvest year of 1909, for example, 1,524 sawmills in the state of West Virginia produced almost 1.5 billion board feet of lumber (Clarkson 1964, Steer 1948).

Ironically, much of what remained and that the loggers cut during this era consisted of softwoods: hemlock, spruce and pine. They also removed large quantities of high quality hardwoods and universally employed clear-cutting throughout the oak-chestnut forest. As in other regions, intense fires consumed the slash left behind by the loggers, at times burning topsoil down to bare rock. Sometimes, farmers intentionally set fires in cut over areas to promote growth of forage for livestock (Luppold 2003a).

The forest that began to regenerate on the cleared sites was dominated by pioneer species, including northern red oak and black cherry. Clear-cutting and fire favored pioneer species, especially oaks. Oaks, especially northern red oak, regenerated on sites where they had previously not existed. The loss of the American chestnut eliminated a fast-growing competitor to the oaks. Drought in the 1930s and the low populations of white-tailed deer in the early part of the century also contributed to the composition of the regenerating forests. The even-aged hardwood stands that have supplied the hardwood industry with raw material for the past half century became established during the era of heavy cutting (Luppold 2003a, 2003b).

The Second Era (1929 to approximately 1970)

The second market era began with the Great Depression. It ran through World War II, the baby boom and ended with the energy crisis of the 1970s and the emergence of a global economy.

The Great Depression brought the relentless harvesting of the previous era to a halt. Demand for wood products declined drastically, allowing forests a chance to recover. In addition, people abandoned large acreages of farmland during the Depression, with large quantities of yellow-poplar regenerating on abandoned farmlands (Luppold 2003a).

Transportation systems were undergoing another change during this era with the construction of more extensive and better roads and an increasing use of trucks. This allowed loggers access to more widespread areas of the region. The diminished supply of timber favored smaller sawmills than those that thrived in the previous era. In addition, the scarcity of huge logs and the relative abundance of smaller sawtimber made the large band saw mills unnecessary. Small, circle sawmills proliferated in the region as many of the older, large bandsaw mills shut down (Luppold 2003a).

During this era, loggers did not practice clear-cutting extensively in the eastern hardwood forest except for residual old-growth stands that had escaped the heavy cutting prior to the Depression. Selective cutting based on diameter and species (diameter limit high grading) was the dominant harvest regime. In other words, they took the big trees of the most valuable species out of the woods. Diameter limit high grading heavily influenced the composition of the forests emerging today.

The primary market for hardwood lumber during this era was the furniture industry. Black walnut and imported mahogany solids and veneer were popular furniture species during the 1930s through the 1960s. Furniture makers used yellow-poplar for core stock (hidden parts, typically covered by veneer) and for veneer used to make plywood. Face veneer of more valuable species such as black walnut covered the yellow-poplar core plies as the visible surfaces in furniture. Companies used maple heavily in the mid 1960s for furniture and kitchen cabinets (Luppold 2003a).

Large quantities of black walnut, maple and yellow-poplar were removed from the forest to meet the demands of the furniture industry. The furniture industry did not use red oak during this era, leaving it largely in the woods. (In fact, foresters were bemoaning red oaks as "underutilized" in the 1940s.) The selective harvest regime of this era allowed the red oaks to grow to merchantable size and allowed shade-tolerant settler species such as red and sugar maple to become established in the forest understory (Luppold 2003a, 2003b, Luppold and Bumgardner 2005).

Lumber production increased along with the production of goods to support the war effort. The return of veterans at the end of World War II boosted the housing market. A boost in new home construction always generates increased economic activity in the wood products industry and production increased as a result.

One of Franklin D. Roosevelt's New Deal programs made significant contributions to forest resources nationally and regionally. The Civilian Conservation Corps (CCC) was created in 1933 to employ young men in public works and conservation projects. The CCC employed nearly three and a half million young men living in camps in a military-like environment. CCC workers planted between 2 and 3 billion trees in reforestation projects. They built roads, hiking trails, picnic shelters, campgrounds and parks. For example, the CCC in West Virginia built a number of facilities in the state parks and forests that the public still enjoys. They restocked streams with fish and completed numerous erosion control projects. The young men of the CCC also proved themselves as an effective fire fighting organization. The

Figure 19.2 Overlook. *Constructed by the CCC at Cooper's Rock State Forest, WV.*

government disbanded the program in 1942 when many, if not most, of the young men of the CCC went to war (Otis et al. 1986, Paige 1985).

The Third Era (approximately 1973 to approximately 1999)

There is no clearly defined point, such as the stock market crash of 1929, that defines when the third hardwood market era began or ended. The transition to this era was driven by federal and international policies that contributed to economic distress in the 1970s and to economic recovery in the 1980s. In 1971, the Nixon administration moved the U.S. dollar off the gold standard and instituted wage and price controls to control inflation. Elimination of the gold standard led to the elimination of the World War II era "Bretton Woods Agreement" that fixed international exchange rates based upon a gold standard. Since then, exchange rates have floated depending upon the relative economic strength of each nation's currency. This opened up opportunities for expanded international trade. Free trade agreements proliferated in the late twentieth century, turning the world into a global marketplace. Wood products were a segment of the global market, and the United States is the most powerful player in that market (Luppold 2003a, 2003b, Luppold and Bumgardner 2006).

As barriers to international trade were removed, hardwood producers increased exports to markets in Asia and Europe. The United States became a major exporter of hardwoods during this era. (Luppold 2003a, Luppold and Bumgardner 2006)

Foreign furniture manufacturers took advantage of open markets and innovations in do-it-yourself assembly, compact packaging and improved shipping to capture an ever-increasing share of the American market. Swedish retailer IKEA entered the U.S. market in 1985 (IKEA Group 2009). Their contemporary styles, inexpensive products and innovative marketing schemes gained acceptance among American consumers. Asian furniture manufacturers followed the IKEA example, and, by 1999, China was emerging as one of the world's major furniture manufacturers and exporters (Luppold 2003b).

The oil crisis, inflation and astronomical mortgage interest rates in the 1970s caused a recession in the housing and lumber markets, but the Reagan tax cuts of the 1980s sparked economic recovery and a rapid increase in housing starts and timber production. This was also the era when the large "baby boom" generation was coming of age and entering the housing market. Furniture remained the leading market for better quality hardwood lumber, but the market became more diverse as the hardwood flooring and kitchen cabinet industries expanded. During this era, red oaks gained great popularity in the furniture, flooring and cabinet industries.

Forests that had regenerated after the era of heavy cutting were maturing and reaching merchantable sizes by the 1970s. As a result, sawtimber supplies had increased. Harvesting and production increased but were nowhere near the intensity of the era of heavy cutting. The predominant harvesting strategy remained selective cutting, but its basis was species and quality (value based high grading) (Luppold 2003a).

Logging removed red oaks in great quantities in the last three decades of the twentieth century. In West Virginia, for example, red oaks accounted for 27 percent of the roundwood (log) production in 1999. The most recent forest inventory, conducted in 2000, indicates that oak is declining in the region. The shift from clear-cutting to selective harvest along with aggressive fire suppression favored the regeneration of settler species as opposed to the oaks and other early-succession species. Increased deer populations throughout the region have severely impacted the regeneration of oaks, a favored browse for deer. There are likely other factors reducing oak regeneration that foresters do not fully understand (Luppold and Bumgardner 2005).

The Present Era (beginning approximately 1999)

The transition to the present market era was gradual and is still occurring. One of the primary driving factors was the very rapid decline of the U.S. furniture industry as exports, particularly from China, have captured markets from domestic manufacturers. An additional factor is the emergence of a hardwood-based engineered wood products industry that began taking shape in the 1990s as hardwoods replaced softwood timber supplies from federal forests that disappeared from the market earlier in the decade (Luppold 2003a, 2003b).

The Internet and e-business have revolutionized the marketing of hardwood products. Global Positioning Satellites (GPS) and Geographic Information System (GIS) software help foresters better understand the changes occurring in forests and aid in the day-to-day business of managing forests and harvesting timber. Log and lumber scanning technologies and Computerized Numerical Control (CNC) woodworking machinery cut costs, reduce waste and produce better quality products. Concepts such as Lean Manufacturing and Just-in-Time inventory strategies are changing manufacturing in the furniture and cabinet industries. Engineered wood products are evolving and changing building construction in ways not seen since Augustine Taylor developed light framing in 1833 (Luppold 2003b).

As this book is being written in the late summer of 2009, the United States is suffering from a severe economic recession. The recession that began with the collapse of the housing market in 2006–2007 has caused disruptions in the forest products industry (Pepke 2008). Mill closures, production cutbacks and layoffs have characterized the past two years. These trends are reminiscent of and may be worse than the economic downturn of the 1970s. It is obvious that the recession is changing the industry, but the extent and character of the change is uncertain.

Industrial land ownership patterns are shifting as wood products companies have created Real Estate Investment Trusts (REITs) or sold land to Timber Investment Management Organizations (TIMOs).

THE FUTURE OF THE CENTRAL APPALACHIAN FOREST

It is difficult to predict the future of the oak-hickory forest. However, policymakers and land managers will face several challenges that will impact the future of the region's forest resource.

Appalachian forests appear to be in a transition from oak-hickory to a more prominent role for maples (Luppold 2003a, 2003b, Luppold and Bumgardner 2005, Smith et al. 2009). If this trend continues, the ecological implications are troubling. Specifically, oaks and hickories are mast producers that support wildlife populations while maple is not. Will industry and policymakers recognize the implications of this ecological change and, if so, how will they respond?

The size of the deer herd is an impediment to forest regeneration and has reduced the diversity of forests (Latham et al. 2005, Rawinski 2008). In 2000 and 2001, the Pennsylvania Game Commission extended its antlerless deer hunting season in an attempt to control deer populations in the state (Wallingford 2007). The change in policy was and remains controversial. Will hunters and the public at large allow other states to follow suit?

Exotic invasive species threaten to disrupt the ecology of the forest type. In particular, the emerald ash borer is established in the region and may cause the decline or demise of ash in the same way the blight led to the decline of the American chestnut. Tree species such as Tree-of-Heaven are taking over ecological niches once occupied by native species. Will the federal and state governments be willing to invest the resources necessary to control invasives? Will environmental organizations commit their considerable public relations and lobbying resources toward solving this problem?

The population of the United States continues to grow and development continues to encroach upon forestland. How will Americans retain forests and wildlands without infringing upon the property rights of citizens?

Concerns over energy and atmospheric carbon have led to numerous well-funded government initiatives—with others still in proposal form—to develop alternative, clean fuels. The impacts of these various initiatives are not without consequences to forest resources. Will the trend of clearing forests to build wind farms on Appalachian ridges continue? Will energy producers clear forests to grow switchgrass or other annual plants for conversion to ethanol? Will they use greater quantities of woody biomass to produce energy? If so, will this be limited to logging or mill residues or will it include whole trees?

These questions remain unanswered, but meeting the challenges of the twenty-first century will require citizens who are knowledgeable and engaged. It will be necessary for citizens to seek factual information and not be misled by paying attention only to points of view of advocates of a single position. This will require effort to locate and learn to critically assess information. It is not a task for the intellectually lazy.

When I was a graduate student, one of my mentors continuously told me to "be skeptical." It was excellent advice that I pass along to the readers of this text. Be skeptical. In the words of Bjorn Lomborg (2001), skepticism is necessary to make sound environmental decisions because we cannot afford to "act on the myths of both optimists and pessimists. Instead we need to use the best information to join others in the common goal of making a better tomorrow."

Recommended Reading

Lomborg, Bjørn. 2001. *The Skeptical Environmentalist: Measuring the Real State of the World.*

The Skeptical Environmentalist is one of the most controversial books published about the environment in the twenty-first century. The book was greeted with both widespread praise and equally widespread criticism (often accompanied by a shocking level of vitriol). The strength of Lomborg's work is his discussion of what constitutes sound science and how advocacy groups on different sides of issues may misuse science to promote their particular positions on issues. Whether one agrees or disagrees with the points made by Lomborg, those who read this book with an open mind will be better prepared to apply reason and skepticism to develop their own conclusions about environmental issues.

Homework

Name: _____   Date: _____

1. Why don't foresters in the Appalachian hardwood region replant trees after harvest?

2. What is an emerald ash borer and why does it cause so much concern among forest ecologists?

Chapter **20**

Conflict over Forests

American forest policy changed radically in the last decade of the twentieth century. Policies formed with passage of the Organic Act of 1897 and articulated by Gifford Pinchot were turned on their head. The vehicle of this transformation was a small owl that lives in the Douglas fir forests of the Pacific Northwest.

Recommended Reading

Chase, Alston. 1995. *In a Dark Wood: The Fight Over Forests and the Rising Tyranny of Ecology.*

Alston Chase holds a Ph.D. in philosophy and gave up an academic career to live a simpler life in the Yellowstone country. His interest in what was happening at Yellowstone National Park inspired him to write *Playing God in Yellowstone,* a book referred to often in this text. His interest led him next to the forests of California and the Pacific Northwest to investigate the conflicts that were taking place over the management of forests. The result was *In a Dark Wood.* This is a book that should be required reading for all forestry, natural resources and environmental science students.

The saga of the northern spotted owl began much earlier. Like other examples of dramatic change that transformed the history of the forest resources of the United States, the spotted owl controversy represented a convergence of a number of societal forces at work in the era following World War II.

MATHEMATICAL MODELS AND FOREST ECOLOGY

The German biologist and philosopher Ernst Haeckel coined the term ecology in 1866 as "the whole science of the relations of the organism to the environment including, in the broad sense, all the 'conditions of existence.'" It was not until after 1900 that ecology became a field for research in the biological sciences. When Frederic Clements (ca. 1900) suggested that the biological community is a complex organism and A. G. Tansley introduced the concept of the ecosystem in 1935, ecology came to represent both the "balance and unity" of nature (Chase 1995).

After World War II, ecologists began to use computer-aided mathematical analysis techniques to develop models that attempted to predict the process of succession within ecosystems. Applying what are essentially mathematical forecasting models to complex natural systems is fraught with difficulty. Scientists must choose the correct statistical principles in developing the models, and they must recognize and acknowledge the probability that results observed in the real world may vary significantly from their predicted results. Most important, natural systems involve many interrelated variables. Those developing models must account for them, correctly describe how they interrelate and employ accurate data to account for each variable. Once the scientist has developed the model, careful observation in the field must verify the results it predicts.

Those who develop forecasting models understandably want to simplify the models. However, this poses the risk of oversimplifying to the point of missing important relationships and phenomena entirely. It is also necessary for scientists to make assumptions, perhaps many assumptions, to fit the pieces together in a viable model. This is why experimental or field data must verify models before they are acceptable.

The Danish statistician Bjørn Lomborg (2001) points out that "to a certain extent all argument relies on metaphors and rhetorical shortcuts." Scientists generally cannot explain all of their assumptions, data and conclusions because they simply lack the "time and space" to do so. They must not allow rhetoric to "cloud reality." It is important to recognize the difference between a justifiable scientific conclusion and a rhetorical flourish that may intentionally or unintentionally alarm or overstate a perceived problem. It is essential to be able to distinguish when what poses as scientific deduction crosses the line to become a value judgment.

The early ecological models were closed-loop systems. To simplify the mathematics, scientists removed variables that they could not predict—disturbance—from the model. In other words, the models assumed that ecosystems were free of outside influences. Without disturbance in the loop, the theoreticians reached similar but erroneous conclusions. Succession is an orderly process. It is predictable. Ecosystems always seek "stability." At this point, many crossed the line separating science from value judgment and concluded that late-succession ecosystems—self-replacing forests for example—represented the true "balance of nature" (Chase 1995).

What the empiricists—the scientists in the field collecting data—were observing contradicted the results obtained by the black box models in the theoreticians' computers. The models were logical and elegant mathematically. But, the empiricists argued, they were "nonsense biologically" (McIntosh 1976). Stability and biological equilibrium did not govern nature. Random disturbance did (Bonnicksen 2000a, Botkin 1990, Chase 1995, Krech 1999)

The debate continues within the scientific community, but the evidence appears clear. The work of historians, archeologists, empirical ecologists and forest scientists supports the conclusion that stable, late-succession forests were more the exception than the rule in the history of the forests of North America. The history of America's forests is a history of disturbance—much of it caused by humans—and regeneration. But the ideas that ecosystems are fragile and that human-caused disturbance can cause ecological disaster are firmly planted in public perception (Bonnicksen 2000a, Chase 1995, Denevan 1992, Krech 1999, Mann 2005).

ECOLOGY, THE PRISTINE MYTH AND BIOCENTRISM

The deductions of the theoretical ecologists seemed to confirm the pristine myth. Without human influence, nature "preferred" self-replacing, late-succession forests. Old-growth and wilderness advocates seized this evidence to advance their political and policy objectives. By the 1960s, the boundaries between science and activism became blurred.

The hypotheses of the theoretical ecologists appeared to add legitimacy to the political and philosophical objectives of environmental, anti-technology, anti-industrial and anti-capitalist movements[1] of the late twentieth century. Publication of ecologist Barry Commoner's *The Closing Circle* by the Sierra Club in 1971 brought the hypotheses of the theoretical ecologists to the public in simple and value-laden rhetoric. He argued that ecosystems became "stressed" and would "collapse" if disturbed. The concept that ecosystems may "collapse" suggested that ecosystems were fragile—a difficult concept for foresters to accept in light of the recovery of forest ecosystems from years of agricultural usage, catastrophic fire and heavy timbering. Commoner's third "law" of ecology transcended science into the metaphysical, "Nature knows best." The genie was out of the bottle (Chase 1995).

The scientific term "ecology" became co-opted into a philosophical school of thought with the emergence of a "biocentric" system of values. In 1973, the Norwegian philosopher Arne Naess presented a paper at the Third World Future Research Conference, "*The Shallow and the Deep: Long-Range Ecology Movements.*" "Shallow ecology" is human-centered concern for the environment—an "anthropocentric" system of values. "Deep ecology" interprets the interdependence of systems ecology as meaning that all living creatures are of equal importance—of equal *value.* This is biocentrism. To the informed public, ecology was no longer just a scientific discipline adhering to scientific method. It had become a "movement" (Chase 1995).

THE MODERN ENVIRONMENTAL MOVEMENT

The modern environmental movement emerged in the 1960s and 1970s. During that era, public attitudes and perceptions shifted from the conservationist philosophy of Gifford Pinchot towards preservation. The public perceived the conservation ethic defined by Pinchot as representing the status quo.

The environmental movement of the 1960s and 1970s emerged to solve very real problems and achieved remarkable success. Critical environmental issues of air and water quality, chemicals in the environment and declining populations of high profile wildlife species were the primary focus of the movement during this period of time (Chase 1995, Moore 2000).

The public called the city of Pittsburgh the "Smoky City" for the clouds of smoke from the city's steel mills. They blamed air pollution levels in Denver and Los Angeles for high levels of respiratory ailments in those cities. In 1970, many people believed that Lake Erie was becoming a "dead lake" and that high levels of industrial and municipal effluents threatened the entire Great Lakes ecosystem. The Cuyahoga River in Cleveland actually caught fire in 1969. Love Canal frightened the public about toxic chemicals in the environment. The plight of the whooping crane, worries about the decline of bald eagle, wolf and California condor populations and growing awareness of the loss of whales brought attention to endangered species.

The environmentalists of the '60s and '70s achieved success after success as Congress passed environmental legislation, state legislatures followed suit and agencies tightened regulations to ensure a cleaner environment. Most indices of environmental quality indicate that the situation is getting better although there is certainly room for further improvement (Lomborg 2001).

---

[1] It is difficult to clearly define different but frequently overlapping motives behind 1960s and 1970s activism. For example, Chase (2003) makes a case that the Unabomber, Theodore Kaczynski, adopted the rhetoric of radical environmentalism as a means to achieve his true objective of dismantling the rapid advance of technology.

Examples of significant gains in environmental policy include passage of the Wilderness Act of 1964, the National Environmental Policy Act (1969) and the Clean Air Act (1970), as well as creation of the Environmental Protection Agency in 1970, the Endangered Species Act (1973) and the Clean Water Act (1977).

PROPHETS OF THE APOCALYPSE VS. THE WORLD'S GREATEST HERO

In the 1960s, strident prophecies of environmental apocalypse came to the public's attention. Pisani (1997) describes this era as one of pervasive pessimism not unlike the pessimism of the late nineteenth century that gave rise to the American conservation movement. Apocalyptic predictions have a long history in Judeo-Christian thought, most recently with the the Y2K scare and worries over global warming. The threat of nuclear war during the Cold War made the concept of the possible annihilation of the human race a worry among a broad segment of the public. Americans built backyard bomb shelters during the 1950s and early 1960s[2] (Simon 1996).

Publication of Rachel Carson's *Silent Spring* in 1962 brought another apocalyptic vision before the public. Carson argued that chemical pesticides were decimating songbird populations. Her book led to the eventual ban of DDT. *Silent Spring* is sometimes said to have marked the beginning of the modern environmental movement. Later evidence refuted some of Carson's conclusions, but the perception became planted in people's minds and perceptions are very difficult to overcome.

A nuclear accident at Pennsylvania's Three Mile Island power plant and the nuclear disaster at Chernobyl in the Soviet Union added to the state of fear and fueled the anti-nuclear movement. Public health scares concerning toxic wastes at the Love Canal, Alar on apples, acid rain, ozone depletion, dioxins and other carcinogenic substances in food and water and global warming have perpetuated the perception of impending environmental disaster.

In 1968, the Sierra Club published *The Population Bomb* by Stanford University ecologist Paul R. Ehrlich. It is obvious that increasing human populations create increased demand for resources. But Ehrlich's message was apocalyptic—world population growth was a "race to oblivion." He reintroduced theories first proposed by Thomas Malthus in 1798 that the Earth had a finite "carrying capacity" for human population. Malthus was an Englishman concerned about the overcrowding of British cities during the industrial revolution. He concluded that eventually, the British Isles would reach their "carrying capacity"—their ability to produce the food and other resources necessary to sustain the human population. Ehrlich's work, as well as subsequent publications, included dire predictions of environmental catastrophe that would occur by the end of the twentieth century if population continued to grow. Few of his predictions have come to pass, but like religious prophets of doom, Ehrlich insists that his predictions are accurate. It's just the timing that was wrong (Bailey 2000, Chase 1995, Simon 1996, 1998).

The media helped to perpetuate alarm and environmental organizations have taken full advantage. Hollywood has also contributed to the culture of gloom and doom with such films as *The China Syndrome, Silkwood, Erin Brockovich, Waterworld, The Day After Tomorrow* and *An Inconvenient Truth*.

---

[2] The author of this book remembers, with some amusement, hiding under a wooden school desk during primary school "air raid drills" in the late 1950s . . . a lot of good that would have done in the event of a real Soviet nuclear attack.

Norman E. Borlaug (1914–2009) stands in stark contrast to Paul Ehrlich and his fellow prophets of the apocalypse. Borlaug graduated from the University of Minnesota in forestry in 1937. After working with the Forest Service, he returned to Minnesota where he completed a Ph.D. in plant pathology in 1942. Borlaug worked as part of a research team with the Rockefeller Foundation in Mexico developing new strains of wheat that increased crop productivity, crop management and disease resistance in Mexico. Borlaug later applied his advances to rice and other crops and was successful in increasing crop production in Asia. Borlaug is credited with saving a billion[3] people from starvation and disease. In 1970, he was awarded the Nobel Peace Prize for his work (Easterbrook 1997).

While Ehrlich was claiming in *The Population Bomb* that attempting to feed humanity was hopeless and hundreds of millions of people would starve to death in the 1970s and 1980s, Borlaug was quietly leading what has come to be known as the "Green Revolution" in agricultural research. Ehrlich singled out India, in particular, for his gloomy predictions of famine and massive human disaster. Apparently Ehrlich never met Norman Borlaug. Borlaug's new strains of wheat and improved cultivation techniques were introduced to India and Pakistan where wheat production more than tripled. "Ehrlich discreetly omitted his prediction about that from later editions of *The Population Bomb*" (Bailey 2000).

Borlaug discussed the impacts of the Green Revolution on land use and forestry in a 2000 interview with Ronald Bailey (2000), stating, "If we grow our food and fiber on the land best suited to farming with the technology that we have and what's coming, including proper use of genetic engineering and biotechnology, we will leave untouched vast tracts of land, with all of their plant and animal diversity." Borlaug went on to claim that without the improved crop yields generated by agricultural research forests would have to be "chopped down" to provide sufficient food for the world's growing population.[4] "This applies to forestry, too. I'm pleased to see that some of the forestry companies are very modern and using good management, good breeding systems."

Borlaug's accomplishments are not universally appreciated. Environmental groups, including Greenpeace and the World Wide Fund for Nature, oppose genetic modification, predicting dire health and ecological consequences as a result of what they describe as "Frankenfoods." A number of nations, including the European Union member nations, have banned certain genetically modified organisms (McWilliams 2009).

Post-Vietnam Radicalization of the Environmental Movement

It is not surprising that the growing sense of alarm over real and imagined environmental issues led to anger and increased stridency among some environmental activists. Earth Day 1970 channeled anti-war fervor toward environmental issues. Foregoing longstanding and staid environmental organizations, the new generation of environmental activists formed new organizations that pushed the envelope of confrontation. It was an angry period in the nation's history.

---

[3] The number one billion is admittedly startling. Some may believe it is a misprint. It is not.

[4] In fact, this is what is occurring in sub-Saharan Africa and in the Amazon basin where farmers without the benefits of modern agriculture have cleared forests to survive.

Greenpeace was founded in Vancouver, British Columbia in 1971 over concerns for the oceanic environment. Soon the Greenpeace vessel "Rainbow Warrior" was interfering with nuclear weapons testing in the Pacific, confronting whaling fleets and saving baby harp seals in the Arctic (Moore 2000). The Animal Liberation Front (ALF) and People for the Ethical Treatment of Animals (PETA) were founded in the United Kingdom in 1976 and in the United States in 1980. A handful of wilderness activists founded EarthFirst! in 1980.

These groups had several things in common. All espouse biocentric philosophies. All adopted militant confrontational tactics used successfully in the anti-war movement, including noisy protests and "street theater" to make their point. All adopted civil disobedience. All of these groups were masterful in generating attention from the television and print media. All are uncompromising in seeking their objectives. As the slogan adopted by EarthFirst! proclaims, "No compromise in defense of Mother Earth!"

ALF, Earth Liberation Front (ELF) and EarthFirst! went so far as to cross the line of civil disobedience to include violence—vandalism, arson, death threats, tree spiking and sending letters and packages laced with razor blades through the mail. The FBI identified these three organizations as domestic terrorist organizations in their 1999 Report on Terrorism (FBI 1999).

As Greenpeace and EarthFirst! grabbed the headlines, the public increasingly viewed the established environmental movement as too conventional. Older, traditional environmental organizations—the Sierra Club, the Audubon Society and the Wilderness Society—became more confrontational in order to maintain their places within the environmentalist movement. In 1996, the Sierra Club adopted a policy of opposing all commercial timber harvest on national forests. In spite of new evidence that the "leave it alone" philosophy applied to western national forests is contributing to the destruction of those forests by catastrophic wildfire, the Sierra Club remains adamant in its stance (Chase 1995).

THE FIGHT OVER FORESTS

As the environmental movement gained victory after victory over issues of air and water quality, nuclear power, chemicals in the environment and other issues, groups began to turn their attention to forests as the next battleground.

Clear-cutting erupted as an issue in 1973 on the Monongahela National Forest near Richwood, West Virginia. The Izaak Walton League successfully sued the Forest Service, arguing that clear-cutting violated the intent of the Organic Act of 1897 by cutting immature, as well as mature, trees. Clear-cutting is a silvicultural regime that favors regeneration of pioneer species.[2] There is no way to disguise the fact that clear-cuts are incredibly ugly. And, like all management tools, loggers can misuse or abuse clear-cutting. Large scale clear-cuts on national forests in the Pacific Northwest came under intense and arguably justifiable criticism from environmental activists and the public in the 1970s and 1980s. Activists successfully turned public opinion against clear-cutting, but foresters insist that clear-cutting is ecologically justifiable—if done right—by mimicking the effects of fire (Chase 1995, Miller 2006, Moore 2000).

Old-growth forests also emerged as an issue. In the 1970s, ecologists, led by Jerry Franklin at the Forest Service's Pacific Northwest Experiment Station in Corvallis, Oregon, were discovering that old growth supported greater biological diversity than previously believed. Franklin and his colleagues recommended protecting and re-creating old growth forests. Differing definitions of what constitutes an old-growth forest cloud the old-growth issue. Furthermore, forest scientists, archeologists and historians dispute the extent of old-growth at the time of European contact claimed by its advocates. But was this a scientific or a values-based recommendation? Was biodiversity threatened by lack of old-growth? Or was forest management as practiced by the Forest Service promoting biodiversity by creating diverse habitats? (Bonnicksen 2000, Chase 1995, Moore 2000)

The Wilderness Act of 1964 led to further conflict. The Forest Service designated 17 percent of national forest lands as wilderness areas in a process known as the Roadless Area Review and Evaluation (RARE I). The Sierra Club and the Wilderness Society were incensed and demanded that the Service set aside more land as wilderness. As the Forest Service began further evaluation (RARE II) to evaluate further lands for wilderness designation, environmental organizations led public relations campaigns, lobbying efforts and petition and letter-writing campaigns to generate support. Their efforts generally met opposition by natural resource industries, local Chambers of Commerce and local governments concerned about the economic impacts of wilderness (Chase 1995).

Controversy also flared up in California as "corporate raider" Charles Hurwitz's Maxxam Corporation acquired the venerated Pacific Lumber Company (Palco) in a hostile takeover in 1985. Founded in 1869, the same family had owned Palco since 1905. Palco owned 197,000 acres of redwood forest and had long demonstrated a commitment to conservation, practicing only selective cutting on its corporate lands. A single redwood tree could be worth $30,000 on the stump at 1985 prices. Its wood is an attractive deep red color, light weight and resistant to decay. But redwoods are large, magnificent trees that are capable of living for centuries.[5] When Hurwitz acquired Palco, he immediately began to liquidate its assets. This meant clear-cutting. The public outcry over Hurwitz's takeover tactics and his disregard for sustainable forest management was fierce. EarthFirst! got involved immediately, organizing protests, blocking logging roads and engaging in lengthy "tree-sitting" on Palco lands—all with the television cameras present and rolling (Chase 1995).

Public sentiment was turning against the forest products industry.

ENTER THE NORTHERN SPOTTED OWL

The environmental activists found their means in the northern spotted owl. Eric Forsman, a graduate student at Oregon State in the 1970s, conducted his doctoral research tracking owls in the old growth Andrews Experimental Forest in Oregon's Cascades. Forsman's was one of the first studies of the owl, its population and habitat. The general belief was that old growth was the owl's "preferred habitat." Forsman concluded that owls had "an extraordinarily large home range" and logging seemed to cause owls to abandon nesting sites (Chase 1995).

What did it mean? Forsman and his colleagues were alarmed at their findings but reluctant to make a leap of faith about the fate of the owl or possible remedies. Evidence to support any conclusion was scanty—owls were known to nest in areas as much as 77 percent clear-cut. Forsman recommended a three hundred acre "buffer" of old growth around known nesting sites.

---

[5] The California redwoods have long been of interest to conservationists and preservationists. Wealthy San Franciscans founded the *Sempervirens* Club in 1901 and the Save the Redwoods League in 1919 to protect the stately giants of the redwood forest. The efforts of these organizations led to the preservation of stands of redwoods near San Francisco in Big Basin Redwoods State Park and Muir Woods National Monument.

In 1977, the Forest Service and the Bureau of Land Management adopted the recommendation of setting aside three hundred acres for each of four hundred pairs of spotted owls. Oregon and Washington state governments appointed groups to further study and recommend strategies for protecting the owl. This decision coincided with "RARE II"—a second effort to inventory potential additional wilderness areas. The Sierra Club and its allies had an opportunity to use the owl to gain its ends in RARE II. Perhaps they could even succeed in shutting down logging in the Pacific Northwest's national forests (Chase 1995).

THE LEGAL WEAPONS

The flurry of environmental legislation in the 1960s and 1970s included several bills that changed the way the Forest Service managed national forests since the time of Pinchot. The National Environmental Policy Act (NEPA) of 1969 established the requirement of preparing detailed environmental impact statements before proceeding with activities that had potential environmental impacts, including timber harvest. The passage of NEPA enabled environmental activists to challenge federal projects on the basis of insufficient environmental impact statements (Chase 1995).

Congress enacted the National Forest Management Act (NFMA) of 1976 in response to the Izaak Walton League winning its suit over clear-cutting in the Monongahela National Forest. The intention of the NFMA was to make clear-cutting legal in national forests while at the same time protecting the forests. It was an exercise in political compromise, but it established a complicated planning process that required that the Forest Service solicit public input in developing forest plans. NFMA made it possible for activists to challenge national forest plans and initiate legal action to block Forest Service timber sales (Chase 1995)

But it was the Endangered Species Act (ESA) of 1973 that became the trump card for environmental activists. Intended to help save romantic species such as the bison and the bald eagle from the perceived threat of extinction, the ESA contains a "citizen lawsuit" clause that permits individual citizens or "public interest" groups (i.e., environmental organizations) to sue the government if they believe the ESA was not being properly enforced. The test case for ESA involved the snail darter, a minnow originally believed to be a separate and rare species but later proved to be a variety of a more common species. The U.S. Supreme Court decision of 1978 stopped building the Tellico Dam on the Little Tennessee River to protect the snail darter, ruling that it was "the plain intent of Congress to halt and reverse the trend toward species extinction, whatever the cost" (Chase 1995, Luecke 2000).

The advantage in determining policies for managing the national forests had shifted away from the professional foresters of the Forest Service and timber companies into the hands of environmental activists and their attorneys.

LISTING THE SPOTTED OWL

The Fish and Wildlife Service lacked sufficient evidence to list the northern spotted owl as endangered.[6] Scientists, including Forsman, agreed. But Andy Stahl of the

---

[6] Later evidence would show that the Fish and Wildlife Service was justified in its reluctance to list the owl. Subsequent studies would provide evidence that there were more owls than previously suspected. Also, owls probably required both old growth and second growth habitat. Forsman, a very careful and competent scientist, still believes that habitat may be a problem but that another problem may be that another owl, the barred owl, is replacing the spotted owl on nesting sites in many areas of the Northwest (Stout 2003).

Sierra Club Legal Defense Fund decided to force the issue through the courts. Stahl obtained Forsman's data through the Freedom of Information Act and enlisted Russell Lande—demographer at the University of Oregon—to prepare a scientific publication documenting that the owl was in peril. Lande based his paper on a theoretical work involving pesticides and insect eradication, concluding that continued logging of old-growth would result in likely extinction of the owl (Chase 1995).

Scientific publications typically receive rigorous "peer review" by other scientists before acceptance for publication. But Lande simply had only Stahl review his paper and he did not submit it for publication in a reputable scientific journal[7] before presenting it in court. Lande told the court that his paper was written "to be distributed by the National Wildlife Federation" and "anybody who requested it." In fact, environmental groups distributed it to the federal agencies with the authority to protect the owl—the Fish and Wildlife Service, the Forest Service and the Bureau of Land Management, and it was entered as evidence in the litigation over the owl (Chase 1995, Stout 2003).

When wildlife biologists read the paper, they heavily criticized it for faulty assumptions, flawed data, poor analysis and unsubstantiated conclusions. Chase calls the report "scientific wool-gathering" based on "scanty evidence" and "false assumptions." Lande underestimated bird populations by at least half (probably one-fourth of actual numbers), assumed that owls absolutely required old growth (not even Forsman agreed), presumed how much old growth forest remained (not a certainty) and assumed that 60 to 70 percent of the pre-settlement forest was old growth (it was more likely 30 percent or less) (Chase 1995, Stout 2003).

The dubious nature of the evidence[8] did not stop environmentalists from pursuing litigation. Armed with the Lande paper, the Sierra Club Legal Defense Fund (SCLDF)[9] and twenty-seven other groups sued the Fish and Wildlife Service under the "citizen lawsuit clause" of the Endangered Species Act in 1988. Judge Thomas Zilly of the U.S. District Court ruled that the Fish and Wildlife Service "was arbitrary and capricious or contrary to law" in not listing the owl as endangered or threatened (Chase 1995).

In subsequent litigation, U.S. District Court Judge William Dwyer halted 163 timber sales in 1989 to protect the owl. In 1991, Dwyer ruled that Forest Service plans for protecting the owl were inadequate, requiring a new environmental impact statement on forest management in the Northwest by August 1983. In response to the courts, the Fish and Wildlife Service listed the owl as "threatened" in 1990 (Chase 1995).

Precedent for further litigation became established and lawsuits a lucrative venture for environmental organizations and their attorneys (Chase 1995, Knudson 2003a). A "fee-shifting" clause in the federal Equal Access to Justice Act authorizes payment of "public interest" plaintiffs' legal expenses when they win a case against the government (Bonine 2009, Luecke 2000, Schenkkan 2002). For example, the government paid a total of $2,140,891 to the Seattle office of the SCLDF for five cases involving the northern spotted owl from 1992 to 1994 (Chase 1995).

---

[7] Lande eventually submitted his paper for publication in a West German journal, toning down his conclusions, and it was finally published three years after he first wrote it.

[8] Sound science requires conclusions supported by a "body of knowledge." This implies more than one paper—usually many more.

[9] The SCLDF changed its name to Earthjustice Legal Defense Fund in 1997

FOREST POLICY IN THE 21ST CENTURY

The spotted owl court decisions have far-reaching ramifications for Americans and their forests. environmental organizations bringing lawsuits paid for by the government invariably stymie timber harvest in national forests. As a result, the balance of power has shifted overwhelmingly away from conservationists toward preservationists. Attorneys and judges are now making forest management decisions on public land, not forest or wildlife managers. Environmental organizations wield an inordinate amount of power, perhaps unmatched since the nineteenth century when industry held free reign, over what happens on public lands. Politics makes Congress impotent to untangle the complex web of regulations it created and the courts exacerbated (Chase 1995).

Timber harvest from national forests fell from 12 billion board feet in 1989 to 18 million board feet in 2003. Between 1990 and 2000, the population of the United States grew by approximately 32.7 million people, increasing national wood consumption by approximately 25 billion board feet per year. Suppliers of wood products have had to turn to other sources to supply the 37 billion board feet to replace the lost sources of supply from federal land and to provide for the increased demand resulting from population growth. The situation forced the industry and American consumers to become more efficient and to seek supplies elsewhere.

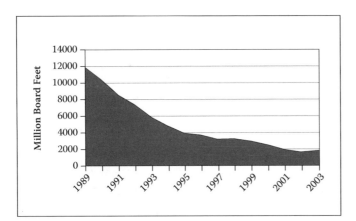

Figure 20.1 **Timber Harvest on National Forests: 1989–2003.**

At the heart of the spotted owl controversy and the fight over forests are questions of ethics and accountability. Differing values drive people. And they may resolve conflicts in different ways. Who is to decide what is right and what is wrong? To date, the debate over forests has been framed as a win-lose ("no compromise") conflict. But is it really? Or are the catastrophic forest fires that have destroyed several million acres of wild land a year in the first decade of the twenty-first century turning it into a no-win situation?

Homework

Name: _____   Date: _____

Please read Dr. Patrick Moore's "Environmentalism for the 21st Century" (*http://greenspirit.com/21st_century.cfm*). What is Moore's position on massive species extinction that environmental activists claim is occurring at the present time and how does he justify his position?

Chapter 21

Fire

Fire sustains life. Humans depend upon it to keep warm, to cook and to generate energy. Our deepest emotional ties are with "hearth and home." Fire is also an essential component of the historical ecology of American forests. Fire renews ecosystems by beginning the process of forest succession and maintaining biological diversity by preserving diverse habitat. Our earliest ancestors understood this and maintained a fire regime to promote plant and animal species upon which they depended for their very survival.

But fire can be a fearfully destructive force of nature. It is at times an unremorseful killer that destroys everything in its path, including life. Humans both need and fear fire.

Table 21.1 *Average Annual Number of Wildfires and Acres Burned by Agency: 1999–2008*

Agency	Number of Fires	Acres Burned
Bureau of Indian Affairs	4,457	225,906
Bureau of Land Management	2,981	1,635,579
Forest Service	9,627	1,375,448
Fish & Wildlife Service	364	636,444
National Park Service	595	112,860
Total Federal	18,024	3,986,237
State/Other	62,177	2,522,430
Total	80,202	6,508,667

SOURCE: NIFC 2009

Wildland[1] fire is one of many contentious issues concerning natural resources in the twenty-first century upon which people with differing attitudes and perceptions—conservationists and preservationists, anthropocentrics and biocentrics—seem unable to agree. From 1999 to 2008, an average of 75,514 wildfires burned 6,508,666 acres annually. Over this decade, approximately 22.5 percent of the wildfires and 61.2 percent of the acres burned were on federal land (NIFC 2009).

CAUSES OF WILDLAND FIRE

Fire requires the presence of heat, fuel and oxygen. Catastrophic fire tends to occur in times of drought and in places where fuel loads are ample. Changes in weather patterns associated with hot, dry wind patterns are strongly associated with severe fires. The El Niño phenomenon and the Santa Ana winds that occasionally blow hot, dry air from the deserts toward the Pacific in Southern California are perhaps the best known examples of nature supplying ideal conditions for catastrophic fire.

Lightning strikes cause thousands of fires annually. Scientists estimate that lightning caused 8,800 wildland fires that burned nearly 1.9 million acres in the United States in 2008. Humans add their own intentional and unintended incendiarism to the mix, causing an estimated 70,000 fires that consumed 3.4 million acres during the same year. Intentional fire, known as *prescribed burning* initiated by public land management agencies, accounted for 7,600 fires that covered 1.9 million acres—remarkably similar numbers to lightning-caused fires (NIFC 2009).

Fuel build up can be associated with numerous natural and human activities. Mortality from insects and fungal diseases can create a heavy concentration of dry fuel. So too can previous fires as partially burned but dead timber can reignite. Historically, there is an association between wildfire and clearing land for agriculture, logging, cutting up the landscape to build railroads and building homes and towns in the woods. Fire suppression, as practiced by the Forest Service and other agencies for the past century, allows the buildup of fuels unless mechanically removed.

Recommended Reading

Moore, Patrick A. 2000. *Green Spirit: Trees Are the Answer.*

Dr. Patrick Moore's book is a concise and clearly written treatise on forest ecology and management. His use of numerous examples and his excellent color photos make the concepts he describes easy to understand. For those wanting to better understand forests and forest management, this book is a good place to start.

The northern spotted owl court decisions beginning in 1989 and subsequent policy changes have reduced timber harvests in national forests to a fraction of what they were in the 1980s. As a result, densely-packed second growth stands have increased the fuel loads on these lands. Densely packed stands contain trees that may not obtain sufficient water, which makes them vulnerable to insects and disease. Insect infestations, fungal disease and storm damage have killed trees, creating large concentrations of dry fuel in some areas.

Different geographic areas tend to experience severe fires in different years. Oregon, Colorado and Arizona experienced a severe fire year and several large fires in 2002. California experienced severe fire years in 2003, 2007 and 2008. Grassland fires swept 907,000 acres near Amarillo, Texas in 2006, accounting for nearly two-thirds of the acreage burned in the state in a particularly bad fire year. Fire hit Alaska hard in 2002, 2004, 2005 and 2009.

---

[1] The government uses the term "wildland fire" to describe fire that occurs in various ecosystems including forests, grassland, chaparral and tundra. The statistics cited in this chapter and elsewhere in this book as wildland fire are not limited to forest fire because the federal wildfire statistics contain no separation of the various affected ecosystems (NIFC 2009).

THE ANCIENT AND FRONTIER FORESTS

Native Americans brought the ancient mastery of fire to the new world. They were prodigious starters of wildland fire. Indigenous burning shaped the landscape, thinning the understory to open the forest, promoting forest types dominated by pioneer species and replacing forest with grassland. The forests that the first Europeans observed were open, park-like and dominated by large trees (Bonnicksen 2000a, Krech 1999, Mann 2005, Pyne 1982, Williams 1989).

European settlers were also prodigious in setting fires to clear the land for agriculture. Land clearing in the New World repeated the process of converting forests to pasture and cropland that had occurred in Europe during the Middle Ages. Scandinavian immigrants to the north woods of America brought practices of swidden agriculture and were in part responsible for some of the worst forest fires in the nineteenth century. Spanish settlers of California and the Southwest brought southern European practices of broadcast burning for improving grazing land. Settlers from Britain, Germany, France and central Europe had little experience in managing fire. The clearing of forest and the cooling of the climate during the Little Ice Age had eliminated widespread wildfires through most of northern Europe several centuries before settlement of the New World (Pyne 1982).

"New World colonists, particularly those from northern Europe, often entered fire regimes unlike any they had known in Europe. In New England, the difference between Old and New was not great, but in the grasslands, and particularly in the South, colonists encountered a fire environment for which they had little preparation. In order to survive, they frequently borrowed the techniques of their Indian predecessors. The frontier thus became a blend of European and Indian fire practices, the one for farms and the other for fire hunting and range" (Pyne 1982).

During this era, Americans were generally unconcerned about wildfire. In many cases, fire in the backcountry affected so few people that many Americans were unaware when large fires occurred. It is also likely that light burning practices of settlers and Indians on the frontier reduced the occurrence of large, catastrophic fire by reducing fuel buildup.

CATASTROPHIC FIRES OF THE 19TH CENTURY

The era of land clearing, heavy logging, rapid industrialization and building of towns in the forest led to changes in burning practices and increased the risks of catastrophic wildfire. People tended to suppress fire near farms and towns for obvious reasons. In the meantime, farms, cut over areas and towns concentrated combustibles.

The result was a series of catastrophic fires in the nineteenth and twentieth centuries. The first such fire event occurred in New Brunswick and Maine in 1825. Settlement of the Pacific Northwest coincided with catastrophic fires in 1849, 1853 and 1868. A number of catastrophic fires occurred in the Lake States in the latter decades of the century associated with a flammable mix of logging, farms, railroads and towns encroaching into the northern forests. The worst was the Great Peshtigo Fire of 1871. More than 1,200 people died when fire consumed the town and 1.5 million acres (NIFC 2009, Pyne 1982).

Local governments in fire-prone regions responded by instituting forest fire prevention. New York State created the Adirondack Forest Preserve in 1885 with organized fire patrols. Other states in the northeast instituted organized fire prevention and fire fighting programs. The creation of the first federal forest reserves in 1891 made fire prevention and fighting a federal priority. But what agency would lead the effort? And what agency would control the forest reserves?

Fire and watershed protection were the critical issues in the debate over forest policy that took place in the late eighteenth and early nineteenth centuries. More than twenty federal agencies had some authority over natural resources with six having authority over forests. The forest reserves were under the Department of the Interior. The Forestry Division was in the Department of Agriculture. The U.S. Geological Survey (USGS) was the finest scientific agency in the federal government of the era. The USGS had conducted extensive surveys of land and resources in the West and possessed unsurpassed expertise on waterways and watersheds. And USGS was in the Department of the Interior—a cabinet-level department separate from the Forestry Division. The National Academy of Sciences committee on forestry believed law enforcement and fire protection were the primary issues concerning the forest reserves and recommended that the Army was best equipped to do the job. It was the widespread concern over fire coupled with the political acumen of Gifford Pinchot that shaped the future of forest policy in America (Miller 2001, Pyne 1982, 2001).

By the eighteenth century, Americans were looking to other European frontiers, particularly British India, as models for managing wildland fire. Sir Dietrich Brandis, a German-born and trained forester, was perhaps the most influential person in creating that model. He was appointed Inspector-general of India's forests in 1864. In 1889 and 1890, a young Yale graduate named Gifford Pinchot traveled to Europe to study forestry at *L'Ecole Nationale Forestière* in Nancy, France. While in Europe, Pinchot traveled through Europe on a tour of forests with Brandis and a group of British students. Brandis became a mentor to Pinchot. Over the next two decades, Pinchot would shape the Forest Service, the national forest system and the forestry profession in America. And fire policy would be central to each (Miller 2001, Pyne 2001).

There was no agreement over how to handle the problem of catastrophic wildfire. Light burning had been the common practice of Indians and European settlers on the frontier. Franklin Hough, the first chief of the Forestry Division, advocated light burning in the Pine Barrens of New Jersey. Light burning was a common practice in the South as well as in Oregon, California and South Dakota. John Wesley Powell also advocated "Indian burning practices." But the European-trained foresters disagreed. Bernhard Fernow, chief of the Forestry Division from 1886 to 1898, was a strong advocate of fire suppression, including banning light burning. Brandis, who instituted fire suppression policies in India, influenced Pinchot's thinking on fire control. It is significant that Europeans, Fernow and Carl Schenck, and the European-trained American, Gifford Pinchot founded the first three American forestry schools. For most of the next century, forestry schools produced graduates of like mindset. In 1905, the forest reserves transferred to the Forestry Division. Later that year, the Forestry Division became the Forest Service, and under Pinchot's leadership fire suppression became the official policy of the federal government (Pyne 2001).

THE FIRES OF 1910

In 1910, wildfires spread across the northern tier of states from the Rockies to New England. The fires in Idaho and Montana were particularly catastrophic. Three million acres burned, principally in national forests. Firefighting efforts were heroic. The new Forest Service sent numerous fire crews into the woods to fight and contain the fires. The fires claimed 84 lives, mostly among the fire crews. The "buffalo soldiers" of the U.S. Army's 25th Infantry Regiment—an all-black regiment—performed heroic service on the fire lines. Railroads and timber companies sent employees out to the fire lines.

The fire crews of the era represented an interesting section of society in the American West. The rangers who supervised them described them as loggers, drifters, drunks and what forester Ed Thenon called "punks . . . with caps on and hands in their pockets all the time, the kind you see around poolrooms and cigar stores" (Pyne 2001). Forester Elers Koch wrote that ". . . most of them sat up all night by the fire, talking mostly about the relative merits of the jails they had been in" (Koch 1998).

The fires of 1910 produced the first legendary hero of the Forest Service's firefighting units. Edward Pulaski was a former miner who had become a ranger. Known to his colleagues and men as "Big Ed," he was a direct descendant of the Polish hero of the American Revolution, Casimir Pulaski. As fires smoldered and spread slowly between Idaho's Couer d'Alene and St. Joe Rivers, Pulaski led 150 men of his fire crews to the fire line. A strong wind fanned the flames and the fire exploded into a roaring inferno that became known as the "Big Blowup." Pulaski and 45 of his men were caught in near total darkness and heavy smoke as the flames raced toward them and trees crashed to the ground around them. One man who lagged behind died when a burning tree fell on him. Pulaski led his terrified crew to shelter in an abandoned mine to wait for the conflagration to burn itself out. A man panicked and attempted to flee, but Pulaski stopped him by the mine entrance with a drawn revolver, threatening to shoot any man who tried to flee. Eventually, Pulaski and the crew succumbed to the heat and lack of oxygen. The first man to regain consciousness left the mine and led a rescue party to the crew. They found Pulaski lying motionless at the entrance to the mine. When one of the crew called out that Pulaski was dead, the men were startled to hear his voice, "Like hell he is." Pulaski later designed a firefighting tool that would bear his name (Pyne 2001).

The 1910 fires also profoundly affected American forest policy. The Weeks Act, authorizing the government to purchase land for the establishment of national forests in the East, had been stalled in Congress for a year. The disastrous impacts of the fires also confirmed, in the minds of the policymakers, that fire suppression was a necessary policy. In 1911, the Weeks Act became law (Pyne 2001).

FIRES AND FIRE SUPPRESSION IN THE 20TH CENTURY

Tactics and strategies to combat catastrophic wildfire changed during the middle of the century. During the Great Depression of the 1930s, the Civilian Conservation Corps (CCC) performed very admirable service on the fire lines. It was also during the 1930s that the Bureau of Land Management and the Forest Service began experimenting with the use of aircraft in fire spotting and fighting. The first smokejumpers, the elite firefighters, first organized in the 1930s. The smokejumpers were similar to the military's paratroopers in both the rigor of their training and their ability to arrive quickly in remote areas.

In 1933, the Tillamook Burn consumed three million acres of forestland in Oregon. Following that experience, the Forest Service adopted a more rigid forest suppression goal known as the "10 A.M. Policy." The goal was to control a fire no later than 10 a.m. the day after it was first reported. With the available labor of the Civilian Conservation Corps and the development of trained firefighting crews within the Forest Service and other federal and state agencies, the task of aggressive fire suppression seemed possible (Temperate Forest Foundation 2007).

Satellite imagery helps firefighters spot and react to fires earlier than ever before. In addition, post-fire assessments employing satellite images enable investigators to assess the ecological and economic damage caused by fire.

The battle against wildfire was also fought on the public relations front. The Forest Service adopted Smokey the Bear to convey its fire prevention message at the end of World War II. A generation of Baby Boomers grew up recognizing Smokey as readily as today's college students recognize Bart Simpson. Disney Studios added its considerable influence in conveying the anti-fire message in the movie *Bambi.* The Forest Service and state forestry agencies carried Smokey's message into schools, to Boy Scouts, Girl Scouts and 4-H Clubs throughout the nation.

By the 1970s, a new generation of foresters began to question the policy of aggressive fire suppression. They were learning that fire was a historic component of forest ecosystems. Foresters had long known that some species of trees require fire to regenerate. Now they were proclaiming that fire was essential to some ecosystems. Critics of federal fire suppression policies found further ammunition to support their arguments after catastrophic fires in the public forests in the West in the 1990s and the first decade of the twenty-first century.

THE FIRES OF THE 21ST CENTURY

The six worst years for wildland fires since the federal government began keeping wildfire statistics in 1960 occurred between 2000 and 2007. More than 9,500,000,000 acres burned in 2006, surpassing the previous record fire year of 2005.

The fire problem is the most severe in the western United States. From 1999 to 2008, 34 percent of the wildfires and 57 percent of the acres burned were in the western regions of the United States, not including Alaska, which accounted for less than 1 percent of the fires but 25.5 percent of the acres burned. The eastern region accounted for 65 percent of the fires and 17 percent of the acres burned. These figures illustrate that fires in the east are generally smaller than those in the west. Fires in remote Alaska tend to be very large. In fact, six of the ten largest wildland fires from 1997 to 2008 occurred in Alaska[2] (NIFC 2009).

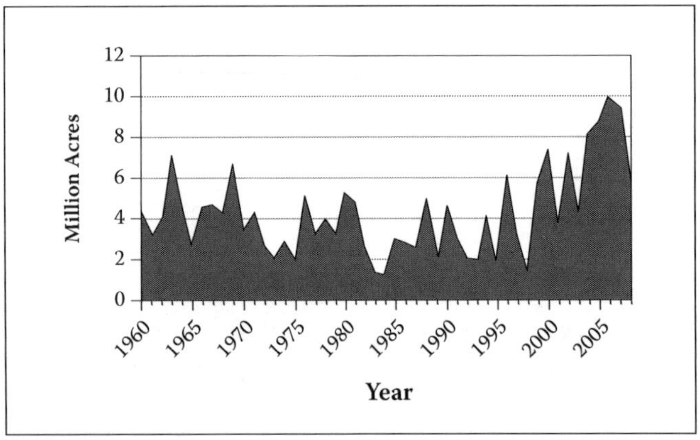

Figure 21.1 Wildland Acres Burned: 1960–2008.

Catastrophic fire is drastically altering some forest ecosystems. Fire has destroyed pine forests in the San Bernardino National Forest, and highly flammable sagebrush and other chaparral vegetation now cover the land. Fire threatens California's ancient groves of giant Sequoias. Beetle-killed conifers in the Lake Tahoe basin pose a serious threat to the area's forests and may ruin years of effort to keep the waters of Lake Tahoe pristine (Bonnicksen 2002, 2003b, 2006).

The wildfire problem is exacerbated in the "urban-wildland interface." The problem is especially severe in California where wildfires frequently threaten and damage

---

[2] Four of the Alaska fires occurred in 2004, including the Taylor Complex Fire that burned more than 1.3 million acres.

Table 21.2 *Average Annual Number of Wildfires and Acres Burned by Region: 1999–2008*

Region	Number of Fires	Acres Burned
Alaska	464	1,672,278
Great Basin (NV, UT, southern ID)	3,547	1,442,858
South (AL, AR, FL, KY, LA, MS, NC, SC, TN, OK, VA, east TX)	37,838	966,700
Rocky Mountains (CO, KS, MT, ND, NE, SD, WY, northern ID)	6,798	802,104
Northwest (OR, WA)	3,984	535,362
California	8,425	497,202
Southwest (AZ, NM, west TX)	4,550	439,674
East (CT, DE, IA, IL, IN, MA, MD, MI, MN, MO, NH, NJ, NY, OH, PA, RI, VT, WI, WV)	14,596	152,489

Source: NIFC 2009

thriving communities adjacent to national forests or other federal land. The southern California fires in October 2007 destroyed at least 3,290 homes and burned more than half a million acres (FEMA 2009). The problem also exists in many areas of the country (EPA 2001). Fires in these areas are a serious challenge for firefighters and emergency response teams. Evacuation of residents is difficult and frequently those fleeing the fire obstruct access to fire and rescue crews. Federal, state and local governments have invested a great deal of effort, to say nothing of taxpayers' money, to educate home and business owners of the best way to reduce fire risk in high risk communities.

Experts generally agree that catastrophic fires are the result of excessive fuel buildup following a century of aggressive fire suppression as well as the absence of forest management on federal land for more than a decade. Others suggest that global warming is

Figure 21.2 Elk Bath. *Sula, MT.*
Photo by John McColgan, Bureau of Land Management, Alaska Fire Service

worsening the problem, but evidence for this is scanty and the claim appears mostly based upon supposition. Aggressive fire suppression eliminated the historic fire regime of light, surface fires that occurred in the west. Lack of management, i.e., timber harvest, has allowed unhealthy, densely-packed stands of timber to grow in previously harvested areas. Trees growing under these conditions have trouble obtaining sufficient water to fend off disease and insect infestation. Areas containing patches of beetle-killed timber are scattered through many western forests, turning those forests into a tinderbox (Bonnicksen 2002, 2003a, 2003b, 2006, Dechter 2008, Gorte 1995, Nelson 2008, O'Toole 2007, Sedjo 2001).

Most everyone agrees that the severity and extent of wildland fire is a problem. However, the process of formulating effective solutions is a mire of finger pointing and political posturing by industry, environmentalists, politicians, scientists and conservative and liberal advocacy groups. Critics of all political and ideological stripes assail the Forest Service and other land management agencies, which certainly are not without fault.

Environmental organizations such as the Sierra Club, the Wilderness Society and the National Resources Defense Council advocate remedial thinning in the urban-wildland interface while adopting a "let burn" policy in remote areas where there is no threat to private property. These organizations are adamantly opposed to commercial logging on public land and view any proposals involving government-private sector partnerships as opening up national forests to the timber industry (Colburn 2002, Knudson 2001b, QLG 2008a).

A number of fire experts advocate light, prescribed burning to reduce fuel buildup and lower the probability of more intense catastrophic fire events. Federal agencies, including the Park Service, adopted prescribed burning as a fuel reduction strategy. Study of prescribed burning in California indicates that it is an effective strategy to reduce fire intensity and severity. If initial fuel loads are too high, it may be coupled with equal effectiveness with initial mechanical thinning (Stephens 2008). Mechanical thinning followed by prescribed burning is credited for lessening the severity and damage in treated areas during the Cone Fire in Northern California in 2002 (Skinner and Ritchie 2008).

Prescribed burning comes with risks. In 2000, a prescribed burn at Bandelier National Monument in New Mexico went out of control, destroying 44,000 acres of forest and 260 homes in Los Alamos. The fire, known as the Cerro Grande Fire, forced 25,000 people to evacuate their homes, damaged an estimated 1,500 Anasazi archeological sites and damaged the Los Alamos National Laboratory. The risk of prescribed fire escaping to become a catastrophic fire is often unacceptable (Bonnicksen 2000b, 2003a).

In addition, burning on a scale necessary to restore national forest lands (an estimated 132 million acres) would release a pall of smoke that would constitute an unacceptable environmental and health cost. Fire, whether a prescribed burn or an unintentional fire, releases huge quantities of carbon into the atmosphere. Lastly, the economic costs of maintaining the status quo—almost a billion dollars a year since 2000 (NIFC 2009)—or restoring 132 million acres at an estimated cost in the tens of billions places a huge burden on taxpayers (Bonnicksen 2003a, 2006, 2008, Dechter 2008, Malmsheimer et al. 2008).

Thomas Bonnicksen and others advocate the concept of restoration forestry. In Bonnicksen's (2003a, 2006) view, foresters would employ prescribed burns sparingly using mechanical thinning to restore the bulk of forests to replicate pre-settlement conditions, i.e., patchy, open and park-like conditions dominated by large trees.

There are drawbacks to mechanical thinning as a means to reducing fuel loads. Roads must be built to access areas to thinning and the impacts of equipment use include "high noise levels, soil compaction, heavy erosion and possible increases in certain pathogens" (Keifer et al. 2000). This is unacceptable in national parks and designated wilderness areas.

In 2003, Congress passed the Healthy Forest Restoration Act, loosening environmental regulations to permit mechanical thinning of overstocked stands and reduction of fuel loads. But the Healthy Forest Act is not perfect, and many widely criticize it. Battles over remediation frequently wind up in the courts where lawyers and judges ultimately decide policy. The experiences of a small, northern California town best illustrate the issues and frustrations experienced in trying to resolve the issue of catastrophic fire.

THE QUINCY LIBRARY GROUP

The town of Quincy is located in the Sierra Nevada Mountains of northern California. The Plumas National Forest surrounds the town, which has been heavily dependent upon the timber industry for its economic prosperity since the early twentieth century. Prior to the 1970s, the Forest Service was heavily engaged in timber sales and promoting what it termed "multiple-use" forestry. The Plumas, as well as the nearby Lassen and Tahoe National Forests, were logged, and the forests of the region mostly consisted of second-growth stands. Following World War II, the Forest Service expanded the rate of cutting, and by the 1970s clear-cutting had become the primary silvicultural regime in the coniferous national forests of the west, including those surrounding Quincy (Colburn 2002).

Criticism of the Forest Service and its timber harvest practices came from within the agency as well as from environmental groups. Ironically, the criticism was not limited to environmentalists but also came from loggers who objected to increased mechanization and lost jobs made possible by adopting clear-cutting as the dominant harvest regime. The Forest Service itself was evolving from the like-thinking elite agency staffed by professional foresters established by Gifford Pinchot to a more diverse group of specialists. Criticism of agency policies was coming from forest ecologists, wildlife biologists, recreation specialists, social scientists and many of the agency's foresters (Chase 1995, Colburn 2002).

The draconian policy changes initiated by the northern spotted owl court decisions had a profoundly negative impact on Quincy and other timber-dependent communities of the west. As jobs were lost, tax revenues dropped and federal subsidies to the area's public schools[3] provided from the receipts of national forest timber sales disappeared, the community went into an economic tailspin. There was a general agreement in the community that the national forests surrounding the town were in bad shape, but no one could agree what to do about it. Quincy was ideologically divided over the forest debate, and the issue had become so heated that the local community was in near chaos. Eco-terrorists—most likely not locals—spiked trees[4] and vandalized logging equipment. Gunshots shattered the Quincy office windows of environmental attorney Michael Jackson (Colburn 2002).

In 1992, county supervisor Bill Coates invited Jackson and Sierra Pacific forester Tom Nelson to a meeting in an attempt to find common ground and to save the community from its own destruction. The meetings soon expanded to include other members of the community and moved to the town's public library. Early meetings were

---

[3] The federal government does not pay property taxes to local governments. To compensate for lost tax revenues, the Forest Service pays a percentage of timber sales receipts from national forests to local communities. When timber sales were drastically curtailed in the 1990s, so did the compensation to support local schools and community infrastructures.

[4] Driving steel spikes into trees was a tactic used by eco-terrorists to intimidate loggers and millworkers. When a saw hits an embedded spike, it literally tears apart, sending lethal fragments flying in all directions. A California sawmill worker was critically injured in 1987 when a saw he was operating hit a tree spike, and a section of the saw blade nearly severed his jugular vein. If it were not for the quick response of coworkers to conduct emergency first aid, he would have died (Chase 1995)

often contentious, degenerating into angry shouting matches. However a process evolved where participants took issues that no one could agree upon off the table. One by one, they discarded issues when they reached no agreement. They eventually discovered that all parties shared a common concern. The surrounding forests and the town were at high risk from catastrophic fire (Colburn 2002).

The Quincy Library Group (QLG), as it came to be known, began working on a plan to alleviate the fire danger in the Plumas. Soon their efforts expanded to include surrounding communities, the Lassen National Forest and part of the Tahoe National Forest. Invitations to participate went out to the Forest Service, to university scientists and policy specialists, to the timber industry and to environmental organizations. While many agreed to collaborate, a few environmental groups stubbornly refused, claiming that the QLG was an industry front group trying to subvert existing law to re-open the national forests to commercial logging (Chase 1995, Colburn 2002).

In 1996, the QLC had drafted a plan that included commercial thinning to reduce fuel buildup, restoring the forest to approximate pre-settlement conditions and providing opportunities for recreation. Frustrated with their attempts to navigate the labyrinth of Forest Service bureaucracy, the group enlisted the support of Congressman Wally Herger and Senators Dianne Feinstein and Barbara Boxer. Boxer dropped her support when pressured by environmental groups and later attempted to block its passage by the Senate. However, Herger and Feinstein were able to garner sufficient support in Congress to pass the Herger-Feinstein Quincy Library Group Forest Recovery Act in 1998 (Colburn 2002).

When President Clinton signed the bill, it appeared that implementation of the plan would begin. However, the Sierra Club, the Wilderness Society, the Natural Resources Defense Council, the Audubon Society and other environmental groups adamantly opposed the plan, claiming that it was in violation of existing law and represented an open invitation for Sierra Pacific to log at its discretion. Lawsuits filed by these groups impede implementation of the QLG plan. The Forest Service also hampers implementation as it tries to find its way amidst a number of federal laws that are often complex and contradictory (Colburn 2002, QLG 2008a).

In July of 2007, lightning strikes ignited the Antelope Fire in the Plumas National Forest, burning 23,420 acres that included areas where the QLG had implemented its fuel reduction plan as well as untreated areas and areas protected for the California spotted owl and goshawk habitat. The areas treated under the QLG plan "had significantly reduced fire behavior and tree and soil impacts compared to untreated areas" (Fites et al. 2007). Untreated areas contributed to the rate of the spread and the intensity of the fire, overwhelming initial attempts to get it under control. Areas under "protection" as threatened species habitat suffered severe damage. Fire crews and two members of a Forest Service Fire Behavior Assessment Team got caught in an area where the fire had crowned and was racing toward them. The fire blocked roads through untreated

Figure 21.3 **Forest Fire.**

© JupiterImages, Inc.

areas, but, fortunately, they managed to escape along a single open road through a treated zone of the forest. In September, another fire broke out in the Plumas. The area contained approximately 64,997 acres that included treated and untreated areas, spotted owl and goshawk protected areas, private land and urban-wildland interface. The post-fire damage assessment came to the same conclusions as those reached from the Antelope fire. Large portions of the untreated areas, including owl and goshawk habitat, experienced 75 to 100 percent canopy cover reduction. Treated areas, however, were too small to do much good in containing and suppressing the fire. The QLG argues that lawsuits and appeals that stalled implementation of their fuel treatment plans contributed to the severity and damage caused by the Moonlight Fire (Dailey et al. 2008, Fites et al. 2007, QLG 2008b).

On March 2, 2009, Sierra Pacific Industries announced the closure of its Quincy small-log sawmill. The company attributed its closure to the economic recession and to litigation by environmental groups that limited its supply of timber. The closure dealt a blow to the QLG and its vision for sustaining the community and its surrounding forests. What happens next remains to be seen (Fragnoli 2009).

The Quincy Library Group is one of many examples of community-based initiatives designed to resolve conflict over the environment and natural resources (Knudson 2001c, Moore 2000). It gained national prominence through its success in winning support of national political figures of both parties and divergent ideological beliefs. It is an example of how people with differing points of view but with a very real stake in the future of their community attempted to overcome the machinery of federal bureaucracy as well as the stonewalling tactics of distant special interest groups to make a difference. Its successes and failures expose flaws within the political and bureaucratic process. But it also serves to show the rest of us a path to solve contentious problems through negotiation and finding common ground (Sedjo 2001).

Homework

Name: _____   Date: _____

Look up the National Interagency Fire Center website at *http://www.nifc.gov/* and answer the following questions.

1. What federal agencies participate in the National Interagency Fire Center?

2. How many wildland fires occurred and how many acres were burned last year in your home state?

   State: _____   Year: _____

   Number of fires: _____

   Number of acres: _____

3. What states are reporting large fires (under wildfire news) on the day you complete this assignment?

   Date: _____

   States:

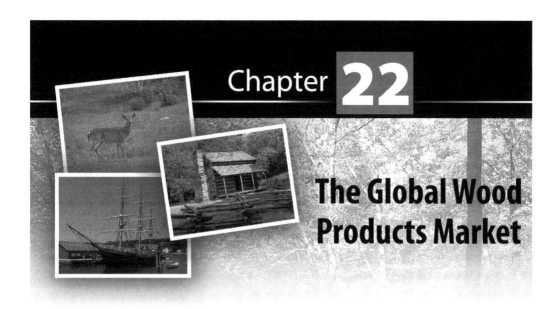

Chapter 22

The Global Wood Products Market

Globalization of the marketplace characterizes the twenty-first century, and will continue to do so. Advanced communication technologies and containerized shipping have lowered the costs of transoceanic shipping. Changes in international policies, including floating exchange rates and international free trade agreements, have eliminated many of the barriers to trade. Wood products are an important part of the international economy (Luppold and Bumgardner 2006, Peck 2001).

A map of global forest cover (FAO 2009) illustrates that the world's forests tend to circle the globe in two wide bands.

A band of temperate forests extends across the northern hemisphere south of the tundra through Alaska and Canada and across northern Eurasia from Scandinavia to Siberia. Forests extend south through British Columbia, along the west coast and through the Cascades, the Sierras and the Rockies in the United States.

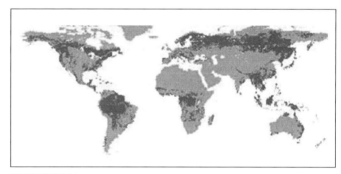

Figure 22.1 Map of the World's Forests.
http://www.fao.org/forestry/country/en/

They also move south along the east coast of Canada and the United States as well as through the Appalachians westward in a broad band across the southern states of the U.S. Forests once covered most of Europe, but they are now limited to bands along the Atlantic coast of Spain and Portugal as well as the Balkans. Softwoods dominate the northern temperate forest. The southern temperate forests are mixed, perhaps with hardwoods dominating.

Tropical forests are located along the Equator with the largest forest in South America with forests extending across Africa into Asia. Forests extend north into China and south into Australia and New Zealand. Hardwood dominates the tropical forest. However, there is a large number of softwood plantations located across the southern temperate zone.

Table 22.1 *Forest Cover by Continent: 2005*

Continent or Region	Land Area (1000 acres)	Forest Land (1000 acres)	Percent Forest Cover
Europe	5,677,787	2,474,498	44.3
South America	4,407,792	2,054,780	47.7
Africa	7,489,700	1,570,137	21.4
Asia	7,850,886	1,412,398	18.5
North and Central America	5,615,472	1,744,191	32.9
Oceania	2,116,245	509,665	24.3
World	33,157,880	9,765,666	30.3
SOURCE: (FAO 2005b)			

Table 22.2 *Most Forest-Covered Countries by Forestland Area: 2005*

Country	Total Land Area (1000 acres)	Forest Land (1000 acres)	Percent Forest Cover
Russian Federation	4,219,423	1,998,564	47.9
Brazil	2,104,073	1,180,417	57.2
Canada	2,463,791	766,358	33.6
United States	2,379,400	748,949	33.1
China	2,371,730	487,514	21.2
Australia	1,898,300	404,457	21.3
Dem. Rep. Congo	579,428	330,158	58.9
Indonesia	470,629	218,676	48.8
Peru	317,585	169,865	53.7
India	812,300	167,293	22.8
SOURCE: (FAO 2005b)			

The Food and Agricultural Organization (FAO) of the United Nations estimates that forest covers 3.952 billion hectares[1] (9.765 billion acres), or 30.3 percent of the Earth's land area. The largest forest is in Europe, with 82 percent of Europe's forests located in Russia.

The United States possesses the fourth largest acreage of forest in the world, behind Russia, Brazil and Canada. According to the USDA Forest Service (Smith et al. 2009), approximately 57 percent of the nation's growing stock is softwood species. The remaining 43 percent consists of hardwoods. Softwood growing stock dominates the Russian and Canadian forests. Hardwoods dominate the Brazilian forests.

---

[1] 1 hectare = 2.47105381 acres = 0.00386102159 square miles

GLOBAL FOREST LOSS

Deforestation, particularly of tropical rainforests, is an issue of worldwide environmental concern. The Food and Agricultural Organization of the United Nations estimates that 13 million hectares (32.1 million acres) of forests are lost every year. Approximately 0.22 percent of the world's forests were lost every year over the decade of the 1990s, but the rate has slowed to 0.18 percent per year from 2000 to 2005 (FAO 2005a). The primary causes are clearing land for agriculture and consumption of wood for fuel in developing countries. In this way, the use of forests in the developing world mirrors what happened in the United States in the pre-industrial era.

The countries with the largest levels of forest loss between 1990 and 2005 are in Latin America, Africa and Southeast Asia. Brazil is the largest single contributor to global forest loss, although a number of countries have lost a greater percentage of their forestland over the past fifteen years. All of these countries experience high levels of poverty and many are war-torn and suffer under totalitarian or unstable governments.

Table 22.3 *Changes in Forest Cover by Continent: 2000–2005*

Continent or Region	Forest Cover Change (1000 acres)	Percent Change
Europe	29,836	1.22
Asia	–7,191	–0.51
North and Central America	–12,209	–0.70
Oceania	–15,469	–2.95
South America	–146,479	–6.65
Africa	–158,021	–9.14
World	–309,539	–3.07
SOURCE: FAO 2005a		

Table 22.4 *Countries with the Greatest Loss of Forest Acreage: 2000–2005*

Country	Forest Cover Change (1000 acres)	Percent Change
Brazil	–104,597	–8.14
Indonesia	–69,367	–24.08
Sudan	–21,832	–11.57
Myanmar	–17,290	–17.84
Dem. Rep. Congo	–17,102	–4.92
Zambia	–16,487	–13.58
Tanzania	–15,281	–14.92
Nigeria	–15,185	–35.66
Mexico	–11,807	–6.92
Zimbabwe	–11,599	–21.11
SOURCE: FAO 2005a		

Table 22.5	_Countries with the Greatest Gain of Forest Acreage: 2000–2005_	
Country	Forest Cover Change (1000 acres)	Percent Change
China	99,210	25.55
United States	10,974	1.49
Spain	10,962	32.91
India	9,296	5.88
Viet Nam	8,817	38.11
Italy	3,944	19.04
France	2,511	6.99
Chile	2,120	5.62
Cuba	1,619	31.83
New Zealand	1,455	7.63
SOURCE: FAO 2005a		

The wood products industry frequently receives blame for forest loss, especially in the tropics. However, only 17 percent of the timber harvested in the tropics goes to the international market. Consumers use an estimated 55 to 60% (or more) of the timber harvested in developing countries for fuel. The U.N. lists five of the countries on the preceding list among the least developed countries. The World Bank lists all as developing countries. The list of countries with the highest levels of forest loss leads to a conclusion: _Poverty_ is the greatest cause of global forest loss (FAO 2007, Lomborg 2001, Moore 2000).

China has adopted aggressive forest preservation policies and has initiated a national reforestation program that increased its forest cover by 25 percent between 1990 and 2005. Other countries showing forest recovery are the United States, Spain, India, Viet Nam, Italy, France, Chile, Cuba and New Zealand.

INTERNATIONAL PRODUCTION OF WOOD PRODUCTS

Wood products comprise approximately 3 percent of the world's economy. Consumers use an estimated 1.7 billion cubic meters (7.2 billion board feet) of wood annually. The forestry sector[2] added an estimated 468 billion dollars (U.S.) to the world's economy in 2006, representing one percent of global Gross Domestic Product. The industry employed almost 14 million people. The furniture industry adds 129 billion dollars and 4.5 million employees (Lebedys 2008).

In 2007, the global production of solid wood products totaled an estimated 4.289 billion cubic meters. Industrial roundwood[3] accounted for 1.705 billion cubic meters, sawn wood[4] accounted for 431 million cubic meters and wood-based panels[5]

---

[2] The forestry sector consists of the forestry, wood products and pulp and paper industries.

[3] Industrial roundwood includes pulpwood, sawlogs, veneer logs and other products, i.e., poles, posts and pilings.

[4] Sawn wood includes lumber and timbers.

[5] Wood-based panels include hardboard, insulating board, medium density fiberboard (MDF), particleboard, plywood and veneer sheets.

accounted for 266 million cubic meters. The remaining 1.886 billion cubic meters consisted of fuel wood (FAO 2007).

Approximately one third of the sawn wood came from Europe and one third from North America (the U.S. and Canada). The United States produced the greatest volume of sawn wood in the world in 2007—approximately 84.4 million cubic meters (37.75 billion board feet), followed closely by Canada, which produced 52.3 million cubic meters (22.2 billion board feet) (FAO 2007).

Industrial roundwood production followed a similar trend with approximately one third of global production coming from the U.S. and Canada and one third from Europe. The United States is the leading producer of industrial roundwood, accounting for 393 million cubic meters in 2007. Canada, the Russian Federation and Brazil each produced between 100 million and 200 million cubic meters of industrial roundwood.

The industry manufactures approximately 40 percent of the wood-based panels in Asia, 32 percent in Europe and 21 percent in North America. China is the world leader in the production of wood-based panels, manufacturing 71 million cubic meters. The United States is second, producing 41.1 million cubic meters in 2007 (FAO 2007).

Approximately 42 percent of the world's fuelwood production is harvested and consumed in Asia, 32 percent in Africa and 15 percent in Latin America. The distribution of fuelwood production indicates the dependence on wood for domestic heating and cooking in developing countries. India, China, Brazil and Ethiopia are the world's leaders in fuelwood production and consumption. The United States ranks eighth in the world in fuelwood use, the most among developed countries (FAO 2007).

Global production of pulp and paper products totaled approximately 560 metric tons in 2007. North America produced 40 percent of the wood pulp and Europe produced 32 percent. Asia produced approximately 37 percent of the paper and paperboard, Europe produced 30 percent and North America produced 27 percent. The U.S. is the leading producer of wood pulp, and the United States and China are the world's leading producers of paper and paperboard (FAO 2007).

INTERNATIONAL TRADE IN WOOD PRODUCTS

International trade in wood products dates back at least five thousand years. History records that the ancient Egyptians received wood from as far away as Crete, Cyprus and Greece. America's involvement in international trade dates from the earliest days of European colonization. The colonists shipped naval stores, masts and timbers to Britain beginning in the early seventeenth century. Just a few decades ago, American imports were largely limited to tropical hardwoods such as mahogany and teak. Canada began to compete on the U.S. softwood lumber market in the 1960s and 1970s (Peck 2001, Williams 1989).

The Food and Agricultural Organization of the United Nations estimates that the global trade in wood products in 2007 accounted for $232 billion U.S. dollars (FAO 2007).

Canada is the leading exporter of wood products in the world with a very high percentage of its exports going to the United States. The forestry sector is essential to the Canadian economy and is its largest employer. Softwood species dominate the Canadian forest—spruce is Canada's primary commercial species—and residential construction materials are their primary products. The United States is the third leading exporter behind Canada and the European Union (FAO 2007, 2009a)

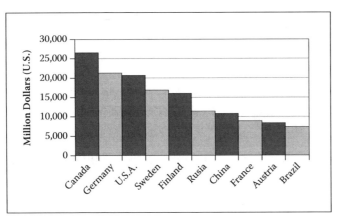

Figure 22.2 Leading Wood Products Exporting Countries: 2007.

The United States has remained the world's largest exporter of hardwood products for a number of years, exporting $1.42 million in shipments of hardwood lumber in 2007. Other significant players in the hardwood export market include the Asian countries of Malaysia, Indonesia and China, as well as Brazil and the western European countries.

European nations represent the most active global region on the wood products export market, accounting for approximately 49 percent of the value of shipments in 2006. Asia accounted for 27 percent and North America (Canada and the U.S) accounted for 15 percent.

The United States has remained the world's leading importer of wood products for a number of years (FAO 2007). Following the cutback in timber harvest on national forests resulting from the northern spotted owl court decisions, the U.S. became a net importer of wood products. While the U.S. has turned increasingly to private land as a source of wood, it has also turned to international sources to supply its needs.

As with exports, European countries represent the largest bloc of importers in the world wood products market. European countries imported approximately 56 percent of the world's total value of shipments of wood products in 2006. North America accounted for 21 percent and Asia accounted for 13 percent of the imports.

China's role as a major importer has grown steadily since the late 1990s. In 2007 it overtook Germany to become second and may equal or overtake the United States in 2008 or 2009. At the same time, China has adopted aggressive forest conservation and restoration policies, and it has aggressively sought to build its economy by building state-of-the-art manufacturing facilities in labor-intensive industries such as shoes, clothing and furniture. In this manner, the Chinese are attempting to employ large numbers of people while increasing the wealth of the nation and its people. Peck (2001) describes China as an "in-transit processor." In other words, they are importing wood to manufacture furniture and other products for the world market. Exports from China increased exponentially since the late 1990s.

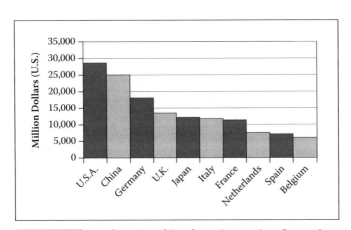

Figure 22.3 Leading Wood Products Importing Countries: 2007.

Because of low wages and state-of-the-art manufacturing facilities, China became the world's largest furniture exporter in 2006, exporting almost 20 percent of the total worldwide value of furniture shipments in 2007 (Grushecky et al. 2006, Lebedys 2008, Luppold and Bumgardner 2006, Pepke 2008, Wang et al. 2008)

The 2006–2007 downturn in the U.S. housing market and the subsequent recession caused major disruptions in the global market for forest products. Falling wood products prices and imports from 2006 to 2007 reflect the downturn.[6] The UN's Economic Commission for Europe predicted a 20 percent decline in North American sawn softwood imports from 2007 to 2008 with a corresponding decline of 22 percent in sawn softwood exports (Pepke 2008).

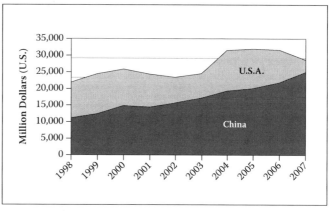

Figure 22.4 Value of Wood Products Imports by the U.S. and China: 1998–2007.

U.S. TRADE WITH CANADA

The trading partnership between Canada and the U.S. accounts for the greatest value of shipments of all goods and services in the world. The trend holds true for wood products. In 2006, approximately 76 percent of the wood products imported by the United States came from Canada.[7] Conversely, Canada shipped approximately 82 percent of its exports of wood products to the U.S. Softwood lumber shipments accounted for $33 billion (U.S.), more than half the value of shipments of all wood products exported by Canada to the United States. The value of wood pulp and paper product shipments from Canada was $16.5 billion, and the value of shipments of wood-based panels was $11.8 billion (FAO 2006).

Canada received 39 percent of the value of wood products exports from the United States in 2006, the greatest value of any country. Shipments of wood products from the U.S. accounted for 87 percent of Canada's imports. Canada is a particularly important customer nation for the U.S. hardwood lumber industry, accounting for $810 million in shipments of hardwood lumber and $3 billion in hardwood industrial roundwood. Canada has traditionally been a trans-shipper of U.S. hardwoods, re-exporting to Europe and Asia (Armstrong et al. 1993, FAO 2006).

In spite of the strong trade relationship, the United States and Canada have been engaged in a bitter trade dispute over softwood products shipped from Canada to the United States since 1982. The dispute centered on claims by U.S. lumber producers that Canadian competitors benefited from unfair government subsidies and were "dumping" product into the U.S. market to undercut U.S. manufacturers. In Canada, the provinces own 71 percent of the forestland and provincial timber sales involve long-term contracts to lumber companies with prices fixed at the time of sale. As a result, Canadian producers have profited as lumber prices have risen over time. In the U.S., public and many private timber sales are short term. Canadians claim that they are able to undersell U.S. producers because their mills are more efficient than those of their U.S. counterparts. The dispute has taken many forms, including tariffs imposed by the United States, compromises that allowed Canada to impose export duties on softwoods, litigation and arbitration under the terms of the North American

---

[6] Data for 2008 were not published at the time this book was written.

[7] Percentages are based on the value of shipments.

Free Trade Agreement (NAFTA) and by the World Trade Organization (WTO). The most recent attempt at resolution was a 2006 agreement that restricts the importation of Canadian softwood lumber to 34 percent of the U.S. market. Alleged failure by four Canadian provinces to uphold the terms of the agreement has caused the dispute to simmer into 2009 (Berry 2006, CBC News 2009, FAO 2009a, Makarenko 2008).

A CASE STUDY IN INTERNATIONAL FORESTRY: NEW ZEALAND

New Zealand is an interesting case study in global forestry. The country consists of two large islands with a total area of 268,680 square miles located in the South Pacific to the east of Australia. It is a parliamentary democracy on the British model. Its population is approximately four million people. New Zealand depends upon agriculture and forestry and has relied upon exports, primarily to the British Commonwealth nations, for its economic prosperity.

Forests cover 20.5 million acres—31 percent of its land area—and range from temperate rainforest to alpine forests to sub-tropical forest. In 2005, 22 percent of New Zealand's forestland was forest plantation. A plantation is a forest where trees are planted and harvested as a crop. Almost 100 percent of New Zealand's timber harvest is from the plantations and 97 to 98 percent of those forests are planted in softwood species. New Zealand produced 4.28 million cubic meters of softwood sawnwood in 2007 and exported approximately 41.5 percent of production. The remaining 78 percent of the forest remains as native or indigenous forest (FAO 2007, 2009b, MAF 1999).

In the 1920s, the New Zealand forest service began replanting hardwood forests that had been logged with non-native conifers. They did some of the planting for the purpose of stabilizing eroded pastureland, but mostly they intended to provide a fast-growing crop of trees to maintain the country's wood products industry. New Zealand foresters experimented with a number of species, but their greatest success came with an unlikely species that would have an impact upon forestry throughout the southern hemisphere (FAO 2005b, 2009b, MAF 1999, Visser 1994).

Figure 22.5 Radiata Pine Plantation. *New Zealand.*

Radiata pine (*Pinus radiata*) is a species of pine native to a very limited range in California where it is more commonly known as Monterrey pine. Within its native range, it is of little commercial value; in fact, an exotic fungal disease threatens it. Radiata pine arrived in New Zealand around 1850 when a planter introduced a seedling that astounded him with its phenomenal growth. Through selective breeding, New Zealand's scientists were able to establish radiata pine plantations that can grow to harvestable size[8] in twenty

---

[8] For example, the author observed a harvesting operation in a radiata pine plantation on New Zealand's South Island where trees were diameters at breast height (DBH) of 24 inches or more were common in a 28-year-old, even-aged stand.

to thirty years. Today, approximately 89 percent of New Zealand's plantations consist of radiata pine (Conifer Specialist Group 1998, Kaiser 1994, MAF 1999, 2009, Visser 1994).

Radiata pine now grows in plantations throughout the southern hemisphere. Another country renowned for its radiata pine plantations is Chile. When radiata was first introduced to the country in 1885, it was planted in mixed stands along with other conifers where it quickly out-competed the other species. Other significant plantations of radiata are in Australia and South Africa (Toro and Gessel 1999, Visser 1994).

For much of its history, most of New Zealand's forests were under government ownership. Prior to 1984, more than half of New Zealand's plantation forests were in government ownership. As part of a program of economic reform, the government sold all but 6 percent of the country's plantation forests to the private sector (MAF 1999).

Figure 22.6 Westland National Park. *New Zealand.*

Approximately 77 percent of the native forest remains in government ownership, much of it dedicated to preservation, heritage and recreation. Much of the native forest is temperate hardwood rainforest and mountain forest located in national parks on the west coast of the South Island. New Zealand accomplished what the United States could not. Economic interests and environmentalists achieved a compromise between preserving native forests while privatizing the planted forests for continuous production of wood products (MAF 1999, Visser 1994).

New Zealand, as an island nation, is noteworthy for the problems it has experienced with exotic invasive species. Approximately eight hundred years ago, humans arrived in New Zealand. The Polynesian Maoris are believed to have brought the first small mammals to the islands. Europeans introduced a large number of additional species, including sheep, cattle and radiata pine, which scientists generally consider beneficial. New Zealanders were not as fortunate with other introduced species.

The only small mammals native to the islands are bats. Without predators, a number of species of flightless birds, including the kiwi[9] and the extinct moa, evolved in New

Figure 22.7 Flightless Bird. *New Zealand.*

---

[9] The kiwi became a national symbol when New Zealand soldiers wore shoulder patches featuring the kiwi. Soon, the soldiers became known as kiwis. It now is the most commonly used nickname for New Zealanders.

Zealand. The introduction of small mammals capable of raiding the ground nests of the flightless birds led to the extinction of some species and placed others on the threatened or endangered lists. Most problematic among the predators are possums, rats and cats. The possum, not to be confused with the North American opossum, is an Australian marsupial. It is particularly detested by New Zealanders for its deleterious effect upon native bird species.

Sheepherders introduced gorse, a plant native to Scotland, as inexpensive forage for sheep. Gorse tends to overrun native plants. It is a particular problem to the forest industry, which must eradicate it before planting radiata pine. The industry also considers broom, another introduced plant, a noxious invader.

FOREST PLANTATIONS

There are 348 million acres of plantation forest in the world. Approximately 46 percent of the plantation area is in Asia and 20 percent is in Europe. Significant areas of the forests of six of the seven continents are planted forests. China has the greatest extent of plantations (77.6 million acres), followed by the United States and the Russian Federation (approximately 42 million acres each) (Bowyer 2001, Del Lungo et al. 2006).

The environmental organization, Worldwatch Institute, estimates that plantations occupying 10 percent of the Earth's forested land can meet the world's wood needs (Postel and Ryan 1991). Yet other environmental groups claim that plantations are not "real forests" and that plantations are "sterile" of biodiversity.[10] Others argue that placing too much reliance on plantations as a source of wood will lower the value of natural forests, making them vulnerable to economic exploitation for other uses such as agriculture or development. Plantation forestry, like many topics pertaining to forestry, can be controversial.

Not all plantations are the same. Some, like the radiata pine plantations of Chile and New Zealand consist of exotic species. Others such as the southern pine plantations of the southeastern U.S. consist of native species. There are plantations of mixed species and plantations where planted trees intersperse within natural forest (Bowyer 2001, Del Lungo et al. 2006).

Critics of plantations cite reduced soil moisture and stream flows, greater risk of pests and disease, soil erosion and reduction of fertility and a lack of biodiversity as drawbacks of plantation forestry. However, evidence indicates that proper design and management of plantations can reduce or alleviate most of these problems. Farmers may establish plantations on land degraded by overuse, especially in the tropics. In cases like this, plantations represent an improvement and likely restore a greater level of biodiversity than under the previous use (Bowyer 2001).

Arguments in favor of plantation forestry hinge on the fact that the Earth's population has grown to 307 billion in August of 2009, and predictions are that it will continue growing, although estimates of how much vary. People will continue to require wood for fuel, shelter, paper and numerous other uses. As the economies of developing countries grow, per capita demand for goods will increase within those countries. We have seen that happen in the last decade with the growing economies of China

---

[10] Some environmentalists are fond of calling forest plantations "tree farms" as a term of derision. The term "Tree Farm" belongs to an organization, The American Tree Farm Association (http://www.treefarmsystem.org/), which advocates sustainable forest management. For example, there is a tree farm south of Morgantown, West Virginia, that is a natural, mixed hardwood forest. To call a forest plantation a "tree farm" is wrong.

and India. It is therefore certain that global demand for wood will continue to grow. And, for reasons that the next chapter will cover, it is unlikely that the wood industry will substitute other materials for wood in any great quantity (Bowyer 2001).

Much like the Green Revolution in agriculture discussed in Chapter 20, plantations offer the advantage of high level productivity on less land. Bowyer (2001) reports significantly higher yields of wood from both tropical and temperate plantations when compared to natural—including managed natural—forests.

When we consider all factors, the expansion of forest plantations is inevitable in light of the growing world demand for wood. The arguments for doing so appear to outweigh the arguments against. Jim Bowyer, a wood scientist who has written extensively on environmental issues pertaining to wood use, puts this debate in perspective: "It is difficult to understand how one can realistically oppose *both* the exploitation of natural forests and development of forest plantations" (Bowyer 2001).

Figure 22.8 Radiata Pine Nursery. *Chile.*

Homework

Name: _____   Date: _____

Look up the FAO's on line database at *http://faostat.fao.org/site/630/default.aspx* and answer the following questions:

1. Follow the ForeSTat link. What is the value of exports of "forest products" from New Zealand each year over the most recent five years? Fill in the answers in the table below.

Value of Exports of Forest Products from New Zealand over the Most Recent Five Years	
Year (most recent year first)	Value of Exports ($1000 US)

2. Follow the Forestry Trade Flows link. What are the top five export destinations in terms of value of shipments of coniferous sawnwood (indicated with a "C" in the FAO database) from New Zealand in the most recent year for which data are given? Fill in the answers in the table below.

Leading Destinations for Coniferous Sawnwood from New Zealand in _____ (year)	
Country	Value of Exports ($1000 US)
1.	
2.	
3.	
4.	
5.	

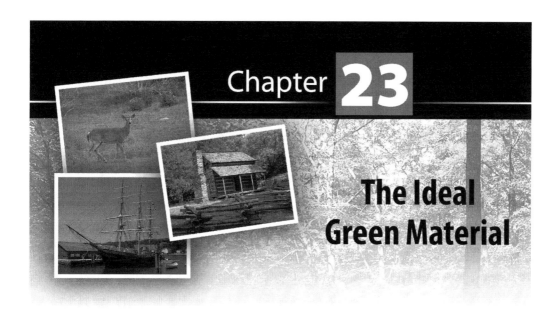

Chapter 23

The Ideal Green Material

The photo of the logging truck with three large logs was taken in 2000 at the Emerald Bay overlook on the west side of Lake Tahoe, California. The other photo is the magnificent view of the lake from the overlook. When I was taking the pictures, I happened to be standing next to two elderly women who were commenting on how horrible it was to cut timber on this spot. I had just taken the picture of the truck and had observed that the trees had been cut down in order to expand the park-ing lot at the overlook. This was not a commercial timber harvest. Of course, I politely interrupted the two women and explained this. They appeared to believe my explanation, but they still expressed consternation about cutting the trees down.

This example illustrates the power of public perceptions. As expressed by the American Institute of Architects (1996), "forest management practices are at the heart of the issue." But is cutting down trees and, by implication, using wood bad for the environment? To rationally answer this question one must carefully examine the options and alternatives of material use.

Increased public awareness of environmental issues has led to a call for green

Figure 23.1 Logging Truck. *At the Emerald Bay overlook, Lake Tahoe.*

Figure 23.2 Lake Tahoe. *From the Emerald Bay overlook, Lake Tahoe, CA.*

energy, green buildings and green materials. But schemes designed to promote green building practices "often reflect more about a sponsor organization's agenda than a true scientifically based environmental footprint" (Lippke 2006). What is truly "green?" How can architects, designers, policymakers and the public make sound, science-based decisions that protect the environment while meeting the basic needs of a growing population? The answers may lie in "Life Cycle Inventory" (LCI) and Life Cycle Assessment (LCA).

LIFE CYCLE INVENTORY/LIFE CYCLE ASSESSMENT

LCI/LCA is a method for quantifying the environmental impacts of material use. The method requires quantifying a wide range of environmental impacts of a material's use from cradle to grave. For example, a wood product's impacts would be quantified from harvest through all stages of manufacture and use, to disposal or recycling. The following table summarizes specific steps that the life cycle and environmental impacts of a product may include (Lippke et al. 2004).

LCI/LCA enables architects and designers to make sound, science-based, environmentally-friendly decisions in choosing and specifying materials and construction methods. It also gives industry a tool to make improvements to their processes and products in order to reduce environmental impacts (Lippke and Edmonds 2006). The model described here may be applied to numerous applications in everyday life such as comparing two materials that may be used in the same application such as a glulam or solid wood beam (Puettmann and Wilson 2005). Scientists have completed two studies of residential construction, one in Canada, and one in the United States, that show similar results when analyzing building systems (CWC 2004, Lippke et al. 2004).

The Consortium for Research on Renewable Industrial Materials (CORRIM)[1] performed the U.S. studies. This is a consortium of universities, government agencies, trade associations and industry. The CORRIM studies analyzed 2,000 to 2,100 square foot, single-family homes in Minneapolis and Atlanta. The non-profit ATHENA Sustainable Materials Institute conducted the Canadian study, which involved a 2,400 square foot home in Toronto. The three analyses compared softwood and engineered wood I-joist frames (all locations), a light steel frame (Minneapolis and Toronto) and a concrete slab floor with concrete block walls (Atlanta and Toronto). The Minneapolis study included several alternatives in wood-based design, such as comparing solid wood floor joists with engineered wood I-joists (CWC 2004, Lippke et al. 2004).

Table 23.1 *Fundamentals of LCI/LCA*

Stages in the Life Cycle	Environmental Impacts
Extraction or Harvest	Embodied Energy
Transportation	Material Usage
Manufacturing	Global Warming Potential
Distribution	Air Pollution
Use	Water Pollution
Maintenance	Solid Waste Generation
Disposal or Recycling	Reuse, Recycling or Disposal

---

[1] The CORRIM website is *http://www.corrim.org/*.

The results of the CORRIM and ATHENA studies illustrate that a wood frame building possesses numerous advantages over the other two systems.

EMBODIED ENERGY

"Embodied energy" is the energy required to produce a material product from raw material extraction to manufacture of the final product. In a residential structure, embodied energy is input in a number of ways. The most obvious is energy consumed to produce the material. Transportation of materials from their source in a mine, quarry or forest to perhaps multiple manufacturing facilities, to a distributor and finally to the job site consumes energy.[2] Construction of the home requires energy inputs that vary from system to system. One must take into account that connecting the various components of the house may involve different energy requirements when comparing wood, steel or concrete structures. Heating and cooling the home requires energy, thus insulation properties are of paramount importance over the life of the building. Different building systems require different levels of maintenance over their life spans, and maintenance requires energy. Finally, the energy consumed in demolishing or disassembling the home at the end of its useful life consumes energy (CWC 2004, Lippke et al. 2004, Winistorfer et al. 2005).

The results of the Canadian and Minneapolis studies indicate that the steel building system embodies 12 percent and 17 percent more energy than the wood frame structure, respectively. The Toronto and Atlanta studies indicate that the concrete structure embodies 20 percent and 16 percent more energy than the wood frame house. The differences are indicative of different designs used in the CORRIM and ATHENA studies. In addition, concrete's thermal properties make it a more efficient material in a warm climate as opposed to a cold climate (CWC 2004, Lippke et al. 2004, Perez Garcia et al. 2005a).

Why does wood perform so well when compared to other materials? "Wood is solar" (Moore 2000). The chemical formulation of wood takes place in the living tree as carbon dioxide and water become converted into complex carbohydrates: cellulose, lignin and hemicellulose in the process of photosynthesis. The sun provides the energy.

Converting raw material into usable products consumes energy. Converting trees into lumber requires energy for harvesting, transporting logs to the mill and to run saws and planers. The most commonly cited estimate is that 70 to 80 percent of the energy consumed in lumber production is expended to dry the wood (Comstock 1975). Drying consumes as much as 87 percent of the energy consumed in the manufacturing of hardwood lumber (Bergman and Bowe 2008). Composite materials such as plywood, particleboard and engineered wood products require more processing steps. As a result, it requires more energy to manufacture these materials (Puettmann and Wilson 2005).

Energy consumption for heating and cooling over the life span of a house is approximately ten times the energy consumed in all other phases of the life cycle assessment (Perez Garcia et al. 2005a). Wood is an excellent thermal insulator. Therefore, one may lessen energy consumption heating or cooling buildings by using wood instead of other materials.

Another energy advantage that favors wood-based materials is the potential for a high level of energy self-sufficiency. Wood industries possess a ready source of industrial

---

[2] For example, shipping by rail requires significantly less energy than shipping an equal distance by road (Puettmann and Wilson 2005).

fuel in the form of mill residues, i.e., sawdust, bark, planer shavings and trimmings. For the most part, they use mill residues to provide heat and process steam for drying lumber and heating buildings.

MATERIAL USAGE

Material usage is difficult to evaluate. Should we measure usage by weight or volume? Wood has a lower density than concrete or steel; thus it stands to reason that assessment based on weight of materials used would favor wood. The ATHENA and CORRIM studies bear this out (CWC 2004, Lippke et al. 2004).

Perhaps a more important consideration in materials usage is the renewability of materials. Wood is a renewable resource. A forest may be clear-cut but, if left alone, a new forest will eventually regenerate to replace the one that was removed.[3] Petroleum (the feed stock for most plastics and a major energy resource) is nonrenewable. Minerals (coal, metallurgical ores, etc.) are nonrenewable.

The new generation of wood composites and engineered wood composites positively impact the material usage equation. Products such as oriented strandboard (OSB) make use of small diameter, low quality logs and may use underutilized species. In the past, loggers would have left much of this material in the woods as logging residue or poorly-formed, low-value trees (Lippke et al. 2004).

Concern over forest sustainability has led to the development of several forest certification schemes to assure consumers that wood products originate in sustainably managed forests. Forest certification is recognized globally, including in U.S. green building codes and green building rating systems such as The National Association of Home Builders (NAHB) National Green Building Program, Leadership in Energy and Environmental Design (LEED) and Green Globes. These schemes include the Forest Stewardship Council (FSC), the Sustainable Forest Initiative (SFI), the American Tree Farm System and the Canadian Standards Association's National Standard for Sustainable Forest Management. Bowyer (2007) and Moore (2002c) argue that sustainable certification schemes exist only for wood products. There is no similar system for mining. Thus, wood is at an unfair disadvantage in the green building rating systems (Bowyer 2007, Lippke 2006, Moore 2002d).

GLOBAL WARMING POTENTIAL

The subject of global climate change is fraught with controversy. It is a complex subject. However, we cannot deny the issue is perceived as a major problem by a significant percentage of the public. Evaluating the issue in terms of a life cycle assessment of materials and building systems is no less complex. Scientists must account for carbon dioxide emissions throughout the life cycle. However, carbon-based materials such as wood sequester, or store, carbon through their life cycles. In addition, trees absorb carbon dioxide as part of the process of photosynthesis. But dead, decaying or burning trees release carbon dioxide into the atmosphere. Forest management can significantly affect the carbon equation.

---

[3] This is why I detest descriptions of forest harvest as "destruction" and "devastation"—even when describing the intensive and widespread clear-cutting and subsequent fires of the era of heavy cutting. The disturbance is temporary. In 1980, Mount St. Helens erupted, creating a moonscape of volcanic ash and fallen timber. Almost thirty years later, the forest is recovering. Clear-cutting a stand of timber and replacing it with a parking lot is destruction. Clear-cutting and replanting or allowing the stand to regenerate is not.

The Canadian (ATHENA) comparison of building systems resulted in 34 percent and 81 percent greater greenhouse gas emissions from the steel and concrete buildings when compared to the wood frame structure, respectively (CWC 2004). The Minneapolis study revealed that carbon dioxide emissions were 26 percent greater in the steel frame house than the wood frame house. The Atlanta study resulted in a 31 percent increase in carbon dioxide emissions in the concrete structure than in the wood frame structure (Lippke et al. 2004) .

A large part of the carbon dioxide emitted in the production of materials occurs in energy production required to manufacture the material. Thus wood, with its lesser embodied energy, requires less consumption of fossil fuels in its manufacture than steel or concrete (Lippke 2006).

Carbon may be sequestered in wood products during their useful life. In addition, carbon may be stored for long periods of time when wood products are buried in landfills or recycled. The length of time that carbon will be sequestered in wood products depends upon the product and its end use. We might expect paper, for example, to remain in use for only a few years and perhaps remain in a landfill for ten years before it decays and emits its carbon. The wood in a house may remain in place sequestering carbon for fifty to several hundred years (Bowyer 2001, Lippke 2006, Malmsheimer et al. 2008).

Forest management has a significant impact on carbon sequestration. Trees take in carbon dioxide in the process of photosynthesis. The faster a tree grows, the more carbon it is absorbing and tying up to create new cells. CORRIM studies determined that actively managed forests sequester more carbon over time. Younger forest patches are growing at a greater rate than older, mature patches. Late transitional and self-replacing forests may be net carbon emitters as a result of the decay of dead timber (Lippke et al. 2004, Malmsheimer et al. 2008, Perez-Garcia 2005b).

Wildfire is a major source of carbon emissions that forest management may reduce. Wildfires that raged through Alaska for two months in 2008 emitted an equivalent quantity of carbon monoxide as all the cars and factories in the continental U.S. over the same period of time. The Angora fire in California in 2007 emitted as much greenhouse gas as 105,500 automobiles emit in a year (Bonnicksen 2008, Malmsheimer et al. 2008, Pfister 2006).

Use of wood as a feedstock for biofuels—particularly mill and forest residues as well as forest thinnings—can substitute for fossil fuels reducing greenhouse gas emissions. A further advantage is that wood use does not take a resource such as corn from the food supply to use as an energy source (Malmsheimer et al. 2008).

The most significant negative pertaining to forestry and greenhouse gas emissions is the loss of forests. An estimated 20 percent of greenhouse gasses have been attributed to deforestation for agriculture and urbanization. Promoting forest management and the use of wood provides economic incentives for people to maintain and expand the world's forests. The advantages in doing so are many (Moore 2000, 2002d, 2006, Malmsheimer et al. 2008).

AIR POLLUTION

The primary air pollutants considered problematic include, but are not limited to, ozone, nitrogen oxides, sulfur dioxides, carbon monoxide, lead and particulates.

The CORRIM study indicates a 14 percent increase in air pollutants when comparing the Minneapolis steel frame house with the wood frame house. Air pollutants were

23 percent greater in the Atlanta concrete house when compared to the wood frame house. The Toronto study reported 10 percent more air pollutant emissions from the steel home and 12 percent more from the concrete home when compared to the wood frame. (CWC 2004, Lippke et al. 2004).

The AIA (American Institute of Architects 1996) points to energy production for the conversion of wood as the primary source of air pollution in the wood industry. One may control particulate emissions in burning wood, and sulfur and nitrogen compounds (problematic with fossil fuels) are negligible. You can minimize emissions by using state-of-the-art, efficient combustion systems and scrubbers or other means of controlling stack gas emissions.

There are several air quality issues that certain segments of the wood products industry must take steps to control.

Wood dust in sawmills and wood shops may cause health problems for workers. Manufacturing facilities may require workers to wear respirators or dust masks. Dust problems are more serious with high extractive species such as black walnut and cedars (American Institute of Architects 1996).

Some of the volatile extractives found in wood may come under EPA regulations for Volatile Organic Compounds (VOCs). For example, α-pinene and β-pinene that exist naturally in southern pines are on the EPA's list of regulated VOCs. An extremely important concept to grasp is that these VOCs occur naturally in the environment. Volatile extractives cause the "pine" odor one smells in a wood shop, during a walk through a forest or from a Christmas tree. Low level exposures to volatile extractives are not a health or environmental hazard. It is when concentrations of VOCs become too high that risks occur. The only such instance that the author is aware of in the lumber industry occurs in kilns drying southern pine. Some states require the industry to monitor emissions and, if necessary, to install scrubbers or other pollution control devices on the vents of their driers or kilns.

Chemical products used in the manufacture of some wood products, including adhesives and coatings, may present air quality problems. Formaldehyde, used in some adhesives, may present a problem in plywood, particleboard and other composite materials manufacture. The problem was prevalent in the 1980s with products that used urea formaldehyde—an adhesive used for interior grades of particleboard or plywood. Although there were complaints about formaldehyde levels in homes, particularly mobile homes, the worst cases of formaldehyde release occurred near the presses in manufacturing facilities. Research revealed that the industry could minimize the problem by carefully controlling the chemical mixture of the adhesive. In some cases, particleboard and plywood mills had to install emission controls. Development of new adhesives has also improved the situation.

Sulfur compounds used in the pulping process are a problem for the paper industry.

WATER POLLUTION

Water pollution issues were more severe with the steel frame house than with either the wood frame or concrete structures studied in the CORRIM and ATHENA research. The steel frame houses in Minneapolis and Toronto exhibited three times the water emissions than the wood frame houses. The concrete house in Toronto resulted in approximately 2.25 times greater water emissions than the wood frame, but the Atlanta houses resulted in identical levels of water emissions. We can explain the differences by the fact that the concrete and Atlanta structures used very different building and product technologies (CWC 2004, Lippke et al. 2004).

The AIA (American Institute of Architects 1996) points to runoff from logging operations as a problem. "Best Management Practices" (BMPs) are logging regulations designed to minimize water quality problems associated with harvesting. The primary problem is in relation to runoff from roads and stream crossings. The BMPs are designed to minimize adverse impacts from roads and other harvesting activities.

Lignosulfates from pulp mills are problematic and heavily regulated.

The chemical treating industry is a primary source of water quality concerns in the wood products industry. As such it is strictly regulated to protect the environment. Regulations include requirements that prevent chemicals from getting into the groundwater, either from point sources or from dispersed sources such as runoff from the plant grounds.

The disposal of treated lumber at the end of its service life is regulated. Companies may not burn treated lumber except under carefully controlled conditions and then only creosote-treated wood. By law, preservative-treated products must be disposed of in a landfill.

In January 2004, the treating industry voluntarily stopped production of wood products treated with Chromated Copper Arsenate (CCA) for all but industrial uses. The removal of CCA was the result of a public health scare over the presence of arsenic in the preservative. Most experts agree that the health scare was greatly exaggerated. However, public perceptions caused by adverse publicity most likely doomed sales of CCA-treated products. As a result, the industry has converted to less toxic (and less effective) substitutes.

SOLID WASTE GENERATION

Historically, the wood industry wasted a high percentage of waste material. The reason is geometry. The industry produces rectangular solids from cylindrical (more or less) raw materials. For example, researchers estimate that sawmills recover only 40 to 60 percent of the volume of a sawlog as usable lumber. The remainder is residue—sawdust, slabs, edgings, trimmings and associated waste.

As one might expect, solid waste generation is the one indicator in the ATHENA and CORRIM assessments where the steel frame houses outperformed the wood frame structure (by 6 percent and 0.9 percent). The two studies generated contradictory results in the comparison of the concrete structure to the wood frame structure because of the different concrete building systems used in Atlanta and Toronto. The more sophisticated Toronto concrete building system generated 16 percent less solid waste than wood, but the traditional concrete block structure in Atlanta generated 51 percent more solid waste than the wood frame structure (CWC 2004, Lippke et al. 2004).

The industry has long sought to add value to their product. Therefore, wood processing research has focused on ways to extend the resource by increasing product yields from harvested timber. The recent widespread use of wood-based composite materials and "engineered wood products" instead of lumber has dramatically increased yields of usable product from raw material. Great progress has occurred doing more with less. Although progress has taken place, there are still opportunities for further improvement. What do we do with sawdust? What do we do with bark?

Wood is biodegradable and combustible. This reduces the problems associated with disposal of wood products at the end of their service life. These characteristics also create opportunities. We may use sawdust, bark and disposed wood as fuel. Bark is frequently sold for mulch.

REUSE, RECYCLING AND DISPOSAL

Except for paper, wood products do not recycle well. Recycling wood building products is labor intensive. Embodied energy is low, which makes the production of wood-based materials from raw material advantageous economically when compared to recycling.

The recycling of wood timbers from old buildings is a growth industry, especially with high-value species. Companies also salvage valuable logs from nineteenth century shipwrecks in the Great Lakes, from dead trees and stumps in the forest and from peat bogs in New Zealand (Carlsen 2008).

The pallet industry is another area of growth for recycling. A shipping pallet is a low value product but a potentially wasteful one. The most difficult problem to solve is one-way shipping of a pallet. The cost of collecting and shipping pallets back to a recycling or concentration center may exceed the cost of making a new pallet. If industry can recycle and reuse pallets, it may conserve resource. Perhaps used pallets can be useful as an energy source.

In 2000, 48 percent of all paper consumption was recovered for recycling. The industry goal is 50 percent. Recycled fiber accounted for 39 percent of all fiber consumed for pulp and paper in 2000. Recycled fiber is used in corrugating medium, newsprint, other printing grades and structural wood fiber products. Impurities (adhesives, plastics, waxes, latex, asphalt, dirt, etc.) must be removed from recycled pulp. There is also a practical limit to how many times one may recycle pulp fibers. Eventually the recycled fibers will disintegrate. Scientists believe that 50 percent recycled content represents the practical maximum rate in paper recycling (Bowyer, et al. 2003).

LIMITATIONS OF LCI/LCA

Life Cycle Analysis produces very favorable results for the use of wood. However, LCA is not without its critics. One of the issues is how the various environmental impacts are weighted to make decisions. For example, one person or advocacy group may place greater importance on embodied energy than global warming potential while another may have distinctly different priorities.

As illustrated in the ATHENA and CORRIM examples, analyses are very sensitive to changes in design and materials selection (Puettmann and Wilson 2005). In addition, outcomes of LCI/LCA are sensitive to location (Lippke and Edmonds 2006).

Others are critical of LCI/LCA analyses for what they do not include. How does one quantify impacts upon wildlife habitat, aesthetics or recreational opportunities?

It seems that environmental concerns over the use of wood generally return to objections to timber harvest. Assessment of the impacts of extraction must account for the size of the area impacted, the permanence of the impact, the intensity of the impact and residual impacts such as water pollution and changes in habitat. When compared to mining, timber harvest is generally more extensive, e.g., it covers a more widespread area. However, mining is generally more intensive, e.g., its localized impact is more severe than that of timber harvest. These differences may be very difficult to weigh and prioritize in a life cycle assessment. We must also consider that we can minimize the negative environmental impacts of both mining and forest harvest operations and that the difference between the worst practices and the best practices in each extraction process may be greater than the differences between the best practices of both (Bowyer et al. 2003, CWC 2003).

Environmental Realities of the 21st Century

More than 6,780,000,000 human beings inhabit the planet Earth. This is more than double the global population fifty years ago. Likewise, the population of the United States has increased over the last half century albeit at a lesser rate.[4]

Growing population demands more resources and produces greater impacts on the environment. We must balance trying to meet the very real human needs for food, shelter, energy and the other goods and services that sustain and enhance human life with protection of the natural environment.

At present, as much wood is consumed globally as "all metals, all plastics, and Portland and masonry cement combined" (Bowyer et al. 2003). To replace wood use with alternative materials would require massive quantities of those materials, most of which carry greater environmental costs than wood. To attempt to do so is impractical if not impossible. LCI/LCA reveals that to do so may also be undesirable. An exception is to substitute other renewable materials such as agricultural residues, for instance corn stalks and straw, to the raw materials mix (Bowyer et al. 2003). Some have suggested growing annual crops such as industrial hemp and kenaf as substitutes for wood in order to "save forests." To do so would most likely result in the conversion of forest to agricultural cropland, thus defeating the purpose of this shift in resource use (Bowyer et al. 2003, Moore 2000, 2002b).

Some argue that Americans should reduce their consumption of wood (and other resources). For example, the size of the average single-family residence in the U.S. has increased dramatically since World War II, a period of time when the average size of an American family has been shrinking. Is this necessary and is it responsible? Paradoxically, developed nations of Western Europe and the United States consume the most, but they also have cleaner environments by most accepted measures. Some experts argue that this is a result of developed countries shifting the burden of

---

[4] The population of the U.S. has grown from 178 million in 1959 to 307 million in 2009.

resource extraction and manufacturing to developing countries. However, is it necessarily a bad thing that countries such as Chile improve their standard of living through a thriving export economy? (Bowyer 2003, Lomborg 2001, MacCleery 1999)

The questions posed in this discussion are many, but wood—and by extension forest management—are, and must remain, a significant part of the solution to sustainably meeting the world's natural resource needs. Wood may not be "the ideal green material," but the evidence indicates that it comes closer than most.

Homework

Name: _____   Date: _____

In his 2003 presentation to the College of Forestry at Oregon State (see Recommended Reading), Dr. Jim L. Bowyer describes two proposed changes in the U.S. tax code that might promote more responsible resource consumption. What are those proposals? Which do you favor and why*?

---

* There is no right or wrong answer to this part of the question.

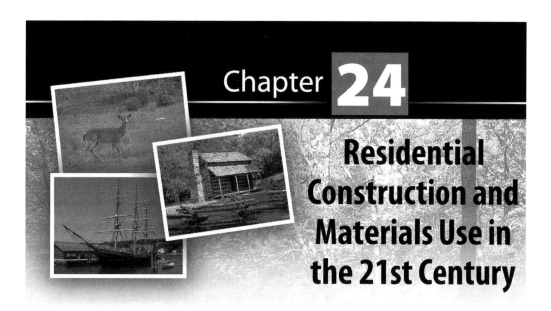

Chapter 24

Residential Construction and Materials Use in the 21st Century

As we enter the twenty-first century, the residential construction industry is going through a transformation as dramatic as the development of balloon frame construction in 1833. Balloon framing developed to adapt to local shortages of wood supplies, expanded demand for housing caused by a growing population and a shortage of skilled labor. The situation today is similar.

Wood supplies are changing in important ways. Increasingly urbanized and affluent societies such as ours value forests as more than a source of raw materials. Recreation, wildlife habitat (including non-game species) and aesthetic qualities of forest viewsheds have become higher priorities than timber harvest on a large portion of our forest lands. Litigation involving the northern spotted owl and other threatened and endangered species has curtailed timber sales on national forests—which is approximately 20 percent of the forested land of the United States. In addition, there are limited supplies of large trees and high quality timber, and where they exist they are more difficult to access. Old growth timber is in short supply, and harvest rotations of second growth are becoming more frequent. As we have seen in the Appalachians, species composition of the forest may also be changing as settler species such as red and sugar maple replace oaks and hickories.

As discussed in previous chapters, the United States is turning increasingly to international sources to meet its needs for wood products. Intensively managed forest plantations, including those in the United States, are meeting a portion of the needs and have potential to meet a greater percentage of the world's wood needs. However, plantations are capable of meeting only a portion of current demand (Bowyer 2001, 2003).

As in the past, human ingenuity must once again prove to be the greatest resource in meeting the growing needs of a growing population. The challenges of the early nineteenth century were met by technological improvements in sawmilling, wood processing, transportation and business models. Augustine Taylor helped solve the raw material problems of the era by developing revolutionary changes in residential construction.

Bernhard Fernow established a "timber science" research program in the Department of Agriculture's Forestry Division between 1886 and 1898. The program sought ways to substitute underutilized resources for heavily harvested species. For instance, the researchers discovered that chestnut oak was an acceptable replacement for white oak as railroad tie material. The Forestry Division's research program also sought to develop new processing technologies and new wood products.

Timber testing continued under the leadership of Gifford Pinchot. In 1910, the U.S. Forest Service established the Forest Products Laboratory[1] in Madison, Wisconsin, to consolidate the wood science research efforts of the Forest Service (Peterson 2003). The Forest Products Laboratory has long conducted research aimed at, as a 1970s promotional brochure put it, "extending the resource."

Specialized academic curricula in wood science and technology began to appear in forestry schools as early as 1929 (Ellis 1964). The demands of World War II and the post-war era led to the creation of twelve forest products programs between 1941 and 1951 at universities in the United States, including the program at West Virginia University in 1947. Important improvements in processing and product development also come from the industry itself.

Fernow was onto something. Throughout human history, improving the manufacture and use of wood—wood science and technology—has been a frequently used and successful solution to the challenges of material supply and use. As we begin the twenty-first century, residential construction is undergoing changes that are the most innovative since Augustine Taylor proposed replacing heavy timber frames and complex joinery with light framing and nailed connections.

RESIDENTIAL CONSTRUCTION IN THE 21ST CENTURY

The transformation of the residential construction industry is the result of the development of a new generation of wood-based composite materials known as "engineered wood products." The principal behind wood-based composite materials is the recombination of small elements of wood into larger products. Engineered wood products recombine materials in a designed fashion to produce structural products.

A number of possibilities exist in terms of composite design. The variables include the geometry of the "furnish" or raw material components, the geometry of the product, the grain orientation of the components and the connectors or various adhesive and pressing variables.

The raw materials (logs) may be broken down into:

- Lumber (2 by 4s, 2 by 6s, etc.)
- Veneer (a thin sheet of wood sliced from a log)
- Particles, chips, flakes or strands (small particles of wood, some with specifically designed geometries)
- Fibers (single wood cells or clusters of cells; pulp)

Recombination of the elements may be into:

- Panels
- Light framing members
- Heavy structural members
- Prefabricated trusses and framing members

---

[1] The website of the Forest Products Laboratory is *http://www.fpl.fs.fed.us/*.

Composite materials, including engineered wood products, offer several general environmental advantages over the use of solid wood products. Perhaps the most important advantage is in reducing the consumption of wood fiber to achieve the same or better results in terms of the structural integrity of a building. In other words, composites are advantageous in an LCI/LCA in terms of materials usage. On the other hand, the additional processing steps required to break down logs into small pieces and reassemble them in usable form, as well as the use of adhesives, adds to the embodied energy, global warming potential and air and water emissions when compared to lumber that requires only sawing, drying and surfacing in processing. Wood composites still outperform metals and masonry products in most facets of LCI/LCA (Lippke et al. 2004, Puettmann and Wilson 2005).

PANELS

Plywood

Plywood is a product manufactured from veneer, thin sheets of wood sliced from a log. Veneer may be sliced on a rotary lathe that produces a continuous sheet of wood or flat sliced, which is analogous to slicing a loaf of bread. The veneer is glued face-to-face in layers with each layer (ply) oriented so that the direction of the grain is at right angles to the sheet below. A press under high temperature and pressure cures the glue. Resulting panels are typically 4 feet wide, 8 feet long and range in thickness from 1/4-inch to 1-1/8-inch. The cross banding of veneer sheets lends the product rigidity, uniform strength and dimensional stability (Bowyer et al. 2003, CWC 2007d).

Builders use plywood in residential construction as subfloor and sheathing (the "skin" of a house). When applied over studs, joists and rafters, plywood acts much as diagonally applied solid wood sheathing did in bracing and stiffening the building structure. Because it is manufactured in 4- by 8-foot panels, it is easier to apply on the building site, thus saving labor costs.

Plywood was one of the first engineered wood products. The idea of laminating sheets of veneer was first patented in 1865 but did not catch on for another forty years. In 1905, a wooden box manufacturer constructed a display of Pacific Northwest woods by gluing veneer sheets for the Lewis and Clark Exposition in Portland, Oregon. The first plywood manufacturing as a commercial product began shortly after in 1907 in

Portland. In the early days, people used plywood for door panels. However, uses expanded to include running boards of automobiles and sheathing and subfloor in building construction. It was not until World War II that plywood became more than a specialty product. The development of waterproof adhesives in the 1930s enabled the U.S. Navy to use plywood to build lightweight craft such as the PT boats that played an important role in campaigns in the South Pacific. The military also used plywood in the construction of fighter aircraft during the war. The

Figure 24.1 Plywood Sheathing and Subfloor.

industry was concentrated in the Pacific Northwest until 1964 when the first southern pine plywood mill opened in Arkansas.[2] Until then, Douglas-fir was the primary species used for the manufacture of plywood. Currently, southern pine is used in the manufacture of approximately two-thirds of the structural plywood made in the United States (Plywood Pioneers 2009).

When we use plywood as sheathing and subfloor, we refer to it as *structural plywood* because it is part of the structure of a residence. Siding or flooring hides it from view in a finished house so appearance is not an issue in its manufacture. On the other hand, the intention is for *decorative plywood*, to be seen. It is manufactured with a face veneer of a high value hardwood species such as black walnut, black cherry or a high value imported hardwood. Typically, the face veneer is very thin, thus allowing greater coverage of surface from a single veneer log. The core plies are of a lower value species, such as yellow-poplar or aspen. Builders use decorative plywood in furniture, kitchen cabinets, interior paneling and flooring.

Figure 24.2 Decorative Veneer (left) and Structural Veneer (right).

Veneer production does not use the entire log. In a rotary peeling process, the log must be rounded, which creates waste. In addition, a cylindrical "peeler core" remains as a byproduct after the veneer peeling process. Veneer logs must be straight and must be of sufficient diameter and quality to produce a sound sheet of veneer of usable size. They are generally the best quality logs coming out of the woods.

Oriented Strandboard (OSB)

Oriented Strandboard (OSB) is an engineered wood product that evolved from particleboard and chipboard in the late 1970s. Particleboard was a low strength product that was first invented in the early twentieth century as a means of making a marketable product from planer shavings, a mill residue. The strands possess a specific geometry designed to achieve the best bonding and product strength. Typically, strands are very thin—approximately 0.03 inches thick, 6 inches in length, and 0.8 to 2 inches wide. The face strands in a panel are oriented so that the grain direction is parallel (or nearly) parallel to the long dimension (usually 8 feet) of the panel. Core strands are oriented nearly perpendicular to panel length. OSB mimics the properties of plywood in its orientation of strands at near-ninety degree angles from face to core. The pressing of panels into solid products is much the same as in plywood manufacture, and, like plywood, panels are typically 4 by 8 feet (Bowyer et al. 2003, CWC 2007c, Timberco 2008).

OSB has replaced plywood as sheathing in most U.S. residential construction. It also competes with plywood for subfloor.

---

[2] Researchers at the U.S. Forest Products Laboratory made southern pine plywood possible by the development of a new adhesive.

Unlike plywood, the whole log (except bark) theoretically goes into the product. Because the log is stranded (chipped) into small strands (flakes), logs can have a small diameter and do not have to be straight. As a result, logs that were unusable for lumber or plywood may be used to produce high quality OSB. In addition, species undesirable for manufacture of lumber and plywood may be used in OSB. An OSB plant in West Virginia, for example, accepts mixed hardwood and softwood logs

Figure 24.3 Mixed Hardwood Strands.

down to 4 inches in diameter, as well as crooked or curved logs that contain numerous knots and other strength-reducing characteristics. An efficient harvesting operation will sort and sell the best quality logs for veneer production and sell lesser quality logs to sawmills for lumber; it will use the poorest qualities logs for OSB production. From a materials usage standpoint, OSB is as close to an ideal wood-based material as we may find at present.

Light Framing Members

Laminated Veneer Lumber (LVL)

The concept behind plywood manufacture led to the development of *Laminated Veneer Lumber (LVL)*. Instead of orienting the plies at right angles to each other as in the manufacture of plywood, LVL is produced by laminating all plies with their grain parallel to the length of the product. Veneer used in manufacture of LVL ranges in thickness from 1/10 to 3/16 inches. Veneer sheets are offset lengthwise as panels form, allowing manufacture of strong products limited in length only by the size of the press (Bowyer et al. 2003, CWC 2007a).

The first use of LVL was during World War II to make propellers for aircraft. Today it is a lumber substitute. Since the 1970s the industry has used it for beams, headers over windows and doors and in engineered wood I-joists. Because strength-reducing defects such as knots and splits are limited to a single thickness of veneer in any one spot, LVL possesses greater and more uniform strength than solid wood. As such, it requires a lesser volume of LVL than lumber to meet the same design specifications in a framing system. Its cost relative to solid-sawn lumber limits its use as a framing material. Species used in manufacture of LVL mainly include southern pine, Douglas-fir, larch and yellow-poplar.

Engineered Wood I-Joists

Engineered Wood I-Joists are so named because their cross section resembles the capital letter "I" and because they are used as a substitute for solid-sawn floor joists in residential construction. The top and bottom of the "I"—the flanges—may be made of sawn lumber, LVL or Oriented Strand Lumber (OSL), a thicker version of OSB but with all strands oriented with the grain parallel to the length of the product. The vertical part of the I-joist—the web—is made from either plywood or OSB (Bowyer et al. 2003, CWC 2007a)

Figure 24.4 *Engineered wood I-joist with LVL flanges and plywood web (left), engineered wood I-joist with OSL flanges and OSB web, and LVL (right).*

An engineered wood I-joist is remarkably strong because of its design, and it requires approximately one half the wood fiber as a solid sawn joist. The use of OSB and OSL in its manufacture offers the additional materials usage advantages of using small diameter and/or poorly formed logs of a wide variety of species.

The growth in use of engineered wood I-joists has been remarkable since they first came on the market in 1969. They currently comprise more than half of all new residential floor framing systems in the U.S. (APA 2005, Leichti et al. 1990)

HEAVY STRUCTURAL MEMBERS

Glulam

Glulam, or glued-laminated timber, is manufactured by laminating solid sawn lumber face to face by laying up the lumber horizontally and clamping the assembled product until the adhesive cures. The lumber used to manufacture glulam may be 2 by 4s, 2 by 6s, 2 by 8s, 2 by 10s or 2 by 12s, depending upon the desired width of the beam or column. The beam may be built up to any desired depth, and the length is limited only by what can legally be transported on the highway to a construction site. When used as a beam or horizontal member in a structure, the individual components are oriented horizontally (Bowyer et al. 2003, CWC 2007b).

Builders can use glulam in heavy post and beam construction and to manufacture heavy trusses with long spans. They can bend it during the laminating process to create arches and curved members. Glulam is used extensively for exposed framing in buildings such as churches, office buildings and sports arenas, and it may be used outside if assembled with waterproof adhesive to support pedestrian bridges.

Figure 24.5 Glulam in a Pedestrian Bridge. *Morgantown, WV.*

Glulam manufacture in the United States typically uses denser, stronger softwood species such as southern pine or Douglas-fir.

Parallel Strand Lumber (PSL)

Parallel Strand Lumber (PSL) is manufactured from thin clipped strips of veneer. The veneer strips pass underneath a waterfall glue spreader and get pressed into a solid structural member through an extrusion process. Mills that manufacture PSL also contain an LVL processing line. Veneer is sorted in these plants with the high quality veneer used in LVL and the poorer quality veneer clipped to make PSL (Bowyer et al. 2003, CWC 2007a).

PREFABRICATED TRUSSES AND FRAMING MEMBERS

Prefabricated Trusses

The truss is a fundamental concept in engineering design. It is essentially a combination of long members connected to form a series of rigid triangles. The Howe truss was an essential element in constructing bridges and trestles in the first transcontinental railroad. Prefabricated roof trusses began to appear in residential houses in the U.S. in the 1950s. By the 1970s, prefabricated floor trusses entered the construction market (Bowyer et al. 2003, CWC 2007e).

Wood trusses most often use 2 by 4 inch (or occasionally 2 by 6) lumber instead of wider and costlier 2 by 8s, 2 by 10s and 2 by 12s required in traditional light framing systems. Sheet metal plate connectors fasten the lumber components of a truss. Wood trusses are prefabricated off the construction site and lifted in place on site with a crane, thus saving time and labor costs on the job site.

Figure 24.6 PSL Beams. *In a pedestrian bridge, West Virginia University, Morgantown, WV.*

A number of truss designs are readily available, giving architects and designers flexibility to create a number of roof configurations in a residence. Trusses may also feature designs that permit storage or extra space in an attic or above a garage.

Figure 24.7 PSL (left) and Glulam.

Figure 24.8 WPC Decking. *In a pedestrian bridge, West Virginia University, Morgantown, WV.*

WOOD-PLASTIC COMPOSITES (WPCs)

Another recent innovation is *Wood-Plastic Composites (WPCs)*. WPCs are hybrid composites combining wood fibers with plastics to manufacture a durable lumber substitute. WPCs have captured a segment of the window and door framing market and are making inroads as a replacement for treated lumber for wood decks and outdoor structures. WPCs may be an opportunity to improve recycling both wood (principally paper) and plastics.

STRUCTURAL INSULATED PANELS (SIPs)

Structural Insulated Panels (SIPs) are prefabricated panels with a rigid foam insulating material sandwiched between sheets of OSB. The panels are precut to size and may contain lumber framing. One can erect them very quickly using a crane. Wall panels may be 4 or 6 inches thick, and roof panels may be up to 14 inches thick.

Figure 24.9 SIP with Insulated Foam Core OSB Cladding. *(Note the channel for wiring.)*

Window and door openings may be cut and framed into SIPs at a factory and channels precut through the insulating material to make the running of electrical wires on the job site easy. Costs of a home constructed of SIPs are comparable to those of a wood framed house (SIPA 2007b).

The U.S. Forest Products Laboratory created the first SIPs in 1935 by gluing plywood to each face of a fiberboard insulating panel. American architect Frank Lloyd Wright employed SIPs in some of his Usonian houses in the 1930s and 1940s. The development of rigid foam insulation in the 1960s enabled the creation of SIPs made of plywood sandwiched around rigid foam insulation. Today SIPs represent a wave of the future that is changing residential construction as radically as Augustine Taylor's idea of using light framing and nailed connections to build houses (SIPA 2007a).

A Few Final Thoughts

The history of America's forest resources is a story of change. This includes how human beings have used the forest and the products that come from the forest to better their lives. It is also a story of how humans have changed the forest, made mistakes and learned from those mistakes in order to become better stewards of the land. Human ingenuity is, as Julian Simon proposed, the greatest resource.

I hope that the last few chapters of this book have convinced you that the use of wood and wood products, as well as scientifically sound forest management, are essential to meeting the resource challenges we face in the twenty-first century. To accomplish this in an environmentally sound manner will require continuous innovation of the kind described in this chapter. There is a lot going on in laboratories and in the field that is just over the horizon in terms of implementation, and there is a lot we have not even dreamed of that can be done.

Where do you fit into this picture[3]?

---

[3] If the profession of wood science and technology is of interest, please visit the website of the Society of Wood Science and Technology at *http://www.swst.org/profession.html.*

Homework

Name: _____ **Date:** _____

Visit each of these websites and write down one thing you learned about wood science from each.

Society of Wood Science and Technology
http://swst.org/

Wood Science and Technology program at West Virginia University
http://www.forestry.caf.wvu.edu/wvu_woodscience/

U.S. Forest Products Laboratory
http://www.fpl.fs.fed.us/

References

Alvarez, M. 2007. *State of America's forests.* Soc. of American Foresters, Bethesda, MD. *http://safnet.org/aboutforestry/StateOfAmericasForests.pdf* (accessed March 22, 2009).

Ambrose, S. E. 2000. *Nothing like it in the world: The men who built the transcontinental railroad 1863–1869.* New York: Simon & Schuster, New York. 431 pp.

American Institute of Architects. 1996. *Environmental resource guide.* New York: John Wiley & Sons.

American Merchant Marine at War. 2009. *www.usmm.org* (accessed June 11, 2009).

Anagnostakis, S. L. 2000. Revitalization of the majestic chestnut: Chestnut blight disease. American Phytopathological Soc., St. Paul, MN. *http://www.apsnet.org/online/feature/chestnut/top.html* (accessed August 10, 2009).

Anderson, K. 2004. *Nature, culture, and big old trees: Live oaks and ceibas in the landscapes of Louisiana and Guatemala.* Austin, Texas: University of Texas Press. 183 pp.

Anderson, L. O. 1970. *Wood-frame house construction.* U.S.D.A. Forest Service, Forest Products Laboratory, Agriculture Handbook No. 73. 223 pp.

APA. 2005. *Wood I-joist floors, fire fighters and fire.* Tacoma, WA: APA—The Engineered Wood Association. Form No. TT–015B.

Armstrong, J. P., T. G. Ponzurick, and W. G. Luppold. 1993. U.S. hardwood lumber exports to Canada: An assessment of market segments. *Forest Prod J* 43(6): 13–18.

Armstrong, W. A. 1986. *The Armstrong borderland.* Bruceton Mills, WV: Scotpress. 166 pp.

Arnold, E., and M. A. Justice. 2003. Urania Lumber Company photograph collection, Library and Archives, Forest History Soc., Durham, North Carolina. *http://www.foresthistory.org/Research/Biltmore_Project/Urania.html* (accessed July 28, 2009).

Bailey, R. 2000. Billions served: Norman Borlaug interviewed by Ronald Bailey. *Reason,* April 2000 Print Edition. *http://www.reason.com/news/show/27665.html* (accessed August 14, 2009).

Ball, J. 2003. Live oak: The ultimate southerner. *American Forests* 109(3), Fall 2003. *http://www.americanforests.org/productsandpubs/magazine/archives/* (accessed June 8, 2009).

Baylor, C. 2006. Mortise & Tenon Joints—Simple and Strong. *About.com*: Woodworking. *http://woodworking.about.com/od/joints/p/MortiseTenon.htm* (accessed June 27, 2009).

Bergman, R. D., and S. A. Bowe. 2008. Environmental impact of producing hardwood lumber using life-cycle inventory. *Wood Fiber Sci* 40(3): 448–458.

Berry, A. 2006. *Branching out: Case studies in Canadian forest Management.* Bozeman, MT: Property and Environment Research Center. 29 pp. *http://www.perc.org/pdf/Canadian Forest.pdf* (accessed August 21, 2009).

Bonnicksen, T. M. 2000a. *America's ancient forests: From the Ice Age to the Age of Discovery.* New York: John Wiley & Sons. 594 pp.

Bonnicksen, T. M. 2000b. *The lesson of Los Alamos.* Heartland Institute, Chicago, IL. *http://www.heartland.org/publications/environment%20climate/article/9686/The_Lesson_of_Los_Alamos.html* (accessed August 29, 2009).

Bonnicksen, T. M. 2002. Saving our giant sequoias: Restoration forestry may be the only way. *Forest Health Organization Magazine.* July/September 2002. *http://www.foresthealth.org/magazine/JulySept01/bonnicksen.htm* (accessed May 14, 2009).

Bonnicksen, T. M. 2003a. Written Statement for the Record of Dr. Thomas M. Bonnicksen. Oversight hearing on crisis on our national forests: Reducing the threat of catastrophic wildfire to central Oregon communities and the surrounding environment. Before the Committee on Resources. United States House of Representatives. August 25, 2003. Redmond, Oregon. *http://resourcescommittee.house.gov/108cong/full/2003aug25/bonnicksen.pdf* (accessed May 14, 2009).

Bonnicksen, T. M. 2003b. Written Statement for the Record of Dr. Thomas M. Bonnicksen. Oversight hearing on forest health crisis in the San Bernardino National Forest. Before the Committee on Resources. United States House of Representatives. September 22, 2003. Lake Arrowhead, California. *http://resourcescommittee.house.gov/108cong/full/2003sep22/bonnicksen.pdf* (accessed May 14, 2009).

Bonnicksen, T. M. 2006. Restoration Forestry. The Forest Foundation: Events and Programs. 6 pp. *http://www.calforestfoundation.org/what_the_experts_say.html* (accessed May 14, 2009).

Bonnicksen, T. M. 2008. *Greenhouse gas emissions from four California wildfires: Opportunities to prevent and reverse environmental and climate impacts.* FCEM Report 2. Auburn, CA: The Forest Foundation.

Borneman, W. R. 2004. *Alaska: Saga of a bold land.* New York: HarperCollins. 640 pp.

Botkin, D. B. 1990. *Discordant harmonies: A new ecology for the 21st century.* New York: Oxford University Press. 256 pp.

Bowden. S., and B. Ward. 2001. *Last chance for victory: Robert E. Lee and the Gettysburg Campaign.* Cambridge, MA: De Capo Press. 640 pp.

Bowen, C. D. 1966. *Miracle at Philadelphia: The Story of the Constitutional Convention May—September 1787.* 1986 Printing. New York: Little, Brown, and Co. 346 pp.

Bowen, C. D. 1986. *The most dangerous man in America: Scenes from the life of Benjamin Franklin.* New York: Little, Brown, and Co. 274 pp.

Bowyer, J. L. 2001. Environmental implications of wood production in intensively managed plantations. *Wood Fiber Sci* 33(3): 318–333.

Bowyer, J. L. 2003. Consumption and the sustainability equation. Transcript, Starker Lecture Series, College of Forestry, Oregon State University, Corvallis, OR. *http://www.cof.orst.edu/starkerlectures/transcripts/2003/bowyer.pdf* (accessed August 19, 2009).

Bowyer, J. L. 2007. Green building programs—Are they really green? *Forest Prod J* 57(9): 6–17.

Bowyer, J. L., R. Shmulsky, and J. G. Haygreen. 2003. *Forest products and wood science: An introduction.* 4th ed. Ames, IA: Iowa State University Press. 554 pp.

Brands, H. W. 2005. *Lone star nation: The epic battle for Texas independence.* New York: Anchor Books. 608 pp.

Burton, O. V. 2007. *The age of Lincoln.* Vancouver, B.C., Canada: Douglas & McIntyre Ltd. 420 pp.

California Resources Agency. 2009. *The California Gold Rush.* California Resources Agency, Sacramento. *http://ceres.ca.gov/ceres/calweb/geology/goldrush.html* (accessed July 25, 2009).

Campbell, R. B. 2003. *Gone to Texas: A history of the Lone Star State.* New York: Oxford University Press. 500 pp.

Carhart, T. 2005. *Lost triumph: Lee's real plan at Gettysburg—and why it failed.* New York: Penguin Group USA. 304 pp.

Carlsen, S. 2008. *A splintered history of wood: Belt sanders, blind woodworkers & baseball bats.* New York: HarperCollins. 432 pp.

Catton, B. 1968. *Grant takes command: 1863–1865.* New York: Little, Brown, and Co. Inc. 556 pp.

CBC News. 2009. Harper 'disappointed' with new U.S. duty on Canadian softwood lumber. Canadian Broadcasting Corporation (April 8, 2009). *http://www.cbc.ca/canada/british-columbia/story/2009/04/08/harper-softwood-227.html* (accessed August 21, 2009).

Chase, A. 1986. *Playing God in Yellowstone: The destruction of America's first national park.* San Diego, CA: Harcourt, Brace and Co. 464 pp.

Chase, A. 1995. *In a dark wood: The fight over forests and the rising tyranny of ecology.* New York: Houghton Mifflin. 535 pp.

Clarkson, R. B. 1964. *Tumult on the mountains: Lumbering in West Virginia: 1770–1920.* Parsons, WV: McClain Printing Company. 410 pp.

Colburn, C. H. 2002. Forest policy and the Quincy Library Group. In *Finding common ground: Governance and natural resources in the American West,* ed. R. D. Brunner, C. H. Colburn, C. M. Cromley, R. A. Klein, and E. A. Olson, 159–200. New Haven, CT: Yale University Press.

Comstock, G. L. 1975. Energy requirements for drying of wood products. In *Wood residues as an energy source*, 8–12. Madison, WI: Forest Products Research Soc.

Conifer Specialist Group. 1998. Pinus radiata. In *IUCN 2009. IUCN Red List of Threatened Species*. Version 2009.1. *www.iucnredlist.org* (accessed August 21, 2009).

Cox, T. 2009. *Railroad land grants. CoxRail.com. http://www.coxrail.com/land-grants.htm* (accessed July 26, 2009).

Crews, E. 2000. The gunsmith's shop. *Colonial Williamsburg J* (Autumn 2000). *http://www. colonialwilliamsburg.com/foundation/journal/Autumn00/gunsmith.cfm* (accessed July 5, 2009).

Crews, E. 2002. Peter Redstone builds a Barton portable: "You really can fall in love with the sound of harpsichord." *Colonial Williamsburg J* (Spring 2002). *http://www.colonial-williamsburg.com/Foundation/journal/Spring02/harpsichord.cfm* (accessed July 5, 2009)

Crews, E. 2003a. Colonial Williamsburg carpenters construct buildings of the past: Reproduction structures offer guests look at trade, hands-on experience. *Colonial Williamsburg J* (Spring 2003). *http://www.colonialwilliamsburg.com/Foundation/journal/spring03/carpenters.cfm* (accessed June 26, 2009).

Crews, E. 2003b. Making circles. *Colonial Williamsburg J* (Autumn 2003). *http://www.colonialwilliamsburg.com/Foundation/journal/Autumn03/cooper.cfm* (accessed July 5, 2009).

Crews, E. 2003c. Plain and neat: Cabinetmakers preserve colonial craftsmanship. *Colonial Williamsburg J* (Summer 2003). *http://www.colonialwilliamsburg.com/Foundation/journal/summer03/cabinet.cfm* (accessed July 5, 2009).

Crews, E. 2004. Wheels and riding carts. *Colonial Williamsburg J* (Winter 2004–2005). *http://www.colonialwilliamsburg.com/Foundation/journal/Winter04-05/wheel.cfm* (accessed July 5, 2009).

Cronon, W. 1983. *Changes in the land: Indians, colonists, and the ecology of New England.* 2003 ed. New York: Hill and Wang. 257 pp.

Cubbage, F. W., J. O'Laughlin, and C. S. Bullock III. 1993. *Forest resource policy.* New York: John Wiley & Sons. 562 pp.

CWC. 2003. *Environmental effects of building materials.* Tech. Bull. No. 2. Canadian Wood Council, Ottawa, Ontario, Canada.

CWC. 2004. *Energy and the environment in residential construction.* Sustainable Building Series No. 1. Canadian Wood Council, Ottawa, Ontario, Canada. *http://www.cwc.ca/NR/rdonlyres/FBEC3574-62E5-44E0-8448-D143370DCF03/0/EnergyAndEnvironment.pdf* (accessed September 18, 2009).

CWC. 2007a. *Engineered Wood Products (EWP).* Canadian Wood Council, Ottawa, Ontario, Canada. *http://cwc.ca/NR/rdonlyres/35C376ED-F20A-43EB-8405-D70C452CAB68/0/EngineeredWoodProducts.pdf* (accessed September 26, 2009).

CWC. 2007b. *Glulam.* Canadian Wood Council, Ottawa, Ontario, Canada. *http://www.cwc.ca/NR/rdonlyres/5B9FFB1C-409C-4B65-BE03-338CC172F5EC/0/Glulam.pdf* (accessed September 26, 2009).

CWC. 2007c. *Oriented Strandboard (OSB).* Canadian Wood Council, Ottawa, Ontario, Canada. *http://www.cwc.ca/NR/rdonlyres/F6074ABC-2FD8-4CBE-A1DE-1AEE5197559E/0/OSB.pdf* (accessed September 26, 2009).

CWC. 2007d. *Plywood.* Canadian Wood Council, Ottawa, Ontario, Canada. *http://www.cwc.ca/NR/rdonlyres/EDAF96EE-EB69-44D4-8557-ED4351D9E32C/0/Plywood.pdf* (accessed September 26, 2009).

CWC. 2007e. *Trusses.* Canadian Wood Council, Ottawa, Ontario, Canada. *http://www.cwc.ca/NR/rdonlyres/828D87E4-76F7-4D1E-A370-F063308312E1/0/ApplicationsHistoryDesign andManufacturing.pdf* (accessed September 26, 2009).

Dahl, B., and D. J. Molnar. 2003. *The anatomy of a park: Essentials of recreation area planning and design.* 3rd ed. Prospect Park, IL: Waveland Press. 200 pp.

Dailey, S., J. Fites, A. Reiner, and S. Mori. 2008. *Fire behavior and effects in fuel treatments and protected habitat on the Moonlight Fire.* Fire Behavior Assessment Team. U.S.D.A. Forest Service, June 2008, 63 pp. *http://www.qlg.org/pub/miscdoc/moonlight_fire_effects_assessment.pdf* (accessed August 23, 2009).

Davis, B. 1988. *The Civil War: Strange and fascinating facts.* New York: Wings. 256 pp.

Deans, B. 2007. *The River where America began: A journey along the James.* Lanham, MD: Rowman and Littlefield. 320 pp.

Dechter, M. 2008. 2008. *Affected environment and environmental consequences: Climate change.* Specialist Report, Butler2-Slide Postfire Fuels Reduction, June 24, 2008. U.S.D.A. Forest Service, San Bernardino National Forest, San Bernardino, CA. *http://www.fs.fed.us/ r5/sanbernardino/documents/ButlerIISlide_climatechange_report.pdf.* (accessed August 29, 2009).

Del Lungo, A., J. Ball, and J. Carle. 2006. *Global planted forests thematic study: results and analysis.* Planted Forests and Trees Working Paper 38. Food and Agricultural Organization of the United Nations, Rome. 168 pp. *http://www.fao.org/forestry/media/ 12139/1/0/* (accessed August 26, 2009).

Denevan, W. M. 1992. The pristine myth: The landscape of the Americas in 1492. *Annals of the Assoc. of American Geographers* 82(3): 369–385.

Dixon, E. J. 2002. How and when did people first come to North America? *Athena Review: J of Archaeology, History, Exploration.* Vol. 3, No. 2: Peopling of the Americas. *http://www. athenapub.com/10Dixon.htm* (accessed May 10, 2009).

Douglass, A. E. 1929. The secret of the Southwest solved by talkative tree rings. *National Geographic* 56(6): 736–770.

Dunkelman, M. 2006. Resurrecting a regiment. *Civil War News,* August 2006. Historical Publications Inc., Tunbridge, VT. *http://www.civilwarnews.com/preservation/154dunkleman. htm* (accessed July 23, 2009).

Easterbrook, G. 1997. Forgotten benefactor of humanity. *Atlantic Monthly,* January 1997. *http:// www.highyieldconservation.org/articles/forgotten_benefactor.html* (accessed August 14, 2009).

Ellis, E. L. 1964. *Education in wood science and technology.* Soc. of Wood Science and Technology. Madison, WI. 187 pp.

Ellis, J. J. 2004. *His Excellency: George Washington.* New York: Vintage Books. 352 pp.

EPA. 2001. Urban Wildland Interface Communities within the Vicinity of Federal Lands that are at High Risk from Wildfire. *Federal Register* 66, no. 160 (August 17, 2001). *http://www. epa.gov/EPA-IMPACT/2001/August/Day-17/i20592.htm* (accessed August 29, 2009).

Eshleman, J. A., R. S. Malhi, and D. G. Smith. 2003. Mitochondrial DNA studies of Native Americans: Conceptions and misconceptions of the population prehistory of the Americas. *Evolutionary Anthropology* 12: 7–18.

Fagan, B. 1990. Tracking the first Americans. *Archeology* (November/December 1990), 14–20). *http://muweb.millersville.edu/~columbus/data/art/FAGAN-02.ART* (accessed May 11, 2009).

Fagan, B. 2000. *The Little Ice Age: How climate made history 1300—1850.* New York: Basic Books. 246 pp.

Fagan, B. 2004. *The long summer: How climate changed civilization.* New York: Basic Books. 284 pp.

FAO. 2005a. *Change in extent of forest and other wooded land 2005; FRA 2005—global tables.* Food and Agricultural Organization of the United Nations, New York, NY. *http://www .fao.org/forestry/32033/en/* (accessed August 19, 2009).

FAO. 2005b. *Extent of forest and other wooded land 2005; FRA 2005—global tables.* Food and Agricultural Organization of the United Nations, New York, NY. *http://www.fao.org/ forestry/32032/en/* (accessed August 19, 2009).

FAO. 2006. *Forestry Trade Flows tables.* Food and Agricultural Organization of the United Nations, New York, NY. *http://faostat.fao.org/site/628/default.aspx* (accessed August 21, 2009).

FAO. 2007. ForesSTAT tables. Food and Agricultural Organization of the United Nations, New York, NY. *http://faostat.fao.org/site/626/default.aspx#ancor* (accessed August 21, 2009).

FAO. 2009. *Forestry Country Profiles.* Food and Agricultural Organization. United Nations. New York, NY. *http://www.fao.org/forestry/country/en/* (accessed March 10, 2009).

FAO. 2009a. *Forest Facts by Country: Canada.* Food and Agricultural Organization of the United Nations, New York, NY. *http://www.fao.org/forestry/country/en/can/* (accessed August 21, 2009).

FAO. 2009b. *Forest Facts by Country: New Zealand.* Food and Agricultural Organization of the United Nations, New York, NY. *http://www.fao.org/forestry/country/en/nzl/.* (accessed August 19, 2009).

Farnham, W. D. 1965. Grenville Dodge and the Union Pacific: A study of historical legends. *J American History* 51(4): 632–650.

FBI. 1999. *Terrorism in the United States: 1999.* U.S. Department of Justice, Federal Bureau of Investigation, Counterterrorism Threat Assessment and Warning Unit, Counterterrorism Division. *http://www.fbi.gov/publications/terror/terror99.pdf* (accessed August 15, 2009).

FEMA. 2009. *2007 California Wildfires: Southern California Recovery from 2007 Wildfires.* U.S. Department of Homeland Security, Federal Emergency Management Administration. *http://www.fema.gov/about/regions/regionix/ca_fires.shtm* accessed August 23, 2009).

Ferling, J. 2003. *A leap in the dark: The struggle to create the American Republic.* New York: Oxford University Press. 576 pp.

Fischer, D. H. 1989. *Albion's Seed: Four British Folkways in America.* New York: Oxford University Press. 972 pp.

Fischer, D. H. 2004. *Liberty and freedom: A visual history of America's founding ideals.* New York: Oxford University Press. 864 pp.

Fites, J., M. Campbell, A. Reiner, and T. Decker. 2007. *Fire behavior and effects relating to suppression, fuel treatments ad protected areas on the Antelope Complex: Wheeler Fire.* Fire Behavior Assessment Team, U.S.D.A. Forest Service, August 2007. 41 pp. *http://www.qlg.org/pub/miscdoc/antelopefireanalysis.pdf* (accessed August 23, 2009).

Fladmark, K. R. 1979. Routes: Alternate migration corridors for early man in North America. *American Antiquity* 44(1): 55–69.

Forest History Society. 2009. *The Forest Products Laboratory.* Forest Service History. The Forest History Soc., Durham, NC. *http://www.foresthistory.org/ASPNET/Places/FPL/FPL.aspx* (accessed July 26, 2009).

Fragnoli, D. 2009. *Mill shutdown: Supply or demand?* Feather River Bulletin, Quincy, CA. March 11, 2009. *http://www.qlg.org/pub/miscdoc/mills/spiq_frb031109b.htm* (accessed August 23, 2009).

Fraser, G. M. 2008. *The steel bonnets: The story of the Anglo-Scottish border reivers.* Skyhorse Publishing. 416 pp.

Frazier, K. 1987. *People of Chaco: A canyon and its culture.* New York: W.W. Norton and Company. 261 pp.

Fuller, J. F. C. 1991. *The generalship of U. S. Grant.* Cambridge, MA: Da Capo Press. 472 pp.

Gaddis, J. K. 2004. *Surprise, Security, and the American Experience.* Cambridge, MA: Harvard University Press. 150 pp.

Gordon, J. S. 2004. *An Empire of Wealth: The Epic History of American Economic Power.* New York: HarperCollins. 480 pp.

Gorte, R. W. 1995. *Forest fires and forest health.* CRS Report for Congress, Congressional Research Service, Washington, D.C. *http://www.cnie.org/NLE/CRSreports/Forests/for-5.cfm.* (accessed August 29, 2009).

Gott, K. D. 2003. *Where the South lost the war: An analysis of the Fort Henry-Fort Donelson campaign, February 1862.* Mechanicsburg, PA: Stackpole Books. 368 pp.

Grant, U. S. 2000. *1885–86. Personal memoirs.* 2 vol. C. L. Webster, New York; Bartleby.com. *http://www.bartleby.com/br/1011.html* (accessed July 20, 2009).

Green, H. 2006. *Wood: Craft, culture, history.* New York: Penguin Group USA. 464 pp.

Greenberg, J. H., C. G. Turner, and S. L. Zegura. 1986. The settlement of the Americas: A comparison of linguistic, dental and genetic evidence. *Current Anthropology* 27: 477–497.

Greene, L. W. 1987. *Yosemite: The park and its resources; a history of the discovery, management, and physical development of Yosemite National Park, California.* U.S. Dept. of the

Interior, National Park Serv., Historic Resource Study series. Denver: Government Printing Office. 3 vol. 1,267 pp. *http://www.yosemite.ca.us/library/yosemite_resources/* (accessed July 28, 2009).

Grushecky, S. T., U. Buehlmann, A. Schuler, W. Luppold, and E. Cesa. 2006. Decline in the U.S. furniture industry: A case study of the impacts to the hardwood lumber supply chain. *Wood Fiber Sci* 38(2): 365–372.

Harlow, W. M., and E. S. Harrar. 1969. *Textbook of dendrology.* 5th ed. New York: McGraw-Hill. 512 pp.

Harman, T. D. 2003. *Lee's real plan at Gettysburg.* Mechanicsburg, PA: Stackpole Books. 160 pp.

Hillstrom, K., and L. C. Hillstrom. 2005. *Industrial revolution in America: Iron and steel, railroads, steam shipping.* Santa Barbara, CA: ABC-CLIO. 877 pp.

Huebner, C. D., C. Olson, and H. C. Smith. 2007. *Invasive plants field and reference guide: An ecological perspective of plant invaders of forests and woodlands.* NA-TP04-05. USDA Forest Serv., Northeastern Research Station, Morgantown, WV. *http://www.na.fs.fed.us/pubs/misc/ip/ip_field_guide.pdf* (accessed August 12, 2009).

IKEA Group. 2009. Our history (1980s). IKEA Group, Leiden, the Netherlands. *http://www.ikea-group.ikea.com/?ID=72* (accessed November 14, 2009).

Illinois State Museum. 2006. Introduction: Definition of a forest. In *Illinois cultural and natural history.* MuseumLink Illinois: A Project of the Illinois State Museum. *http://www.museum.state.il.us/muslink/forest/htmls/intro_def.html* (accessed March 22, 2009).

Jacobs, J. 2002. *PaleoAmerican origins: Review of hypotheses and evidence relating to the origins of the first Americans. http://www.jqjacobs.net/anthro/paleoamerican_origins.html* (accessed May 15, 2009).

Jolley, H. E. 1998. The cradle of forestry: Where tree power started. *Forest History Today.* Forest History Soc., Durham, NC. *http://www.foresthistory.org/Publications/FHT/FHT1998/Jolley.pdf* (accessed August 2, 2009).

Kaiser, J. A. 1994. Radiata pine: a perfect plantation timber. *Wood & Wood Products.* March 1, 1994. *http://www.allbusiness.com/furniture-related/office-furniture-including/434930-1.html.* (accessed August 21, 2009).

Keifer, M. B., N. L. Stephenson, and J. Manley. 2000. Prescribed fire as the minimum tool for wilderness forest and fire regime restoration: A case study from the Sierra Nevada, California. In eds. D. N. Cole and S. F. McCool, 266–269. Proc. RMRS-P-000, *Wilderness science in a time of change.* USDA Forest Serv., Rocky Mountain Research Station, Ogden, UT. *http://www.fs.fed.us/rm/pubs/rmrs_p015_5/rmrs_p015_5_266_269.pdf.* (24 August 2009)

Kellogg, R. S. 1909. *The timber supply of the United States.* For. Resour. Circ. 166. USDA Forest Serv., Washington, D.C. 24 pp.

Knudson, T. 2001a. Environment, Inc. (Third of five parts). Litigation central: A flood of costly lawsuits raises questions about motive. *Sacramento Bee,* Sacramento, CA, April 24, 2001.

Knudson, T. 2001b. Environment, Inc. (Fourth of five parts). Playing with fire: Spin on science puts national treasure at risk. *Sacramento Bee,* Sacramento, CA, April 25, 2001.

Knudson, T. 2001c. Environment, Inc. (Fifth of five parts). Seeds of change: Solutions sprouting from grass-roots efforts. *Sacramento Bee,* Sacramento, CA, April 26, 2001.

Koch, E. 1998. *Forty years a forester: 1903–1943.* Missoula, MT: Mountain Press Publishing Company. 206 pp.

Kraft, S., and G. Chappell. 1999. *Historic railroads in the national park system and beyond.* CRM No. 10, U.S. Dept. of the Interior, National Park Serv., Washington, D.C. *http://crm.cr.nps.gov/archive/22-10/22-10-2.pdf* (accessed July 25, 2009).

Krech, S. 1999. *The ecological Indian: Myth and history.* New York: W.W. Norton & Co. 318 pp.

Langguth, A. J. 1989. *Patriots: The men who started the American Revolution.* New York: Simon and Schuster. 640 pp.

Lassoie, J., R. Oglesby, and P. Smallidge. 1998. Roots of forestry education in America: Trials and tribulations at Cornell University. *Forest History Today,* Forest History Soc., Durham, NC. *http://www.foresthistory.org/Publications/FHT/FHT1998/cornell.pdf* (accessed August 2, 2009).

Latham, R. E., J. Beyea, M. Benner, C. A. Dunn, M. A. Fajvan, R. R. Freed, M. Grund, S. B. Horsley, A. F. Rhoads, and B. P. Shissler. 2005. *Managing white-tailed deer in forest habitat from an ecosystem perspective: Pennsylvania case study.* Executive summary. Report by the Deer Management Forum for Audubon Pennsylvania and Pennsylvania Habitat Alliance, Harrisburg, PA. *http://pa.audubon.org/docs/deer_report/ExecutiveSummary.pdf* (accessed August 13, 2009).

Laurie, M. V. 1964. Forestry education in America. *Forestry* 37(2): 137–144.

Lebedys, A. 2008. Contribution of the forestry sector to national economies, 1990–2006. Food and Agricultural Organization of the United Nations, Forest Economics and Policy Division, Working paper FSFM/ACC/08, Rome. 180 pp. *ftp://ftp.fao.org/docrep/fao/011/k4588e/k4588e00.pdf* (accessed August 25, 2009).

Leichti, R. J., R. H. Falk, and T. L. Laufenberg. 1990. Prefabricated wood
I-joists: an industry overview. *Forest Prod J* 40(3): 15–20.

Levin, M. R. 2009. *Liberty and tyranny: A conservative manifesto.* New York: Threshold Editions. 256 pp.

Lewis, L. 1950. *Captain Sam Grant: 1822–1861.* New York: Little, Brown, and Co. 512 pp.

Lienhard, J. H. 1991. *George Perkins Marsh. Engines of Our Ingenuity,* No. 595. *http://www.uh.edu/engines/epi595.htm* (accessed July 27, 2009).

Lienhard, J. H. 1993. *Balloon frame houses. Engines of Our Ingenuity.* University of Houston, Houston, TX. *http://www.uh.edu/engines/epi779.htm.* (13 July 2009)

Lienhard, J. H. 1999. *The Erie Canal. Engines of Our Ingenuity.* No 1420. University of Houston, Houston, TX. *http://www.uh.edu/engines/epi1420.htm* (accessed July 13, 2009).

Lienhard, J. H. 2007. *Continuous saws. Engines of Our Ingenuity.* No. 2258. *http://www.uh.edu/engines/epi2258.htm* (accessed July 25, 2007).

Lippke, B. 2006. The unseen connection: Building materials and climate change. *California Forests* 10(1): 12–13.

Lippke, B., and L. Edmonds. 2006. Environmental performance improvement in residential construction: The impact of products, biofuels, and processes. *Forest Prod J* 56(10): 58–63.

Lippke, B., J. Wilson, J. Perez-Garcia, J. Bowyer, and J. Meil. 2004. CORRIM: Life cycle environmental performance of renewable building materials. *Forest Prod J* 54(6): 8-19.

Lomborg, B. 2001. *The skeptical environmentalist: Measuring the real state of the world.* New York: Cambridge University Press. 540 pp.

Luecke, D. 2000. The law and politics of federal wildlife preservation. In *Political environmentalism: Going beyond the green curtain,* ed. T. L. Anderson, 61–120. Stanford University, Stanford, CA: Hoover Institution Press.

Luppold, W. G. 2003a. Is the hardwood market entering a new era? Part I. *Hardwood Market Report* 81(41): 11–14. *http://www.ahc.caf.wvu.edu/usdafs/web_Documents/567.pdf* (accessed August 11, 2009).

Luppold, W. G. 2003b. Is the hardwood market entering a new era? Part II. *Hardwood Market Report* 81(42). *http://www.ahc.caf.wvu.edu/usdafs/web_Documents/568.pdf* (accessed August 11, 2009).

Luppold, W. G., and M. S. Bumgardner. 2005. Are we transitioning from an era of oak to an era of maple? In Proc of the Southern Forest Economics Workshop, 185–196. Baton Rouge, LA, April 18-20, 2005. *http://www.ahc.caf.wvu.edu/usdafs/web_documents/634.pdf* (accessed August 12, 2009).

Luppold, W. G., and M. S. Bumgardner. 2006. Two eras of globalization and hardwood sawtimber demand. *Hardwood Matters.* September 2006: 10–11. National Hardwood Lumber Association, Memphis, TN. *http://www.ahc.caf.wvu.edu/usdafs/web_documents/662.pdf* (accessed August 13, 2009).

MacCleery, D. W. 1994a. *American forests: A history of resiliency and recovery.* Forest History Soc., Durham, NC. 58 pp.

MacCleery, D. W. 1994b. *Understanding the role the human dimension has played in shaping America's forest and grassland landscapes: Is there a landscape archaeologist in the house?* USDA Forest Service. Eco-Watch (2/10/94). *http://www.fs.fed.us/eco/eco-watch/ew940210.htm?presettlement+forest+density#first_hit* (accessed June 5, 2009).

MacCleery, D. W. 1999. Is the shift to "ecological sustainability" or ecosystem management on U.S. public lands merely a sophisticated "NIMBYism" masquerading as a "paradigm shift"? or Aldo Leopold's land ethic: Is it only half a loaf unless a consumption ethic accompanies it? *Eco-Watch*, 4/11/99. *http://www.fs.fed.us/eco/eco-watch/consumption_ethic2.html* (accessed August 19, 2009).

MAF. 1999. Forestry resources. New Zealand Ministry of Agriculture and Forestry, Wellington, NZ. *http://www.maf.govt.nz/forestry/resources/* (accessed August 21, 2009).

MAF. 2009. *A national exotic forest description: as at 1 April 2008.* New Zealand Ministry of Agriculture and Forestry, Wellington, NZ. 64 pp. *http://www.maf.govt.nz/mafnet/publi-cations/nefd/national-exotic-forest-2008/nefd-2008.pdf* (accessed August 21, 2009).

Makarenko, J. 2008. *The Canada-US softwood lumber dispute.* MapleLeafWeb, Department of Political Science, University of Lethbridge, Lethbridge, Alberta, Canada.

Malhi, R. S., J. A. Eshleman, J. A. Greenberg, D. A. Weiss, B. A. Schultz-Shook, F. A. Kaestle, J. G. Lorenz, B. M. Kemp, J. R. Johnson, and D. G. Smith. 2002. The structure of diversity within New World mitochondrial DNA haplogroups: Implications for the prehistory of North America. *American J of Human Genetics* 70: 905–919.

Malmsheimer, R. W., P. Heffernan, S. Brink, D. Crandall, F. Deneke, C. Galik, E. Gee, J. A. Helms, N. McClure, M. Mortimer, S. Ruddell, M. Smith, and J. Stewart. 2008. Forest management solutions for mitigating climate change in the United States. *J Forestry* 106(3): 115–173.

Mann, C. C. 2002. 1491. *Atlantic Monthly* 289(3): 41–53.

Mann, C. C. 2005. *1491: New revelations of the Americas before Columbus.* New York: Alfred A. Knopf. 65 pp.

http://www.mapleleafweb.com/features/the-canada-us-softwood-lumber-dispute#history (accessed August 21, 2009).

McClintock, M. 2000. Putting a new spin on saws. Washington Post (June 8, 2000). *http://www.washingtonpost.com/wp-adv/specialsales/homefashion/post77.html* (accessed July 26, 2009).

McCullough, D. 2001. *John Adams.* New York: Simon & Schuster. 751 pp.

McCullough, D. 2005. *1776.* New York: Simon & Schuster. 386 pp.

McIntosh, R. P. 1976. Ecology since 1900. In *Issues and Ideas in America,* eds. B. J. Taylor and T. J. White, 353–372. Norman, OK: University of Oklahoma Press.

McWilliams, J. E. 2009. The Green Monster: Could Frankenfoods be good for the environment? Slate (January 28, 2009). *http://www.slate.com/id/2209168/* (accessed August 14, 2009)

Miller, C. 2000. What happened in the Ranier Grand's lobby? A question of sources. *The Journal of American History* 86(4): 1709.

Miller, C. 2001. *Gifford Pinchot and the making of modern environmentalism.* Washington, D.C.: Island Press/Shearwater Books. 458 pp.

Miller, C. 2006. *Will the Forest Service celebrate its bicentennial?* Forest History Soc., Durham, NC. *http://www.foresthistory.org/Events/Miller%20Lecture.pdf* (accessed August 14, 2009).

Moffatt, A. 2008. *The reivers: The story of the border reivers.* Edinburgh, Scotland: Birlinn Books. 321 pp.

Moore, P. A. 2000. *Green spirit: Trees are the answer.* Greenspirit Enterprises Ltd., Vancouver, BC, Canada. 150 pp.

Moore, P. A. 2002a. *Environmentalism for the 21st century.* Greenspirit: For a Sustainable Future. *http://www.greenspirit.com/21st_century.cfm?msid=29&page=1* (accessed August 11, 2009).

Moore, P. A. 2002b. *Hemp.* Greenspirit: For a Sustainable Future. *http://greenspirit.com/key_issues.cfm?msid=50&page=1* (accessed August 19, 2009).

Moore, P. A. 2002c. *Trees are the answer.* Greenspirit: For a Sustainable Future. *http://www.greenspirit.com/trees_answer.cfm* (accessed August 17, 2009).

Moore, P. A. 2002d. Where's the green steel? *Los Angeles Times,* March 26, 2002. Reprinted on Greenspirit: For a Sustainable Future. *http://www.greenspirit.com/logbook.cfm?msid=27* (accessed August 17, 2009).

Moore, P. A. 2006. Forest management: Part of the climate change solution. *California Forests* 10(1): 8–9.

Morris, E. 2001. *Theodore Rex.* New York: Random House. 784 pp.

National Park Service. 2009. Gettysburg National Military Park, Pennsylvania. U.S. Dept. of the Interior, National Park Serv., Gettysburg, PA. *http://www.nps.gov/gett/index.htm* (accessed July 23, 2009).

Nelson, R. H. 2008. *Fire in the national forest system.* Property and Environment Research Center, Bozeman, MT. PERC Reports: Volume 26, No. 2, June 2008. *http://www.perc.org/ articles/article1063.php* (accessed August 29, 2009).

*New York Times.*1903. Cornell School of Forestry suspended: Action followed failure of state to provide means for its support. *New York Times* Archives. June 18, 1903. *http://query. nytimes.com/mem/archive-free/pdf?_r=1&res=9A05EEDB1339E333A2575BC1A9609C 946297D6CF* (accessed August 1, 2009).

NIFC. 2009. Fire information—Wildland fire statistics. U.S. National Interagency Fire Center, Boise, ID. *http://www.nifc.gov/fire_info/fire_stats.htm* (accessed September 29, 2009).

Nix, S. 2004a. *A brief history of United States forestry: From Pleny to Gifford Pinchot. About. com:* Forestry. *http://forestry.about.com/library/weekly/aa072098.htm.* (31 July 2009)

Nix, S. 2004b. *The first North American forestry school. About.com:* Forestry. *http://forestry. about.com/library/weekly/aa100102a.htm* (accessed July 31, 2009).

Orfield, M. N. 1915. *Federal land grants to the states with special reference to Minnesota.* Studies in the Social Studies, No. 2. University of Minnesota, St. Paul, MN. 275 pp.

Otis, A. T., W. D. Honey, T. C. Hogg, and K. K. Lakin. 1986. *The Forest Service and the Civilian Conservation Corps: 1933–42.* FS-395, USDA Forest Serv., Washington, D.C. *http://www. nps.gov/history/history/online_books/ccc/ccc/index.htm* (accessed August 31, 2009).

O'Toole, R. 2007. *The perfect firestorm: Bringing Forest Service wildfire costs under control.* Policy Analysis No. 591. CATO Institute, Washington, D.C, 16 pp. *http://www.cato.org/ pubs/pas/pa591.pdf* (accessed August 29, 2009).

Paige, J. C. 1985. *The Civilian Conservation Corps and the National Park Service, 1933–1942: An administrative History.* U.S. Dept. of the Interior, National Park Serv., Washington, D.C. *http://www.nps.gov/history/history/online_books/ccc/ccct.htm* (accessed August 13, 2009).

Panshin, A. J., and C. deZeeuw. 1980. *Textbook of wood technology.* 4th ed. New York: McGraw-Hill. 722 pp.

Peck, T. 2001. *The international timber trade.* Abington, U.K.: Woodhead Publishing Limited. 325 pp.

Pepke, E. 2008. *Global trade of wood and paper products—An overview.* Proc of the 51st Annual Convention of the Soc. of Wood Science and Technology, Universidad del Bío-Bío, Concepción, Chile, November 10–12, 2008. *http://www.swst.org/meetings/AM08/ presentations/pdfs%20of%20ppts%20global%20trade/1_PepkeGlobalTrade091108.pdf* (accessed August 21, 2009).

Perez-Garcia, J., B. Lippke, D. Briggs, J. B. Wilson, J. Bowyer, and J. Meil. 2005a. The environmental performance of renewable building materials in the context of residential construction. *Wood Fiber Sci* 37, CORRIM Special Issue, 3–17.

Perez-Garcia J., B. Lippke, J. Comnick, and C. Manriquez. 2005b. An assessment of carbon pools, storage, and wood products market substitution using life-cycle analysis results. *Wood Fiber Sci* 37, CORRIM Special Issue, 140–148.

Peterson, J. 2003. Giant minds, giant ideas: The USFS Forest Products Laboratory at Madison, Wisconsin. *Evergreen Magazine* November 2003. *http://evergreenmagazine.com/magazine/ article/GIANT_MINDS_GIANT_IDEAS_The_USFS_Forest_Products_Laboratory_at_ Madison_Wisconsin.html* (accessed November 12, 2009).

Pfanz, H. W. 1993. *Gettysburg: Culp's Hill and Cemetery Hill.* Chapel Hill, NC: University of North Carolina Press. 528 pp.

Pfister, G. 2006. Forest management: part of the climate change solution. *California Forests* 10(1): 8–9.

Philbrick, N. 2006. *Mayflower: A story of courage, community, and war.* New York: Penguin Group USA. 461 pp.

Pielou, E. C. 1991. *After the ice age: The return of life to glaciated North America*. Chicago, IL: University of Chicago Press. 366 pp.

Pinchot, G. 1998. *Breaking New Ground (Commemorative Edition)*. Washington, D.C.: Island Press. 542 pp.

Pisani, D. J. 1997. Forests and conservation: 1865–1890. In *American forests: Nature, culture, and politics*, ed. C. Miller, 15–34. Lawrence, KS: University Press of Kansas.

Plywood Pioneers. 2009. Milestones in the history of plywood. Plywood Pioneers Association, American Panel Association, Tacoma, WA. *http://www.apawood.org/plywoodpioneers/history.htm* (accessed September 27, 2009).

Porter, H. 2000. Campaigning with Grant. Bison Books (reprinted from a series of articles published in 1896–97 in *The Century*). 618 pp.

Postel, S., and J. C. Ryan. 1991. Reforming forestry. In *State of the World, 1991*, ed. L. Brown, 74–92. New York: W.W. Norton and Company.

Puettmann, M. E., and J. B. Wilson. 2005. Life-cycle analysis of wood products: Cradle-to-gate LCI of residential wood building materials. *Wood Fiber Sci*, 37 CORRIM Special Issue, 18–29.

Pyne, S. J. 1982. *Fire in America: A cultural history of wildland and rural fire*. Seattle, WA: University of Washington Press. 654 pp.

Pyne, S. J. 2001. *Year of the fires: The story of the great fires of 1910*. New York: Penguin Group USA. 322 pp.

QLG. 2008a. Implementation trends. The Quincy Library Group, Quincy, CA. *http://www.qlg.org/pub/act/implementation.htm* (accessed August 23, 2009).

QLG. 2008b. The Moonlight Fire and DFPZs. The Quincy Library Group, Quincy, CA. *http://www.qlg.org/pub/act/moonlight.htm*. (accessed 23 August 2009)

Rawinski, T. J. 2008. Impacts of white-tailed deer overabundance in forest ecosystems: An overview. U.S. Department of Agriculture, Forest Service, Northeastern Area State and Private Forestry, Newtown Square, PA. *http://michigansaf.org/Tours/05Deer/USFS-2008.pdf* (accessed August 13, 2009).

Reiger, J. F. 1997. Wildlife, conservation, and the first forest reserve. In *American forests: Nature, culture, and politics*, ed. C. Miller, 35–47. Lawrence, KS: University Press of Kansas.

Ross, C. D. 2000. *Trial by fire: Science, technology, and the Civil War*. Shippensburg, PA: White Mane Publishing Company. 215 pp.

Sadler, J. 2006. *Border fury: England and Scotland at war 1296–1568*. Harlow, U.K.: Pearson Education Ltd. 656 pp.

Schlosser, S. E. 2008. *American folklore: Paul Bunyan. http://www.americanfolklore.net/paulbunyan.html* (accessed July 8, 2009).

Schenkkan, P. 2002. Citizen Suits. In *The Endangered Species Act: Law, policy, and perspectives*, eds. D. C. Baur and W. R. Irvin, 415–439. American Bar Association. *http://books.google.com/books?id=qtNkfFZ68NgC&source=gbs_navlinks_s*. (accessed August 14, 2009).

Schneider, P. 1998. *The Adirondacks: A history of America's first wilderness*. New York: Holt Paperbacks. 416 pp.

Sears, S. W. 2003. *Gettysburg*. New York: Houghton Mifflin Co. 623 pp.

Sechrest, L. J. 1998. *American shipbuilders in the heyday of sail: Their rise and decline*. Working Papers. Ludwig von Mises Institute, Auburn, Alabama. *http://mises.org/journals/scholar/sechrest2.PDF* (accessed June 10, 2009).

Sedjo, R. A. 2001. *The national forests: For whom and for what?* Issue Number PS-23, Property and Environment Research Center, Bozeman, MT. *http://www.perc.org/pdf/ps23.pdf* (accessed August 29, 2009).

Sheldon, G. 2003. *When the smoke cleared at Gettysburg: The tragic aftermath of the bloodiest battle of the Civil War*. Nashville, TN: Cumberland House Publishing. 288 pp.

Sides, H. 2006. *Blood and thunder: The epic story of Kit Carson and the conquest of the American West*. New York: Anchor Books. 578 pp.

Simon, J. L. 1996. *Hoodwinking the nation*. New York: Transaction Publishers. 154 pp. *http://www.juliansimon.com/writings/Truth_Shortage/* (accessed August 14, 2009).

Simon, J. L. 1998. *The ultimate resource 2*. Princeton, NJ: Princeton University Press. 778 pp. *http://www.juliansimon.com/writings/Ultimate_Resource/* (accessed August 20, 2009).

SIPA. 2007a. *The history of SIPs*. Structural Insulated Panel Association (SIPA). Gig Harbor, WA. *http://www.sips.org/content/about/index.cfm?PageId=37* (accessed September 27, 2009).

SIPA. 2007b. *What are SIPs?* Structural Insulated Panel Association (SIPA). Gig Harbor, WA. *http://www.sips.org/content/about/index.cfm?pageId=7* (accessed September 27, 2009).

Skinner, C., and M. Ritchie. 2008. *The Cone Fire: A chance reckoning for fuel treatments.* U.S. Joint Fire Science Program, Fire Science Brief, Issue 4, January 2008. 6 pp. *http://www.firescience.gov/projects/03-2-3-20/03-2-3-20_brief.pdf* (accessed August 24, 2009).

Skousen, W. C. 1981. *The 5000 year leap: A miracle that changed the world.* 7th ed. National Center for Constitutional Studies, Malta, ID. 337 pp.

Smith, W. B., P. D. Miles, C. H. Perry, and S. A. Pugh. 2009. *Forest resources of the United States, 2007.* A technical document supporting the Forest Service 2010 RPA assessment. Gen. Tech. Rep. WO-78. USDA Forest Serv., Washington, D.C. 336 pp. *http://nrs.fs.fed.us/pubs/gtr/gtr_wo78.pdf* (accessed September 30, 2009).

Snyder, M. 1999. Still growing after 100 Years: Weyerhaeuser Company celebrates its centennial. *Forest History Today* (Fall 1999), 2–8. Forest History Soc., Durham, NC. *http://www.foresthistory.org/Publications/FHT/FHTFall1999/stillgrowing.pdf* (accessed July 28, 2009).

Spence, W. P. 1993. *Residential framing: A homebuilder's construction guide.* New York: Sterling Publishing Co. 320 pp.

Srodes, J. 2002. *Franklin: The essential founding father.* Washington, D.C.: Regenry Publishing. 450 pp.

Steer, H. B. 1948. *Lumber production in the United States: 1799–1946.* Miscellaneous Publication No. 669, USDA Forest Serv., Washington, D.C.

Stephens, S. 2008. *Chainsaws or driptorches: How should fire risk be reduced?* U.S. Joint Fire Science Program, Fire Science Brief, Issue 6, March 2008, pp. 1–6. *http://www.firescience.gov/projects/99-S-01/supdocs/99-S-01_99-S-01_BMV.pdf* (accessed August 24, 2009).

Stephenson, W. 1989. *I remain unvanquished: The incredible, 1,000-year history of the Armstrong family.* Great Northern Pulp and Paper Group, Etobicoke, Ontario, Canada. 183 pp.

Stevens, S. K. 1964. *Pennsylvania: Birthplace of a nation.* New York: Random House. 401 pp.

Stout, B. B. 2003. *The Northern Spotted Owl: An Oregon View 1975-2002.* Victoria, B.C., Canada: Trafford Publishing. 176 pp.

Taylor, A. 2001. *American colonies: The settling of North America.* New York: Penguin Group USA. 544 pp.

Temperate Forest Foundation. 2007. Wildland Fire. Temperate Forest Foundation, Portland, OR. *http://www.forestinfo.org/discover/wildfire.htm.* [accessed 18 August 2009]

Timberco. 2008. *History of Oriented Strand Board.* OSB Guide, Timberco, Inc., dba TECO, Sun Prairie, WI. *http://osbguide.tecotested.com/osbhistory* (accessed September 27, 2009).

Toll, I. W. 2006. *Six frigates: The epic history of the founding of the U.S. Navy.* New York: W. W. Norton & Co. 592 pp.

Toro, J., and S. Gessel. 1999. Radiata pine plantations in Chile. *New Forests* 18(1): 33–44.

Trudeau, N. A. 2002. *Gettysburg: A testing of courage.* New York: Harper/Collins. 720 pp.

Turner, D. 1999. The thirteenth fire. *Forest History Today* (Spring 1999), 26–28. Forest History Soc., Durham, NC. *http://www.foresthistory.org/Publications/FHT/FHTSpring1999/Turner.pdf* (accessed December 13, 2009).

Turner, F. J. 1921. *The frontier in American history.* New York: Henry Holt and Co. Hypertext version by M. W. Kidd (1996), University of Virginia, Charlottesville, VA. *http://xroads.virginia.edu/~HYPER/TURNER/* (accessed July 24, 2009).

U.S. Fish and Wildlife Service. 2008. *Short History of the Refuge System: The Early Years (1864–1920).* U.S. Fish and Wildlife Service, U.S. Department of the Interior, Washington, D.C. *http://www.fws.gov/refuges/history/over/over_hist-a_fs.html* (accessed July 30, 2009).

U.S. Forest Service. 1920. *Timber depletion, lumber prices, lumber exports, and concentrations of timber ownership.* Report on Senate Resolution 311, June 1, 1920, USDA Forest Serv., Washington, D.C.

U.S. Forest Service. 2008. Land area reports (LAR)—As of Sept. 30, 2008. USDA Forest Serv., Washington, D.C. *http://www.fs.fed.us/land/staff/lar/2008/lar08index.html* (accessed August 1, 2009).

U.S. Forest Service. 2009. Forest health protection. USDA Forest Serv., Northeastern Area, Newtown Square, PA. *http://na.fs.fed.us/fhp/index.shtm* (accessed August 11, 2009).

Van Oosterhout, T. 2008. *Schoonerman: Schooner and Tall Sailing Ships. http://www.schooner man.com/home.htm* (accessed June 16, 2009).

Van Ophem, M. 2001. *The iron horse: the impact of the railroads on 19th century American society.* Department of Alfa-informatica, University of Groningen, Netherlands. *http:// odur.let.rug.nl/~usa/E/ironhorse/ironhorsexx.htm* (accessed July 25, 2009).

Visser, R. 1994. New Zealand forestry and the forest code of practice. In *Forest codes of practice: Contributing to environmentally sound forest operations,* eds. D. P. Dykstra and R. Heinrich. FAO Forestry Paper No. 133, Proc of an FAO/IUFRO meeting of experts on forest practices, Feldafing, Germany. December 11–14, 1994. *http://www.fao.org/docrep/ W3646E/w3646e09.htm#new%20zealand%20forestry%20and%20the%20forest%20code %20of%20practice* (accessed August 21, 2009).

Wallingford, B. D. 2007. *Deer and deer management in Pennsylvania.* Pennsylvania Game Commission, Harrisburg, PA. *http://www.pgc.state.pa.us/pgc/cwp/view.asp?a=465&q= 171167* (accessed August 13, 2009).

Wang, J., J. P. Armstrong, J. Wu, and W. Lin. 2008. *An analysis of Appalachian hardwood markets in China.* 51st Annual Convention. Soc. of Wood Science and Technology, Universidad del Bío-Bío. Concepción, Chile. November 10–12, 2008. *http://www.swst. org/meetings/AM08/proceedings/WS-55.pdf* (accessed August 21, 2009).

Webb, J. H. 2004. *Born fighting: How the Scots-Irish shaped America.* New York: Bantam Dell Publishing Group. 400 pp.

Wildlife Society. 2005. *A brief history of the Wildlife Society.* The Wildlife Soc., Bethesda, MD. *http://joomla.wildlife.org/index.php?id=13&option=com_content&task=view* (accessed August 5, 2009).

Williams, G. W. 2001. *References on the American Indian use of fire in ecosystems.* USDA Forest Serv., Washington, D.C. *http://www.wildlandfire.com/docs/biblio_indianfire.htm* (accessed May 15, 2009).

Williams, M. 1989. *Americans and their forests: A historical geography.* New York: Cambridge University Press. 599 pp.

Winistorfer, P., Z. Chen, B. Lippke, and N. Stevens. 2005. Energy consumption and greenhouse gas emissions related to the use, maintenance, and disposal of a residential structure. *Wood Fiber Sci* 37, CORRIM Special Issue, 128–139.

Wisdom, H. W, and C. D. C. Wisdom. 1983. Wood use in the American furniture industry. J Forest History 27(3): 122–125.

Woodworth, S. E. 2005. *Nothing but victory: The Army of the Tennessee 1861–1865.* New York: Alfred A. Knopf. 784 pp.

Yetter, G. H. 1988. *Williamsburg before and after: The rebirth of Virginia's colonial capital.* Williamsburg, VA: Colonial Williamsburg Foundation. 198 pp.

Youngquist, W. G., and H. O. Fleischer. 1977. *Wood in American life: 1776–2076.* Forest Products Research Soc., Madison, WI. 192 pp.

Zinnen Jr., R. O. 1991. City Point, the tool that gave General Grant victory. *Quartermaster Professional Bull.*, Spring 1991. *http://www.qmfound.com/citypt.htm* (accessed July 19, 2009).